A NEW HISTORY OF
THE IRISH IN AUSTRALIA

ELIZABETH MALCOLM is an honorary professorial fellow and was formerly Gerry Higgins Professor of Irish Studies at the University of Melbourne. She has published on policing, mental health, gender and popular culture in Ireland, as well as on the Irish diaspora in both Britain and Australia.

DIANNE HALL is an associate professor at Victoria University, Melbourne. She has published widely on the Irish in 19th-century Australia, as well as on gender, religion and violence in Ireland.

D1610626

A NEW
HISTORY
OF THE
IRISH
IN
AUSTRALIA

ELIZABETH MALCOLM
& DIANNE HALL

CORK UNIVERSITY PRESS

Contents

SECTION THREE: POLITICS

First Published in Australia and New Zealand by
NewSouth Publishing
University of New South Wales Press Ltd
University of New South Wales
Sydney NSW 2052
AUSTRALIA
newsouthpublishing.com

First published in Ireland by
Cork University Press
Youngline Industrial Estate
Pouladuff Road, Togher
Cork T12, HT6V, Ireland

A New History of the Irish in Australia

ISBN 9781782053057

British Library Cataloguing in Publication Data

A CIP catalogue record for this book is available from the British Library.

Typeset by Avril Makula
Cover design Peter Long
Cover images Background by Dmytro Shvetsov and Celtic cross by VitAnGen,
    Shutterstock
Printed in Poland by HussarBooks

Acknowledgments

We would like to thank the Australian Research Council for funding the research on which this book is based. Additional data was collected by Dianne Hall during a project funded by the Leverhulme Trust (UK) and led by Lindsay Proudfoot, then of Queen's University, Belfast. We are grateful to Dr Proudfoot for his continuing support and for allowing us access to his unpublished research materials. Our universities – Victoria University, Melbourne, and the University of Melbourne – provided us with facilities and support throughout the project. In addition, Victoria University contributed funding, teaching relief and research leave for Dianne Hall.

We were fortunate to work with a dedicated and gifted group of research assistants at different times over the course of the project. Sarah Pinto collected large numbers of cartoons from newspapers before they were digitised. Liam Byrne, Catie Gilchrist, Antoine Guillemette, Molly Lukin, Lee-Ann Monk and Brett Wright helped us to locate further sources and to manage our research data.

Colleagues have also been generous with their time and expertise in giving advice, sharing research, answering questions and reading drafts. We particularly want to thank: Philip Bull, Liz Conor, Phillip Deery, Frances Devlin-Glass, Charles Fahey,

Mark Finnane, the late Angela Gehrig, Stephanie James, John Lack, Marilyn Lake, Barry McCarron, Chris McConville, Rónán McDonald, Val Noone, Eunan O'Halpin, Robert Pascoe, Robin Sullivan, Rodney Sullivan, Roger Swift, Christina Twomey and Ciarán Walsh. Thanks also to Rachel U'Ren for giving Dianne the library of Australian history journals that her mother, Nancy, had collected.

The encouraging responses received from interested audiences when we presented our research have also been appreciated. We would especially like to thank those attending conferences organised in conjunction with the Irish Studies Association of Australia and New Zealand (ISAANZ) and participants in the Melbourne Irish Studies Seminars (MISS) at Newman College, University of Melbourne.

Elizabeth Malcolm would like to thank Hartley and Robert for making the trials of book production easier. She also wishes to dedicate her work to her three Irish women ancestors who made the long voyage from Ireland to Australia: Margaret Cooke, a Famine orphan, who left County Kildare in 1848; Ellen Byrne, who left Dublin city in 1875; and Letitia Storey Johnston, who left County Fermanagh with her family in 1925.

Dianne Hall would like to thank the Hynds O'Flanagan family, who have welcomed her to their home in Dublin over many years. Mary McGee sparked Dianne's early interest in history, as did Leila Hall's stories of relatives who had left Ireland for Queensland during the 19th century. She also wishes to thank Louise, Rowan and Jack for patiently putting up with her preoccupations when writing this book and always being ready to show her that there is more to life.

Introduction:
The Irish in Australia

St Patrick's Day in Brisbane in March 2018 saw a joyous and colourful celebration of Irish identity and its popular symbols. A large parade through city streets featured the Queensland Irish Association pipe band, enthusiastic Irish dancers and an agile child on a unicycle wearing a large green leprechaun-style hat – all cheered on by laughing crowds waving shamrock-shaped balloons. In similar scenes that day in many Australian cities and towns, there were also family events, concerts of Irish music and outdoor tables at Irish-themed pubs, crowded with patrons drinking beer coloured green to mark the occasion.[1]

The celebratory atmosphere of Brisbane's St Patrick's Day parade presented Irishness as a happy and positive aspect of Australia's modern culture. But not only do large numbers of Irish Australians – and many non-Irish Australians as well – enjoy the festivities held on 17 March each year, in recent decades Irish immigrants' achievements have been rewarded with some of the country's highest official accolades. The 2010 Australian of the Year was Irish-born Melbourne-based psychiatrist, Professor Patrick McGorry, a leading campaigner for improved mental health services for young people. Twenty years earlier,

Sister Angela Mary Doyle RSM, a hospital administrator and outspoken advocate for people with HIV/AIDS, was named the 1989 Queenslander of the Year.[2] Listing influential Irish-born Australians could fill many pages, while a similar listing of notable Australians of Irish ancestry would be far longer and would include thousands of women and men representing all aspects of Australian life.

Yet this story of success and celebration is in stark contrast to how earlier generations of Australians, especially those of British birth or descent, understood Ireland and the Irish. Exactly 170 years ago, the arrival of Catholic Irish immigrants – people from backgrounds similar to those of McGorry or Doyle – provoked a Melbourne newspaper to warn against an influx of 'hordes of useless and lawless savages', who threatened to transform the colony into a 'Province of Popedom'. Another Melbourne paper was at the same time characterising Aboriginal people in similar terms, describing them too as 'lawless savages'.[3] The transformation of Irish-born immigrants from 'useless ... savages' into honoured citizens highlights the vast distance that they and their children travelled during the course of the 19th and 20th centuries in the public consciousness of most Australians. From being widely perceived as alien and menacing, today the Irish are included alongside the English, Scots and Welsh as founding peoples of modern Australia, even if they often disappear into broader categories like 'British' and 'Anglo-Celtic' in histories of Australian colonisation and settlement.

The current St Patrick's Day celebrations of Irishness are therefore rather different from earlier such festivities. Gatherings and parades, beginning in the 1840s and extending into the 1920s, were often controversial and sometimes violent.[4] Many Irish Australians argued strongly that there was no contradiction between being loyal Australians within the British Empire, while remaining proud of their Irish heritage and acknowledging it publicly each year on 17 March: in effect, they were asserting a form of multiculturalism. But most of their Protestant neighbours of English and Scottish descent perceived Irishness very differently: to them it denoted disorder, disaffection, poverty and religious oppression and constituted an existential threat to Australia's Protestant British identity.

The Irish diaspora

The Irish-born and their descendants have always formed a substantial minority within Australian society.[5] At the time the colonies federated into the Commonwealth of Australia in 1901, Catholic Irish immigrants and their Australian-born offspring made up around 23 per cent of the total non-Indigenous population.[6] In numerical terms, far more Irish people emigrated to the United States (US) or Britain than to Australia during 1800–2000, but they never formed as large a proportion of the population in those countries as they did in Australia.[7]

Migration, however, is not just about numbers, percentages and the movement of bodies through physical space from one place to another; perhaps more importantly, it is also about transferring and adapting ways of imagining the world. One of the most interesting, though often most elusive, aspects of migration is the process by which deep-rooted old-world beliefs and practices were reinforced, reconstituted or disregarded in the rapidly evolving circumstances of the new world. The Catholic Irish, who began arriving in Australia in large numbers first as convicts from the 1790s and then as free immigrants from the 1830s, were the bearers, according to the leading historian of the Irish in Australia, Patrick O'Farrell, of a 'distinctive cultural tradition, world-view, historical experience and sense of values', not merely different from, but fundamentally 'hostile' to the traditions and values of the English- and Scottish-born majority of colonial society.[8] Thus, historians of the Irish outside Ireland have emphasised that the Irish migration experience cannot be fully understood without a thorough appreciation of the culture from which the immigrants came and with which they maintained contact.

The concept of the 'diaspora' as applied by historians in recent decades to the overseas Irish envisages a web of complex relationships across space and time – a multi-national, multi-generational network – connecting immigrants and their offspring to their original homeland, as well as to Irish immigrant communities in other places. From the early 19th century onwards, information circulated through this network by means of newspapers, letters and personal visits to keep immigrants in touch with happenings in Ireland and elsewhere in the diaspora. Immigrants also established or joined ethnic associations – some local, others national and even international – that aimed to preserve their culture and identity and to promote Irish political causes. And, of course, immigrants usually continued to mark St Patrick's Day as an annual national festival.[9] It is a mistake therefore to treat Irish immigrants solely in relation to the host societies in their new homelands, for they in fact inhabited a large multi-dimensional landscape.[10]

The Irish diaspora in Australia

If the diaspora was a complex space, the Irish who moved through it were a complex people. While contemporaries and historians alike have generally employed the single, unqualified word 'Irish' to describe all those born in Ireland who arrived in Australia over several centuries, and often their descendants as well, key distinctions among the Irish are crucial to any understanding of their experience in Australia. People born in the four provinces of Ireland – Munster, Ulster, Leinster and Connacht – who arrived from the end of the 18th century onwards, were a diverse group, divided by gender, class, religion, language, identity, loyalties and historical antecedents – as well as by whether or not they were free or convicts. Included amongst them were members of the Protestant Anglo-Irish elite, who maintained close social, cultural and political ties with England. Men from this group occupied positions of power and influence throughout the British Empire, including in the Australian colonies. Below the Anglo-Irish in class terms, but also essential to the imperial workforce, were middle-class Protestant and Catholic men employed in the armed forces, the professions and the civil service or engaged in business and commerce.

The final and largest group of immigrants were Catholic men and women from poor rural backgrounds, many of whom, especially before the 1840s, were likely to have been Irish-speaking. From the 1830s, in the records of assisted immigration schemes, these Irish were identified as mostly being labourers and servants. It was primarily this last group that was targeted by the Melbourne *Argus* when it warned in 1848 about the threat posed by 'hordes' of 'lawless savages' coming from the south and west of Ireland.

There were also three markedly different phases of migration by the Irish to Australia, although the phases did overlap to some degree. The first involved forced migration. Between 1791 and 1867, around 48 000 Irish-born women and men were transported to the Australian colonies as convicts. Irish men made up nearly 30 per cent of all male convicts, while Irish women comprised upwards of 40 per cent of female convicts. So there is a major Irish story to tell in terms of convict history: a story in which women feature prominently.[11] The second phase of Irish migration saw large numbers of free settlers arrive, keen to pursue opportunities in the colonies denied to them in Ireland. These mostly young, single women and men either paid their own fares or, more often, were partially funded by one of many government and private assistance schemes. Such schemes, which operated at the same time as Indigenous dispossession, were designed to populate the supposedly 'empty' lands of Australia with British and Irish farmers and also with female household servants, most of whom would in time graduate to become settlers' wives. Overall, between 1830 and 1914, proportionately more Irish took up offers of assisted passages to Australia than did immigrants from more prosperous parts of the United Kingdom, like England, Scotland and Wales.[12]

Although the period of Irish assisted immigration and free settlement included the years of the Great Famine in the late 1840s and early 1850s, far fewer Famine refugees reached Australia than arrived in the US or Britain. Most would have lacked the financial resources, and many perhaps the physical resources as well, to qualify for an assisted passage. However, the impact of the Famine can certainly be detected in a jump in the proportion of Irish convicts being transported, the majority sentenced for crimes against property.[13] Of the nearly 20 900 convicts sent to Australia during 1846–53, 45 per cent of the women and 33 per cent of the men were Irish born.[14] In addition, in 1848–50 the colonies received 4100 so-called 'Famine orphans': destitute teenage girls confined in Irish workhouses who were shipped to Australia by the British government in order to ease pressure on the overcrowded workhouse system and to provide female labour for the colonies.[15] So, although Irish Australia did not exhibit the intense bitterness of Famine memory that came to characterise Irish America, it was by no means totally immune from the trauma suffered by Famine survivors.[16]

These large influxes of both convict and free immigrants meant that by 1901, as we have seen, the non-Indigenous Australian population was about one-quarter Irish. Census data does not distinguish Irish-born Protestants from Irish-born Catholics, but historians have estimated that around 25 per cent of Irish immigrants to Australia were Protestants.[17] We also know that, prior to 1945, the majority of Australia's Catholic population were of Irish birth or descent. Irish-born Protestants and their children, on the other hand, formed a minority, although often a distinctive and influential one, among the Protestant population, who were mostly of British birth or descent. All in all, from the 1790s up to the 1920s, perhaps 400 000 Irish-born people landed on Australia's shores, around 12 per cent of whom were convicts and the rest free immigrants, and approximately 75 per cent were Catholics.[18]

Changes to Commonwealth immigration policies, com-bined with political developments in Ireland itself, meant that far fewer Irish people immigrated to Australia during the course of the 20th century. So it is fair to say that the landscape of Irish Australia was effectively laid out before 1914, even though there have been significant changes to it since. The 20th century witnessed a third phase of Irish immigration, with a relatively small but steady trickle of immigrants who were motivated to leave their now partitioned homeland by economic or political upheaval. Those coming from Northern Ireland, which remained part of the United Kingdom after 1922, qualified for assistance under various Anglo-Australian migration schemes, but intending immigrants from the independent south of Ireland usually had to fund their own travel.[19] At the start of the 21st century, the collapse of the Irish Republic's economy in 2008 following the excesses of the boom period known as the 'Celtic Tiger' decade produced a marked upsurge in immigration. This time, though, the new arrivals, many of whom were highly educated young people, generally considered themselves only temporary immigrants, and most intended to return to Ireland once the economy had recovered and the job market improved.[20]

Patrick O'Farrell's two colliding 'cultural forces'

Patrick O'Farrell synthesised the broad parameters of Irish immigration and settlement in Australia in his *The Irish in Australia*, first published in 1986. Since then, there has been a steady stream of research that has amplified, extended and debated O'Farrell's core findings, so that knowledge of the Irish from the perspectives of demography, geography, religion and politics is now reasonably detailed.[21]

In his book, O'Farrell made a series of striking claims concerning the role that Irish immigrants and their descendants had played in shaping the society and culture of settler Australia.[22] According to him: 'The distinctive Australian identity was not born in the bush, nor at Anzac Cove: these were merely situations for its expression. No; it was born in Irishness protesting against the extremes of Englishness.' O'Farrell had in mind a specific type of Irishness: not that of the Protestant Anglo-Irish or Ulster Scots-Irish, but that of those he called the 'Gaelic Catholic Irish'. It was the existence of this large 'insubordinate' minority, always ready to challenge Protestant English authority, that, according to O'Farrell, helped foster in colonial Australia 'a general atmosphere in which exclusion, discrimination and rigid hierarchies became increasingly less possible to sustain'. He argued that settler Australia had two markedly different histories, and it was the 'tension, abrasion and sometimes collision' between the 'cultural forces' of Protestant Englishness and Catholic Irishness that, 'far from being divisive, became the main unifying principle of Australian history'.[23]

In writing his book, O'Farrell deliberately adopted a confrontational approach, determined upon challenging much of the existing historiography. On the one hand, he was reacting against the standard general histories of Australia emanating from non-Irish sources that either ignored the Irish by subsuming them into broader categories or relegated them to the subaltern status of troublesome and disruptive outsiders. But he was also reacting against earlier populist works, often written by Irish and Catholic authors, which he saw as informed by a pious and naive Catholic nationalism.[24] In this latter category, O'Farrell directed his fire mainly at the writings of two men, both journalists, JF Hogan and PS Cleary.

The first publication to carry the title *The Irish in Australia* appeared in London almost exactly a century before O'Farrell's book. Its author, James Francis Hogan (1855–1924), a young journalist, had been born in Ireland but raised in Victoria, and he went on to sit in the British House of Commons during the 1890s as a home rule member representing County Tipperary. His 1887 book largely ignored the convict history of the Irish and instead offered a fulsome celebration of the colonial achievements of prominent Irish men, viewed from a Catholic nationalist perspective.[25] Yet Hogan was no political radical: he looked forward to a self-governing Ireland taking its place alongside the self-governing Australian colonies as a loyal member of the British imperial family.[26]

Patrick Scott Cleary (1861–1941), born in Melbourne to Irish immigrant parents, pursued a career in Sydney Catholic politics and journalism. In 1913, he helped establish the Catholic Federation in New South Wales (NSW) to lobby for the restoration of government aid to church schools and, in 1922, he became the editor of the church-owned *Catholic Press*. The title of the 1933 book he published about the Irish in Australia clearly revealed his approach: *Australia's Debt to Irish Nation-Builders*.[27] Like Hogan, Cleary devoted most of his book to praising the achievements of Irish male immigrants, but, whereas Hogan had little to say about convicts, Cleary included a chapter on male convicts entitled 'Irish Exiles'. He justified the use of the word 'exiles', instead of 'convicts', because he claimed that most of these Irish men were 'political victims', 'poor fellows' provoked into rebellion by the 'abominable injustice' and 'wickedness' of British rule.[28] According to this view, the Irish were not *really* criminals at all and were thus free of the so-called 'convict stain'. Numbers of later works, published well into the 1980s and focusing especially on those transported for political offences, followed Cleary's lead in rejecting the word 'convict' and substituting instead 'exile'.[29]

O'Farrell, however, emphatically rejected the notion of Irish 'exiles', estimating that as many as 80 per cent of the nearly 50 000

Irish convicts transported to Australia were 'ordinary criminals, mostly thieves', with 'many' of the women being 'prostitutes as well'. Political offenders, despite the attention paid to them by Irish-Australian writers, were few: probably less than 600, he thought.[30] This was not a judgment calculated to please many Australians proud of their Irish heritage and increasingly of their Irish convict ancestry as well.[31] As a consequence, despite his flattering claims for Irish influence, O'Farrell's work was by no means wholeheartedly embraced by the Irish-Australian community.[32]

British, Catholic or Anglo-Celtic?

Many writers on Australian history have not embraced O'Farrell's ideas either; some in fact have shown little interest in the Irish at all. In 2005, for example, a collection of essays published under the title *Australia's History* claimed to offer a 'compelling' and 'up-to-date account' of current 'issues and debates in Australian history' intended for both 'students and general readers'. Yet no work dealing with the Irish in Australia was cited in the book's bibliographies and, in the discussion of immigration, the Irish were largely subsumed into the category 'British'. In all, the book contained only a handful of fleeting references to the Irish, which collectively portrayed them as 'other'. They were generally perceived, readers were told, as 'violent, impulsive, degraded and unregulated' and, as a result, were 'systematically poorly treated'.[33] Nearly twenty years after the initial publication of *The Irish in Australia*, this collection, intended for a large audience, ignored O'Farrell's work entirely.

Nor has the situation changed much over the past decade. The massive 1200-page, two-volume *Cambridge History of*

Australia, published in 2013, also relegated the Irish to a very minor role. In the index to the first volume, there were just eight entries on the Irish, compared with 42 on the Chinese; in the index to the second volume, there were no entries on the Irish at all. These volumes continued to deal with the Irish much as mainstream Australian historiography had before 1986: that is, they were consigned to the category 'Catholic' and treated in the context of religious history. And, as in the 2005 collection, this treatment was far from flattering, with Irish Catholics often associated with sectarianism.[34] Ethnicity was here subsumed into religion and Irishness into Catholicism, just as other historians chose to subsume Irishness into Britishness. Either way, the Irish-born and their Irish-Australian descendants disappeared into larger groups, stripped of much of their distinctive cultural identity.

Recently too, in the field of Australian studies, the Irish and Irish Australians have been disappearing into another larger 'imagined community'. The old categories 'British' and 'Catholic' are increasingly being superseded by a new one, 'Anglo-Celtic' – an identity that will be discussed in more detail in the epilogue to this book.

Some historians have, however, acknowledged deficiencies in the way mainstream Australian history has handled the Irish. In 1988, John Rickard recognised that a 'myth' of British 'homogeneity' had been 'manufactured' about pre-1945 Australia, despite there being major ethnic differences within Britain between the English, Scots and Welsh. As for the Irish, Rickard characterised their situation in Australia as 'peculiar', because they had, 'against their will', been 'designated "British"'.[35] Ann Curthoys also demonstrated an appreciation of this anomaly when she acknowledged that the 'high Irish proportion always meant that the Australian population could not be the replica of Britain many wanted it to be'.[36] In a recent discussion of post-1945 immigration, John Hirst included some interesting thoughts about the Irish as an ethnic, as well as a religious, group. He noted that in colonial Australia the term 'British' included the Irish, but he recognised that the Irish in Ireland certainly did not consider themselves British, while 'no one in England or Scotland thought of the Irish as British' either. Australian usage of the word 'British' to include the Irish was, as Rickard had remarked, 'peculiar'.

But Hirst went on to claim that Irish Australians themselves were 'in two minds about the offer to be included as British'. When the British were busy 'suppressing' Irish nationalism, the offer tended to be rejected. However, towards the end of the 19th century, when the British Liberal Party embraced the cause of Irish home rule, Hirst believed it became much easier for the Australian Irish to identify as 'British'. From the 1870s onwards, though, the issue of state aid to Catholic schools emerged to foster divisions along religious rather than ethnic lines and Hirst argued that by the early 20th century, 'Catholics and Protestants were beginning to live more apart'. He was not necessarily describing residential segregation here, but rather that important aspects of their lives were conducted separately. Children were taught in either the state or the Catholic school system. Catholics and Protestants tended to work in different areas of employment, even in different parts of the public service, while their social and leisure activities were largely conducted separately as well.

Hirst, who was certainly no fan of the Catholic Irish, wrote that they were a 'disruptive' factor, responsible for creating ethnic and religious divisions in Australia that would not otherwise have existed. Yet, the 'commitment to containing old-world disputes or overcoming them was very strong', and Australians developed 'a way of being good neighbours despite their differences'. This good neighbourliness, Hirst argued, had its roots in 'egalitarianism' and male mateship, plus economic prosperity. And he concluded on an optimistic note, suggesting that the largely peaceful resolution of, first, the Irish-British schism and then the Catholic-Protestant one gave Australians a 'good preparation' for the task of successfully 'accommodating' the post-1945 waves of immigrants.[37] Although more critical of the Irish than O'Farrell, Hirst nevertheless agreed with him that, in the long run, the divisions and tensions generated by the presence of the Irish had proved to be a positive phenomenon. Other historians, however, were far less sanguine about the Irish influence on Australia.

Sexism, sectarianism and sedition

If Hirst considered the Catholic Irish a generally 'disruptive' force in 19th- and early 20th-century Australia, others have portrayed them far more negatively. One historian who dealt with the Irish as both an ethnic and religious group was Miriam Dixson. Like O'Farrell, she accepted that Irish influence on Australian colonial society was profound, but to her mind it was profoundly damaging, especially for women.

Dixson devoted a chapter to the Irish in her pioneering book on Australian women's history, *The Real Matilda*, first published in 1976. In that she quoted approvingly historian Russel Ward's argument that 'Irish working-class attitudes' were an 'important ingredient' in developing the 'distinctive Australian [mateship] ethos'.[38] She also went on to endorse what she called the English view of the Irish as 'not-quite-Western' and 'primitive in the sense of pre-modern', at the same time quoting Manning Clark to the effect that the English considered 'there was nothing but the shade of a Catholic's skin to distinguish him from an aborigine'.[39] Dixson believed that what the Irish essentially contributed to the mateship ethos was a pre-modern 'clan-based collectiveness', of which misogyny was a major characteristic. Drawing upon the work of the psychiatrist and post-colonial theorist Franz Fanon, Dixson argued that 'the Irish male, like the black, became a "victim" of English colonial arrogance'. Irish men in turn imposed the 'humiliation and blighted self-image' on women that imperialism had forced upon them. In addition, 'Irish fear of sexuality', a product of their Catholicism, had helped 'shape the curiously low standing and impoverished self-identity of Australian women'.[40] Dixson showed sympathy for the Irish women as 'victims' of British imperialism, but none for Irish men, whom she believed were substantially responsible for Australia's deep-seated misogynist culture.

Whereas Dixson held the Irish responsible in large part for Australia's macho sexist culture, other leading historians blamed them for introducing additional undesirable traits into Australian society. In his history of Victoria, first published in 1984 and reissued in a new edition in 2006, Geoffrey Blainey included three entries in the index under the heading 'Irish': 'Catholic church', 'negative nationalism' and 'sectarianism'. He informed readers that sectarianism involved 'Ireland versus the Rest', as well as 'Ireland versus Ireland', meaning Irish Catholics in conflict with British Protestants as well as with Irish Protestants. Either way, sectarianism was portrayed as essentially an Irish phenomenon. The chapter on religion was titled 'Sunshine and Moonshine', for, after treating the 'sunshine' of religion, Blainey moved on to the 'moonshine' of alcohol. Here too the Irish figured prominently, being described as 'strong drinkers'. In addition to fostering sectarianism and alcoholism in Australia, the other main achievement of the Irish, according to Blainey, was to introduce what he called 'negative nationalism'. The Irish brought this 'noisy' creed 'ready-made' to Australia, and its chief characteristic was a bitter 'dislike of England'. Blainey contrasted this with 'positive nationalism', which was 'home-grown' and expressed a healthy love for Australia. He ignored O'Farrell's claim that the Irish had played a crucial role in developing Australian nationalism.[41]

Blainey was in fact following a well-trodden path in his treatment of the Irish. Many earlier, similarly Anglophile historians had also expressed hostile views, seeing in the Irish a threat to English authority in Australia that had to be defeated. English-born Sir Ernest Scott, professor of history at the University of Melbourne during 1913–36, had, like Dixson and Blainey, a decidedly jaundiced view of the Irish. Most of the time he ignored them altogether, choosing to characterise Australia's colonisers simply as 'British'. But, occasionally, events forced him to take account of the Irish. Then he viewed them through the eyes of their English rulers. Relying on the hostile accounts of NSW governors John Hunter and Philip Gidley King, Scott described Irish prisoners transported in the wake of the 1798 Rebellion as '[r]ebels by life-long disposition, bitter enemies of ... authority'. Their 'violent hatred' of British rule threatened 'desperate things' and the 'wildest anarchy' in the new colony. Scott made no attempt to understand the causes of Irish disaffection, instead portraying the Irish as an innately 'turbulent' and 'seditious' people, and agreeing with Hunter and King that their '"restless and diabolical spirit" had to be stamped out by vigorously exemplary means': that is, Scott wrote, by 'the cat and the gallows'.[42]

Negative readings of the part the Irish played in the Australian story have continued. In a keynote address to the 2010 annual conference of the Australian Historical Association, the Australian-born, Oxford-based historian, Ross McKibbin, offered a comparison of Britain and Australia. He agreed that Irish influence was important, but, like a number of Australian historians, he did not consider this influence to have been at all constructive. McKibbin highlighted, among other differences, those between the Australian and British labour parties. The Australian Labor Party (ALP), he argued, unlike the British party, was and remains highly factionalised – sometimes cripplingly so. In seeking the origins of this flaw, McKibbin pointed to the Catholic Church. The Catholic hierarchy in Britain had always been largely British-born and therefore 'more anxious to conciliate and ... more cautious'. By contrast, the Irish dominated the Australian hierarchy up until the middle of the 20th century. And until the 1960s the Catholic Church remained very active in Australian politics, campaigning to restore state aid to church schools – an issue that had been resolved in Britain as far back as 1902. Moreover, the ALP had always depended more upon Catholic votes than did the British Labour Party. On top of this, the ALP had proved more susceptible to communist infiltration than had the British party. Consequently, Irish clergy, most famously Melbourne's Archbishop Daniel Mannix, played an interventionist role in Australian political affairs that had no parallel in Britain. Having helped split the ALP during the 1950s and given it a factionalised character, many Catholics then moved on, said McKibbin, into conservative politics, especially during the prime ministership of Robert Menzies, who had finally in the early 1960s given the church the state aid it had fought so long and hard for. But, among conservatives too, Catholics often proved a divisive force.[43]

A new history of the Irish in Australia

Popular appreciation of the Irish remains strong in Australia today, as the widespread celebrations on 17 March each year demonstrate. Nevertheless, negative assessments persist among some historians, while anti-Irish jokes remain popular, as we shall see in our epilogue. O'Farrell's 1986 book won prizes when first published and it was subsequently re-published in two further editions. Both in Australia and overseas, the book is generally accepted as a seminal work. Yet its impact on the writing of Australian history has obviously been limited. Currently there is no clear consensus among historians as to the role or significance of the Irish and their descendants in the making of modern Australia.

The present book, as its title implies, aims to take a 'new' look at the history of the Irish in Australia – 'new' in various respects. The book draws on previously unused source materials; it examines topics not studied in the past; it takes approaches not attempted before; and it draws upon the latest research published, not only in Australia, but in Ireland and other parts of the Irish diaspora as well. Nevertheless, the book does not aspire to be a comprehensive account, as others, notably O'Farrell and Chris McConville, have produced.[44] It is concerned with certain themes and topics: some dealt with previously, but others not, or at least not previously dealt with in Australia. We interrogate issues to do with race, gender, crime, mental health, employment, politics and religion. The book is informed by new and important research published by Irish-Australian scholars since the 1980s and by major new works produced overseas, notably in Ireland, Britain, the US, New Zealand and Canada. We discuss circumstances in Ireland and other parts of the diaspora when relevant to the Irish experience in Australia. While focusing on the Irish in one country, the book still aspires to have a diasporic or transnational dimension by situating the Australian Irish in much broader contexts.

This book asks rather different questions from those that O'Farrell asked more than a generation ago, yet his work remains fundamental. Even if some of his answers no longer seem convincing, his courage in posing such challenging questions and the intellectually stimulating responses he offered cannot help but impress. For readers today, though, whether they are Irish Australians or Australians with no Irish ancestry at all, the long journey of the Catholic Irish from unwelcome 'savages' to respected citizens provides a compelling story and, moreover, one with considerable contemporary relevance. Today Australia is a nation of immigrants – 49 per cent of the population were either born overseas or have at least one parent born overseas – just as it was during the 19th century.[45] Then the Irish, and especially the Catholic Irish, challenged the majority society with their difference, just as today other immigrant groups offer rather similar challenges. The story of how the Irish overcame often intense hostility to eventually become recognised as Australians holds out many lessons, not only about the past but potentially for the future as well.

SECTION ONE:
RACE

CHAPTER 1
The Irish race

That the Irish were different seemed self-evident to Australian settlers of English and Scottish origin or descent. Historians have usually thought the main points of difference were religion and class: that the Irish were predominantly Catholic, while most colonists were Protestant, and that many of the Catholic Irish were poor. These were indeed major points of difference and ones that cannot be dismissed. However, were they the only ones? If this is so, what of press comments in 1864 about the very public divorce of middle-class Irish Protestants, Henrietta and Robert Molesworth? In its remarks the Melbourne *Age* suggested that even though some 'latitude' should be given to those who came from a country where 'people and pigs huddle together promiscuously', the behaviour of the couple exceeded 'the licence of that primitive and innocent' society. As historian Frank Bongiorno has pointed out, for the Molesworths, their sin was 'racial not religious'.[1] Clearly it was not just religion and class that marked the Irish out as different; there was something else, and for some this difference could still be perceived in later generations. The writer Jack Lindsay in his memoirs described the sculptor Guy Lynch, whose grandparents were Irish, as having an 'Irish-Australian face, rough and tough, of the wildwood, yet sensitive'.[2] These comments point to a focus on perceived physical differences: deeply rooted, unavoidable and often couched in the terminology of race. In this chapter we will trace this thread of racialisation from negative stereotyping in the convict era to the positive interpretations of Irish distinctiveness advanced by increasingly confident Irish Australians in the latter part of the 19th century.

From the beginning of European settlement in Australia, there has been a constant stream of writing about the inferiority of the Irish. The Anglican clergyman Samuel Marsden was scathing in his criticisms of the moral shortcomings of the Irish convicts he encountered.[3] When large-scale immigration of free settlers started, the conservative Melbourne *Argus* castigated the Irish as 'lawless savages', whose arrival threatened to destroy the Anglo-Saxon racial character of the colony.[4] In 1881, Melbourne businessman and journalist AM Topp, who had been born in England, declared that: 'It cannot be too strongly impressed upon the minds of Englishmen that the Irish are not a mere variety of their own race.'[5] Over 90 years later, when Patrick O'Farrell started to publish research on the Irish in Australia, he received a letter claiming: 'These [Irish] natives were a long way back in evolution, stupid, stubborn, strong physically and very dull.'[6] Even after an independent Ireland had weathered major economic, political and social storms during the 20th and early 21st centuries, jokes and political comment assuming Irish stupidity continued to be popular in Australia. In 2011, Tony Abbott, then federal Opposition leader, found it acceptable to try to score political points against the Labor Party by claiming that it was behaving a 'bit like the Irishman who lost 10 pounds betting on the Grand National and then lost 20 pounds on the action replay'.[7]

Many more such examples could be cited, but in this book we are more interested in exploring what such attitudes have meant for the Irish in Australia. Equally important, what were the implications for Australia when such a large minority, considered 'alien' by many, formed a significant proportion of the founding settlers? During the 19th century, the Catholic Irish were widely despised and feared, yet at the same time there was never any real prospect of excluding them from the Australian colonies or from the rights guaranteed to subjects of the British crown. Indeed, by the end of the 19th century, increasing numbers of Irish-Australian writers were claiming that the distinctiveness of the Irish was a positive attribute that should be celebrated, not condemned. This chapter will navigate a path through these numerous disjunctions and argue that racial theories about the Irish, both positive and negative, are as essential to understanding the Irish in Australia as are religion and class.

Race and the Irish

Throughout the 19th century, Europeans worked to make sense of the world around them in light of new discoveries and ideas. As they expanded their colonies and gained knowledge of different peoples, they increasingly attempted to categorise and explain observed differences between societies in terms of race.[8] This was no benign endeavour. Dividing peoples into racial hierarchies allowed them to intellectually justify exploiting, colonising and devastating societies composed of those deemed to be at the bottom of such hierarchies.[9]

Nineteenth-century European race theorists created different categories based on investigating the physical, cultural and moral differences they perceived in those around them. They looked for and found such differences amongst groups within the British Isles and in Europe and then encountered many more at the outer reaches of the empire.[10] When we try to make sense of the way writers understood these differences, and the implications of their work, the task is complicated as words shift meaning, particularly the word 'race'. This word was generally deployed when writers wanted to explain perceived differences using factors such as physiology, anatomy, biology, history, culture, class and morality.[11] Historian Catherine Hall, following the sociologist Stuart Hall, has suggested that two broad categories of meanings were involved when 19th-century writers used the word 'race'. The first involved biological markers of difference and the second cultural markers. These two meanings were effectively two different 'registers' of racial thinking: ones for which in the 21st century we would use different words, most likely 'race' and 'ethnicity'. However, the registers of meaning in the word 'race', as used by 19th-century writers, were often not separate but instead used simultaneously and interchangeably. This means that the word and the concepts it tried to capture were inherently unstable and they shifted to accommodate changing political, cultural and social circumstances.[12] As postcolonial theorist Robert Young put it: 'Race has always been culturally constructed. Culture has always been racially constructed.'[13] The concepts of 'race' and 'culture' were so firmly entwined they are difficult to disentangle.[14]

The question of whether during the 19th century the Irish were considered to be racially different from the English, and from other Europeans as well, has been the subject of considerable academic debate since the 1990s, when American scholar Noel Ignatiev published his provocatively titled book, *How the*

Irish Became White.[15] The scholarly context in which Ignatiev framed his arguments is often referred to as 'whiteness studies'. Scholars in this field argued that in order to fully understand the historical and contemporary intricacies of racial thinking, the term 'white' needed to be seen as a racial term just as much as 'black' or 'coloured'.[16] In his book, Ignatiev claimed that during the mid-19th century the working-class Catholic Irish were subject to discrimination that kept them at the bottom of the American economic and social class system, competing for jobs in the big cities of the east coast with poor, recently emancipated African Americans. In a society where skin colour had become a crucial marker separating slaves from citizens, the working-class Irish pushed to be recognised as different from African Americans and more like white working-class Americans of British or northern European descent. They achieved this through becoming increasingly involved in anti-abolitionist politics, using overt violence against African Americans and competing directly with black people for menial jobs. Ignatiev argued that, for the Irish to be accepted as white, they had to be seen to be doing 'white man's work', which by definition was work from which black men were excluded.[17] Once the Irish had displaced African Americans from a range of low-paid jobs, these then came to be redefined as 'white' jobs, confirming black exclusion. By such means, the Irish asserted and gained membership of the racial category 'white' with all its social, cultural and economic benefits, at the expense of African Americans.[18]

Ignatiev's book has been influential outside the United States (US), although some historians have challenged his arguments and his work is situated very firmly within the context of 19th-century American labour history.[19] Questions regarding Irish racialisation and whiteness are different in Britain and different again in Australia. In Britain there has long been disagreement among scholars as to whether racialisation existed at all and, if so, what its consequences were. Some have argued that religion and class were more significant factors in promoting anti-Irish sentiment than race.[20] In summing up these debates, historian Michael De Nie suggested that race was rather 'a metalanguage in Anglo-Saxonist discourse, a vehicle for expressing multiple anxieties and preconceptions, among them class concerns and sectarian prejudices'.[21] In other words, the 'language of race' could be used to express religious and political differences, as well as perceived racial ones.

However interpreted, it is clear that hostile attitudes towards the Irish as a people and a culture have a long intellectual history and this is especially true in Britain. The English began their conquest of Ireland in the late 12th century and their hostility towards the Irish intensified during the conflicts of the Tudor and Stuart periods, which saw the whole of Gaelic Ireland finally brought under the control of the British crown.[22] For centuries the English perceived the Irish as primitive, treacherous, violent, lazy and stupid. Such stereotypes were often gendered: Irish men were feminised as treacherous and Irish women masculinised as violent.[23] Irish insistence on clinging to Catholic 'superstition' in the face of the Protestant Reformation only served to confirm their intractability in Protestant British eyes.[24] The bloody rebellion of 1798, when the Irish not only fought to overthrow British rule but allied themselves with the traditional enemy, France, only further entrenched notions of Irish barbarity amongst Britain's ruling classes and in British popular culture as well. During the 19th century, Catholic Irish immigrants to Britain swelled what had earlier been a small, select group of Catholics into large, mainly working-class Catholic communities based especially in the big urban centres. There Irish workers competed with the English for jobs. The rise of Irish republicanism in the form of the Fenian movement, funded largely by Irish Americans, saw bombing campaigns and assassinations carried out in England during the 1860s and 1880s. The Irish had imported their disloyalty and political violence into the very heart of the empire. Negative racial stereotyping of the Irish did not end when the south of Ireland gained its independence in 1922, but continued throughout the 20th century and especially when the Troubles broke out in Northern Ireland during the late 1960s.[25] As sociologist Steve Garner has pointed out, 'racialisation of the Irish in Britain involved focusing on difference in three overlapping arenas: religion, class and race'.[26] The ingredients were the same as in the US, but the mix was rather different in Britain since the Irish were not competing for jobs against black people during the 19th and early 20th centuries. They were competing against and attracting hostility from the white British working class.

The racialisation of European settlers, in particular the Irish, has not attracted the same scholarly attention in Australia, where academic interest in recent decades has focused on the role that racial theories played in dispossessing Indigenous peoples and excluding Asians.[27] Patrick O'Farrell, when he was writing in the 1980s, certainly recognised that in colonial Australia the Irish were perceived in racial terms, but he preferred, he said, to deal with 'the higher ground of the anti-Irish argument', which was religion.[28] However, in his last, unfinished work before his death in 2003, O'Farrell was more careful in defining these terms. He argued then that the word 'sectarianism' was by no means restricted to religion; it was all-encompassing and included 'a tangle of history, culture, race, religion, politics, class status and possessions'.[29] Since O'Farrell's death, some scholars have approached the Irish in Australia through the lens of the international debates on racialisation and whiteness, relying for much of their information on O'Farrell's own research. In a 2005 article, cultural studies scholar Jon Stratton claimed that the Irish had largely achieved full acceptance as white by the time of Federation, when the borders of the new state were closed to 'coloured' races, but remained open to the previously despised Irish.[30] Historian Ann McGrath, in her analysis of relations between the Irish and Indigenous Australians, criticised the inclusion of the Irish among white settlers without differentiation, and called for further work to break down this category. A 'renewed emphasis is now required', she wrote, 'not only on the difference of the Asian, Pacific and other ethnic groups that settled in Australia, but on difference amongst the British colonisers in various timeframes'.[31] In an earlier article, historian Ann Curthoys had echoed the need to analyse difference amongst the so-called 'British', and proposed unpacking the category of 'British' to recognise the varied regional and class groups who made up 'white' settlers. However, although she mentioned the Irish, the main focus of her argument was on English settlers who came from different regions.[32]

In Australia, the initial reliance on convict labour and then on only small numbers of non-European workers meant that the dynamics of labour competition between non-Europeans and the unskilled working-class Irish were different from those in the US and Britain. The Catholic Irish were a foundation settler group. They were not newcomers moving into a longstanding Protestant society, as they were in the US; nor were they the largest group of immigrant workers, as they were in Britain. In Australia all settlers were new arrivals. But although the circumstances were different, similar theories and attitudes about race and the Irish had been imported into Australia. AM Topp, in his 1881 polemic about the unfitness of the Irish to participate in English legal and political institutions, buttressed his arguments with the work of English and German historians, combined with information about the Irish in the US.[33] Racialised stereotypes of Irishness based on physical appearance also circulated by means of newspapers and magazines and, as we shall see in later chapters, local Australian content was shaped by material drawn from British and American publications. So the transnational context of ideas about Irishness is important to any discussion of the Irish in Australia; equally important, though, are the specifics of the Australian context. We will consider both in turn.

Transnational race science and the Irish

The transnational context includes negative English attitudes towards the Irish arising from their long and brutal conquest of Ireland, which English immigrants took with them as mental baggage to all parts of the British Empire. Such longstanding attitudes were bolstered during the 19th century by theories developed in the emerging fields of ethnology, anthropology and race science. These theories argued that there were fundamental differences between human groups based on inherited physical features bound up with cultural and moral differences.[34] There was much debate and disagreement, and the Irish in particular posed problems. They were widely perceived as different from the British and from other western and northern European peoples, and this fact puzzled scholars who were striving to develop race theories they thought would prove the superiority of white Europeans.[35]

In 1850, Robert Knox, a Scottish physician and anatomist, published a book about European races based on a series of lectures he had delivered over the previous five years.[36] The Irish and the Celts were far from the only focus of Knox's work, but his assertions about them were hotly debated, particularly his argument that, because of racial deficiencies, the Irish could not 'comprehend the meaning of the word liberty'.[37] Knox had set out to prove that 'the European races, so called, differ from each other as widely as the Negro does from the Bushman; the Caffre from the Hottentot; the Red Indian of America from the Esquimaux; the Esquimaux from the Basque'.[38] For Knox, the most successful European race was the Scandinavian or Saxon one, of which the Anglo-Saxons were the most important branch. Knox was perfectly aware of the political implications of his theories and was forthright in prescribing what the Saxons of England should do about the Celts of Ireland. The Irish race, he wrote, 'must be forced from the soil; by fair means, if possible; still they must leave. England's safety requires it.'[39] In his conception of the Irish Celts as a race, Knox merged physical characteristics with moral traits. According to him: 'The Celtic race presents the two extremes of what is called civilized man; in Paris we find the one; in Ireland, at Skibbereen and Derrynane, the other. Civilized man cannot sink lower than at Derrynane.'[40] Here he was referring to two places which would have been familiar to his audience. The small town of Skibbereen in County Cork, which had recently been devastated by famine, had been the subject of a series of widely publicised illustrated newspaper articles. Derrynane in County Kerry was the birthplace and home of Daniel O'Connell, the leading Catholic Irish politician of the first half of the 19th century, a campaigner for Catholic rights and for Irish self-government.

In singling out Skibbereen and Derrynane, Knox was forging a link between abject Irish economic failure and dangerous Catholic political aspirations.

For Knox and others like him, a key factor distinguishing the Irish from the English was the refusal of the former to be governed by English common law, which he believed to be the fairest and most civilised legal code in the world.[41] This meant that the Irish had to be ruled firmly and by force if necessary. Knox's influence on anthropological thinking about the Irish as a race can be seen in lectures given at the Anthropological Society in London in 1868. A paper delivered by anthropologist J Gould Avery claimed that the disordered political state of Ireland during the 1860s was due to racial differences between the Saxon and the Celt and that the 'peculiarities of the Irish character are not due to political causes ... but they are racial, hereditary and irradicible [sic]'.[42] While some in the audience disagreed with the tone of this paper, there were others who agreed wholeheartedly. Captain Bedford Pim RN announced that: 'The Irish question was simply a race question ... the Celt was a different being to the Saxon.'[43]

Knox, in teaching anatomy in Edinburgh, had used the physical characteristics of skulls to categorise people by race. In doing so, he was following in the footsteps of other craniologists, including a number in the US who were also working to prove the inferiority of the Celtic Irish.[44] Publications by Knox and others, including Darwin's disciple Thomas Huxley, influenced medical practitioners as well as political commentators. One doctor noted Huxley's work on Irish and English racial differ-ence when seeking to explain why the Irish tended to succumb to 'granular' disease of the eyes more than did the English.[45] After the 1850s, the 'science' of measuring skulls and skeletons, as well as eye and hair colour, was developed further to try and provide quantitative proof of profound racial differences.[46] Scientists collected skulls and skeletons from graves, hospitals and asylums, often without consent, in Europe and throughout much of the colonial world, and took elaborate measurements. While much of this work eventually focused on identifying the alleged inferior characteristics of non-European racial groups, there was a strand of this research that included the Irish and the British in its calculations.[47]

One of the most influential of these researchers was the English doctor John Beddoe, who was active in the Ethnological Society and Anthropological Society from the 1860s until his death in 1911.[48] He devoted himself to uncovering physical differences amongst the peoples of the British Isles and in 1885 he published the results of decades of work in his best-known book, *The Races of Britain*. During his extensive travels, Beddoe collected data on the inhabitants of Ireland, England, Scotland and Wales, to whom he applied his 'Index of Nigrescence', a measurement of hair and eye colour. From this he concluded that the inhabitants of the western coasts and islands of Ireland were racially closer to African than to European populations.[49] Generally speaking, Beddoe imposed few overt value judgments on his voluminous statistical findings, although on occasion he did annotate human 'types' he had found in Ireland. Of one type, common in the Scottish highlands and Irish west, which he identified as resembling prehistoric Cro-Magnon man, Beddoe wrote: 'the intelligence is low, and there is a great deal of cunning and suspicion'.[50] In his memoirs, he recalled meeting people in County Sligo whom he considered 'a primitive race, swarthy and sombre of feature with high cheekbones and reminding me of a common Welsh type'.[51]

Beddoe and other anthropometric researchers who measured heads and heights and interpreted hair and eye colour were influential in the latter half of the 19th century and into the early decades of the 20th century. One of the pioneers of English anthropology, who began his career in anthropometry, was English-born Alfred C Haddon, who during the 1880s and 1890s worked in Dublin.[52] Haddon made his most important contribution to anthropology during two expeditions to the islands of the Torres Strait in 1889–90 and 1898–99. But as well as studying the people of the Torres Strait, Haddon was simultaneously conducting anthropometric and ethnographic research on the people of the west of Ireland.

Haddon's initial thinking on race was influenced by the Irish ethnologist John Grattan and by John Beddoe and later Francis Galton, the pioneer of eugenics, with all of whom he was in friendly correspondence and at times collaboration.[53] Building upon their methodologies, he used physical measurements in his search for definitive examples of racial types. During his first trip to the Torres Strait in 1888–89, he concluded that contact with European civilisation had already irrevocably changed the islanders' original way of life – to the islanders' detriment. Back in Dublin, he continued his interest in looking for 'original' peoples by next travelling to the west coast of Ireland, where he interviewed many Aran Islanders, photographed them, measured their skulls, noted their hair and eye colours and collected skulls surreptitiously from their graveyards. He then returned to his laboratory in Dublin convinced that he had found what he had failed to find in the Torres Strait: an isolated people, racially distinct and uncontaminated by outsiders.[54] With grants from the Royal Irish Academy, Haddon established an anthropometric laboratory at Trinity College, Dublin. Between 1894 and 1901, he was also working part-time at the University of Cambridge, which helped fund a second and more extensive Torres Strait expedition in 1898–99.[55]

Throughout Haddon's writings, his use of the term 'race' was somewhat ambiguous, for at times he was referring to cultural groups and at other times to physiological similarities. When he came to define 'race' in *The Races of Man and their Distribution* (1909), he stated that the Irish were not a separate race, but were instead a subset of the Mediterranean race and so distinct from Anglo-Saxons.[56] He had obviously accepted the categorisation, popular at the time, of Europeans into Nordic or Aryan, Alpine and Mediterranean, with the English belonging to the superior Nordic group, while the Irish were among the inferior Mediterranean peoples. Haddon was not hostile towards those he met and studied in the west of Ireland, but he certainly considered them backward, needing to be persuaded to have photographs and measurements taken and tricked so that he could acquire their ancestors' skulls. In many ways he saw the Aran Islanders as more primitive than the people he had encountered on the islands in the Torres Strait. In a letter to his son in 1890, he wrote: 'The people here as a rule, live in worse houses than the people of Torres Strait and they do not keep them anything like so clean and tidy as the black savages do.'[57] But at the same time, he spoke admiringly of the physical characteristics and wisdom of some of the Aran Islanders and conceded that the British had governed the Irish badly.[58] Haddon used much the same techniques in all his ethnographic work, whether he was in Ireland, the Torres Strait or later Borneo, measuring, photographing and collecting examples of folklore, cats' cradles, spades and carts, demonstrating – to his own satisfaction at least – that many objects and stories were similar across different racial groups.[59] During the 1880s and 1890s, Haddon clearly saw no contradiction in simultaneously researching peoples living on islands off the west coast of Ireland and off the north coast of Australia. According to his theories, which reflected much contemporary racial science, both peoples belonged to less advanced races than his own and he was intrigued by the similarities and differences he believed he had discovered between them.

Nineteenth- and early 20th-century anthropologists and ethnologists, like Beddoe and Haddon, were sure that they were describing reality when they assigned different human groups to racial categories and hierarchies. Scientists disagreed as to the exact nature of the categories and where different groups should be placed, but there was general agreement that Teutonic/Anglo-Saxon/Germanic/Nordic peoples were at the pinnacle of the racial hierarchy due to their capacity for reason, hard work, high culture and civilised values. There was just as much general agreement that the 'savages' who still lived on the lands these same Anglo-Saxons were now colonising were towards the bottom of the hierarchy and, amongst these, 'Tasmanians' were often situated at the very bottom. As many scholars have shown, such racial theories justified confiscating indigenous lands and systematic attempts to reshape if not eradicate indigenous societies.[60] Scholars disputed where the Irish sat exactly in terms of racial hierarchies, but it was never as low as the 'Tasmanians' and nor were the Irish subjected to the same degree of violent colonisation during the 19th century as were Indigenous Australians.

The 'low' Irish in colonial Australia

The Irish were negatively stereotyped in racial terms both explicitly and implicitly in 19th- and early 20th-century Australia, as we shall see throughout this book. In this section, we examine aspects of the way the Irish were overtly racialised during the colonial period. Race and religion were closely intertwined in negative attitudes towards Irish immigrants and not only did officials, politicians and commentators hold these widely, so did neighbours and even sometimes, tragically, family members too.

Thousands of Irish convicts, transported to the eastern Australian colonies between 1791 and 1853, were distinguished from their fellow prisoners by their ethnicity, religion, culture, language and sometimes by their race as well. About 29 500 male and 9100 female convicts were sent directly from Irish courts, while about another 8000 of the Irish-born came from Britain. Since they made up around 28 per cent of the total convict population, the Irish were impossible to ignore.[61] To many British colonial officials, they were the lowest among the low convict population. David Collins, captain of marines and deputy judge-advocate during the 1790s, was particularly outspoken. He employed traditional anti-Irish terminology in describing Irish convicts as 'ignorant', 'obstinate', 'cunning', 'restless' and 'diabolical'. They were so ignorant as to be scarcely human, according to Collins. After reporting that a group of Irish convicts had tried to escape in 1798, he wrote in exasperation: 'Could it be imagined ... there was existing in a polished civilized kingdom a race of beings (for they do not deserve the appellation of men) so extremely ignorant, and so little humanized as these were, compared with whom the naked savages of the mountains were an enlightened people.'[62] Another strident critic of Catholic Irish convicts was the Reverend Samuel Marsden. According to him, the Irish were a 'most wild, ignorant and savage race'.[63] Some, on the other hand, saw the Irish in rather more benign terms, as 'simple, innocent and as tractable as a child'.[64] Yet this paternalistic view was still in keeping with assigning the Irish to the lower levels of racial hierarchies and it justified the colonial state in directing and monitoring Irish convicts' lives both during and after their sentences.[65]

Once free settlers began to immigrate on a large scale during the 1830s, mainly funded by government schemes of assistance, the Irish proved particularly adept at managing the complex bureaucratic processes involved in such schemes. This prompted much public debate over the quality of the immigrants arriving, and many people objected to the Irish on the grounds of religion as well as their innate racial inferiority. Indeed, the two were closely intertwined. One of the loudest critics of Catholic Irish immigration was Scottish-born Presbyterian minister and politician John Dunmore Lang, who throughout his long career opposed increased migration from Ireland for fear that the 'low' Catholic Irish might corrupt if not swamp Protestant and British colonial society.[66] Immigrants from Ireland, however, showed no sign of heeding any of Lang's diatribes, if they were aware of them, for they continued to arrive in large numbers from the 1830s up until the 1880s, taking full advantage of the various assisted migration schemes then available, their numbers declining only when such schemes were curtailed.[67]

That the Irish had rejected Protestantism and chosen to remain Catholic was often ascribed to basic flaws in the moral character of their race. They were incapable of seeing the shortcomings of Catholicism, while the church's teachings in turn helped blunt their reasoning powers. As one newspaper commentator put it in 1891: 'He [the Irishman] has an imperfect conception of causation, in common with the inferior races of man, due almost entirely to his religion.'[68] But for this writer, the Irish, unlike other low and 'inferior' races, had the chance of advancement if only they could be freed from Catholic indoctrination. A decade earlier, in two articles in the *Melbourne Review*, AM Topp had expressed a similar view: that state education could eliminate the disastrous consequences of the inferiority of the Irish 'race' in Australia.[69] Topp was indebted to Edward Augustus Freeman, the English liberal historian of Anglo-Saxonism, who combined contempt for the Irish with support for Irish home rule, on the basis that the Celtic Irish should be left to settle their own affairs.[70] Topp might have agreed with leaving the Irish to themselves, but was faced with the problem, as he saw it, that the Irish could not be isolated in the colonies and must therefore be educated out of their undesirable mental and moral characteristics. Topp's assessment of the Irish threat was certainly mediated by political concerns, especially concerns about Irish republican violence during the early 1880s, nevertheless, he was forthright in his opinion that the Irish were a race of 'morally, socially and intellectually' inferior people.[71]

Ideas about the savage nature and low moral character of the Irish were not, of course, restricted to newspaper commentators, government officials or Protestant clergy. As we shall see in a later chapter, there were always employers who would not hire Irish workers because they perceived them as unreliable and untrustworthy. That such attitudes seeped into personal and even family relationships is perhaps not surprising. Insults like 'dirty Irish' were thrown about during disputes, some of which ended up in the courts. In 1865, for example, two female neighbours faced a Bendigo magistrate on charges of offensive language. Mrs Scott had called Mrs Webb a 'dirty Irish beast' and accused her of being of 'low Irish extraction' and of only knowing how to live on 'potatoes and buttermilk'. In addition, she had alleged that Mrs Webb had left illegitimate children behind her in Ireland. Mrs Webb in response flung at Mrs Scott that at least Irish men were better than the Chinese men some members of Mrs Scott's family had married.[72] Courts and newspapers usually treated such exchanges with amusement, however, there were more disturbing cases as well. An Irish woman living in Adelaide, Julia Meadows, attempted in 1869 to get a court order restraining her husband from beating her. She claimed that he had told her he would 'never wash again until I have dirtied myself with your dirty Irish blood'.[73] In a tragic and widely reported case of family violence near Wollongong in 1877, an English-born man killed his two children and himself, leaving a note blaming his Irish-born wife. 'I love my little children too much to leave them to their brutal mother,' he wrote, 'that dirty, drunken, selfish, and unfeeling Irish savage.'[74] People used the culturally available vocabulary of the time to express personal and family conflicts, and notions of the 'dirty' and 'savage' Irish were clearly readily to hand in colonial Australia.

The Irish and other races

Commentators on the expanding British imperial world of the 19th century often compared Europeans to Indigenous peoples, Asians and Africans. In the US too, people often compared European immigrants and African Americans during the mid and late 19th century. In such discourses, the Irish sometimes constituted a liminal category: they were European and were accepted by most people, although not by all, as 'white', yet at the same time, they shared characteristics with groups who were not European and definitely not 'white'.

In the 1830s, for example, one official defended the living conditions of slaves in the West Indies on the grounds that: 'I have seen more Misery in Ireland in One Day than I have seen in the West Indies during my Service there.' Wesleyan missionary the Reverend John Barry, who had worked in Kingston and Spanish Town, reported to the British House of Commons that 'Negroes' were 'just the same as other men', possessing 'as high a Degree of Intellect as the Irish Peasantry'.[75] Other writers did not intend their comparisons of the Irish with Indigenous or black peoples to flatter either group. The French anthropologist Armand de Quatrefages wrote that the Irish reminded him 'of the very lowest tribes of Australia'.[76] English novelist Charles Kingsley, on a visit to Ireland in 1860, was deeply unsettled by the sight of what he called 'white chimpanzees'. If 'they were black', he wrote, 'one would not feel it so much, but their skins, except where tanned by exposure, are as white as ours'.[77] In 1843, Scottish-born Dr Alexander Thomson of Geelong, a member of the New South Wales Legislative Council representing the Port Phillip district (now Victoria), gave evidence before a select committee investigating immigration. In answer to one question, he said he had encountered many immigrants from the south of Ireland 'who are utterly useless; in point of intellect they are inferior to our own aborigines'.[78] A somewhat similar comparison was made by James Bonwick when he wrote in 1863 that '[Aborigines] pronounce English far better than half the Scotch or Irish emigrants'.[79] All such comments comparing the Irish to black people, whether in the West Indies or Australia, reflected minds that perceived the Irish as being closer to the people of colour at the bottom of the racial hierarchy than to the white people at the top.

Many leading proponents of racial science abhorred the idea of interracial marriage, or 'miscegenation' as it was then often termed. But a few thought that the mixing of the races might prove beneficial in certain circumstances. In 1864, an anonymous American pamphlet entitled 'Miscegenation' praised interracial marriage, specifically identifying the Irish as a group that might benefit from it:

> He [the Irish man] was originally of a coloured race, and
> has all the fervid emotional power which belongs to a people
> born in or near the tropics. His long habitation north,
> however, and the ignorance in which he has been kept by
> misgovernment, have sunk the Irishman below the level of the
> most degraded negro.[80]

Intermarriage between the Irish and black people, according to this writer, would likely improve the Irish. The pamphlet outraged a reviewer in the *British Anthropological Review*, who, after quoting it at length, claimed that it was too painful to read.[81] The pamphlet circulated widely before it was revealed to be a hoax concocted by members of the Democratic Party who wanted to influence the 1864 presidential election.[82] But by then its arguments had been summarised in the *Sydney Morning Herald*, based on a report appearing in the London *Times*.[83] The Australian press showed a marked interest in American race relations. In 1867, for example, the Melbourne *Argus* and other colonial papers reprinted statistics on the 'coloured' population of New York from the London *Pall Mall Gazette*. After listing 82 'miscegens' families, the article continued: 'although the Irish are loudest and most forward in their declarations of hostility to the negroes, in almost every case of miscegenation the parties are Irish and blacks, so nearly akin is hate to love'.[84]

There was clearly a widespread belief that 'miscegenation' mostly occurred between black people and the Irish, and such alliances were not considered to reflect well on either group. Later chapters will discuss marriage between the Irish and Indigenous Australians and Chinese immigrants, but it is worth emphasising here that, although the Irish were ridiculed for intermarrying with African Americans and the Chinese in both the US and Australia, there were no race laws preventing them from marrying non-Europeans. But such laws were often applied to people of colour in both countries. This difference points to the fact that the Irish, despite their perceived racial inferiority, were still generally considered to be white and thus not targeted by laws intended to control non-white races.

The Irish: a superior race?

While theories and attitudes that relegated the Irish to the lower levels of different racial hierarchies persisted into the early 20th century, from at least the mid 19th century Irish people had begun to argue forcefully against such stereotyping. As members of the Catholic Irish community acquired education, employment, prosperity and confidence in Australia, so they angrily refuted the many attempts made to characterise them as 'low' or as sharing characteristics with the 'native blacks'.

In 1881, Topp's widely publicised anti-Irish articles met with strong opposition. The Melbourne Catholic *Advocate* reported rather gleefully that Topp had been snubbed in the streets of

Melbourne. It also published a letter from Topp's lawyer brother repudiating his ideas as likely to 'embitter sectarian and racial prejudices'.[85] An Irish immigrant, Joseph O'Brien, writing in the same journal, also quickly challenged Topp's arguments. He highlighted the fact that the English were a racially mixed people and went on to claim that their behaviour both at home and in acquiring an empire was far worse than anything the Irish had ever done.[86] O'Brien's swift intervention was typical of Irish and Irish Australians' responses to racial slurs. If required to look at themselves as a race, the Irish saw only positives where many English writers saw only negatives. Then the Irish used these to argue with increasing force in favour of self-government.

From the 1880s onwards, a cultural movement which scholars call the 'Gaelic Revival' emerged in Ireland and spread through the diaspora. It aimed to restore pride in Gaelic history, literature, language and sport.[87] Organisations and clubs which strove to foster pride in Irish culture and history formed in Australia during the 1880s and 1890s. The Melbourne Celtic Club, various Sydney Irish associations, the Perth Gaelic League and the Queensland Irish Association were part of this movement.[88] Some members of these organisations read a small, attractively bound book published in 1899 that argued the Irish were racially superior. Its author, the distinguished Irish-language scholar and historian, Father Edmund Hogan, was a member of the audience at a public lecture given in Dublin in 1893 by Alfred C Haddon and the next day he passed on to Haddon his own research on the positive connotations of Irish physical characteristics.[89] Hogan finally published this research in an 1899 book, *The Irish People, their Height, Form and Strength*, in which he noted approvingly that Haddon had shown the Irish were physically superior, or at least not inferior, to other races. Hogan's book was an extended refutation of what he called scurrilous views about the 'degeneracy' of the Irish 'race', appearing in commentaries, satires and cartoons outside Ireland, particularly in English magazines like *Punch* and American ones like *Puck*. These, Hogan complained, 'invariably represented the Irishman as of a low savage type'.[90] As we will see later, Hogan might also have included in his list of objectionable publications Australian periodicals like *Melbourne Punch* and the Sydney *Bulletin*. Hogan's book was well known in Australia through the excerpts from it that appeared in the Catholic press.[91]

Those, like Hogan, who were writing within the optimistic glow of the Gaelic Revival assumed that the Catholic Irish and their descendants were physically and morally distinct. Irish nationalists and republicans joined him and his Irish-Australian readers in seeing only positive Irish characteristics in the differences between Celts and Anglo-Saxons. Towards the end of the 19th century, race was becoming an increasingly essential feature of arguments that Ireland should have more political independence.[92] That the Irish race was distinctive, both physically and culturally, and that it had an illustrious history, long predating the arrival of the English in the 12th century, was seen as prima facie evidence that Ireland deserved a measure of self-government. A homogenous Irish race was 'in keeping with contemporary European nationalist criteria for a territory to become a self-governing polity'.[93]

The *Advocate* in Melbourne, as well as other Australian Catholic newspapers, regularly reprinted articles on the findings of anthropometric studies that showed the Irish were physically stronger, taller and generally more able than the English. As one such article put it, these studies 'successfully vindicate the claims of Irishmen to be very unlike what the "savage representations of the comic journals" describe them to be'.[94] By claiming that the Irish were members of the Aryan or Indo-European family of races, supporters of Irish home rule argued that they were white and, as such, they, like white colonists in South Africa, Australia, New Zealand and Canada, deserved a measure of self-government.[95] As the Irish home rule politician John Dillon explained to a New Zealand audience in 1899, the Irish deserved home rule because 'we are white men'.[96] Whiteness and the right to self-government went hand in hand. Thus, even if the Irish were not Anglo-Saxons or even Protestants, their perceived whiteness meant that they were entitled to rule themselves, though of course only within the confines of the British Empire.

We have seen that 'race' was an ill-defined and slippery concept during the 19th century, the period when the Irish were settling colonial Australia. It could encompass physiology, culture, religion and morality, often in the same scholar's work. In the latter part of the 20th century, the meanings of 'race' solidified under the weight of the horrifying consequences of colonisation, eugenics and Nazi racial ideology. 'Race' or 'racism' came to mean believing that human diversity derived 'from separate racial stocks having distinctive attributes', especially physical characteristics, that were 'usually considered to stand to one another in relations of superiority and inferiority'.[97] We can definitely find the antecedents of such beliefs in 19th-century racial theories about the Irish, while there are also numerous instances of the Irish being included in the category 'white'. For many, the Irish were a liminal people, uncomfortably close in physical appearance and character to Indigenous Australians and other non-white peoples, yet, at the same time, similar in significant ways to the white British. In settler colonies like

Australia, as well as in Britain and the US, there was never any question that the Irish would be denied legal rights or targeted for the sort of extermination, exclusion or assimilationist policies that were applied to indigenous and Chinese peoples. In fact, as we shall see in the following chapters, many Irish Australians supported and participated in the policies and actions of British settler colonialism aimed against Indigenous and non-European populations. Perhaps it is most helpful to think of the Irish as a group who played a significant role in delineating the boundaries of what it meant to be white in Australia.

CHAPTER 2

The Irish and Indigenous Australians: friends or foes?

There is all sortes black & white misted & married together
& Living in pretty Cotages Just the same as the white people
... There are verry rich fancy John white girls marrid to a black
man & Irish girls to [too] & to Yellow Chinaman with their
Hair platted down there [their] black back.[1]

Biddy Burke, a domestic servant, was obviously fascinated by the differences between Brisbane and her native Galway when she wrote to her brother John in Ireland in 1882, two years after she had emigrated with another brother, Patrick. She appears to have seen 'verry rich ... white girls' married to 'black' men and 'Irish girls' married to 'Yellow' Chinese men as different, but marvelled at both types of marriage. Not all newly arrived Irish immigrants reacted in this way, however. Mary O'Brien, living near Rockhampton during the 1860s, had been far more alarmed when she noticed a young Aboriginal man peering into the back of her hut while she was home alone with her young baby.[2] As we saw in the previous chapter, contemporary hierarchies of race often placed the Irish below the British and other northern

Europeans and closer to people of colour. Yet the Irish-born and their children, although discriminated against and subjected to racial stereotyping, were generally classed as white Europeans when compared with Indigenous Australians or Chinese immigrants. This chapter investigates the many ways in which the Irish interacted with Indigenous peoples during the 19th and 20th centuries.

The Irish as colonised and colonisers

Although British colonists in Australia often looked down on the Irish as an inferior, homogenous group, there were always major differences among Irish immigrants along lines of class, religion, culture and gender, as well as where they originated from in Ireland: whether rural or urban areas and the North or the South. There were also differences in how poor Catholic Irish immigrants responded to the abrupt switch from being members of an oppressed majority in Ireland to being part of Australia's dominant white colonial class, especially in relation to the country's Indigenous inhabitants. It could be argued that migration transformed the Irish from the colonised into the colonisers.

However, debates over whether Ireland should be classed as a colony at any time in its history remain unresolved.[3] There is little doubt, though, that during the 1801–1922 Anglo-Irish union, when the British Empire was at its height, England was the dominant partner in the political and economic relationship between the two countries.[4] Although Ireland did elect representatives to the British parliament, its interests were wholly subordinated to Britain's. Whereas most Irish immigrants seeking a better life headed across the Atlantic to the United States, large numbers from all classes also populated the British Empire.[5] Many travelled as settlers, seeking economic opportunities and new homes; some worked as itinerant seamen and miners; others pursued careers in colonial administration, medicine, the law, the military and the police; still others went as missionaries and clergy to serve their churches overseas; and, in the case of the Australian colonies, thousands had no choice, being transported for criminal offences.[6]

The Catholic Irish were prepared for these varied roles partly through a national system of education that had been introduced in 1831. National schools aimed to ensure that Irish children learnt the English language and, in addition, that they learnt the values and virtues of British imperialism. It was in such schools that Irish pupils read books informing them that, although Australian Aboriginal people were 'among the lowest and most ignorant savages in the world', they could still be civilised by the British. School books praised the growth of empire and encouraged positive attitudes in their young readers towards emigrating to colonial Australia.[7] Once out of Ireland, the Catholic Irish would become colonisers, even as they continued to carry the stigma of Irishness with them into the largely Protestant and British-dominated Australian colonies.

Irish-Indigenous families

The interactions between Irish settlers and Indigenous peoples have attracted limited historical analysis to date, although Bob Reece and Ann McGrath have both published interesting studies.[8] Both commented on contemporary positive relationships that existed between Indigenous and Irish peoples, based at least in part on a recognition of shared injustice, dispossession and colonial oppression. Family histories and autobiographies of Indigenous Australians chronicle intimate relationships between Irish men and Aboriginal women, resulting in supportive families that survived even in the face of official discrimination. A continuing sense of past injustices was undoubtedly enhanced by political activists from the 1960s onwards, when many interpreted the conflict in Northern Ireland as a struggle against colonialism: a struggle like those by other colonised peoples, including Indigenous Australians. Both Reece and McGrath warned, though, that this contemporary appreciation of family histories and a common cause masks a more complex and troubled history, one that also features Irish-born settlers dispossessing and killing Aboriginal people or turning a blind eye to the violence used against them.

Respected elder Billy Lynch, the son of Irish convict shoemaker Maurice Lynch and a Gundungurra woman whose name has not survived, was born in 1839 and lived much of his life in the Blue Mountains west of Sydney. He was doubtless one of many children of such relationships between convicts and Aboriginal people during the early years of British and Irish settlement. Before his death in 1913, he played a part in developing the town of Katoomba and preserving Aboriginal community life in the mountains.[9] During the early years of the 20th century, Indigenous activists Val and Joe McGinness and their siblings were raised west of Darwin by their Irish-born father Stephen, a miner, and their mother Alyandabu (known as Lucy), a Kungarakany woman. Joe McGinness remembered being told stories about evil spirits as a child, drawn from both parents' cultures, which were designed to frighten him into good behaviour.

But when their father died in 1918, the children were taken from their mother and institutionalised.[10] Many Indigenous people who have investigated their family histories have discovered Irish backgrounds. For example, Jimmy Governor, who was executed in 1901 for murdering members of several farming families in northern New South Wales (NSW), had an Irish grandfather, as did his young wife, Ethel Page. But the rest of Ethel's family were white, while Jimmy's were Aboriginal, and at Jimmy's trial the defence cited hostile responses to their marriage as among the motives for his attacks.[11]

If Catholic-Protestant marriages between white people were frowned upon, various colonial and state Aboriginal protection Acts placed official barriers in the way of marriages between whites and Indigenous peoples. Yet relationships continued to occur nonetheless.[12] Relationships between Irish women and Indigenous men were generally less common than those between Irish men and Indigenous women. One of these less common families were the Sharps of Victoria's Colac region. In 1874, Catherine McLaughlin, an Irish domestic servant, married Richard Sharp, an Aboriginal man. Their struggles to maintain themselves in the difficult middle space between marginalised poor working-class whites and the Aboriginal community meant they had frequent contact with the Victorian Board for the Protection of Aborigines and with the managements of nearby Christian missions. In some of these contacts, especially arrangements for payments and contract negotiations, the authorities bypassed Richard in favour of Catherine. Although she was a woman and Irish, the white authorities obviously considered her better equipped to manage money than her Indigenous husband.[13]

Many other families can trace their origins to Irish-Australian men working on farms and pastoral stations and living with Indigenous families in rural and regional Australia during the early and middle years of the 20th century. It is possible that some of these positive relationships were fostered by the curriculum taught in Catholic primary schools. For instance, book 4 of the 1908 *Approved Readers for Catholic Schools in Australasia* informed Catholic children that Aboriginal people had been honest and trustworthy before contact with 'our civilisation'. And the textbook went on to praise Indigenous Australians' 'fine sense of manliness' and 'their respect for the aged, their ready care of the sick'.[14]

Tantalising snippets of evidence also survive within language studies, suggesting that early encounters between Indigenous peoples and the Irish – perhaps Irish convicts working as itinerant shepherds and stockmen – may sometimes have been close and friendly. Irish-language words for items such as a shoe (*pampúta*) and a stick or cudgel (*waddy*) have been recorded among Aboriginal languages in south-west NSW. It is also possible that the well-known word 'didgeridoo' derives from an Irish term, *dúdaire dubh*, meaning a black trumpet.[15] Other records of words, phrases and pronunciation suggest close contact between Indigenous Australians and Irish people speaking Hiberno-English, particularly in areas of early settlement around Sydney.[16] While analysis based on language transfer can only be speculative, the evidence does suggest that Indigenous communities and speakers of either the Irish language or Hiberno-English engaged in prolonged enough information exchanges to have an impact on Indigenous languages.

The Irish in Australia's frontier wars

Evidence is more plentiful, though, that Irish immigrants and their offspring were involved in the 19th- and 20th-century frontier wars between white settlers and Aboriginal people that occurred at different times throughout much of Australia. Some among the Irish fought to take Aboriginal land and secure it for themselves, but there were others who attempted to mitigate violence or bring perpetrators to justice. The subject of Irish immigrants' participation in frontier violence has been relatively neglected in accounts of the Australian-Irish experience, although Reece and McGrath, and more recently the president of Ireland Michael D Higgins, have certainly referred to it. We know that there were many men of Irish birth or descent among squatters, convict herdsmen and stockmen, farmers, pastoralists, selectors, police forces, magistrates, state officials and missionaries – all groups that were actively involved in violently dispossessing and dispersing Indigenous communities.[17] But much more research is needed before we can create a full picture of the precise role of the Irish in the frontier wars.

Evidence makes clear that Irish convicts and free settlers reacted in different ways to their new colonial environments and to the people they encountered in them. Some, such as Bridget Burke, met the first dark faces they saw with interest and curiosity; others perceived only savagery and a threat to their hard-won property. Still others appear not to have seen Indigenous Australians at all, or perhaps only at the periphery of their vision. Irish nationalist poet Eva Doherty continued to write poetry after she and her husband arrived in Queensland in 1860, but she saw her new home as 'untainted' by 'shadows dark ... cold and soulless'.[18] Some Irish immigrants, on the other hand, experienced a complex mix of alarm at material threats alongside cultural inquisitiveness. George Fletcher Moore, a Tyrone-born Protestant lawyer and landowner, settled in Western Australia in 1830. He initially established good relations with some of the local Indigenous peoples and became interested in their culture, publishing a book in London in 1842 on Aboriginal languages. But, as he sought to increase his landholdings, he came to see the Indigenous community as a barrier to his ambitions. He concluded that they would have to be coerced into recognising English common law that governed property rights. They were, he wrote, 'troublesome friends and dangerous enemies'.[19] And in 1834 he took part in a controversial punitive attack that came to be known as the 'battle' of Pinjarra.[20]

One of the most notorious Indigenous massacres in Australian history took place in June 1838 at Myall Creek in northern NSW. A group of 11 stockmen, all of whom except their leader were convicts or ex-convicts, killed at least 28 Aboriginal women, children and elderly men who had been living near an outstation on a squatter's property. Four of the stockmen were Irish-born and three of these were among the seven men eventually executed for the crime. But, in addition to the Irish among the perpetrators, Irish men were also to the fore among the police, magistrates, lawyers and judges who captured and prosecuted them. It was due to the determined efforts of the local Irish-born police magistrate, Captain Edward Denny Day, that the massacre was thoroughly investigated and those responsible apprehended.[21] The NSW attorney-general, Irish-born JH Plunkett, was instrumental in prosecuting the arrested men, assisted by his fellow graduate from Trinity College, Dublin, Roger Therry. In addition, the judge at the first trial, the colony's chief justice Sir James Dowling, was the London-born son of Irish parents. But the two trials and the executions were conducted in the face of formidable opposition from the NSW settler society.[22]

Plunkett, a supporter and friend of the Irish nationalist leader Daniel O'Connell had arrived in Sydney from Ireland in 1832, bringing with him a strong sense of the injustices that had long afflicted his homeland and a determination to make NSW a fairer place.[23] The dreadful events at Myall Creek encapsulate much about the multifaceted Irish-Indigenous encounter. Some, like the executed convicts Ned Foley and James Oates and ex-convict John Russell, appear to have had little compunction about hunting down and killing groups of defenceless Indigenous people. However, it should be noted that the massacre was directed by the stockmen's boss John Henry Fleming, an Australian-born squatter's son, who escaped prosecution. Denny Day, Plunkett and Therry certainly worked hard, in the face of public outrage, to ensure that those responsible were brought to justice, even if Fleming, who had ordered the massacre, ultimately escaped. While there were intense protests at the prosecution of white men for the murder of black people, some people expressed sympathy for those killed. This is evidenced by an emotionally charged poem, 'The Aboriginal Mother', written by Irish-born Eliza Dunlop and published in the Sydney *Australian* in December 1838, less than a week before the executions.[24]

Myall Creek was one of the very rare occasions during the whole of the 19th century on which white men were punished for murdering Indigenous people. In his 1887 book, *The Irish in Australia*, James F Hogan eulogised Plunkett, while describing the massacre as an 'outrage' and an 'atrocity'. But, for Hogan, Aboriginal people were still 'savages', 'hapless creatures' and a 'dying race'. He also claimed that after Plunkett's successful prosecution, 'the poor blacks were in the future treated more like human beings and less like legitimate game for every white scoundrel in possession of a gun'. Significantly, he did not mention that some of the killers were Irish-born, saying only that a party of ten 'Europeans', whom he described as 'horrible offenders', had carried out the attack. Hogan rarely uses the term 'European' in his book, so this was presumably a way to avoid admitting that, like Plunkett, some of the perpetrators were Irish.[25] In general, Hogan's book had little to say about the Irish as convicts, instead celebrating the achievements of Irish free settlers and, largely by omission, suggesting that the Irish took no part in past atrocities.

The frontier wars were by no means over, whatever Hogan had so confidently asserted in 1887. They continued for many years, especially in parts of Queensland, Western Australia and the Northern Territory. In all these conflicts the Irish or Irish Australians played a part, suggesting that they found no common ground with Indigenous peoples, seeing them only as obstacles standing in the way of economic development. Peter Gifford, for example, has researched accounts of the ill-treatment and murder of Mirning people during the 1880s in the Eucla area of the Nullarbor Plain near the Western Australia and South Australia border. Those mainly responsible were a Scottish station owner, William Stuart McGill, and his business partners, Ulster-born William and Thomas Kennedy.[26]

In 1926, nearly 90 years after Myall Creek, another notorious massacre took place in the north of Western Australia at Forrest River. Here a party of local men and police attacked an unknown number of Indigenous people, including women and children, in retribution for the murder of pastoralist Frederick Hay by Andeja elder Lumbulumbia or Lumbia.[27] There were several men with Irish names in the attacking party, including

Irish-Australian Patrick Bernard (known as Barney) O'Leary, who occupied a nearby property he had called 'Galway Valley'. O'Leary was made a special constable for the purposes of the expedition, along with Richard John Jolly. The two full-time policemen in charge were constables Denis Hastings Regan and James St Jack. Hay's partner, Leonard Overheu, and Daniel Murnane, along with Aboriginal trackers, made up the rest of the group. While there is no definite information on the backgrounds of Murnane, Regan and Jolly, their names suggest that, like O'Leary, they came from Catholic Irish families. At the royal commission into the incident, Regan was described as inexperienced, but O'Leary had spent many years tracking Aboriginal people in Western Australia and Queensland.[28] The white men were not charged with murder as there was no evidence to link them to any identifiable victim. Recently, historians have re-examined evidence presented to the royal commission, as well as that given by local Indigenous people but not presented. This has led to the suggestion that Jolly, O'Leary, Murnane and Overheu were linked as they, along with the murdered Hay, were all veterans of the 1915 Gallipoli campaign.[29] It is possible therefore that loyalty to an old army mate was one of the motivations behind the punitive expedition. Certainly, while O'Leary demonstrated an attachment to his Irish background in the name he gave to his property, his principal loyalty might well have been to his fellow Anzacs.

Although not all Irish pastoralists reacted with the savagery of Barney O'Leary, many were implicated in widespread frontier violence and dispossession. Patrick Durack adopted a relatively benign approach to the Indigenous peoples who lived on the land he claimed, but other members of his extended family were both more violent and more willing to overlook violence. From unpromising beginnings as poor County Clare immigrants, who first arrived in NSW in 1849 and later made some money on the goldfields, the Duracks went on to create a pastoral empire stretching across Queensland and Western Australia. As they developed their vast properties, they depended heavily upon the skills of their Aboriginal stockmen. Patsy Durack always acknowledged how much he owed his stockmen, particularly Pumpkin, a Bootnamurra man from near Cooper's Creek in Queensland, who was instrumental in the success of the Durack holdings on the Ord River in Western Australia. In her 1959 history of the family, *Kings in Grass Castles*, Mary Durack recalled her grandfather saying that: 'It is the blessing of Almighty God they are kindly and childlike savages.'[30] But, as well as quoting these paternalistic sentiments, Durack also mentioned in passing the 'inevitable unauthorised punitive expedition' against those Indigenous people who resisted the advance of the Durack empire – the word 'inevitable' makes for chilling reading.[31]

Enough was known or assumed about Catholic Irish pastoralists for the Sydney *Bulletin* to caricature them in an 1897 cartoon entitled 'The spread of the gospel'. This shows 'Kieran Dalton, a wealthy back-block settler', in conversation with Father O'Mahony, described as 'a bit of a wag'. When O'Mahony queries the light skin of the many children playing in the dirt outside the homestead, Dalton informs his 'reverence' that their colour is due to 'the spread of the gospel to be sure'.[32] This 'joke' about the number of children Dalton had fathered with Aboriginal women reflected the reality in many outback places and Catholics, like the fictional Dalton and O'Mahony, were well aware of it. But for the real children and their mothers, their situations were often no laughing matter. While some children were acknowledged

THE SPREAD OF THE GOSPEL.

FATHER O'MAHONY (a bit of a wag): "How do you account for the exceptionally pale color the natives around your homestead, Da. on?"

KIERAN DALTON (a wealthy back-block settler): "Why, your reverence, to the spread of the Gospel, to be sure."

A cartoon in the Sydney *Bulletin* drawing attention to the Catholic Irishness of a pastoralist and a clergyman, who are joking about white men fathering numerous children with Aboriginal women. But the reality of the situation for the women and children was often far from funny.

Source: 'The spread of the gospel', *Bulletin*, 11 December 1897, p. 27.

by their Irish fathers, even if only unofficially, many suffered. In 1912, three-year-old Clancy McKenna, son of Morris McKenna, an Irish-born station manager working near Nullagine in the Pilbara region of Western Australia, was evicted at gunpoint along with his Nyamal mother Nyamalangu (called Nellie) and her husband. Clancy, like so many others, was labelled a 'half-caste': in other words, 'a whitefella today and a blackfella tomorrow'.[33]

By 1912, the policy of removing lighter-skinned children from their Indigenous families and sending them to schools on missions and reserves was widespread throughout Australia. It was carried out in the belief that the 'full-bloods' were doomed to disappear and that the 'half-castes' needed to be assimilated into the white community by being trained for menial employment as servants and labourers. AO Neville, the government official in charge of Aboriginal affairs in Western Australia during the early part of the 20th century, argued forcefully that 'half-castes' required urgent attention. It is possible that he viewed children of mixed Irish and Indigenous descent as particularly problematic. In his 1947 book *Australia's Coloured Minority*, he included numerous photographs of 'half-castes': some were impromptu pictures, while others were formal studio family portraits. Only with one photograph did Neville add further details about the family. The picture was captioned: 'Half Blood – (Irish-Australian father, full-blood aboriginal mother) Quadroon daughter (Father Australian born of Scottish parents: mother no. 1) Octaroon grandson (father Australian of Irish descent: mother no. 2)'. While this information may simply have reflected the details available to Neville, it is also possible that he was making a point about the frequency with which Irish-Australian men created these, as he saw it, undesirable families.[34]

One such mixed-race child was Bill Brock Byrne, whose father Stan Byrne was the Irish-Australian owner of 'Tipperary', a station near the Daly River in the Northern Territory, and whose mother was Jessie, a Daly River Indigenous woman. When interviewed in 2013 for an Irish television documentary, he recalled his father with fondness and then spoke of how, when he was seven, he and his two sisters were removed from their home and their mother and sent to a Catholic mission. There they remained throughout their childhoods; there too Bill's name was changed from 'Byrne' to 'Brock' and he was forced to stop speaking his Aboriginal language and to learn English.[35]

The Irish as Indigenous scholars, administrators and missionaries

As well as making up a proportion of station owners and managers and the police, there were also Irish Australians among the anthropologists who studied Indigenous peoples and provided the theoretical justification for government policies that dispossessed Aboriginal people of their land and removed their children. The Cavan-born parents of Frank Gillen had immigrated to South Australia in 1855, where he was born that same year. His brothers were involved in the colony's Irish and Catholic social and political affairs, while Gillen worked as an operator on the overland telegraph line between Adelaide and Darwin. For most of the 1890s he was employed as the postmaster in Alice Springs, until ill-health forced him to move south to Moonta, west of Adelaide. During his years in the outback, Gillen demonstrated concern for Aboriginal welfare, later saying with some pride that: 'I was never obliged to fire a shot at the blackfellow.' In his additional roles as supervisor of Aboriginal people and a magistrate in Alice Springs, Gillen created controversy in 1891 when he tried unsuccessfully to convict a notorious mounted constable, WH Willshire, of the murder of two local Indigenous men.[36]

Gillen also found time to become an authority on Aboriginal languages and customs and to begin a voluminous correspondence with the Melbourne-based anthropologist Baldwin Spencer. The two collaborated on important books, notably *The Native Tribes of Central Australia* (1899) and *The Northern Tribes of Central Australia* (1904).[37] From the outset of their friendship, Gillen provided Spencer with vital contacts amongst Aboriginal peoples and much information about languages and customs. In one of his letters, he described how he had met several elders, who 'were delighted to find a white man who did not look upon their customs as being hideous and their beliefs wicked'.[38] Yet, at the same time, Gillen identified with his Irish origins, supporting the campaign for Irish home rule and signing his letters to Spencer with the word 'slainthe' (in Irish *sláinte*), meaning 'good health', while joking about Spencer's belief in English superiority over the Irish.[39] Gillen during his lifetime never received the public recognition for his work he had hoped for. This he attributed, at least in part, to anti-Irish feeling among the Adelaide establishment and to his attempt to convict Willshire of murdering Aboriginal people.[40]

Daisy Bates was another Irish anthropologist who lived among and studied Indigenous peoples during the first half of the 20th century in Western Australia and South Australia. Her journalism and books describing customs, beliefs, languages and stories were popular at the time and for decades afterwards. She expressed in her writings, and especially in her influential

1938 book *The Passing of the Aborigines*, her disdain for what she termed 'miscegenation' and her conviction that 'full-blood' Indigenous people were dying out.[41] She was a controversial figure who throughout her long life obscured her origins as Tipperary-born Margaret Dwyer, the daughter of a Catholic shoemaker, instead presenting herself as the privileged child of the Anglo-Irish gentry.[42] In a decidedly contradictory fashion, while she stressed the advantages of an Anglo-Irish background and an English education, she used her supposed Celtic Irishness to claim 'affinity' with Aboriginal people. She based this claim on shared characteristics she detected between Irish and Indigenous society, such as strong oral traditions and kinship ties, a powerful sense of place and a belief in the supernatural.[43] She saw similarities, for example, between the Irish blackthorn stick, the shillelagh, and the Indigenous waddy, both of which could be used as weapons.[44] She suggested that it was her Celtic heritage that enabled her to understand the unspoken emotions expressed in an initiation corroboree she had witnessed.[45] On first meeting Bates in 1932, the journalist Ernestine Hill, who later became her friend, wrote that Bates's Irishness accounted for her 'lifetime loyalty to the lost cause of a lost people with all their sins and sorrows in her always loving heart and mind'.[46] As well as writing for the press, Bates, who corresponded with AC Haddon, gave lectures emphasising the 'innate racial affinity' between the Irish and Indigenous Australians. In support of her theories, she pointed out that both peoples were 'lighthearted, quick to take offence and quick to forgive'.[47]

Some Irish Australians living in Perth did not, however, appreciate Bates's analysis. In December 1905, the *West Australian* published a rather gossipy article by 'Alpha' reporting on a lecture Bates had given. 'Alpha' compared the customs of the

Indigenous people Bates was studying with those of the Irish. 'The national weapon, the shillalagh has its counterpart in the walga or dowak of the native', claimed 'Alpha', 'and with both the traditional rule is the same – if one sees a head "hit it", and any member of a strange tribe is first of all hit "over-the-head" and then asked his business.'[48] The Perth branch of the Gaelic League was quick to react, passing a resolution at its next meeting: 'That we consider a paragraph by "Alpha", ... in which a comparison is drawn between the Irish people and the aborigines of West Australia, insulting to the Irish race.'[49] This was followed by a detailed riposte in the Catholic *West Australian Record* from 'An Irish Irelander', who may have thought that 'Alpha' was Bates, for the writer claimed that, although 'Alpha' 'had been long enough among the blacks' to know them, she obviously did not know the Irish.[50] In 1910, another similar lecture by Bates provoked more critical responses from Irish Australians. One letter writer said it was regrettable that Bates had 'stooped to insult a large section of the community by comparing the despised blackfellow with the Irish'.[51] Bates was a complex woman whose reputation suffered in the decades after her death, particularly since her sensationalist claims about Aboriginal cannibalism and motherhood were thoroughly discredited.[52] However, she obviously interpreted much of what she observed in Indigenous societies through a lens at least partially informed by her personal memories of Ireland and by romantic understandings of Celtic Irishness. But, at the same time, there were many Irish Australians who did not share her views and, indeed, who considered them deeply offensive.

When we come to scrutinise Irish and Irish-Australian political leaders and public administrators for their actions towards Indigenous peoples, it is obvious that many pursued an assimilationist agenda like that adopted by those of British birth or descent. All agreed that Aboriginal people were dying out and that they needed to be segregated on reserves to protect them. This policy also conveniently removed Aboriginal people from lands coveted by white settlers, controlling their movements, forcing them to adopt a European lifestyle and educating their children in Christian religion and culture. John O'Shanassy, the first Catholic Irish premier of Victoria, campaigned for office in the 1850s on a democratic platform of extending the franchise to miners on the goldfields. During his second term as premier in 1858–59, his government established a select committee to enquire into 'the condition of aborigines'. The committee's report recommended increased aid for Indigenous communities, as well as the creation of reserves.[53] Soon afterwards, a delegation of leaders from the Kulin people arrived in Melbourne to lobby the minister for lands, the former Young Irelander Charles Gavan Duffy, for a grant of land along the Goulburn River to be used for hunting and raising crops. Duffy was convinced by Kulin arguments and ruled in their favour. But his decision came to nothing because competing pastoral interests, headed by Protestant Irish-born squatter and land speculator Hugh Glass, prevailed.[54] It is possible that Duffy did not prioritise the request of the Kulin elders for a Goulburn River reserve, since at the time he was battling in an increasingly difficult political environment to secure land reform for white small farmers, many of them Irish.

John O'Shanassy became increasingly conservative as he grew older, supporting policies favouring large pastoralists, whose ranks he joined in 1862 when he acquired 'Moira', a substantial property in the Riverina region. But he found himself at odds with Methodist missionaries who in 1874 had gained some land from 'Moira' for the Maloga Mission. O'Shanassy and his son

John resented their poorly paid local Indigenous labour force leaving 'Moira' to live with the missionaries at Maloga and they tried to prevent further land being allocated to the mission.[55] During the first decade of the 20th century, James Connolly, whose Irish-born parents had initially settled in the 1860s near Warwick on the Darling Downs in southern Queensland, was responsible as Western Australian colonial secretary for establishing the first Aboriginal reserve in the Kimberley region, at Moola Bulla north-west of Halls Creek. He aimed to preserve Aboriginal hunting grounds, hoping thereby to reduce raids on neighbouring cattle stations. Cattle-spearing and white reprisals did decline, but the reserve soon degenerated into a mere feeding depot and a place of detention.[56]

Some of the senior public servants who headed Aboriginal protection agencies in various of the colonies and later the states were Irish or Irish Australian. These included Roscommon-born Catholic William Cahill, who arrived in Queensland in 1878, having previously served as a policeman in the Royal Irish Constabulary (RIC). He joined the Queensland public service and, in 1905, was appointed commissioner of police and a 'protector' or supervisor of Aboriginal people, positions he held until 1916.[57] In Queensland, police already had extensive powers over the Indigenous population, but Cahill, described as a 'martinet', modelled the Queensland force on the RIC and sought even further coercive powers.[58] Cornelius O'Leary was another Queensland public servant appointed a protector of Aboriginal people. He was the Australian-born son of Irish immigrants and, after 1922, he was a protector in various districts, including the Torres Strait, Cape York and Palm Island. In 1943, he became the Queensland director of 'native affairs' and based himself, not in Brisbane, but on Thursday Island. O'Leary was a firm believer in education for Indigenous and Islander peoples and he instituted many measures designed to ensure that they would be integrated into white Australian society. In doing so, he was highly paternalistic, regarding himself as a strict but fair father figure. But many of his initiatives, including the Aboriginal Welfare Fund, which deprived Indigenous workers of their wages, have since been heavily criticised.[59] At the time, though, many white people thought him too lenient and claimed that his policies risked white safety in North Queensland. But overall, there seems little evidence that Irish-Australian politicians or public servants did much other than follow the standard oppressive policies towards Indigenous Australians that prevailed at the time.

Irish and Irish Australians also interacted with Indigenous peoples in the mission field. Like Protestant British and Irish missionaries, the Catholic Irish focused on salvation through converting Indigenous peoples to Christianity, which entailed attempts at 'civilising' them by stripping them of their traditional beliefs and customs. But during the 19th century, the Catholic Church was not as active in the field of Indigenous missions as were many of the Protestant churches. The Catholics were not as well resourced and what resources they had, they largely devoted to providing churches, schools, hospitals and other institutions for their mainly working-class Irish and Irish-Australian adherents. Some bishops, notably English-born Archbishop John B Polding of Sydney, tried to obtain permission and funding from Rome for Indigenous missions, but these efforts were largely in vain. In pastoral letters, though, Polding condemned the violence used against Aboriginal people and urged Catholics to act with compassion towards them.[60] The most enduring 19th-century Catholic Aboriginal missions operated in Western

Australia from 1847 onwards, with the Spanish foundation at New Norcia north-east of Perth being the best known.[61]

The Irish-born bishop of Perth, Matthew Gibney, encouraged Catholic missions and was vocal in criticising white treatment of Aboriginal workers and their communities in the north of the colony. In 1892, he entered into a heated public correspondence with a Protestant squatter, Charles Harper of De Grey Station near Port Hedland. In his letters, published in the *West Australian*, Gibney denounced the inhumane punishment of Aboriginal people for stealing sheep. Harper had contrasted the actions of white people in northern Australia with the atrocities committed by nationalists in Ireland, which he claimed Gibney had not condemned. Gibney sought to refute the comparison by writing:

> the few real atrocities in Ireland were those of the weak against the strong, and [they were] founded on centuries of misrule. Not so with the white settlers whose deliberate murders in no single instance met with the punishment that invariably overtook the blackfellow convicted of a similar crime against the invaders of his country.[62]

In Gibney's mind, there could be no parallel between the violent actions of Irish nationalists protesting British 'misrule' in Ireland and the 'deliberate murders' by settlers of Indigenous people who had committed minor offences against property laws that they probably did not even understand.

During the 20th century, Catholics became more actively involved in Indigenous missions, with the laity, female religious and European male orders taking the lead. For example, Francis McGarry, the son of Irish-Australian parents, worked from 1922 for the St Vincent de Paul Society in Sydney, before in 1935 joining

Father PJ Moloney, who was establishing an Aboriginal mission near Alice Springs in the Northern Territory. In 1942, McGarry was appointed a protector of Aborigines, moving to work in 1945–48 in the Tanami Desert region of central Australia.[63] After 1900, female Catholic religious worked with European male orders in missions in the Kimberley region of Western Australia, on Bathurst Island near Darwin, on islands in the Torres Strait and on Palm and Fantome islands off the Queensland coast. But when northern Australia was threatened by invasion during the Second World War, many missions had to be closed or moved.[64]

There were also Protestant missionaries of Irish birth or descent, many of whom were women working alongside their husbands or on their own.[65] Isabella Hetherington, a nurse, had read about the plight of Australia's Indigenous peoples while still in Ireland. After arriving in Melbourne, she joined the Australian (United) Aborigines' Mission in 1906 and spent the rest of her life working on missions run by various Protestant denominations, accompanied by her adopted Aboriginal daughter Nellie. Retta Long, nee Dixon, the Australian-born daughter of Irish Baptists, who began mission work among Sydney's Aboriginal communities in the 1890s, was instrumental in setting up the Aborigines Inland Mission in 1905. She too conducted missionary work throughout the remainder of her life. Both women criticised the government policy, widespread at the time, of forcibly removing so-called 'half-caste' children from their Indigenous families.[66]

The connections forged in Australia between the Irish and Irish Australians, on the one hand, and Indigenous peoples, on the other, were profoundly shaped by colonialism. For many, this involved Irish violence against Aboriginal people or indifference to their sufferings. But for some, there were personal friendships and familial relationships. Since the 1960s, politics have emerged as another notable link. Many Irish, Irish-Australian and Indigenous political activists have found common cause. In 1972, during the early days of the Aboriginal Tent Embassy in Canberra, a visiting group of Irish Republican Army supporters showed their solidarity with Indigenous struggles by donating an Irish linen handkerchief.[67] Gary Foley, one of the founders of the Tent Embassy, later recalled that the fight for civil rights by Northern Irish Catholics during the late 1960s and early 1970s inspired him and other campaigners for Aboriginal rights.[68] Yawuru elder Patrick Dodson, chosen as a senator for Western Australia in 2016 and the first Aboriginal man to be ordained a Catholic priest, has also spoken of the influence of the Irish on his career, through both his own Irish family background and his contacts with Northern Irish political campaigners.[69] On a visit to Ireland in 2000, Dodson met Michael D Higgins, an academic, former cabinet minister and a member of the Irish parliament. A year later, Higgins celebrated the centenary of Australia's Federation in a statement that, among other things, encouraged 'the Australian nation, at the beginning of its new century, to seek ... arrangements and discussions in order to further secure and protect the rights, identity, culture and traditions of the Aboriginal people'.[70] In November 2017, when Higgins, by then president of Ireland, made his first official visit to Australia, he used a speech to the Western Australian parliament to acknowledge the role of the Irish in injustices committed against Aboriginal people during colonisation.[71]

Although, as the previous chapter demonstrated, British immigrants and their Australian descendants frequently saw the Irish in terms of racial stereotypes, Irish immigrants were in fact a varied group, exhibiting major differences in class, religion, gender and place of origin. For this simple reason alone, the Irish-Indigenous encounter has been a very varied affair and, given the current lack of adequate research, it is impossible to generalise about it confidently. However, what is apparent is that some Irish immigrants identified with the dominant white settler society and participated in efforts to dispossess Aboriginal peoples of both their lands and their cultures. These included members of the Perth Gaelic League, who reacted angrily in 1905 to a suggestion that the Irish and Aboriginal peoples might have things in common. Like Gaelic League members in Ireland, they were proud of their Irishness, their rich history and culture, which meant in their eyes that they were 'white', not 'black', and therefore their homeland deserved self-government. Others around the same time, such as Frank Gillen, while maintaining a sense of Irish identity and supporting the cause of Irish home rule, nevertheless tried to understand and help Indigenous peoples. While we may never know what most Irish Australians who created families with Indigenous women and men thought about their Irish roots, we do know that many such families existed and significant numbers of them thrived despite very unfavourable circumstances. Irish people were part of the story of Australian colonisation in all its complexity.

CHAPTER 3

The Irish and the Chinese in white Australia

Biddy Burke was as fascinated by the Chinese people she first saw when she arrived in Brisbane in 1880 as she was by 'black' people. She wrote to her brother in wonder at encountering Irish girls married to 'Yellow Chinaman with their Hair platted down there [their] black back'.[1] Yet to many Australians of British birth or descent, Biddy, a servant girl from a small townland in rural County Galway, probably seemed almost as strange and foreign as any 'Yellow Chinaman'. In 1896, a cartoon in the Sydney *Bulletin*, simply entitled 'Foreigners', showed two idle shop-keepers separated by a wall: one a Chinese man standing in front of a laundry; the other a stereotyped Irish man called 'Mick', smoking a pipe and leaning against the wall.[2] The cartoonist portrayed both men as foreigners in terms of their racial features and behaviour, in particular their laziness. Yet, while readers of the *Bulletin* might have agreed that Irish and Chinese immigrants were equally foreign, many Irish men and women were very determined to proclaim their difference from Chinese laundry men, miners, market gardeners, furniture makers and hawkers. These Irish immigrants would have approved the actions of their

FOREIGNERS.—(A Melbourne Sketch from Life.)

Although most Irish Australians supported the white Australia policy and restrictions on 'coloured' immigration, publications like the Sydney *Bulletin*, even as late as the 1890s, were still portraying the Irish as 'foreigners' and drawing racialised parallels between them and the Chinese.
Source: 'Foreigners', *Bulletin*, 4 July 1896, p. 13.

fellow immigrants in California, who from the 1850s onwards were at the forefront of anti-Chinese riots and campaigns for tighter restrictions on Chinese entry into the United States (US).[3]

The field of Chinese-Australian studies is now a large one and includes much valuable research, not only on efforts to restrict Chinese immigration, but on the varied connections and networks that developed between and among Australians of European and Chinese origin.[4] Yet historians have shown surprisingly little interest to date in interactions between Chinese and Irish Australians, although there are some important studies particularly of Chinese-Irish marriage patterns.[5] Malcolm Campbell's comparative work examining the Irish on the Australian and Californian goldfields has produced insights into Irish attitudes towards the Chinese.[6] In addition, Barry McCarron's 2016 doctoral thesis comparing Irish and Chinese immigrants in countries around the Pacific Rim has opened up new avenues of research both in Australia and internationally and, hopefully, it will prompt historians to investigate sources further for the history of Irish and Chinese Australians. McCarron's work is especially significant because he has used Chinese-language sources to examine Chinese-Australian attitudes towards the Irish.[7]

In this chapter, however, we plan to concentrate on how non-Irish observers viewed the Irish in relation to the Chinese and what similarities they detected between the two peoples. We also want to consider the ways in which Irish Australians strove to distinguish themselves from the Chinese. The disjunction between these two viewpoints tells us much about the shifting position of the Irish: they were outsiders in Protestant British Australia, yet, at the same time, they enthusiastically supported restrictions on Chinese immigration and the white Australia policy.

Chinese and Irish miners on the goldfields

In the mid and late 19th century, large groups of Chinese men were living and working on the goldfields of Victoria, New South Wales (NSW) and Queensland.[8] Small numbers had arrived before the early 1850s, mostly as indentured servants, but once gold was discovered in both NSW and Victoria, the Chinese population increased rapidly, reaching 38258 by 1861. After a series of Acts were passed restricting immigration, 29627 Chinese-born immigrants remained in Australia in 1901, with the largest group (34.5 per cent of the total) living in NSW. As a whole, though, at the time of Federation the Chinese community made up only around 0.8 per cent of the total Australian population.[9] But these overall figures mask major regional differences. On the Victorian goldfields in 1857, for example, the overwhelmingly male Chinese miners comprised 19 per cent of the total male population.[10] Many Chinese immigrants did not remain in the colonies, however. Between 1852 and 1889 in Victoria, 40721 Chinese arrivals by sea were recorded, but 36049 departures as well.[11] This was in part because it was common practice for Chinese men to come to Australia for relatively short periods to look for gold or work, sometimes on contract, and then return to their families in China.[12]

On the Australian goldfields, as in California, interactions between the Irish and Chinese ranged all the way from friendly co-operation to full-scale bloody riots. Tempers were easily aroused in the crowded and competitive living and working conditions, and fights over the placement of claim pegs or access to water frequently ended up in the courts. When the *Bendigo Advertiser* reported one such court case in September 1857, the writer gave full rein to his stereotyped opinions regarding both groups. Thomas Young, who was described as 'a native of the fighting county of Kerry', brought a case for assault against four 'Mongolians' and was represented in court by Counsellor O'Loughlin. The fight at Peg Leg Gully, near Eaglehawk, started when Young and a fellow Irish miner marked out land for a puddling mill. 'A large number of the long-tailed race' had objected, according to the *Bendigo Advertiser*, claiming the land belonged to them, and a brawl had ensued in which Young was injured. After representations by Counsellor Lysaght for the Chinese, the magistrate dismissed the case. But he rebuked what he called 'these rebellious Irishmen' for trespassing on a Chinese claim and for taking 'the law into their own hands'. He urged the police to monitor Peg Leg Gully, as it was obviously a 'rowdy place', and he threatened both parties 'with the utmost rigor of the law' should there be any further clashes.[13] In this instance, lawyers with Irish names represented both sides – testifying to the significant number of Irish lawyers then practising in Victoria – and press reporting of the case relied heavily on racial stereotypes. Such small-scale disputes between Irish and Chinese miners were common throughout the 1850s and 1860s, with both parties quick to take their arguments to the courts.[14]

On the NSW and Victorian diggings, well-organised groups of Irish miners protected their claims against outsiders, and against the Chinese in particular. Men from County Donegal, known as 'Donegallers' in NSW, and men from County Tipperary, known as the 'Tipperary mob' in Victoria, proved formidable opponents. There were suggestions that some of these groups were 'oath-bound', which means that they might have had links with Irish secret societies.[15] As at Peg Leg Gully in 1857, clashes were frequently between only a handful of men, but sometimes they could grow to involve hundreds. The largest disturbance in which Irish and Chinese miners took part was a series of organised attacks on Chinese mining camps in 1861 that began and ended at Tipperary Gully on the Lambing Flat goldfield west of Sydney.[16] The NSW fields had seen an increase in Chinese numbers during the late 1850s after Victoria and South Australia began restricting Chinese arrivals.[17] When the Lambing Flat field had been proclaimed in November 1860, it was the biggest to be opened in several years and, by late January 1861, it was home to around 9000 eager miners who had high hopes of success.[18]

While a number of historians have studied the events at Lambing Flat, the important role Irish miners played in them has attracted little attention in most accounts. But Irish men were among the white miners' leaders and also took a prominent part in subsequent calls for politicians to restrict Chinese immigration.[19] James Torpy, a Cork-born Protestant, headed the Miners' Protective League at Lambing Flat and worked assiduously to deny Chinese men access to the goldfields in order to protect the European monopoly of the diggings.[20] The League's complaints were ostensibly over access to relatively scarce resources, such as water, which it alleged the Chinese were exploiting unfairly.[21] During a series of riots stretching from January to July 1861, Tom McCarthy, the Irish-born chairman of the Lambing Flat Riot Committee, carried a notorious banner reading 'Roll up Roll up No Chinese'.[22] Several thousand white miners, including Irish men carrying large wooden sticks, or shillelaghs, marched to attack the Chinese camps under a variety of banners, including English and American flags and green flags incorporating Irish symbols, of which the harp was one. Through such displays, the Irish linked their cultural heritage to the fight to maintain their mining rights alongside fellow white miners from England and the US. Large gatherings and processions featuring Irish banners had been used in Ireland during the early 1840s by Daniel O'Connell in his campaign to repeal the Act of Union between Ireland and Britain.[23] While there is no direct evidence that the Lambing Flat miners were involved in any of O'Connell's political rallies, they would certainly have known about them and been familiar with the tactic of displaying Irish symbols as a way of promoting solidarity and allegiance to a common cause.

The particular antipathy that existed between Irish and Chinese miners was well known and was acknowledged in popular literature. This can be seen in Edward Dyson's 'A golden shanty', which appeared as the title short story in the *Bulletin*'s 1889 Christmas anthology. An Irish publican named Michael Doyle is portrayed as conducting a long-running dispute with local Chinese diggers, who he believes are robbing him. The Doyle family reflects familiar anti-Irish stereotypes: Mrs Doyle is a fat, lazy slattern; the children are a 'tribe of dirty, unkempt urchins'; while Michael himself is a boastful, 'scraggy' little man who struggles to eke out a bare living. Nevertheless, he looks down disdainfully upon the Chinese as a 'plague' of 'perfidious, heathern [sic] ... Chows' – the fact that they are teetotallers does not help matters. When some of these 'haythen furriners' laugh at him, Michael loses his temper and attacks them violently. However, the 'battle' goes against the 'Irish cause' until 'Mrs Mickey, making a timely appearance, warded off the surplus Chinamen by chipping at their skulls with an axe-handle'.[24] The story incorporates a longstanding gender reversal stereotype of the Irish man as weak and cowardly, like a woman, and the Irish woman as aggressive and violent, like a man.

Chinese men, Irish women and their children

One of the most persistent fears expressed in newspaper articles, political debates, cartoons and popular literature was that Chinese men were not only using unfair tactics on the goldfields, but that they were also seducing and corrupting white women.[25] This fear was encouraged by the fact that virtually all Chinese immigrants were single men, even though a significant proportion of them had wives and families back in China.[26] There were few single women on the goldfields and white miners resented what they saw as Chinese competition for them. When discussing the 1861 Lambing Flat riots in his posthumously published recollections, Irish miner Tom McCarthy highlighted the threat of 'white slavery': the fear that white women were being forced into prostitution. According to him: 'Procuresses were everywhere about in the pay of the Chinese to entrap young girls' to be kept 'by the heathens without the slightest fear'.[27] Similar fears echoed throughout the rest of the century and not only on the goldfields. Journalists and politicians sought evidence to prove their belief that Chinese men were involved in prostitution rackets and in seducing vulnerable white women through drugs and promises of easy money.[28]

As the alluvial goldfields became less profitable and Chinese miners were generally excluded from working for the quartz-mining companies, they left Australia in large numbers for New Zealand or California or to return to China. Some remained, however, many moving to work in cities and towns as merchants, storekeepers, market gardeners, hawkers and labourers.[29] By the 1890s, small numbers were also employed in the furniture trades.[30] Many of these occupations brought Chinese men into contact with single white women, especially domestic servants.

As early as the 1850s, there were reports of Chinese men marrying or living with European women and such reports increased as more Chinese immigrants moved to the cities.[31] The Australian situation appears different from that on the Californian goldfields, where marriages between the Chinese and American-born women were rare and were eventually prohibited by law.[32] In California, the authorities allowed Chinese prostitutes to immigrate rather than permitting marriages between Chinese men and American women. But this was not the path followed in Australia.[33]

William Lew Shing, a native of southern China, was one of the Chinese men who married on the goldfields. His wife was Irish-born Brigit Garvan. Married in Ballarat, William and Brigit then moved to the Tasmanian tin mines in around 1877, before settling in Melbourne in 1893 and running a small business.[34] The numbers of Chinese-Irish marriages were certainly believed to be much greater than they actually were. Articles in the press often expressed the view that nearly all the women who married Chinese men were Irish, at the same time bemoaning the fall in social status and the corruption in morals that such marriages entailed for them. While marriages had to be registered, non-marital relationships between Chinese men and British, Irish or Australian women did not. When we look at sources such as Chinese-Australian family history, police reports and newspaper articles, we find that many such relationships existed, although they are impossible to quantify.[35] Life stories preserved by the descendants of such women as Margaret Fulham show some of the complexities of these relationships. Born to Irish parents on the voyage to Australia, Margaret was 35 years old, had been married three times and had nine children, when she met Billy Ah Pan in Singleton, NSW. Although the couple never married, presumably because she was still married to her third husband, they had a further three children together.[36]

Work done by historians Kate Bagnall on NSW and Pauline Rule on Victoria shows that the number of Chinese men marrying was always relatively small: around 400 in NSW before 1888 and 700 in Victoria before 1901.[37] During the 1850s and 1860s there was some basis for the belief that Irish women were marrying Chinese men in larger numbers than might be expected given their proportion of the female population. Between 1855 and 1860 the Victorian statistician recorded 59 marriages by Chinese men, with 28 (47 per cent) of the brides being Irish-born.[38] English- and Australian-born brides each made up around 20 per cent of the total. This may in part reflect a higher number of Irish women living and working on the goldfields because, after the 1860s, the number of Chinese-Irish marriages declined sharply.[39] One of these marriages took place in 1868, when young Irish woman Margaret Hogan married Canton-born George Bakhap. She had already given birth to an illegitimate son, Thomas, two years before in the Ballarat Benevolent Asylum. The family moved to Tasmania, where Thomas Bakhap grew up fluent in Cantonese as well as English. In later life, he did not discourage the belief that he was half Chinese. Throughout his political career, first as a member of the Tasmanian parliament and from 1913 as a federal senator for Tasmania, he was considered one of Australia's foremost experts on China.[40] Bakhap's Irish mother, Margaret Hogan, like Margaret Fulham, seems to have established a secure family life with a Chinese husband after a number of initially difficult years in Australia.

Outsiders, though, tended to see only well-worn stereotypes of impoverished Irish women and alien Chinese men, neither of whom were likely to be improved by marriage between them.[41] The idea of an Irish domestic servant marrying a 'Celestial' created an obvious frisson of racial anxiety. During the 1850s, a Scottish visitor to the goldfields named Just noted that the 'few' Chinese men who married in Victoria usually took 'Irish girls' for their wives. And he went on to ponder: 'What the future character of the offspring of such unions may be, is an interesting question for those curious on the subject of races; but certainly the Celtic and Mongolian character combined will be something new in the history of mankind.' He took for granted that such children would remain in Australia, for – employing the word 'ladies' with obvious irony – he went on: 'I suspect these Irish ladies would not be made very welcome in the land of the "Celestials".'[42] On his visit to the Victorian goldfields in 1867, the English Liberal parliamentarian Sir Charles Dilke showed an interest in Chinese-Irish marriages, comparing the two groups very unflatteringly on several occasions. He had arrived via the US, where he was horrified by the numbers and influence of the Irish and the Chinese. His aim to create a 'Greater Britain', which would include the white settler colonies, excluded not only the Chinese and 'coolies', as he called Indians, but the Irish as well. Near Bendigo, when he went into a baker's shop to buy a roll for his lunch, the woman serving him 'shuddered when she told me of one or two recent marriages between Irish "Biddies" and some of the wealthiest Chinese'.[43] PH Parker, an English diplomat who had visited Australia briefly, reported in 1902 a conversation he had had in Ballarat with an English miner working for a Chinese employer. His informant told him that the Chinese were 'not bad fellows', but they 'plays old 'Arry with our women'. Their soft-spoken ways were especially popular with Irish girls, who 'gets kind of fond o' them'.[44]

A strong perception obviously existed that it was mostly Irish women who married or cohabited with Chinese men, even though the statistics do not support this view. In 1875, the Victorian statistician HH Hayter noted that, although many women were living with Chinese men, there had only been 183 marriages of Chinese men during 1866–75. He went on to say that it was 'very generally believed' that the 'majority' of women who married Chinese men were Irish. But he then demonstrated that this belief was not supported by the evidence. During 1866–75 in Victoria, 53 per cent of the brides of Chinese men were Australian-born, 22 per cent were English-born and only 12 per cent were Irish-born.[45] Further statistical data from Victoria and Queensland during the 1880s confirmed that the brides of Chinese men were mostly Australian-born.[46] That the number of Irish women marrying Chinese men declined between 1850 and 1886 is to be expected, partly because the Irish-born immigrant population was aging. It is also likely that some of the increasingly Australian-born wives of Chinese husbands after the 1860s had Irish parents, but it is impossible to say exactly how many.

Even with colonial statisticians publishing data aimed at refuting the belief that Chinese men mostly married Irish women, popular opinion was not to be swayed, and nor was the press that helped form it. In 1882, a letter to the editor of *Australian Town and Country Journal* was at pains to point out that 'white' women who cohabited with Chinese men were not English, as had been stated in a previous article; on the contrary, they were '95% Irish'.[47] In May 1888, in the midst of the controversy known as the *Afghan* crisis, when first Victoria and then NSW refused to allow Chinese immigrants to disembark from the ship *Afghan*, newspapers gave free rein to their anti-Chinese prejudices and fantasies.[48] The writer of an article in the Melbourne *Leader* remarked that 'all Chinese who have married in Victoria have chosen Irish wives'. He then went on to illustrate this remark with an anecdote about an Irish domestic servant he had employed who had left his household to marry a 'purveyor of vegetables'. She had loudly praised her husband who, she said, 'has never as much as blacken[ed]' my eye'.[49] A week later in Adelaide, AE McDermott wrote to a local newspaper crossly challenging the assertion that only Irish women married Chinese men, citing figures from the *Victorian Year Book* of 1886–87 to prove his point.[50] Yet, despite the efforts of Irish men like McDermott and of the colonial statisticians, the popular belief in large numbers of Chinese-Irish marriages persisted throughout the rest of the century and beyond.

Whereas during the 1850s a visitor could only speculate about the future character of the Australian-born children of Chinese-Irish marriages, later writers sometimes met such children in the flesh. In a 1908 article, the socialist playwright Louis Esson described his encounter with a 'half-caste "Pat"' employed as a waiter in an all-night Chinese restaurant in Little Lonsdale Street, Melbourne's notorious 'Little Lon' Chinatown area. The waiter, wrote Esson, was an 'astonishing person, half Chinese, half Larrikin. Talkative, confident … he professes great faith in China, and, like most half-castes, his sentiments are all Celestial'. Reflecting the widespread belief that many larrikins were Irish Australians, Esson noted that Pat the waiter talked in Australian and larrikin slang, with some Chinese words mixed in. He claimed his Chinese ancestors had been great warriors: his clan, he said, 'eats gunpowder and drinks blood'. But, despite Pat's preference for China, Esson presented him as a mostly Irish rather than Chinese stereotype, for, as well as being full of boastful 'blarney', according to Esson, he was an inveterate liar.[51]

Chinese-Australian commentators also appear to have seen the children of Chinese men and their Irish wives as having particular issues with their identity. In 1898, the Sydney-based *Chinese Australian Herald* published a letter from a Queensland reader complaining that the children of Irish mothers, unlike Pat the Melbourne waiter, tended to identify with their mothers – to consider themselves Irish – and not with their Chinese fathers.[52]

Speculation about the identity of Chinese-Irish children did not just occur in newspapers and periodicals: a comic hybrid character with an identity problem also appeared on the Australian stage. Between 1914 and 1927, amateur theatre groups in a number of NSW and Victorian country towns performed a short farce entitled *Patsy O'Wang*.[53] The play had been written in 1895 by a prolific American playwright, Thomas Stewart Denison, who published it in a collection of his short pieces intended for amateur theatrical groups.[54] The action takes place in a sanatorium run by Dr Fluke, who has two Irish servants, Norah and Mike, described in the script as 'conventional Irish with a thick brogue'. Against the wishes of his wife and servants, Dr Fluke decides to employ a Chinese cook, as he is dissatisfied with Norah's culinary skills. The cook, Chin Sum, is from Hong Kong, but only his mother was Chinese, his father being a 'wild Irish' artillery officer named Hooligan. Chin Sum's character is deeply conflicted. While he drinks strong tea his Chinese nature remains dominant, but should he drink whiskey – which he does when drunken Mike leaves out a bottle – then he becomes an Irish man called Patsy O'Wang. Even his speech changes: from Chinese pidgin English he switches to the 'good English with little if any brogue' learnt from British army officers in barracks. Like Just and Esson, Denison seems to have perceived the combination of Irish and Chinese parentage as unnatural and so the character, and even the speech, of Chin Sum/Patsy O'Wang alternates between two incompatible stereotyped identities. As a Chinese man he is docile and polite, but as an Irish man he is wild and unpredictable. By the end of the play, Patsy has determined to remain Irish and to venture upon a career in politics, despite Mike's comment: 'Faith, I'll niver vote a shplit ticket, half Irish half Chinay.'[55] This portrayal of stereotypes clearly appealed to Australian audiences as the play proved popular. When it was performed in 1914 at the Windsor Literary Institute near Sydney, many of the women in the audience kept up an 'incessant roar of laughter, at times increasing to screams'.[56]

Australian public opinion, and American as well, perceived Chinese men both as sexual predators and as alarmingly attractive to white women due to their domesticity and willingness to do women's work.[57] During the 1870s and 1880s several journalists explored inner-city Sydney, investigating its impoverished and seedy underworld at length. In the series 'After dark', published in the *Sydney Morning Herald* in 1873, a journalist interviewed several women married to Chinese men. One, a young Irish-Australian woman who married aged 15 and now had three children, explained that her husband was 'good to her, and she had no reason to complain'.[58] In another lengthy report in 1888, a reporter for the *Sydney Illustrated News* interviewed an Irish-born woman married to a Chinese man, who contrasted the comfortable life she currently led with what she believed would have been her fate had she married an Irish man. Her husband, Ah Moon, she said: 'earns the bread, he does half the housework, he walks the floor all night with the babies'. Opium, she admitted, made 'the place smell', although you soon got used to it and 'a bad smell is better than a broken head, and that is what I would get if it was whiskey'.[59] Significantly, although these articles interviewed a range of women living with Chinese men, it was only Irish women's ethnicity that was ever specified, other women being described more vaguely as 'European' or 'white'. Reports such as these contributed to the popular notion that it was Irish and Irish-Australian women who mostly married or lived with Chinese men, at the same time reinforcing stereotypes of drunken and violent Irish men.

Colonial stereotypes were never rigidly fixed, however, but shifted and developed in different ways over time. As the century wore on, cartoonists and comic writers were as likely to show Bridget, the typical Irish servant, rejecting 'John the Chinaman' as marrying him. Relations between the Irish and the Chinese had become complex and such interactions offered lots of comic opportunities, especially for verbal humour based on miscommunication. A cartoon in the *Bulletin* in 1899 shows a servant, 'Bridgetta', asking 'John' if he is 'mallied'. He answers, 'No feah—me no mally wife'. Then he tries to reassure 'Blidget', in case she believes he is rejecting her, by saying that some 'udder man makee you happy some day'. John in this cartoon has stereotyped Chinese facial features, hair and dress and speaks in broken English. The two bags he carries on a pole indicate his occupation as an itinerant hawker. Relations between the two characters are finely balanced. The servant's Irishness is indicated by her name, although she prefers 'Bridgetta' to mere 'Bridget', but, unlike John, her face and body are not racially caricatured. Her occupation is signalled by her maid's uniform and the duster in her hand. She stands on the front step of the house above John in the street and looking down upon him. Unlike him, she has access to the Australian home, even if only as a servant. She talks to John in a friendly and rather personal manner, which her middle-class mistress would be unlikely

CONSOLA-
TION.

BRIDGETTA : " You mallied
man, John ? "

JOHN : " No feah—me no mally wife ; too muchee
spendum money. But you no cly, Blidget—
some udder man makee you happy some day."

In this complex cartoon, an Irish female servant guards a white middle-
class home against the entry of a Chinese male hawker, yet the two discuss
marriage in a friendly fashion. The conversation points to the widespread,
although erroneous, belief that Irish women were especially prone to marry
Chinese men.
Source: 'Consolation', *Bulletin*, 11 November 1899, p. 11.

to have done. Bridget the archetypal Irish servant is very obviously a liminal figure in this cartoon, literally standing on the threshold of domestic white respectability, but talking to an alien 'other' in the street. The two characters are joined in conversation, but simultaneously divided by space and verbal misunderstanding.[60] Chinese-Irish relations, although less violent than on the goldfields, remained fraught.

The Irish and the Chinese labour threat

While Australians of British birth and descent insisted that it was mostly Irish women, rather than members of their own community, who married or lived with Chinese men, many Irish Australians actually agreed that the Chinese were a threat that had to be contained if not eliminated entirely. In 1850, an Irish immigrant living at Moreton Bay, in what would soon become Queensland, wrote to the Sydney *Freeman's Journal*, complaining that 'the loathesome idolaters from China' and 'the cannibals from the South Seas' were likely to be tolerated, 'but let the afflicted poor of Erin but appear, and [British settlers] will immediately howl and bark at them'.[61] This Irish man was writing before restrictions were placed on Chinese immigration and at a time when there was an outcry in the colonies against large numbers of young Irish girls arriving from workhouses in famine-stricken Ireland. Nevertheless, he was drawing a very clear line that placed the poor 'afflicted' Irish on one side, separate from 'loathesome' Chinese 'idolaters' and Pacific Island 'cannibals' on the other.

The first attempt to restrict Chinese immigration was made in NSW in 1851 by Henry Grattan Douglass, a Dublin-born

Protestant doctor, who denounced what he called the 'slave trade' in Chinese labourers. But the pastoralists who dominated the Legislative Council simply laughed at him and he was forced to withdraw his motion.[62] Douglass had supporters though. The *Freeman's Journal* regretted that Australia's 'inoffensive race of savages' had not been trained as shepherds and instead squatters were bent upon importing 'vile and vicious Asiatics'.[63] The politician and writer Daniel Deniehy, whose parents were Irish convicts, also denounced Asian immigration to NSW throughout the 1850s.[64] Plans to bring in indentured Indian 'coolie' labour were 'diabolical', he wrote in 1854, since 'freedom cannot exist in the pestiferous atmosphere of slavery'.[65] Deniehy wanted a poll tax placed on the increasing numbers of Chinese miners, arguing in 1858 that unlimited immigration 'would impart to the country a barbarous and degraded aspect'.[66] In the NSW Legislative Assembly in October 1860, amid widespread concern over Chinese immigration, Deniehy warned that, in 'this most English of colonies', there was 'gradually growing up a race of barbarians of a far worse stamp than the negroes' of the US. If immigration was allowed to continue at its present levels, the Chinese would become such a numerous 'inferior and degraded caste' that they could 'jeopardise the free working of our political institutions'.[67] Within months anti-Chinese riots had broken out at Lambing Flat and, in October 1861, NSW finally introduced an act limiting Chinese immigration – a step most other colonies had already taken.[68]

In contrast to Deniehy, his good friend William Bede Dalley, also the son of Irish convicts, spoke against later attempts to restrict Chinese immigration. In 1881, he opposed a measure aimed to deny basic rights to the Chinese and, although not wholly successful, he did get the bill's provisions modified.[69]

Dalley, however, was speaking in very different circumstances from those Deniehy had faced 20 years earlier: the goldfields were no longer attracting large numbers of Chinese miners and Chinese merchants had established successful businesses in a number of Australian cities. With a reputation as the colony's leading lawyer and orator, Dalley opposed the proposed bill as a represenive of a group of wealthy Sydney Chinese merchants. Alarmed by an outbreak of smallpox that was blamed on the Chinese, Henry Parkes had proposed an Act to automatically quarantine Chinese immigrants on arrival, as well as to end their rights to buy land and be granted naturalisation. Members of the Legislative Council supported Dalley and blocked these particular clauses, although further restrictions on Chinese numbers were carried. Dalley's opposition to the 1881 legislation was based on his belief that no government should be able to deny basic rights to residents, whatever their race, or to ban property transactions.[70]

Some clergy, middle-class Catholics and left-wing activists protested against restricting immigration, but they were in a decided minority and became less vocal as time went on. By 1866, the *Freeman's Journal*, which Dalley had bought by 1864, had changed its tune on the Chinese and was arguing for the repeal of the 1861 Act limiting their numbers. While having 'no great admiration for the Chinese in a moral ... sense', a writer – who may well have been Dalley himself – stressed that they were 'hard-working, industrious and useful ... colonists'.[71] Cardinal Patrick Moran, archbishop of Sydney, who was eager to foster good relations with the Chinese as he wanted to send Catholic missionaries to China, expressed similar sentiments in a contro-versial interview he gave in Adelaide in 1888. He too suggested that the hard-working Chinese were an asset to the Australian colonies and should not be barred.[72] However, the mood of the public was decidedly against Chinese immigration in the wake of the *Afghan* crisis and Moran's comments provoked a storm of indignation in the press. The *Bulletin* published several striking cartoons mocking him as the 'Chow's Patron'.[73] In following years, although Moran's opposition to immigration restriction became more muted in public, Chinese community leaders nevertheless recognised in him a sympathiser. Thus the *Chinese Australian Herald* urged its readers to vote for Moran when he stood unsuccessfully in 1897 as a delegate to the federal convention.[74] And, when the NSW Chinese Anti-Opium League was seeking support in 1905 for its efforts to combat opium addiction and other social problems among the Chinese community, it turned to Moran, who agreed to endorse its campaign.[75]

Other Irish Australians also criticised the upsurge in support for restricting immigration around the time of Federation. Bernard O'Dowd, who was raised by Catholic Irish-born parents in Beaufort in central-western Victoria, abandoned his family's faith later in life and in 1907 became a founder member of the Victorian Socialist Party.[76] Frank Bongiorno has argued that O'Dowd's early writings suggest he was repelled by, rather than sympathetic to, the Chinese he met during his youth in the gold-mining districts around Beaufort and Ballarat. But O'Dowd's attitude to the Chinese seemed to change after he moved to Melbourne and became interested in Eastern philosophy and mysticism as a member of the Theosophical Society.[77] He then used the radical newspaper he founded, *Tocsin*, to advocate for racial equality and to attack race-based immigration policies. Although there was debate amongst socialists and trade unionists over restricting immigration in the years before Federation, there were few who agreed with O'Dowd and his arguments were not popular.[78]

Irish-born politicians often deferred to their working-class constituents when they argued in favour of legislation to limit the numbers of Chinese and other immigrants of colour. Nowhere was this clearer than in Queensland, where Donegal-born John Murtagh Macrossan represented North Queensland mining communities in the colony's Legislative Assembly from 1873 until 1891.[79] He resolutely opposed Chinese immigration, particularly when the Palmer River goldfields on Cape York attracted large numbers of Chinese miners during the 1870s and 1880s.[80] According to him, 'one Chinaman in the colony is one too many'; he considered them 'one of the greatest evils which is looming in the distance to the European people'.[81] But Macrossan was by no means always consistent in his policies.[82] For example, he supported restrictions on 'Kanaka' or Pacific Islander labour, yet wanted to allow indentured 'coolie' Indian labourers to work in the sugar cane industry. In taking this position, he exasperated those Queensland politicians opposed to any form of 'coloured' labour.[83] Macrossan's views were informed by the widely held belief that white men were racially unsuited for work in industries based in northern Australia due to the tropical climate, thus making it essential to hire people of colour for such work.[84]

Macrossan was just one of the more outspoken Irish and Irish-Australian leaders who opposed Chinese immigration. Others included Patrick Garvan in NSW, as well as John Talbot, head of the NSW Trades and Labor Council, both of whom were prominent during the anti-Chinese crisis of 1888.[85] Such men were convinced that the Chinese and other people of colour constituted a major threat to the white working class because they were willing to accept lower wages and poorer working conditions and they would not join a trade union.[86] The

This Brisbane newspaper cartoon reflects fears in the labour movement during the 1890s depression that just as the Catholic Irish had been excluded from jobs in the past by 'No Irish Need Apply' signs, so in the future white men would be similarly excluded in favour of 'cheap coloured' labour.

Source: 'The bushman's future', *Worker*, 14 May 1892, p. 1.

Queensland labour newspaper, the *Worker*, while sympathetic to Irish nationalism, was at the same time fiercely opposed to non-white immigrant labour – a position that doubtless appealed to many working-class Irish Australians. The paper often featured striking cartoons. One published in 1892, entitled 'The bushman's future', shows a thin Australian worker confronted by a large sign, reading: 'Wanted, shearers and station hands, No White Men Need Apply'. Around the sign, plump black workers cut sugar cane and a Chinese man pans for gold in a stream.[87] The cartoon assumes the paper's readers were familiar with the notorious 'No Irish Need Apply' signs and advertisements (see chapter 6). It seems to be saying that while the Irish have escaped one form of employment discrimination due to their Irishness, they are now facing another form as white men challenged by 'cheap coloured' labour.

Irish Australians in white Australia

Support for restrictions, if not outright bans, on Chinese immigration was strong among Irish Australians, and not only those belonging to the working class. Irish-born John Coffey, a wealthy landowner in the Wimmera district of western Victoria, was, according to his 1908 obituary, an 'enthusiastic believer in a white Australia', who had boasted that he never employed 'coloured labour'.[88] In the years around 1900, letters to Catholic newspapers in all states, and reports in the same papers covering meetings of Catholic clubs and societies, showed widespread support for limits to immigration by people of colour and especially by the Chinese.

The Catholic Young Men's Society (CYMS), a self-improvement organisation backed by the church with branches in most cities and regional centres, regularly held debates and hosted lectures on topics of particular interest to young Irish Australians, rather than to their Irish immigrant parents.[89] The society's membership consisted of men who were generally ambitious to better themselves and perhaps to make a mark on society. A number of these youthful debaters, notably James Scullin, Australia's first Catholic prime minister, went on to become influential politicians.[90] Debates on Chinese immigration were held in Melbourne and in towns throughout Victoria during the 1880s. At Woodend near Melbourne in 1888, for example, a newspaper report noted that although 'both sides were well supported', the general feeling of the meeting was in favour of restrictions on Chinese immigration.[91] Twenty years later, in 1909, the Perth branch of the CYMS was treated to a long lecture asserting that 'the white Australia policy was the most inspiring ideal which had ever been adopted by a country at the dawn of its nationhood'. The speaker, JJ Simons, founder of the youth organisation the Young Australia League, who later became a Labor politician, explained that the US, where lynchings and interracial violence were common, offered the best evidence that white and black could not live together.[92]

When it came to ensuring that the Australian colonies were reserved for white workers alone, Catholic Irish Australians argued that they were no different from Australians of Protestant British descent. They bolstered such arguments by protesting against attempts to divide them from their fellow Australians on the basis of what they labelled spurious racial or ethnic differences. In December 1880, on the day that state funding for Catholic schools ceased in Queensland, Brisbane's Bishop James Quinn protested in a letter to the minister for instruction, Arthur Palmer, himself an Armagh-born Protestant. In his letter, Quinn argued that the new funding model effectively established one education system for English and Scottish pupils and another for Chinese, Irish and Polynesian children. We 'can see no reason why Irish children should be treated so', complained Quinn. The bishop was pointing out that, by not funding Catholic education, the government was relegating Catholic Irish-Australian children to the same outsider status held by racial minorities of colour. This was especially harsh, wrote Quinn, in light of the fact that it was 'the blood of the Irish' shed in battle, not that of 'coloured' people, on which the 'greatness of the English' had been built.[93]

There were many voices calling for Catholic Irish Australians and Protestant British Australians to co-operate over the issue of Chinese immigration – some of which were rather unlikely. In 1871, the NSW politician Henry Parkes, normally a fierce critic of the Irish, was out of favour and needed Irish-Australian electoral support. In a letter, Parkes told the Irish-born Victorian politician, Charles Gavan Duffy, that he would 'fervently pray to God that a way may be found out for your race to mix with mine as fellow citizens'. If barriers prevented those of British and Irish descent becoming 'one Australian people', Parkes wrote, 'we shall end up a factious & senseless rabble'. Parkes was an opportunist, known for shifting allegiances to suit his own political purposes, and he was no genuine friend of the Catholic Irish.[94] However, the sentiments he expressed to Duffy were frequently echoed in the press, especially in statements about leaving 'old world' problems behind – notably problems like the ancient enmity between the Irish and English – in order to build a new united country. By joining with Protestant British-Australian workers in opposing so-called 'cheap' Chinese labour, Catholic Irish-Australian workers identified with the principles of a white Australia policy.[95]

Catholic newspapers editorialised in favour of white Australia on various grounds, notably because of racial differences between white people and the Chinese, the need to ensure social harmony and the threat of competition from cheap labour.[96] The Adelaide Catholic paper, the *Southern Cross*, argued in March 1906 that although allowing 'coloured' workers into Australia might in the short term speed economic development: 'Wisdom suggests that we should be content to go slow and keep the race pure ... all rapidity of progress would be bought dearly if it cost the hybridisation of our people and the variegation of their colour'.[97]

Irish Australians also drew parallels between Britain's refusal to grant home rule or self-government to Ireland and its refusal to allow the Australian colonies to control their own immigration policies. In 1897, the NSW government tried to pass legislation aimed to bar all people of colour from immigrating to the colony, but the British colonial secretary, Joseph Chamberlain, rejected the measure and NSW was forced instead to substitute a measure that allowed African and Asian British subjects to immigrate if they passed a writing test in any European language. In an editorial, the *Freeman's Journal* fumed against Chamberlain and the NSW government, which, in bowing to his demands, was 'guilty of a humiliating act of treason against Australian freedom'. Australia should not, the editorial went on, 'be dirtied by the feet of Asia and Africa'. The writer strongly objected to the 'habits, modes of life' and 'morality' of the 'alien ... dark hordes of the British Empire'. They were 'indigestible', he announced, 'or can only be assimilated with danger to the racial purity which is summed up in the demand for a "White Australia"'. Britain was wrong to refuse Ireland home rule, but it was right to deny autonomy to the peoples of its Asian and African possessions because they were 'unfit for the art of self-government'. Yet, if such people were allowed into the Australian colonies, they would be able to participate in self-government.[98] The *Freeman's Journal* leader writer was well aware that much of the rhetoric surrounding opposition to Irish home rule was couched in terms of the Irish people's unfitness for the 'art of self-government'. Therefore, he was careful when denying political rights to the 'coloured' subjects of the British crown to exempt the Irish, making plain that Ireland had a right to home rule, just as Irish Australians were wisely exercising colonial self-government in supporting the white Australia policy.[99]

In the years around Federation Australians began using words like 'whites', 'Australians' and 'Europeans' more frequently to refer to themselves, rather than 'English', 'Anglo-Saxons' or even 'British'. This shift in thinking allowed the Catholic Irish more space within British Australian society, a society that saw itself as now less threatened by the Irish and more threatened by what the *Freeman's Journal* had called the 'dark hordes of the British Empire'.[100] Such developments were clear in the parliamentary debates over the 1901 Immigration Restriction Bill, during which words like 'white' and 'Australian' were used far more frequently than 'British' or 'English'.[101] Irish-Australian politicians were in step with public opinion when they supported restrictions on 'coloured' and Chinese immigration during these debates, while at the same time, many continued to call for Irish home rule.

The Galway-born Catholic lawyer and conservative federal senator for South Australia, Patrick McMahon Glynn, combined strong support for Irish home rule with more moderate support for legislation to restrict immigration by people of colour.[102] He was not alone. Dublin-born Protestant lawyer Henry Bournes Higgins, a liberal member of the lower house of the federal parliament, spoke during the second reading of the Immigration Restriction Bill in 1901. He did not want, he said, to see 'the Empire ... dragged into complications arising out of this coloured race question', so steps needed to be 'taken speedily for the purpose of preventing these people from coming to our shores'.[103] Higgins, Glynn and others, including the *Freeman's Journal*, saw no contradiction in their support for Irish home rule and their opposition to allowing people of colour to immigrate. Political rights were the domain of white people, they believed, and the Irish in Australia had been exercising the right of self-government successfully since the 1850s; there was thus no reason to deny the same right to the Irish in Ireland.

In October 1905, the Australian federal parliament passed a motion in support of home rule for Ireland proposed by Irish-Australian members Higgins, Glynn and Hugh Mahon, amongst others.[104] But the motion heightened tensions over Irish politics, with Australian opponents of home rule speaking out against it. Tensions increased at the end of the year when a United Kingdom general election returned a Liberal government to power: a government that had Irish home rule on its legislative agenda. After one Melbourne rally against home rule in December 1905, the Catholic *Tribune* commented in a widely reprinted article: 'We may categorise the anti-Home Rule party as also the anti-Catholic party, the anti-White Australia party ... the pro-cheap labour party.'[105] Catholic Irish Australians who supported Irish home rule now considered themselves the champions of a white Australia.

Just as those who opposed home rule for Ireland used arguments based on race, so those who supported it also used the idiom of race to justify their claims. In the words previously quoted of the Irish home rule leader, John Dillon, before a New

Zealand audience in 1899: the Irish deserved self-government because 'we are white men'.[106] These debates continued during the first decades of the 20th century. WA Osborne, the professor of physiology at the University of Melbourne, had formed his opinions about the Catholic Irish while growing up as a Protestant in Belfast. He strongly opposed home rule and, in 1918, published a booklet expressing the view that the Irish ranked 'very low among the white races for their contribution to civilization'.[107] Osborne obviously saw the Irish as white, but there was a hierarchy of white races and in that the Irish for him sat 'very low'. At this time too, Irish nationalists continued to use the vocabulary of shared whiteness in their demands, not merely for self-government, but now for Irish independence from Britain. In 1919, Erskine Childers claimed that 'Ireland is now the only white nationality in the world ... where the principle of self-determination is not, at least in theory, conceded'.[108] This rhetoric was quickly and enthusiastically picked up in Australia at the Irish Race Convention held in Melbourne in 1919, where 'self-determination for the last of the small white nations which languishes under the oppressors' heel' was a major topic of discussion.[109]

Federation marked a shift, if not a definitive turning point, for Catholic Irish Australians. In general, they now enjoyed better economic and social prospects than had their Irish-born immigrant parents. They facilitated the journey towards these better prospects in part by separating themselves from other persecuted minorities like the Chinese. Irish Australians, with a few notable exceptions, supported efforts to create an exclusively white Australia and, in doing so, they strongly resisted attempts to divide them from Protestant British Australians on grounds of race and link them to 'inferior' immigrants of colour. But, although the Catholic Irish had fought hard and largely successfully to claim a place for themselves inside the walls of white Australia, there were still many who distrusted them. As war clouds gathered after 1900, Protestants and loyalists of British descent were concerned about Catholic allegiances: could they really be relied upon to fight for Britain in a war involving the Catholic powers of Europe? And there were many like Osborne, who, while they now recognised the Celtic Irish as among the white races, still insisted on Irish inferiority: they were white, but their whiteness was different from and inferior to British and British-Australian whiteness.

CHAPTER 4

Irish immigration, 1901–39: race, politics and eugenics

Hostility to the Catholic Irish and to Irish immigration did not end in 1901, although many Irish Australians had hoped that their support for Federation and for the white Australia policy would change attitudes and lead to their full acceptance within British-dominated Australian society. Race-based thinking about the Irish continued to be important, although not as significant as it had been during the 19th century. Sectarianism too remained influential and the politics of Ireland itself proved periodically disruptive. But a new factor to emerge was the pseudo-science of eugenics. New also was an Australian federal government armed with wide-ranging powers to exclude and deport immigrants under the 1901 *Immigration Restriction Act* and its many subsequent amendments. This chapter will investigate how continuing prejudice against the Irish meant that they were sometimes barred from Australia during the inter-war period and on occasion deported if they did succeed in gaining entry.

Two white races: the Mediterranean
and Nordic Irish

By the late 19th century, as we have seen, the Catholic Irish and their descendants were generally accepted as white. Yet there were varieties and degrees of whiteness: the Irish could be white, but at the same time not quite white enough.[1] Questions as to where exactly the Irish fitted in the perceived hierarchy of races remained unresolved even up to the 1930s. Ulster-born WA Osborne, professor of physiology at the University of Melbourne from 1903 to 1938, was no admirer of his Catholic fellow countrymen – his *Australian Dictionary of Biography* entry commented that his 'antagonism to Catholics and southern Irish was of Paisleyite dimensions'. He strenuously opposed Irish nationalism and equally strenuously supported the campaigns aimed to introduce conscription in 1916–17, while abusing Melbourne's Archbishop Daniel Mannix as the 'hooligan of Maynooth'.[2] Osborne was also active in the eugenics movement, being on the committee of the Eugenics Education Society, established in Melbourne in 1914. The society's president was fellow Melbourne University professor, the biologist and anthropologist Baldwin Spencer, while its vice-president was Dr William Ernest Jones, Victoria's inspector-general of the insane. Another member of this distinguished and influential committee was the former prime minister Alfred Deakin.[3]

In the wake of the bitter 1917 conscription controversy, Osborne published a booklet entitled *What We Owe to Ireland*. It contained lists of famous Irish men who had made major contributions to politics, warfare, science, industry, the law, art, music and literature. Not surprisingly perhaps, the overwhelming majority were Protestants and many had, like Osborne, been born in the province of Ulster.[4] Osborne explained to his Australian readers that they should be careful how they used the term 'Irish' because the people of Ireland exhibited a 'wide racial disparity'. There were in fact three racial groups in Ireland, according to Osborne: 'Ulstermen, Protestant Anglo-Irish, and Catholic Irish, or simply Irish'. The 'racial affinities' of Ulstermen were with Scotland. The Protestant Anglo-Irish were 'more akin to the English in race'. They were 'great sportsmen' and 'excellent army officers', but they also took 'easily to literature' and were 'admirable speakers'. The Catholic Irish, on the other hand, were 'mostly darker in complexion', and an 'upturned nose and longer upper lip' were important facial indicators of their distinctive racial origins. Osborne had nothing good to say about this 'simply Irish' group, concluding that they were a 'race low in the scale of civilization', noted especially for their poverty, superstition, criminality, addiction to alcohol, fondness for 'political agitation' and incapacity for 'sustained mental activity'. At the same time, he admitted that 'any anthropological analysis of their racial status' was currently a 'matter of enthusiastic disagreement amongst experts'.[5]

Osborne obviously reflected the hostility to the Catholic Irish then prevalent among the Ulster Protestant community and also very evident in Protestant British Australia during the Great War. But we should not dismiss him as merely an isolated bigot. He was actively involved in scholarly debates surrounding race and whiteness and, in 1911, he had attended the International Race Congress held in London.[6] He was also right when he said that experts continued to hotly debate the 'racial status' of the Catholic Celtic Irish. During the mid 19th century, as discussed in a previous chapter, influenced no doubt by the mass migration of the Famine period, both British and American race scientists had located the Irish low in their various hierarchies, well below the British and Americans of British descent.[7] But towards the end of the century, as some former Irish immigrants prospered and as new waves of poor immigrants emerged from eastern and southern Europe, so assessments of the Irish as a race began to change.

In 1899, William Z Ripley, a Harvard University economist, published a highly influential book entitled *The Races of Europe*. In this, building on previous racial hierarchies, he suggested that there were three major European races. Using physical characteristics such as shape of head, facial features, hair and eye colour and stature, Ripley classed Europeans as either Teutonic, Alpine or Mediterranean. He struggled, however, to decide in which group to place the continental and insular Celts. Ripley incorporated John Beddoe's 'Index of Nigrescence' into his work, which as we have seen defined the Celtic Irish as of African origin. This pointed towards them being, like the Spanish and Italians, Mediterranean people, the most 'inferior' of the three categories. As well as physical characteristics, Ripley also used temperament and language in his categories. The English were Teutonic, his highest category, but due to the 'profound contrast' of 'temperament' between the English and the Irish, Ripley believed the Irish could not possibly be Teutonic.[8] But during the early decades of the 20th century, other race scientists were not so sure.

Based on intelligence testing, which had been used to screen nearly two million American army recruits in 1917–19, Carl C Brigham of Princeton University published a book in 1923 entitled *A Study of American Intelligence*. It contained bar graphs illustrating the average intelligence of 20 groups of recruits, categorised by ethnicity and colour. At the top were men born in England, while at the bottom were 'negroes'. Irish-born recruits were number 12 on the list, below northern Europeans and white Americans, but ahead of eastern and southern Europeans and well ahead of African Americans. Other research on intelligence published around the same time also positioned the Irish in a liminal space between the northern Europeans and the eastern and southern Europeans. Using Ripley's three racial categories, Brigham went on to assess what he called the 'blood' of the different nationalities. He chose, however, to substitute the term 'Nordic' for 'Teutonic', undoubtedly due at least in part to sensitivities in using a word associated with the Germans, so recently at war with Britain and the United States (US). He then concluded, without much explanation, that the Irish were 70 per cent Mediterranean, but also 30 per cent Nordic: the latter group being the product of centuries of English and Scottish settlement in Ireland.[9]

Scholars of race in Australia followed these debates closely and, as Osborne shows, some were aware that classification of the Catholic Irish was open to debate. Osborne believed that, as a Protestant Ulster man, he was purely Nordic or Aryan: indeed, he considered himself a 'fine example of the Nordic type'.[10] When Osborne spoke of 'whites', race historian Warwick Anderson believes he meant Nordics or the inhabitants of Britain, excluding Alpine groups and those designated Mediterranean.[11] Thus, although acknowledged as white, for Osborne the Celtic Irish, like southern Europeans, represented a racially inferior variety of whiteness. Osborne's views were not unusual, however, for, as Anderson has shown, other scholars connected to Melbourne University responded along similar lines to new theories in race science emerging from the US.[12]

Jens Sorensen Lyng had migrated to Australia from Denmark in 1891, eventually finding employment as a statistician. Funded by a scholarship at Melbourne University, he wrote a book in 1927 entitled *Non-Britishers in Australia*. The work was updated and republished in 1935 with a foreword by Ernest Scott, the university's English-born professor of history. Scott was obviously a firm believer in racial difference, if not hierarchy. In his foreword, he quoted French race theorist Arthur de Gobineau, who wrote an influential essay in 1853 on the inequality of races, extolling the superiority of the Aryan race. Gobineau had claimed that: 'If a nation goes down, the reason is that its blood, the race itself, is deteriorating.'[13] It was 'quite certain', said Scott, that different races possessed 'different physical, moral and temperamental characteristics'. But when it came to deciding whether the 'Nordics', 'Latins' or 'Celts' exhibited greater courage, energy, tenacity, endurance and capacity for solving problems, Scott demurred, expressing a reluctance to generalise as to which was the superior race.

Perhaps Scott's hesitancy was because Lyng had warned in his introduction against what he considered the German and American practice of 'race-worship': extolling the virtues of one race at the expense of another. However, this did not stop him from critiquing the 'temperamental characteristics' of certain races, including the Irish.[14] Lyng's work reflects some of the confused thinking evident in early 20th-century Australia over where the Catholic Irish fitted in terms of racial and ethnic categories. By 'non-Britishers' in the title he meant those, like himself, who had not been born in Britain or Ireland and had not descended from British or Irish immigrants. His title in effect classed the Irish as 'British', although by the time he was writing the south of Ireland had won political independence and was no longer ruled by Britain. In terms of colour, Lyng judged the Irish to be 'white', but he believed that they displayed an inferior variety of whiteness.

He divided Australia's European communities along national or ethnic lines, devoting chapters to Germans, Italians, French, Scandinavians and others. But these were followed by a separate chapter on the Jews and further chapters on races he defined by colour: 'Yellow' (Chinese, Japanese), 'Brown' (including Turks, Arabs, Afghans, Indians and Malays) and 'Black' (Melanesians, Aboriginal people). Although he employed national categories for 'whites', Lyng argued that 'nationality ... founded on political boundaries' was 'ever changing' and thus ephemeral. For him, 'racial characteristics' were more significant, since they 'passed from generation to generation' and were 'subject only to modification by environment during a long period of time'.[15]

In line with the work of Ripley and Brigham in the US, Lyng suggested that the 'white race, while representing ever so many nationalities, only embraces three sub-races – the Nordic or Aryan race; the Alpine (mainly Slavs); and the Mediterranean'. The 'true' Nordics were 'tall and blond' and displayed a 'restless, creative energy'. The Alpine peoples were darker, shorter and stockier and, although sturdy and tenacious, they were 'stolid and unimaginative'. Inferior to both was the Mediterranean race. These people were even shorter, thinner and swarthier, with highly 'emotional' and 'unstable' temperaments. They could be joyful, artistic and 'quick-witted', but they lacked discipline and required strong leadership if they were to succeed. Lyng produced maps and graphs charting the territories of the three races in continental Europe and the British Isles and showing their distribution across the six Australian states. Employing data from the 1891 census, he calculated that 'white' Australians were about 82 per cent Nordic, 13 per cent Mediterranean and 5 per cent Alpine. Lyng considered the English, Scots, Anglo-Irish and Protestant Northern Irish to be Nordic, like Germans and Scandinavians. But the Catholic Irish and the Welsh were Mediterranean, like Spaniards, southern Italians, Greeks, north Africans and the Jews. Lyng endorsed Osborne's view that in effect the Catholic and Protestant Irish were different races: the former being Mediterranean and the latter Nordic.[16] Lyng seemed quite comfortable with treating the Catholic Irish as ethnically 'British', while at the same time claiming that they belonged to an entirely different racial category from the British, and an inferior one.

By the 1920s and 1930s, race science was not as negative about the Catholic Irish as it had been during the mid and late 19th century. Nevertheless, some of those who were considered experts in the field were still arguing that fundamental racial differences existed between the Irish and the English and, by extension, their descendants in Australia. This they did while, like Lyng, subsuming the Irish with the English into the national category 'British'. It was all a bit of a muddle really. Meanwhile, in 1935, the same year that Lyng's book was republished in Melbourne, a very different book appeared in London with the title *We Europeans*. It flatly rejected the notion that there were three different European races. It slammed 'racial biology' as a 'vast pseudo-science', serving 'to justify political ambitions, economic ends, social grudges, [and] class prejudices', and it nailed its political colours to the mast when it ridiculed Nazism. The authors urged that the word 'race' be 'banished' from academic discourse and the term 'ethnic group' substituted instead.[17] The book's authors were Julian Huxley and AC Haddon. Eighty years old at the time, Haddon, the influential former professor of anthropology at Cambridge University, had begun his career, as we saw in chapter 1, conducting research during the 1880s and 1890s, in the west of Ireland and in the Torres Strait.[18] In Australia it would not be until after

1945 that scholars completely abandoned the idea of separate European races and conceded – at long last – that the Irish and English were not distinguishable by race.[19]

Politics and the 1922 *Empire Settlement Act*

While academics and theorists disagreed over the different categories of white Europeans, Australian immigration authorities were putting the race-based tenets of the 1901 *Immigration Restriction Act* into practice. Although generally classed as white and British at the time of Federation, Irish immigrants were not immune from the various restrictions that the Act and its many amendments contained. In the years after Federation, hostility to the Catholic Irish-Australian community was most often grounded in politics and religion, and it was a hostility that extended to Irish immigrants as well. Prime Minister WM Hughes's allegations during the conscription plebiscite campaigns of 1916–17 that Irish Australians were not fully behind the war effort and instead supported pro-German Irish republicanism – referred to as Sinn Féin – were widely accepted in conservative circles, not only in Australia but in Britain as well. Therefore, after the war, when Australia and Britain came to negotiate new immigration arrangements, they attempted to exclude the Catholic Irish from any scheme and, in some cases, the Protestant Irish as well.

James Connolly, the son of an Irish immigrant labouring family, had been a minister in Western Australian Liberal governments before serving as the state's agent-general in London during 1917–23.[20] After the end of the war he wanted to attract Irish-born British army veterans to settle in Western

Australia, but the British government's Overseas Settlement Committee (OSC), an arm of the Colonial Office, opposed this. Connolly believed the British wanted former Irish soldiers to go to the US rather than to Australia. Certainly, WM Hughes, who was keen to welcome British ex-soldier immigrants, made plain that he drew the line at Catholic Irish ex-soldiers, even those who had served Britain loyally in the war. Ultimately, around 35 000 British-born veterans and their families were helped to immigrate to Australia in 1919–21.[21] More controversial were British attempts in 1922–23 to assist members of the disbanded Royal Irish Constabulary, including former Black and Tans, to find employment after the end of the Irish War of Independence. Whereas Hughes did not want Irish ex-soldiers in Australia, the labour movement did not want Irish ex-policemen. The *Australian Worker*, having in 1921 called the new federal police force 'Hughes's Black and Tans', in the following year strongly opposed allowing former Irish policemen to immigrate. But with 13 000 to 15 000 policemen on its hands, the British government, and especially the OSC, pressed the dominions to accept them as immigrants under the 1922 *Empire Settlement Act*. Australian officials were reluctant, however, pointing out that due to depressed economic conditions state police forces were not hiring men and, when they did resume recruiting, they would give preference to Australian ex-soldiers. Fear of protests against Irish police immigrants at a time of heightened sectarian tension also undoubtedly shaped official policy and, in the end, Australia only accepted 433 former Irish policemen.[22]

The OSC, while keen to encourage Irish police emigration, echoed Hughes's fears about the threat both Sinn Féin and Bolshevism posed to Australia. In April 1920, Terence Macnaghten, a senior Colonial Office official, wrote: 'In Australia the situation is extremely difficult. The Labor Party ... has gone out of hand and under the control of Sinn Fein and Bolshevist elements whose whole purpose is anti-Imperial.' According to him: 'The better elements in Australia are endeavouring to combat the tendencies referred to, and are anxious for settlers of the right type.' And, of course, the 'right type' of immigrant was definitely not Irish and Catholic. In a later memo dealing with Australia, Macnaghten wrote: 'There is evidence that for the past 50 years Roman influence has been exerted to introduce a large Roman Catholic element. There has probably been active recruiting in Ireland.' The result was that: 'a large part of the population is of low Irish origin, disloyal, Sinn Fein and even Bolshevist'.[23] Macnaghten's hostility to further Catholic Irish immigration to Australia is perhaps understandable in the circumstances. He was writing in London in 1920–21, at a time when the British government was conducting a war in Ireland against the Irish Republican Army and Sinn Féin – a war that the British were not winning.

The 1922 *Empire Settlement Act*, which was intended to promote assisted immigration from the United Kingdom (UK) to dominions like Australia, did not cover the recently created Irish Free State, although it did cover Northern Ireland. However, citizens of the Free State who had been resident in the UK for at least six months could qualify for subsidised migration. This provision allowed young working-class Irish women who had been employed for a time in Britain to come to Australia on assisted passages. Thus 'Bridget', the archetypal Irish domestic servant, who had first reached Australia during the 1830s, was still arriving a century later, albeit in much reduced numbers.[24] Prime Minister Stanley M Bruce, whose father had been born in County Leitrim, approached the Free State government in early

1924 about setting up a separate Irish-Australian immigration scheme, but the new Irish administration, preoccupied with internal affairs in the aftermath of war and civil war, was not interested. It did however introduce provisions that allowed some Free State residents to apply for rebates on fares to Australia.[25] It is clear though that, in the inter-war period, Australia was not particularly interested in attracting Catholics from the south of Ireland. Thus, of the nearly 215 000 assisted immigrants who arrived between 1921 and 1930, the overwhelming majority were English or Scottish, with a small contingent from Northern Ireland among them.[26]

By the 1920s, Irish immigration to Australia had been in decline for many years. The peak had been back in the 1850s, when some 100 000 immigrants arrived from Ireland. In 1891 the census registered the highest number of Irish-born people living in the country at around 229 000, or 6.1 per cent of the total non-Indigenous population. Two decades later, in 1911, Irish numbers had nearly halved to 141 000 as the immigrants of the 1850s died out and there were few new arrivals to replace them.[27] After Federation, precise immigration figures are more difficult to come by. The Australian authorities adopted the practice of lumping the Irish in with the British under the heading 'British' or 'UK and Ireland', while in Britain and Ireland immigration figures were given for Australia and New Zealand combined, sometimes designated 'Australasia' – and none of the different sets of figures agreed anyway.[28] Numbers fluctuated considerably after 1901, with a rise in 1911–14, after several states reintroduced assisted migration schemes, and a trough in 1917–19.[29] By 1924–30, only about 900 immigrants on average were arriving each year from the Irish Free State and, during 1931–39, even that modest figure collapsed to an average of a little less than 200 per annum.[30]

According to the 1933 Australian census, there were some 79 000 Irish-born immigrants living in Australia, making up a mere 1.2 per cent of the total non-Indigenous population.[31] By that stage, with a major worldwide depression and no government funds available to subsidise travel, immigration to Australia had become almost impossible for the majority of people living in the impoverished south of Ireland.[32] However, even those with the resources and determination to reach Australia's shores were not necessarily guaranteed a welcome, or even permission to land.

The 1901 *Immigration Restriction Act*, eugenics and Irish deportations

Opposition to Catholic Irish immigration in early 20th-century Australia was not based on politics alone. The *Immigration Restriction Act* of 1901 succeeded in largely preventing immigrants of colour from entering the country for over half a century. But this legislation, with its numerous subsequent amendments, went significantly further than that. Paragraph 3 of the Act meant that intending immigrants could be refused admission, firstly, if they failed a dictation test in any European language – amended in 1905 to any 'prescribed' language.[33] But further subsections, which increased in number over time, specified a series of other grounds for exclusion. The original 1901 Act allowed exclusion, for example, if a person was likely to become a charge upon the public purse, if they suffered from insanity or 'idiocy', and if they had a 'dangerous' infectious disease, which usually meant tuberculosis (TB) or syphilis.[34]

When the Act was being debated, the government indicated that the dictation test would only be used to exclude 'coloured' immigrants, not 'whites'. But, in 1903, George Reid, a former premier of New South Wales, who was then leader of the federal free trade opposition and who would later be Australia's high commissioner in London, raised the issue of the test in relation to the Irish. Reid's father, a Presbyterian minister, brought the family to Australia from Scotland in 1852 and worked with the Reverend John Dunmore Lang at Sydney's Scots Church. Hostility to the Catholic Irish ran deep in Reid's family and, as premier in 1894–99, he was noted for his sectarian approach to politics.[35] He enjoyed the support of both the Orange Order and the Protestant Defence Association, so much so that the Sydney Catholic press considered free trade and anti-Catholic sentiment went 'hand-in-hand'.[36] During the 1903 federal election, when campaigning as a free trader against Alfred Deakin's protectionist government, Reid criticised the 1901 Act, while maintaining that he strongly supported the white Australia policy. But the 'Aliens Restriction Act', he complained, was excluding 'our people'. Despite a low British immigration rate and a declining Australian birth rate, Deakin had, according to Reid, placed a 'gaol wall round Australia against our fellow countrymen'. By 'our people' and 'our fellow countrymen', Reid made clear he meant 'Britishers'. A British man could be shipped 'home' merely because he might be in 'indifferent' health or have little money, and, if he did manage to get ashore in Australia, he could be gaoled for six months.[37] As for Irish men being excluded, Reid pointedly remarked that they could be asked to do a dictation test in Italian. Most newspapers reporting Reid's speech did not mention the latter comment, but the Sydney *Freeman's Journal* was furious, stating emphatically, and mangling its grammar in the process: 'The alien *Restriction Act* does not subject Irishmen to a language test as proof of his [sic] fitness as an immigrant to Australia.'[38] It understood what Reid was implying. He was including the Irish not in the category of 'our people', who might be excluded due to poverty or illness, but relegating them to the category of 'coloureds' and 'aliens': those liable to be excluded by the language test. Nothing came of Reid's remarks as he lost the election, but they did indicate that some Australians persisted in viewing the Catholic Irish as 'aliens'.

Major amendments to the immigration Act in 1912 extended the additional grounds listed in paragraph 3 even further. Poverty and physical or mental illness were retained, but now an immigrant could be refused admission: under section 3(c) if they were an 'idiot, imbecile, feeble-minded person, or epileptic'; under section 3(d) for having any 'serious transmissible disease or defect'; and under section 3(g) for having any other 'prescribed disease, disability or disqualification'.[39] When these proposed amendments were debated in the federal parliament in 1912, several Catholic members spoke out strongly against them. Irish-born Senator Patrick McMahon Glynn of South Australia, the most senior non-Labor Catholic federal politician, joined Dr William Maloney, Labor member for Melbourne, in claiming that the changes proposed were too sweeping and, moreover, they smacked of eugenics. According to Maloney, if the proposed sections were to be applied to Australians emigrating, then 95 per cent of people would not be allowed to leave the country. Glynn had criticised the original 1901 bill for discriminating against immigrants with little money. In 1912, he described the amended bill as 'too drastic' and dismissed eugenics as not scientifically proven. When he was briefly minister for external affairs in 1913–14, Glynn amended instructions relating to section 3(g) to make them less wide-ranging by specifying the particular diseases or disabilities for which customs officials could exclude people. He wrote that he wanted to make the section less 'a matter of eugenics'.[40] However, subsequent amendments to the Act only widened its scope further. By the early 1920s, among those who could be excluded were people accused of 'moral turpitude' or of advocating the overthrow 'by force' of the government of 'any civilized country' and absolutely anyone deemed by the minister to be 'undesirable'.[41]

The eugenics movement, which was supported by prominent doctors, academics and politicians, believed that some in the population – mainly members of the working class – suffered from hereditary mental and physical defects, and it was vital that these people be identified and controlled in order to prevent racial 'degeneration'. Moreover, many eugenicists were convinced that those they called the 'feeble-minded' tended to have large families. This, combined with the fact that the birth rate, especially among the middle class, was falling before 1914, led some alarmists to allege that Australia was heading for what in the US was called 'race suicide'.[42] How the existing 'feeble-minded' population was to be reduced and ultimately eliminated was much debated. Policies involving contraception and sterilisation, sometimes termed 'negative eugenics', were proposed. Such suggestions attracted the ire of the Catholic Church, which became a firm and sometimes outspoken opponent of eugenics.[43] Glynn and Maloney were reflecting Catholic views in their attacks on the 1912 immigration bill. Eugenicists, in turn, hit back at the church for selfishly and recklessly encouraging large families among its mainly working-class parishioners, who were overwhelmingly of Irish descent.[44] The church, it was claimed, was only interested in quantity, in increasing Catholic numbers, not in the genetic quality of the Australian population. In the US, some eugenicists also attacked Catholic clergy for their celibacy.

Priests were labelled 'dysgenic' because they were an able and educated group who refused to reproduce, while encouraging the 'unfit' to have as many children as possible.[45] Historians of eugenics generally agree that this strong Catholic opposition impeded the movement's progress in Australia, probably more so than it did in Britain or the US.[46] Although eugenicists argued among themselves as to how the quality of the population should be improved, they did agree that immigrants exhibiting hereditary mental or physical defects must be barred from the country. They were suspicious of immigration in general, one leading supporter of eugenics claiming that the 'Australian babe' is 'Australia's best immigrant'.[47]

It was mainly the Chinese who were refused admission to Australia under the 1901 *Immigration Restriction Act*, and this was done via a dictation test. An official of the Department of External Affairs claimed in 1906 that: 'No white man has ever been prevented from landing in Australia by that act.' But he went on to warn that if a 'white person came sick, and absolutely poor, and therefore likely to become a burden on the state', then that person would not be allowed to land.[48] Official guidance to customs officers informed them that 'white men' suffering from mental or physical illnesses could be allowed entry on one condition: if they paid a substantial bond, which in 1911 amounted to £500.[49] So rich 'white men' had the power to circumvent the health provisions of the Act, but the poor did not.

As Table 1 opposite demonstrates, from 1911, and especially with the passage of the 1912 amended Act, the numbers of those being excluded who were described as 'British' jumped substantially. This was at least in part because immigration from the UK had risen sharply in 1910-12.[51] 'British' meant British subject, but the majority of people in this category

Table 1: Numbers and percentages of British immigrants refused admission to Australia, 1902–39[50]

DATES	TOTAL REFUSED	BRITISH REFUSED	PERCENTAGE OF REFUSED BRITISH
1902–10 (excluding 1906)	1169	13	1.1
1911–14	433	124	28.6
1915–22	419	30	7.2
1923–29 (excluding 1925)	330	77	23.3
1930–39	330	78	23.6
Total	2681	322	12.0

had been born in either Britain or Ireland. Of the handful of British subjects excluded before 1911, nearly half were barred on grounds of poverty. But from 1911–12 onwards, exclusions on the other, often eugenicist, grounds provided for under paragraph 3 of the Act increased significantly. During 1911–14, having a 'transmissible defect' or being 'feeble-minded' or suffering from insanity accounted together for 53 per cent of British exclusions, while only 12 per cent were excluded on grounds of poverty, with a further 12 per cent barred for being prostitutes. Immigration was relatively low during the war years, but rose again after 1918, promoted by funding offered under the 1922 *Empire Settlement Act*.[52] Among British exclusions in 1923–29, the largest single group was barred on grounds of insanity or 'feeble-mindedness' (30 per cent), followed closely by poverty (29 per cent), while a handful were refused entry as 'undesirables' (5 per cent). In addition, during the 1920s and 1930s, the dictation test started to be used for the first time to exclude immigrants classed as 'British', with 9 per cent of those barred during each decade being refused entry because they had failed the language test. The immigration authorities were beginning to use the test at this time, particularly against those they deemed to be political radicals.[53]

Science and population historian Alison Bashford was correct therefore when she argued recently that:

> In the Australian context ... historians will typically claim that the immigration restriction act was 'eugenic' *because* it excluded coloured aliens. And yet immigration restriction was far more strictly 'eugenic' because it excluded 'unfit' (insane, idiotic, feeble-minded, deaf, epileptic) whites, almost all of whom were from the United Kingdom and Ireland ... whites only, but only (mentally) fit whites were admitted.[54]

Even though the number of Irish immigrants was not particularly large after 1900 and shrank even further during the 1920s and 1930s, it is apparent that some Irish-born immigrants who tried to enter Australia were rejected under the immigration Act. Between 1901 and 1957, a total of 3290 intending immigrants were turned away: 41 per cent were rejected on grounds other than the dictation test and, of the total rejected, about 13 per cent were classed as 'British'.[55]

Although it is not possible to establish the exact number of Irish-born people in this group of excluded 'British' immigrants, we can assume that the Irish were likely to have been barred especially because they were poor, were believed to have been suffering from a serious physical illness or were considered to be insane or 'feeble-minded'. By Australian standards at the time, the south of Ireland was a poor country with serious public health problems. It had very high rates of both TB deaths and mental hospital committals. In 1925–27, for example, annual average TB deaths per 100000 of population were 152 in Northern Ireland

and 150 in the Irish Free State, as against 58 in Australia.[56] In the mid 1940s life expectancy at birth in the south of Ireland was 60.5 years for men and 62.4 years for women; the comparable Australian figures were 66.1 and 70.6 years.[57] Committals to mental hospitals in the south of Ireland during the 1930s were the highest in Europe and by the mid 1950s probably the highest in the world. Studies of England and the US have shown that the immigration authorities were on the alert for health problems amongst Irish immigrants, and it is highly likely that the same was true of Australia.[58] But more research is required to reveal the numbers and details of Irish immigrants excluded on grounds of poverty or illness. In addition, we currently know little about those excluded after 1912 under eugenicist criteria, having been assessed as 'feeble-minded' or 'mentally deficient' or as exhibiting some other hereditary mental or physical 'defect'.

Even if immigrants were granted entry to Australia, though, they could still be deported subsequently. In 1923, at a time of civil war in Ireland, two republican representatives on a fundraising tour were deported for sedition because of their attacks on the new Irish Free State. The case demonstrated that not only immigrants but even short-term visitors could be deported under the sweeping powers contained in the immigration Act; and they could be deported for political as well as health and eugenicist reasons.[59] In July 1925, the Act was amended during a period of labour unrest and major strikes, with changes made especially to paragraph 8. These allowed the government to deport any person not born in Australia who, in the minister's opinion, was during a 'serious industrial disturbance' considered to be 'prejudicing or threatening ... peace, order or good government'. This included any such person who was 'hindering or obstructing' the 'transport of goods or the conveyance of passengers'.[60] The amendments were aimed mainly against the Seamen's Union, whose federal president, Cork-born Tom Walsh, had immigrated to Australia in 1893. A foundation member of the Australian Communist Party in 1920 along with his wife, the English suffragist Adela Pankhurst, Walsh fought hard to improve the pay and conditions of seamen. But at the behest of shipowners, the Bruce government deregistered the union in 1925 and tried to deport Walsh and another European-born union official, using the newly amended immigration Act. Defended by HV Evatt, who had failed to prevent the expulsion of the Irish envoys in 1923, Walsh's deportation was overturned on appeal to the High Court, which ruled that, as he had arrived in Australia before 1901, the Act could not be applied to him retrospectively.[61]

Deportations normally occurred, however, if immigrants became a charge upon the public purse within three years of their arrival – extended to five years in 1932. Becoming a burden on the taxpayer usually meant that a recent immigrant had been convicted and imprisoned for a criminal offence or they had been committed to a public institution, such as a mental hospital or TB sanatorium. In her study of patient deportations from the Claremont Mental Hospital near Perth during the inter-war years, medical historian Philippa Martyr found consistent patterns in overseas-born patients expelled from the country. A substantial majority were young, single male labourers suffering from what was then considered an incurable psychotic illness. In ethnic terms, by far the most likely patients to be deported were Italians, followed at a distance by the Irish and then finally the British. Despite restrictions, there had been an upsurge in Italian immigration during the 1920s, with many finding work in Western Australia, northern Queensland or the Riverina district of NSW. However, they were by no means welcomed.

WA Osborne, who regarded southern Italians as a Mediterranean race, with similar shortcomings to the Catholic Irish, labelled them a 'racial menace' and a 'new young Frankenstein'. The Labor Party also opposed southern European immigration, with the *Australian Worker* describing Italians and Maltese as 'inferior races' who were only 'part white'.[62] A major race riot occurred in Kalgoorlie in January 1934 when an Australian miner died after a fight with an Italian barman.[63] The high numbers of Italians deported from Claremont doubtless partly reflected this hostility. But Irish deportations were also significant. For, whereas only a handful of female patients were deported, 30 per cent of them were Irish, mostly domestic servants.[64]

Eugenics was a controversial issue in Western Australia at the time, with 'exhaustive' though ultimately unsuccessful efforts being made in 1929–30 to get a 'mental deficiency' bill through the parliament. This bill allowed for the sterilisation of those deemed 'mentally defective' or 'feeble-minded'.[65] Martyr says that she found no eugenicist terminology in the papers of the 14 psychiatric deportation cases that she sampled and studied in detail, some of whom were Irish. But this terminology is apparent in cases of other Irish immigrants. For example, Irish-born Robert Ignatius O'Connor, aged 29, had arrived in Fremantle from England as an unassisted immigrant in June 1927. However, he was quickly admitted to Wooroloo sanatorium. O'Connor was obviously a seriously ill man, for he had previously been treated for TB while serving in the army.[66] He was therefore assessed as likely to become a 'permanent charge' upon state funds and, later that year, he was deported. Dr Robert M Mitchell, the government medical officer who examined O'Connor, was not only concerned about his TB. In his report, Mitchell noted that O'Connor was 'mentally inefficient at present' and was 'probably a mental defective'. O'Connor admitted to 'self abuse' and had 'accompanying mental stress'. Mitchell obviously diagnosed O'Connor in eugenicist terms as a 'mental defective', as well as being a victim of TB. On both grounds under the *Immigration Act 1901–25*, he was liable to deportation.[67] Another case is that of John Dillon, who arrived in Melbourne as an assisted immigrant in September 1929. He had a sister living in the city and quickly found employment. But he was unable to retain a job for long, going through three in as many months, before being admitted to Royal Park Mental Hospital in April 1930. His sister told the authorities that her brother was 'mentally afflicted' and she wanted him returned to the care of their parents in Ireland. The medical report described him as 'confused' and 'restless', and concluded that he was 'of a low type of general intelligence'. Dillon was deported.[68]

Some Irish immigrants were obviously being assessed and deported under the eugenicist provisions of the immigration Act. But it is TB that looms especially large in Irish deportations during the late 1920s and early 1930s. This is not surprising given that Ireland at the time was experiencing a TB epidemic, which would not peter out until the 1950s.[69] A major Irish report on the problem published in 1954 noted that there had been arguments 'for many years' that the 'susceptibility of the Irish to tuberculosis' was a 'racial factor', since they appeared to have less resistance to the disease than 'other nations or races'.[70] Indeed, John Beddoe had claimed in his 1885 book, *The Races of Britain*, that there was a correlation between the incidence of diseases, including TB and cancer, and the darker races like the Celtic Irish.[71] With such views prevalent, it is not surprising that Australian immigration and health authorities checked Irish immigrants especially closely for symptoms of TB.[72] But their checks were not always successful, as the following case shows.

Cork-born Jeremiah McCarthy, a 26-year-old veteran of the Irish army, arrived in Melbourne in February 1927 as an unassisted immigrant. But in April 1929, while working as a barman, he was admitted to the Austin Hospital for Chronic Diseases. Doctors there diagnosed him as suffering from pulmonary TB, probably contracted in 1918, the disease having spread recently to one of his kidneys. Told in October that he would be deported under the immigration Act for becoming a permanent charge on the state within three years of his arrival, McCarthy absconded from the hospital. He appears to have sought the help of Labor politician Frank Anstey, who had just been appointed minister for health in the recently elected Scullin Labor government. Anstey, believing McCarthy had been in the country for around five years, made representations on his behalf, but withdrew these when informed that McCarthy had in fact arrived in 1927. McCarthy also wrote to the Melbourne collector of customs claiming that he was receiving £1 a week from Ireland and had applied to the Irish Department of Finance for an army disability pension. 'I only ask for a fair chance', he wrote, 'and [to] be left in the country at peace until the result of my pension comes.' His file noted that he had no relatives in Australia, but that his mother and sister derived an income from running a small hotel in Cork. McCarthy was traced in November 1929 by Detective Inspector James Gleeson of the Customs Department to a house in the Melbourne working-class suburb of Northcote. He was clearly in poor circumstances. He had recently suffered a haemorrhage, had 'little clothing' and 'only one thin singlet'. Gleeson took McCarthy to a doctor, who declared him fit to travel, and then spent 11 shillings buying him underclothes, before putting him aboard a ship bound for England.[73]

During the early decades of the 20th century, race scientists continued to have difficulty categorising the Irish, who were still widely seen as different from the English and other northern European peoples in their physical characteristics and temperament, as well as in their greater susceptibility to serious diseases of the body and mind. Many believed them closer to southern Europeans, like the Italians. The Irish were certainly white, but not quite as white as the British. It seems ironic then that, whereas most Irish Australians strongly supported the white Australia policy and the exclusion of immigrants of colour, persistent fears about Irish racial inferiority and Irish disloyalty to Britain left immigrants from Ireland vulnerable to the draconian provisions of Australia's immigration legislation, passed primarily to keep out Asian people. Unfortunately due to lack of research on this topic, we cannot say at present with any confidence how many Irish immigrants were denied entry or deported during the inter-war period, or the precise grounds on which they were excluded. But it seems clear that race, eugenics, politics, poverty and poor health were all factors ensuring that, as so often in the 19th century, Irish immigrants continued to be far from welcome in Australia during the first half of the 20th century.

SECTION TWO:
STEREOTYPES

CHAPTER 5

Irish men in Australian popular culture, 1790s–1920s

Debates surrounding the physical and temperamental characteristics of the Irish were reflected in popular culture by a dazzling array of visual and aural stereotypes. Irish characters were everywhere in colonial Australian publications and entertainments. With their distinctive and readily recognisable faces, bodies, dress and speech patterns, they were a gift to cartoonists and satirical writers. Drawings of the Irish in illustrated periodicals, descriptions in novels, poetry, short stories and songs, as well as portrayals on the stage, offered a wealth of humour, political satire and social commentary. This was not true only of the Australian colonies of course: stock Irish figures were ubiquitous throughout the 19th-century Anglophone newspaper and entertainment worlds. But for audiences to instantly identify a character as Irish and also to appreciate the meaning of a joke or satire, a generic Irishness had to be widely understood.[1] Certain personal qualities were characteristic of this broad Irish stereotype, especially ignorance, violence, laziness, stupidity, cunning and clannishness. At the same time, however, there were a limited number of specific Irish types that writers, actors and cartoonists came to rely heavily upon: types that reflected particular situations and also gender differences. This chapter will explore the portrayal of three key types of Irish men: the violent terrorist, the stupid gullible labourer and the crafty politician.

Firstly, though, it is important to appreciate how widespread these popular stereotypes were during the 19th century. In cartoons, racial or ethnic difference was indicated in the way bodies were drawn and in speech patterns reproduced in captions.[2] Similarly, in literature and on the stage, physical appearance was crucial, although here speech was generally more important than it was in cartoons. Contemporaries often interpreted physical features, especially facial features, as outward indicators of a person's inner moral character or worth. 'Physiognomy', as this pseudo-science was called, can in fact be traced back to classical Greece, but it enjoyed wide acceptance from the 18th century onwards and proved an enormously useful tool for artists who wanted to show character visually.[3] In caricatures or cartoons, they exaggerated aspects of the anatomy, often drawing them as unusually large or distorted in some way. Similarities to animals might also be hinted at, especially animals noted for human qualities, such as bravery (lion) or stupidity (sheep) or stubbornness (mule). These caricatures might then be placed alongside what was perceived to be the 'normal' or 'natural' standard, thus drawing attention to any deviations.[4] For the intended humour or satire to work, however, stereotypes had to be readily recognisable. They had to reflect, even if in a distorted manner, realities their audience was familiar with and, for these stereotypes to persist, they had to be capable of capturing changing meanings over time.[5]

Visual stereotypes embedded in 19th-century English-language print culture moved through global information networks, both from the metropolitan centre to the colonial periphery and also around the interconnected periphery. Cartoonists and satirists in Australia were heavily influenced by styles emerging from Britain, but they were frequently familiar with developments in New Zealand, Canada and the United States (US) as well.[6] In part this was due to the simple fact that many illustrators had been trained and commenced their careers outside Australia. As illustrated periodicals became increasingly popular from the 1840s, colonial editors recruited specialist cartoonists from abroad, some of whom carved out long and successful careers in Australia.[7] For instance, English-born Tom Carrington, trained in London under the Cruikshank family of illustrators, had tried his luck unsuccessfully on the goldfields before having his first drawings accepted by *Melbourne Punch* in 1866. Others, like American-born Livingston Hopkins ('Hop') and English-born Phil May, were actively sought out and enticed to Sydney with generous job offers by the *Bulletin*'s William Traill in the mid 1880s.[8] Towards the end of the century, home-grown cartoonists were taking over from this first generation. One of these was Tom Durkin, born to Irish parents and a self-educated artist, who worked on the *Bulletin* as well as on his own short-lived publications, *The Ant* and *The Bull Ant* (1890–92).[9] As we shall see later, Durkin's cartoons provide some of the most striking racially stereotyped images of the period.

If cartoons reflected broad understandings of stereotyped racial characteristics, the same can be said of the written word and the stage. Writers and actors too were linked into global networks. Many of Australia's first writers were born overseas and even when living in Australia sought overseas publication, usually in London. Actors too were usually born outside the colonies and Australian-based theatre companies began mounting tours to overseas destinations from an early date. Not until towards the end of the century were most writers and actors working in Australia native-born.[10] Colonial Australia's major theatre impresarios, such as George Coppin, George Darrell, Alfred Dampier, Bland Holt and JC Williamson, were all either English or American and most took their plays to New Zealand, sometimes to Asia, and often to Britain and the US as well, where, like the magazine editors, they sourced new talent. English-born Coppin, for instance, who had toured Ireland in comic roles in his youth during the 1830s, brought out to Australia leading Irish-born Shakespearian actors, like GV Brooke in the 1850s and Charles John Kean in the 1860s, while it was he who in the early 1870s invited American-born JC Williamson and his Irish-American actress wife, Maggie, to Australia for the first time.[11]

In colonial Australian culture, whether in pictorial, written or stage form, the basic norms against which characters were usually measured were middle class, English and Protestant.[12] The English themselves were certainly not immune from satire, the effete English 'new chum' unable to cope with tough Australian bush life being a perennial target of Australian-based humorists.[13] But the mocking of the English was comparatively mild in comparison to the savage physical satire and offensive names employed by writers and cartoonists against Australian racial or ethnic minorities, including the Irish. In cartoons, Indigenous Australians and Pacific Islanders often appeared with enormous lips, as well as very black skin and frizzy hair; Jewish men were portrayed as old and swarthy, invariably with huge noses and sometimes with big bellies and thin legs; and

Chinese men, aside from their pigtails and distinctive clothing, usually had round, flat faces and narrow, squinting eyes.[14]

The Irish stereotype, in both its visual and written forms, did not exist in isolation; it operated in a world peopled by numerous other racial or ethnic stereotypes, with which it shared characteristics and on occasion interacted. Like Aboriginal people, the Irish were perceived as lazy and stupid; like the Chinese, they stuck together in clans and were devious and cunning. However, unlike the Jews, they were feckless and prone to squander any money that came their way, usually on drink. We shall see that Australian cartoonists sometimes sought to convey their messages by employing more than one stereotyped character in a single drawing and mocking the interactions between, say, an Irish woman and a Chinese man (see also, page 89) or an Irish man and an Aboriginal woman. In a sense the artist was able to double the potential for entertainment by satirising two groups in the one drawing.

The Fenian: the Irish man as terrorist

By no means all Irish stereotyped figures were intended to be comic; some were literally terrifying. Throughout the English-speaking world from the 1860s until at least the end of the century, one of the most recognisable visual images of male Irishness was the figure of the Fenian. The Fenian appeared frequently, especially during the 1860s and 1880s, in cartoons published in illustrated newspapers and magazines. The component parts of the Fenian stereotype developed from varied sources stretching back centuries.[15] But perhaps the most direct sources were drawings made by leading English satirists, like James

Gillray and Isaac Cruikshank, commenting upon the failed 1798 Rebellion led by the United Irishmen.[16] Isaac's son, George, in his illustrations for WH Maxwell's hostile 1845 account of the rebellion, took depictions of fearsome rebels much further by giving the insurgents grotesque faces. In an attempt to convey the frenzied violence of the Irish, who, according to Maxwell's account, spared neither man, woman nor child, Cruikshank drew them with simian or ape-like facial features. The ferocity of these illustrations has been compared to Goya's horrifying Peninsular War series, *Disasters of War*.[17] Cruikshank's message was unmistakable: only creatures more animal than human could possibly inflict such gruesome and pitiless carnage.[18]

Caricatures of later Irish republicans, in particular members of the Fenian Brotherhood established in Ireland and the US in the late 1850s, have echoes of Cruikshank's animal-like United Irishmen.[19] The signifiers of Irishness used in depicting the Fenian frequently focused on the face. They included an overhanging brow, a heavy receding prognathous jaw, a wide mouth with thin lips, small eyes set close together and large low-hanging ears. Such ape-like features were often combined with others that suggested immorality and dissipation. These included the collapsed nose common to victims of syphilis and the rotten teeth, unruly hair and dirty skin suggestive of drunkards, paupers or vagrants.[20] Such physical signs of racialised Irishness were enhanced by stereotyped clothing and accessories, many based on descriptions or pictures of the Irish peasantry.[21] The clothes, including a swallow-tail coat, breeches and stockings, brogues and a tall hat – all shabby, battered and torn – were increasingly anachronistic by the second half of the 19th century. Such dress had, however, become an important signifier of Irishness and so was retained by cartoonists even when it had actually ceased to be worn in Ireland itself and had probably seldom been worn in Australia. The Fenian also usually carried distinctive accessories associated with male Irishness, such as a clay pipe, a bottle of whiskey and a blackthorn stick or shillelagh. The stick symbolised aggression, but the violent character of the Fenian might be further underlined by a pistol or dagger stuck in his belt or, especially during the 1880s, by a bomb in his hand. All in all, the Fenian embodied the perceived violence and menace of the Irish working-class male, made infinitely more dangerous because this brute had been politicised into a terrorist.

In the late 1860s the violent activities of Fenians in Ireland, Britain and North America prompted a wave of press outrage, expressed in editorials and articles, but, most strikingly, in illustrations and cartoons.[22] Illustrators, while clearly influenced by earlier depictions of the United Irishmen, also drew heavily upon the popular evolutionary theories of the time. This allowed them to follow Cruikshank's lead and offer their audiences a menagerie of terrifying Fenian apes. Some of the most influential of these illustrations appeared in London *Punch*, where for instance monstrous Fenians were shown threatening the pathetic, innocent figure of the maiden Hibernia in cartoons such as 'The mad-doctor'[23] and 'The Irish "Tempest"'.[24] But, when cartoonists presented their bloody-minded Fenians in conjunction with other characters, they could often convey quite complex and even contradictory messages.[25]

At the height of the international Fenian scare, in March 1868, one of Queen Victoria's sons Prince Alfred was shot and wounded while attending a picnic lunch at Clontarf Beach on Sydney Harbour. The would-be assassin, Dublin-born Henry James O'Farrell, was immediately apprehended, and his claim – almost certainly spurious – to be a Fenian sparked intense fear of Irish violence throughout the Australian colonies. Even O'Farrell's swift conviction and execution did not stem the panic, partly because the crime was exploited for political advantage by the New South Wales (NSW) colonial secretary, Henry Parkes, who coveted the premiership. Despite attracting suspicion and ridicule for his theory of a widespread Fenian conspiracy – mocked as the 'Kiama ghost story' – the scare, nevertheless, helped Parkes achieve his goal: in 1872 he embarked on the first of his five terms as premier of NSW.[26]

At the time *Melbourne Punch* published two interesting cartoons that emphasised the threat Fenianism posed, while simultaneously subverting it. The caption under the first, 'Another daring attempt on the part of a Fenian to overthrow the British Empire' (see page 138), was intended ironically. We can identify the heavily armed Fenian figure by his typically Irish clothing, although his striped breeches hint at an Uncle Sam or American connection, for Fenianism was largely funded from the US. To remove any doubt as to identity, the cartoonist has added a sprig of shamrock to the figure's hat band. While his face, which resembles O'Farrell's, is half hidden by his hat, what one can see of it is certainly menacing. The cartoon thus encourages fear of the violent Fenian, but also undercuts this by suggesting cowardliness. The Fenian's large pistol is pointed at the back of a tiny child, oblivious to danger and innocently playing with a small spade. Young Prince Alfred, the queen's child, was enjoying himself at a beach when he was shot in the back. At the height of the crisis, it appears that *Melbourne Punch* was trying to reassure its readers by suggesting that the Fenian bogey-man was not as formidable as he might first appear: Irish men were certainly violent and dangerous, but underneath their bluster they were actually cowards, for they preyed upon the defenceless.[27]

ANOTHER DARING ATTEMPT ON THE PART OF A FENIAN TO
OVERTHROW THE BRITISH EMPIRE.

In a reference to the attempted assassination of Prince Alfred at a Sydney beach in 1868, this cartoon depicts an Irish Fenian about to shoot an innocent child in the back. But, as the cartoon's ironic title reassuringly implies, such cowardly terrorist attacks were unlikely to seriously challenge British imperialism.

Source: 'Another daring attempt on the part of a Fenian to overthrow the British Empire', *Melbourne Punch*, 19 March 1868, p. 89.

Another *Melbourne Punch* cartoon by Tom Carrington appeared ten days later with a somewhat similar message and captioned 'The state of the case'.[28] Here we see two very different faces of Irish Australia confronting each other. On the right is a heavily armed Fenian, his face grotesque, with swarthy skin, sunken eyes and protruding bad teeth. Opposite him, also clothed in largely Irish dress, is a handsome figure with regular facial features, identified in the caption as a 'Well-to-do Irishman'. Rather than a weapon, this man carries a rake; beside him are bushels of harvested wheat or barley; behind him stands a family farmhouse. In the caption, the 'Rabid Fenian' invites the prosperous Irish farmer to 'join us', but the farmer rebuffs him, saying in very moderate dialect: 'Here I have me bit of land, me home, wife and childer; shall I raise my hand against a Government under which I have prospered so well?' Again *Melbourne Punch* seemed bent upon playing down the threat that Parkes in NSW was determined to play up. If the Irish prospered economically as small farmers, the paper suggested, they would become deaf to the message of violent revolutionary Fenianism.

The Fenian panic faded during the 1870s, but outrage at alleged Fenian excesses returned to the pages of *Melbourne Punch*, to the new *Bulletin* in Sydney and to other illustrated periodicals whenever there was an upsurge in political violence in Ireland. During the 1880s Fenians were active in the Irish Land War, a campaign for land reform and ultimately for Irish home rule. At the same time, some Irish-American Fenians began a bombing campaign in England itself.[29] This violence was a long way from Australia's shores, nevertheless, conservative politicians and Protestant clergy feared the power of Catholic Irish-born immigrants and Irish Australians, who made up nearly a quarter of the total population. Virtually all the adult men in this group had been enfranchised since the 1850s, and Catholic leaders were eager to organise what their enemies termed the 'Catholic vote'. As a result, colonial Australia was not immune to the violent political passions that characterised both Ireland and England during the 1880s.

Sometimes the Fenian stereotype was used to comment on political events in the United Kingdom or to criticise fundrais- ing visits to Australia by Irish nationalist politicians.[30] But more often it was deployed to attack domestic leaders with Catholic Irish backgrounds by linking them to political extremism. In an 1882 Carrington cartoon that appeared in *Melbourne Punch*, see opposite 'The hoof of a foreign despotism', a tall, heavily armed, powerful Fenian figure dominates the scene. He is easily recognisable by his dark complexion, prognathous jaw, shaggy hair and long Irish-style fustian coat; in addition, on his hat he sports a band labelled 'Murder' and a feather labelled 'Disloyalty'. To ensure the audience was in no doubt as to the Fenian's intentions or his local affiliations, under his arm he carries a bag labelled 'Dynamite', while sticking out of his coat pocket is a copy of the *Advocate* newspaper. This was Melbourne's leading Catholic journal, which, while sympathetic to Irish nationalism, followed the Catholic Church's line in opposing Fenianism.

The Fenian character in the cartoon dominates the smaller figure of John Gavan Duffy, a member of the Victorian Legislative Assembly, who is reading from a scroll signed by several other politicians of Irish birth or descent. In the background of the picture are various banners labelled 'Treason', 'Home Rule', 'No Rent' and 'No Landlords' – all referring to the violent land struggle then reaching a climax in Ireland. Also lurking in the background is John's father, former Victorian premier and Irish

"THE HOOF OF A FOREIGN DESPOTISM."

Mr. *JOHN GAVAN DUFFY, M.L.A.* (*Reading from the Fenian Address*).—" Your self-reliance, indomitable courage, and perseverance are regarded with admiration and pride by your kindred abroad. The manifestation of these virtues, so conspicuous in your calm, unyielding resistance to coercion, strengthens the strong claim you have on us for support. The prudence and firmness with which you are acting is to us an assurance that victory will soon reward your heroic constancy."

In this cartoon, unscrupulous Irish-Australian Catholic politicans and newspapers consort with the monstrosity that is Fenianism. John Gavan Duffy attacks British rule in Ireland during the Land War as 'a foreign despotism', while his father Sir Charles hypocritically enjoys a 'Saxon' knighthood and pension.

Source: 'The hoof of a foreign despotism', *Melbourne Punch*, 8 June 1882, p. 5.

nationalist leader, Charles Gavan Duffy, pictured with a paper under his arm labelled, with heavy irony, 'Pension from Brutal Saxon'. By 1882 the older Duffy was enjoying retirement in the south of France on a substantial government pension, having accepted a knighthood from the British crown in 1873.[31] Yet, in a speech bubble, Sir Charles, with blatant hypocrisy, declares of his son: 'My own boy, I taught him that'. The cartoon is a comment on what became known as 'The Grattan Address', a document signed in early 1882 by a handful of Victorian Catholic politicians and addressed to the people of Ireland. The address, which described British rule in Ireland as 'foreign despotism', infuriated conservatives in Australia, who saw in it a mark of disloyalty at a critical time, when Britain was under attack from Fenian bombers and assassins.[32] As Parkes had demonstrated in NSW in 1868, the spectre of Fenianism could be exploited to stir up public anxiety in Australia and to smear political opponents. But, whereas in 1868 *Melbourne Punch* and its leading cartoonist, Tom Carrington, appeared intent on calming the hysteria, by 1882, they had obviously joined the likes of Parkes and others in seeking to exploit Fenianism in order to tarnish the reputations of Catholic politicians. The change was almost certainly due, in part at least, to the fact that in 1882 Victoria had a Catholic Irish premier. He will be discussed later in this chapter and also in chapter 9.

During the 1880s and 1890s the Fenian stereotype offered a rich resource to satirists in a variety of different political contexts. When Irish Australians donated money to support the Irish home rule party, which after 1885 was in alliance with the British Liberal Party, they were accused of disloyalty and of funding Fenianism.[33] When Australian contingents began to be committed to imperial conflicts overseas, whether in the Sudan in 1885, in South Africa in 1899–1902 or in China in 1900, the bogey of Fenianism and questions as to where Irish loyalties really lay were usually resurrected.[34]

Of the nearly 800 men sent from NSW to the Sudan in March 1885 to bolster the faltering British campaign against the Islamist Mahdi in the wake of the fall of Khartoum, about a quarter were Catholics. They were dispatched on the initiative of William Bede Dalley, the colony's acting premier and a staunch Catholic of Irish convict parentage, and they sailed with the blessing of the Catholic archbishop of Sydney, Patrick Moran.[35] However, the *Bulletin* and *Melbourne Punch*, which both opposed Australian intervention, used the episode as an opportunity to question the fighting qualities of the Irish and to imply Irish support for Islamic fundamentalism. Hop's well-known cartoon, 'The roll-call', depicting the sorry return of a contingent in May and featuring the 'Little Boy at Manly', satirises both Dalley and Moran. It also shows the contingent bringing back with it cases of whiskey, while one soldier, with markedly Irish facial features, lies sprawled on the ground, drunkenly grasping a whiskey bottle in his hand.[36] *Melbourne Punch* also made fun of the Irish over the Sudan contingent, but it focused on claims that 1000 Chicago Fenians had voiced sympathy for Muslim opponents of the British Empire and had offered to fight for the Mahdi. A mock news report appeared about 'Gineral' Moriarty and his Fenian army. Moriarty is described in the item as dressed in an Irish uniform of '[g]reen swallow-tail coat, breeches, stockings and shoes. Time-honoured black hat ... red waistcoat and brass buttons. Arms – a wee taste of a stick' and a rifle. His first order to his men is to buy whiskey and his second is to hold a banquet, at which they all get drunk and fall to fighting among themselves. On the wharf preparing for departure, there is another 'nice shindy' that leaves 100 of the 'bhoys ... insensible' and the rest in gaol.[37]

Modern studies of Fenianism in Australia have concluded that it was never a significant force in colonial politics nor a major military threat either, yet fear of the Fenian, as manipulated by political opponents of the Irish, did exert influence.[38] The Fenian character encapsulated key features of the more general Irish stereotype, particularly as it related to working-class men. Prominent among these were violence, cruelty, irrationality and cowardice. Thus critics of Irish or Irish-Australian involvement in colonial politics found in the Fenian stereotype an extremely useful weapon with which to contest Catholic political aspirations.

The comic Irish man: Paddy, Constable O'Grady and Ginger Mick

If the Fenian was a monstrous terror, Paddy was a hilarious buffoon. Yet the two figures were closely connected, for many of the visual cues used to identify the Fenian were also employed when portraying the comic Irish man. These included simian-ised facial features and distinctive peasant clothing. The comic Irish man was stupid and ill educated, although sometimes he exhibited an element of instinctive wit and cunning. His amusing feeble-mindedness could be portrayed visually, and frequently also in what he said and how he said it, as well as what he did. His dialect was replicated in brief cartoon captions, but it could be given freer rein for comic effect in stories or on the stage for, unlike the Fenian who usually let his deeds speak for him, Paddy had a great deal to say for himself: he was the prime exponent of the 'blarney'.

The comic or 'stage' Irish man has a very long history: scholars have traced the character back to Shakespeare, and he continued to appear regularly in English theatres throughout the 17th and 18th centuries.[39] Even after the stereotype of the Irish terrorist emerged, the comic Irish man did not lose his popularity. The character could be young or old and he was usually, although not invariably, working class. In Australia he might be called Paddy, Pat or Mick, or occasionally nicknamed Red or Ginger if he had red hair. He spoke with an Irish brogue, often a heavy one, in a dialect of English influenced by the Irish language and now known as Hiberno-English. He frequently wore stereotyped Irish peasant clothes and he had a marked fondness for drink and for fighting. His facial features, if simianised, were usually more chimpanzee-like than ape-like: in other words, they were cheeky and cunning rather than fierce and menacing.

'Tim's prediction' is a typical cartoon of the comic Irish man genre. A small drawing, it appeared in 1896 on the *Bulletin*'s 'Personal items' page.[40] Mick, the comic Irish character, is being addressed by a contractor on a building site, while in the background the body of his workmate Tim is being carried away. Mick stands with bended knees and stooped back, one of his long fingers touching his mouth as he speaks. The stance and gesture, together with Mick's receding forehead, upturned nose and sunken eyes, all suggest chimp-like stupidity. The Irishness of the illustration is reinforced by the caption, in which Mick's speech features elongated vowels meant to convey the Irish brogue: 'Faith, sur, it was only yesterday poor Tim tould me this job would be the death of him. Tim whatever else was no loir.' It is not the speech patterns alone that point to Irishness, but also the odd logic of the pun on the idea of the job being the 'death' of Tim. 'Tim's prediction' was drawn by Tom Durkin, who, as already mentioned, was himself of Irish parentage. Durkin's caricatures were very popular, and he was particularly adept at depicting racial stereotypes in physical terms. Not only his Irish, but his Jewish subjects too, were unmistakable, as in the 1897 cartoon, 'At the pawnshop door', where Isidore Wolfenstein is shown in conversation with Mick O'Hooligan.[41] As they glare into each other's eyes, their distinctive racialised facial profiles are thrown into sharp contrast: Isidore's enormous projecting nose and receding chin and Mick's small turned-up nose and his heavy jaw.

The jokes associated with the comic Irish man on the page and also on the stage are often what were known as Irish 'bulls'. These can be traced back in popular literature in England to the 17th century.[42] They involve a logical absurdity or incongruity, although, as the early 19th-century Irish novelist Maria Edgeworth acknowledged in her book on the subject, how they actually work is not easily described. She resorted to examples, rather than clunky definitions, for an explanation – and so shall we.[43]

Rolf Boldrewood's *Robbery Under Arms* was first serialised in the press in 1882–83, then published as a book in 1888, before finally being adapted for the stage in 1890. In all these forms the story proved extremely popular with Australian audiences. A number of Irish characters appear in the novel, mainly as bushrangers, and the hero Dick Marston, who joins a gang of bushrangers, is half Irish – as was Boldrewood himself.[44] However, when the story was turned into a play and staged by Alfred Dampier, not only was the ending changed to allow Dick to live rather than be killed, but two new characters were added to the plot who had not appeared in Boldrewood's original work. Both were comic Irish policemen: troopers O'Hara and

Maginnis. As historians of the colonial stage have noted, such 'low' comic characters were essential in melodrama in Australia from the advent of commercial theatre in the 1830s up to the First World War, for Australian audiences always demanded a good laugh even amid the most heart-rending of dramas.[45] Many of these 'low' characters were Irish and much of the humour they generated was in the form of comic dialogue and jokes, especially bulls.[46] Thus Trooper Maginnis advises his colleague O'Hara that capturing bushrangers is difficult: according to him, 'it'll be much easier for a needle to go into the eye of a camel'. Later he informs O'Hara that: 'Australia's no place for a poor man unless he has plenty o' money.' When actually menaced by bushrangers, O'Hara instructs Maginnis on how they should defend themselves: 'We'll forrum oursilves into a holly shquare,' he says. The clever Aboriginal character, Warrigal, gets the better of these dim-witted Irish men, but he does so with a bull. When O'Hara laughs at him for wearing only one spur, Warrigal replies that if: 'One side o' [his horse] go t'other side go too.'[47]

The Maginnis–O'Hara duo proved so popular with audiences that other playwrights and theatre managers, particularly those staging plays about the Kelly gang in the 1890s and 1900s, sought to emulate their success. But, for copyright reasons, names were sometimes changed, so in later bushranger dramas we encounter pairs of comic troopers called Moloney and Murphy or Mulligan and Flanigan. Nevertheless, the humour is much the same. In Arnold Denham's 1899 *The Kelly Gang*, alongside the real-life Irish policemen who had clashed with Ned Kelly – Fitzpatrick, Kennedy, Lonergan and McIntyre – there are two fictional 'Bould Sons of Erin' named O'Hara and McGuinness. Trying to justify his sore bum after a short ride, O'Hara explains: 'I can ride alright but sure the horse wont keep still.' Hearing a kookaburra laugh when he makes this remark, an alarmed O'Hara asks McGuinness: 'What the divil is that?' McGuinness mocks the ignorance of his recently arrived Irish colleague, informing him that it is a kangaroo and that: 'them same Kangaroos can fly faster than a swallow'.[48]

Stupid Irish policemen were a staple of visual and verbal humour for cartoonists as well as for dramatists.[49] This portrayal of the police in Australia as largely Irish-born accurately reflected the composition of colonial forces in the latter half of the 19th century, for most contained large numbers of Irish men; in some colonies, such as Victoria for example, they at times formed the majority of the force.[50] Visual depictions of the police often showed them with comic Paddy characteristics. Police incompetence could thus be explained by Irish stupidity or, more disturbingly, perhaps by ethnic solidarity, with Irish police colluding with Irish criminals, as was frequently alleged during the Kelly outbreak in Victoria in 1878–80.[51]

One of Tom Durkin's illustrations in the *Bulletin* in 1897 indicates how persistent this negative portrayal of Irish policemen was. 'A natural query' (see opposite) shows 'P.C. O'Grady' in conversation with a 'colored gentleman' wearing a turban. O'Grady is fat, with a heavy jaw and tiny nose, while his tall helmet tilts awkwardly forward, nearly covering his eyes. His appearance is obviously not calculated to inspire confidence in his intelligence, and his thick brogue adds to that impression. When the Indian character reports that a man has 'blackened mine eye', O'Grady asks: 'Phwich wan?' This is one of those drawings that deploys two racial stereotypes interacting with each other. The Indian is very dark-skinned, and the cartoon's title accepts it is therefore 'natural' that O'Grady cannot detect which of his eyes has been blackened. Yet, at the same time,

A NATURAL QUERY.

COLORED GENTLEMAN: *"An' den he blackened mine eye"*——
P.C. O'GRADY: *"Phwich wan?"*

Here the fat Irish policeman has simianised facial features, but his stance and expression are now comical rather than menacing. His large unwieldy helmet tilts towards the thin Indian's equally unwieldy turban, hinting perhaps at similarities amid the obvious racialised differences depicted.
Source: 'A natural query', *Bulletin*, 7 August 1897, p. 11.

O'Grady's appearance and speech are in line with the stereotype of the intellectually challenged Irish policeman.

The comic Irish man was clearly not as frightening a figure as the Fenian; nevertheless, reflecting the general Irish male stereotype, he could still behave very violently at times. This violence though was not motivated by any desire to overthrow the government: it was instead often the result of an alcohol-fuelled craving for fun or mischief-making, particularly around the time of St Patrick's Day. The swarthy, paunchy Mick of the 1881 cartoon, 'A reminiscence of St Patrick's Day'[52] has a bulbous nose, a clear indication of his fondness for alcohol; his clothes are unkempt and he has a rather shambolic air about him. His Irishness is made apparent by the shillelagh he is brandishing in his left hand, as well as by his Irish speech idioms. He tells his unnamed friend: 'Begorra, they foined me foive pounds for sphlitting the polisman's skull, but, be the powers, I laid him up for a month.' He personifies the widespread belief that Irish men loved to fight. Violence for them was recreational and thus they often fought for no discernible reason except for the sheer fun of it.

But the violence of the comic Irish man was not directed solely against other men in drunken brawls or against the police; more disturbingly, women and children could also fall victim to it. Irish husbands beating their wives – and vice versa – was a source of much amusement in many cartoons. Even children did not always escape the Irish man's innately violent nature. A pair of cartoons was published in 1895 in the Queensland *Warwick Argus*, entitled 'A slight turn'.[53] In the first, a small boy, described in the caption as a 'Wicked Youth', is shown following close behind a workman and attempting to stick a piece of paper to his back with 'Kick Me' written on it, while calling out mockingly,

'Irish! Irish!' The man, who is identified as Murphy, walks with bent knees like a monkey and displays typical stereotyped Irish facial features, including a prognathous jaw, a small upturned nose and a receding forehead. He also wears characteristic Irish clothing and smokes a pipe. Murphy is obviously a building labourer for on his shoulder he is carrying a wooden hod full of mortar or plaster, while the background shows house-building in progress. In the second picture, Murphy, while asking 'Phat's thot?' in response to the child's taunts, tips his hod backwards, dumping its contents over the head of his small assailant. The cartoon seems to suggest that Murphy does this out of clumsiness and stupidity, rather than malice, but it is clear that his action has seriously injured the child.

Over time in Australian popular culture the comic Irish male figure became less distinctively Irish, reflecting in part the rapid decline in the numbers of Irish-born people in Australia after the early 1890s.[54] Visually, the peasant clothing largely disappeared and the distorted facial features became far less pronounced. Yet the verbal humour, especially the jokes and bulls, persisted.[55] Now, however, they were often associated with Australian-born working-class male types, like the small rural selector or the young urban larrikin. What scholars call a 'nativisation' process was clearly underway.[56] The selector and the larrikin in many instances probably had Irish-born immigrant parents; some of the writers who caricatured them in stories, poems and plays during the first third of the 20th century certainly did. Examples of Australian humour with recognisably Irish roots include: Steele Rudd's *On Our Selection* (1899) and *Our New Selection* (1903), out of which emerged several films and comic strips and the long-running *Dad and Dave* radio serial;[57] CJ Dennis's *The Moods of Ginger Mick* (1916); many of the works of AB 'Banjo' Paterson;[58]

and the comic strip begun by Jimmy Bancks in 1921–22 featuring Ginger Meggs and his arch rival Tiger Kelly.

AH Davis, who wrote under the pen-name 'Steele Rudd', had an Irish-immigrant mother. He gave his character Dad Rudd an Irish saint's name, Murtagh, and a selection on the Darling Downs in southern Queensland, an area noted for heavy Irish settlement, where Davis himself had grown up.[59] The fictional Rudd family's neighbours include dozens of other small selectors, the majority with unmistakably Irish surnames. Not surprisingly, Dad's favourite songs are all Irish: 'The wild colonial boy', 'The wind that shakes the barley' and 'The rocky road to Dublin'. Given such a context, it is hardly surprising that Dad, with his pig-headed self-confidence, violent temper and extraordinary gullibility, displays many features of the comic Irish male stereotype.[60] CJ Dennis, both of whose parents were Irish-born, locates his larrikin character, Ginger Mick, in areas of working-class, inner-city Melbourne that boasted large Catholic populations. With his red hair and love of boozing and brawling, Mick the rabbit-oh is another recognisable version of the comic Irish man.[61]

Neither Rudd nor Dennis had much to say about religion. Both implied their characters were not especially interested in that sort of thing, but were probably vaguely Protestant. This avoidance of Catholicism is doubtless because sectarianism remained a potent and divisive force in Australia after 1900, and thus an overtly Catholic Dad Rudd or Ginger Mick, accurately reflecting their Irish roots, would have made them far less acceptable comic characters for Australian audiences, most of whom were Protestants. Jimmy Bancks, who had an Irish-born father, was somewhat more forthright in his Ginger Meggs comic strips. It is apparent that Ginger comes from a Protestant family – he attends Sunday school and his father is a freemason – while his enemy Kelly, portrayed as a violent bully, is clearly a Catholic.[62] But, while evident, religion is not foregrounded. So, in the transformation of the comic Irish man into a comic Australian character, the Irish man lost not only his distinctive face, clothing and brogue, but his religion as well.

The Irish politician: the premier, the pig and Ned Kelly

As we have seen with regard to the Fenian, the Australian press and local politicians were very ready to deploy negative Irish stereotypes in order to score points against political opponents. The higher up in the world of colonial politics or the labour movement Irish-born or Irish-Australian leaders rose, the more ferocious were the attacks launched against them. Politicians of every persuasion were of course caricatured, but the motives of few were as seriously impugned as those of the Irish. That their racial character wholly unfitted them for peaceful, democratic-style colonial politics was a not uncommon allegation.[63] Satirists in colonial Australia were obviously influenced by political developments overseas, especially in Ireland and the US. In Ireland, Daniel O'Connell had pioneered large-scale political agitation beginning in the 1820s and this was continued by the home rule movement from the 1870s onwards, especially under the leadership of Charles Stewart Parnell during the 1880s. Irish politics produced controversial and divisive leaders. In the US, the growing power of the Irish within the Democratic Party after the Civil War, symbolised for many by New York's corrupt Tammany Hall, helped cement the unsavoury popular image of the Irish politician as an unscrupulous and unprincipled operator.[64] When we consider how Irish-Australian politicians were represented in the colonial press, we need to bear this background in mind.

One popular mode of attack in cartoons was to graft some of the physical features of the Fenian stereotype onto a recognisable portrait of a particular Catholic politician to suggest that both shared such innate Irish racial characteristics as violence, treachery and duplicity. In Victoria, the Irish reached the top of colonial politics relatively quickly: three Catholic Irish-born men, John O'Shanassy, Charles Gavan Duffy and Bryan O'Loghlen, all occupied the premiership between the 1850s and the 1880s, despite often intense opposition.[65]

Whereas O'Shanassy, a grocer before he entered Victorian politics, was usually caricatured dismissively as a gruff, ignorant peasant, the backgrounds of Duffy and O'Loghlen invited more severe censure. Both had been active in O'Connellite politics in Ireland during the 1840s. Duffy, as editor of a leading nationalist newspaper, had even been prosecuted for treason more than once in connection with the 1848 Rebellion, although he was always acquitted. It was therefore easy for their opponents in Victoria to represent both as similar to O'Connell or later Parnell and to the Irish-American politicians of Tammany Hall. That is, they were cynical and hypocritcal rabble-rousers, playing on the discontents of ignorant people to advance their own personal interests at the expense of the majority non-Irish society.[66]

From the 1860s into the early 1880s, *Melbourne Punch* was full of cartoons, articles and comic verses attacking the characters of first Duffy and then O'Loghlen, as well as other Irish-born politicians, like the former Eureka Stockade leader Peter Lalor – the 'Irish Brigade', the journal scornfully labelled them. Duffy's brief tenure as premier (1871-72) was clouded by bitter sectarian controversy, especially over the issue of state aid to Catholic schools.[67] Shortly before he became premier, it was rumoured that he intended to run for the speakership of the Legislative Assembly. This claim prompted an 1871 cartoon by Tom Carrington, entitled 'The new speaker?' (see page 156). Duffy is depicted emerging from under the bed of the sleeping retiring speaker, Sir Francis Murphy. As his name suggests, Murphy was Irish-born, but, unlike Duffy, he was a conservative Protestant doctor whose loyalty to the crown had never been questioned. Duffy is dressed in the Irish-style costume that at the time was associated with Fenianism, while in his hand he grasps the parliamentary mace like a weapon. Coming so soon after the Fenian scare of 1868, the drawing's gestures towards Fenianism would have been apparent to a contemporary audience. In heavy brogue, Duffy threatens his main rival for the position, Captain Charles McMahon, the former chief of police and another conservative Irish Protestant, who is shown in the process of trying on the speaker's robes and wig. 'Ah thin, Captain Darlint, [says Duffy] yee can dhrop thim things like a hot sphud. It's meself that's had my oie on thim for a toime past, and bedad I aint a going to be chated out ov 'em now.' In fact, Duffy did not contest the speakership, which went to McMahon, although he did eventually occupy the office in 1877-80. Alfred Deakin later claimed that this cartoon had particularly angered Duffy.[68] Yet, during the late 1870s and early 1880s, Sir Bryan O'Loghlen suffered far worse at the hands of *Melbourne Punch* cartoonists.

O'Loghlen was rather unfortunate in the timing of his political career. He served as attorney-general during the Kelly outbreak (1878-80), while his premiership (1881-83) coincided with the Irish Land War, in which Fenians played a leading and

THE NEW SPEAKER?

Mr. Duffy (from beneath the bed)—"AH THIN, CAPTAIN DARLINT, YEZ CAN DHROP THIM THINGS LIKE A HOT SPHUD. IT'S MESELF THAT'S HAD MY OIE ON THIM FOR A TOIME PAST, AND BEDAD I AINT A GOING TO BE CHATED OUT OV 'EM NOW."

Three Irish-born men are depicted: the one asleep is the current speaker of the Victorian Legislative Assembly; the other two are aspirants for his job. But it is the Catholic nationalist, Charles Gavan Duffy, who is singled out for stereotyping, not his Protestant loyalist rival. Duffy skulks under the bed, emerging in Irish garb to threaten violence.

Source: 'The new speaker?', *Melbourne Punch*, 30 July 1871, p. 100.

often violent role. *Melbourne Punch* took full advantage of both situations in order to smear the mild-mannered barrister as a friend to outlaws and rebels, as well as a master of political chicanery. In the late 1870s O'Loghlen appeared frequently in cartoons, poems and squibs as 'Bryan O'Larrikin', portrayed as being in league with that other well-known Irish larrikin, Ned Kelly.[69] Some cartoons, however, suggested that O'Loghlen was even more of a problem for the colony than was Kelly. In Tom Carrington's 1879 cartoon, 'The "Berry Blight" on the ballot box' (see page 158), a fat, stooped O'Loghlen appears with a ballot box under one arm and a whip labelled 'Press Gag' under the other. Beside him stands a tall, slim, well-armed Ned Kelly. O'Loghlen tells Kelly: 'I'm doing a bit in your line', meaning he is stealing a ballot box. But Kelly demurs: 'No, Mr Chief Secretary, *not* in my line. Bad as I am, I don't do a widow out of her money, or rob any man of his political rights. I'm a cut above you yet.'

Another interesting O'Loghlen cartoon, appearing early in 1883 at the time of an election, was entitled 'A new departure'.[70] This term had originally been introduced to characterise the informal alliance Fenians and Irish nationalist politicians, led by Parnell, entered into secretly in 1878–79 to facilitate the Land War.[71] In the drawing O'Loghlen is depicted in Irish peasant attire, with a stick tucked under his arm, sitting beside a pig in a farmyard. He pats the pig fondly on the head, saying: 'Now, me friend, you just keep a troifle in the background. O'ime going to run on me "personal popularity" ticket this toime.' But a poem below the cartoon titled 'Non Possumus' makes clear that O'Loghlen has no chance of fooling voters into believing that he has severed his links with his corrupt and violent Irish past, symbolised by the pig. And, indeed, the election was a disaster for O'Loghlen for, not only was his government defeated, but he

THE "BERRY BLIGHT" ON THE BALLOT BOX.

Sir B. O'L.—" HULLO, MR. KELLY, I'M DOING A BIT IN YOUR LINE."

Ned Kelly.—" NO, MR. CHIEF SECRETARY, *not* IN MY LINE. BAD AS I AM, I DON'T DO A WIDOW OUT OF HER MONEY, OR ROB ANY MAN OF HIS POLITICAL RIGHTS. I'M A CUT ABOVE YOU YET."

Bryan O'Loghlen was often accused by his political enemies of assisting Ned Kelly, but here an upright, well-dressed Kelly is depicted as a 'cut above' the fat, shambling O'Loghlen, who robs widows of their money and men of their political rights. According to this cartoon, the Irish politician was a bigger criminal than the Irish-Australian outlaw.

Source: 'The "Berry Blight" on the ballot box', *Melbourne Punch*, 27 February 1879, p. 85.

lost his own seat. The poem asks: 'Will he wash? Will he clean? Can the brush make him white?'; and answers its own question with an unequivocal 'no': not until it says 'the negro turns white'. O'Loghlen, like most Catholic politicians, was assuredly very black in the eyes of *Melbourne Punch* and nothing could possibly ever make him white.

From black ape to white grub

The terrorist Fenian, the stupid Paddy and the corrupt Irish politician appear repeatedly and relentlessly in the pages of Australian popular illustrated magazines from the 1850s up to the 1920s. We have gathered hundreds and hundreds of these drawings, yet our collection is by no means exhaustive, for we have not researched all such publications nor covered all the years between 1850 and 1930. In addition to a substantial body of cartoons, periodicals also published many more jokes, poems and stories satirising the Irish. And then there were the caricatures contained in novels and plays. The stage Irish man – and, to a lesser extent, woman – was a stalwart of colonial melodrama, even being added to the cast, as we have seen, when not in the original source on which a play was based.

Donald Horne, later an influential editor of the *Bulletin*, who grew up during the late 1920s and early 1930s in a NSW country town, vividly illustrates the impact of such stereotyping on the mind of a child. It was, he writes, 'in our distinction from the Catholics (who made up about a fifth of the town) that we members of the Ascendancy most clearly characterized ourselves'. Among freemason families, like his own, 'it is doubtful that we considered Catholics to be fully human'. Their faces were 'coarser than ours – more like [the faces of] apes'. And he went on: 'I can still see my childhood image of a Catholic child: flat-nosed, freckled, scowling, barefooted, tough – and as white-skinned as a grub (a white skin was an evil in a sun-worshipping society)'.[72] It is striking that Horne's aversion to these Catholic children was so strong that, even nearly 40 years later, he could still picture them clearly in his mind.

The Irish community was by no means quiescent in the face of such a barrage of negativity. During the 1830s and 1840s, for instance, there were a number of riots at theatres when Irish members of the audience objected to how they or their church were being represented on the stage.[73] The Catholic press also on occasion published leading articles and letters to the editor complaining about particular plays, cartoons or reports. For instance, the farce *Muldoon's Picnic*, first staged in New York in the late 1870s and claimed as a source for Steele Rudd's *On Our Selection*, proved very popular with Australian audiences. But, in 1905, when Melbourne's Gaiety Theatre decided to put it on for St Patrick's Day, the Catholic *Advocate* was incensed. According to the paper, the play was a 'vile representation in which the stage Irishman indulges in his usual burlesquing of the Irish character and Irish customs'. It called on Irish men and women not to attend the performance and, referring vaguely to recent events in America, it warned that those who were satirising the Irish might soon be 'taught a useful lesson'.[74] This presumably was a reference to theatre riots, as in the US violent Irish protests at their portrayal on stage were not uncommon.[75] But there is little evidence that such Catholic responses had much impact on the level or intensity of hostile stereotyping. Certainly *Muldoon's Picnic* played successfully in Australian theatres for many years and was still being fondly recalled as late as the 1940s.[76]

Anti-Irish satire, as we have seen, did not always originate from non-Irish sources. Some artists, writers and actors of Irish birth or descent were complicit in the stereotype. Cartoonists like Tom Durkin and actors like GV Brooke made good livings out of employing comic Irish figures in their works. But some writers, like some newspapers, took an explicit stand against Irish stereotyping. However, in defending the Irish, they sometimes resorted to demeaning other races. Ernest O'Farrell, whose parents were Irish immigrants, wrote under the pen-name 'Kodak' an interesting story for a 1918 collection edited by Ethel Turner and intended to raise funds for Australian troops. The title of his story, 'And the Singer was Irish', is ironic, for the man singing sentimental Irish ballads in the street – ballads that move an Irish immigrant named Donovan almost to tears – is in fact an African American. When, after first hearing the singer, Donovan actually sees him, he immediately knocks the man down, demanding: 'What right has a nigger to sing an Irish [song]?' Arrested by a constable and hauled off to a police station, the station sergeant immediately rebukes the constable and releases Donovan. From his speech it is clear that the unnamed sergeant, who threatens 'to lay a charge of insultin' behavior against the nigger', is Irish. Both he and Donovan are in no doubt that a black man has no right to attempt to assume an Irish identity by singing Irish songs.[77]

Stereotypes are not immutable: over time they flex and adjust themselves in response to the pressures of changing circumstances. So the stereotypes of the 1840s or 1850s were not exactly the same as those of the 1900s or 1910s. Most obviously, the Irish-Australian community transitioned from being predominantly Irish-born in the 1850s and 1860s to being largely Australian-born by the end of the century. The physical stereotype, especially the simianised facial features, went into decline from the 1880s. Donald Horne, describing growing up in the 1920s and 1930s, does not talk about the Irish at all, but instead about 'Catholics'. It is notable though that he still imagines them with the ape-like facial features previously ascribed to the Irish Fenian. That particular image lingered and occasionally re-surfaced in cartoons as late as 1920.[78] Yet, it appears somewhat anomalous because in the next breath Horne describes Catholic children, not as black, but as strikingly white. However, using a term of abuse common amongst Australian children at the time, it is the 'evil' whiteness of a miserable 'grub'; it is not 'our' healthy, 'sun-worshipping' whiteness.

Just as caricatures damaged the political fortunes of some Irish politicians, so racial and ethnic stereotypes also undermined the employment prospects of many Irish men and women. The stereotypes we have discussed in this chapter have been those of Irish men. There were different, though related, stereotypes employed to portray Irish women, which we will consider in the following chapter.

CHAPTER 6

Employment:
Bridget need not apply

During a mining boom in Australia in 2012, a Perth builder put an advertisement for a bricklayer in the free online paper *Gumtree*, specifying 'No Irish'. The incident was widely reported in the Irish-Australian press and then in the Irish press, with a comment from the Australian ambassador to Ireland stressing that the ad did not comply with Australia's anti-discrimination law.[1] The builder's response was very similar to that of many employers a century and a half earlier: he said that the Irish were not reliable, they exaggerated their experience, and he just did not want to employ them. In their reactions, the Irish-Australian press and the ambassador too responded in ways similar to earlier Irish Australians protesting against job discrimination. They also demonstrated their awareness of the historic context of signs and advertisements specifying 'No Irish Need Apply', which had appeared throughout the English-speaking world during the 19th century and were widely remembered from the 1950s and 1960s in England.[2]

'No Irish Need Apply' (NINA) advertisements for employees or tenants drew on stereotypes of the ignorant and untrustworthy Irish dating back to at least the early 19th century. The physically racialised Irish stereotype we saw in the last chapter, displayed most strikingly in cartoons of the ape-like Fenian, was generally masculine. Yet caricatures of Irish women were also common in illustrated periodicals, in fiction and on the stage.[3] Though not usually as physically grotesque as some of the Irish men, Irish women were represented as sharing qualities with their men like stupidity and cunning and sometimes a fondness for alcohol and violence. The most frequently caricatured Irish woman in Australian popular culture during the 19th century and later was the young Irish domestic servant, usually called 'Bridget'. There was a second less common stereotype, often designated 'Mrs Murphy'. She was an older version of Bridget after she had married or been widowed, often now portrayed as making a little extra cash taking in washing. The Catholic Irish themselves recognised that one of the consequences of all these caricatures was that Irish women and men were often excluded from jobs by advertisements employing variations on the phrase 'No Irish Need Apply'. The phrase became so widely known that it entered the rhetoric of the Irish when they challenged restrictions on immigration or attempts to exclude them from political influence. In this chapter we examine advertisements that included it, alongside cartoons of Bridget, in order to chart attitudes towards and discrimination against Irish workers, particularly female servants. We also examine how the Catholic Irish used NINA in a wide range of political contexts to undercut its effectiveness and turn it into a rallying cry against discrimination and injustice.

'Bridget', the Irish domestic servant

The stereotype of the incompetent, lazy, feckless and truculent Irish female servant was commonplace in public discourse in Britain, the United States (US) and Australia.[4] It reflected in general terms the myriad tensions inherent in the master/mistress-servant relationship. A particularly vivid description of the perceived difficulties of Irish domestic servants in Australia was provided by English-born journalist Richard Twopeny in his 1883 *Town Life in Australia*. He was not overly impressed with the quality of any of the colonial servants he encountered, but he reserved his most pithy criticisms for the Irish. 'Unfortunately, four-fifths of our servants are Irish – liars and dirty,' he wrote. Although the Irish were 'less impertinent than the colonials', a major problem was that the typical Irish servant had 'as often as not never been inside any other household than her native hovel, and stares in astonishment to find that you don't keep a pig on your drawing-room sofa'. Twopeny then listed the faults of various inept Irish servants, including one who put the soup, meat and pudding for the day all into one pot to serve.[5]

Recently arrived from a small Irish tenant farm, Bridget's ignorance, her unfamiliarity with the ways of middle-class households and with Australian conditions were the subject of many cartoons. In 1883, in the *Bulletin*'s 'Holy Moses!' (see page 166), a terrified Bridget, grasping a toasting fork, perches precariously on a chair while a large lobster, which has escaped from its basket, runs amok in the kitchen.[6] Bridget's facial features proclaim her Irishness: she has a heavy jaw and receding forehead, as well as small eyes and a turned-up nose. Her inexperience and naivety are apparent in her anguished query: 'How am I to shkin that?' But when in due course Bridget became

BRIDGET: "Holy Moses! How am I to shkin that?"

Irish immigrants' unfamiliarity with the middle-class colonial kitchen is mocked in this cartoon. The servant Bridget, clearly identified as Irish by her name, face and speech, displays her ignorance in wanting to 'shkin' a lobster: a creature obviously new to her.

Source: 'Holy Moses!', *Bulletin*, 23 June 1883, p. 16

more familiar with Australian household routines, instead of improving, she invariably became an even more troublesome employee. In 1889, 'Her day out', also from the *Bulletin*, satirised Bridget's insistent demand for time off work. Thus, on arriving at the gates of paradise, she stops to question St Peter as to 'how many nights out yez give every wake'.[7]

Bridget's inadequacies as a servant were also chronicled in popular verse:

> Biddy Murphy was a spinster
> Who to Melbourne – years ago –
> Emigrated – out of Leinster –
> Like a number more we know
>
> ...
>
> Soon a lady fine engaged her –
> Found her but a useless jade –
>
> ...
>
> Ere a week had passed she'd broken
> Half the things about the place;
> Insolently oft had spoken –
> Had become a sore disgrace.

Having left Ireland full of dreams of an easy well-paid job or marriage to a rich digger, Biddy Murphy's incompetence condemns her in the end to charwoman's work, scrubbing floors, her fantasies turned to mere 'bubbles' in her 'fuming washing tub'.[8]

Given this stereotype, it is perhaps understandable that when we look at newspapers from the 1850s onwards, we find employment ads like the following:

> WANTED in a family about three miles from Melbourne, a respectable Young Woman as Housemaid; must understand waiting at table. Apply this day to Symons and Perry, Bourke street. No Irish need apply.[9]

This family did not want a 'Bridget', an Irish servant who did not understand the niceties of waiting at middle-class tables and was demonstrably vastly different from themselves. The family used a phrase widely known in the United Kingdom (UK) and US to bar applicants before they reached the front door, to ensure that they did not have to endure Bridget's incompetence within the walls of their home.

'No Irish Need Apply' in the US and UK

NINA ads originated in England in the early 19th century and spread with English settlers to the new world. Facilitated in recent years by large-scale digitisation of newspaper archives, historians in the UK and US have been interested for some time in the significance of NINA signs and advertisements. Richard Jensen investigated 19th-century American NINA signs and ads in a 2002 article. He argued that the 'memory' currently held by many Irish Americans of their parents or grandparents telling them about NINA signs and ads was a myth and, in fact, there were no verifiable signs in windows. He conceded, however, that there may have been some handwritten ones for female domestic servants, but he discounted these. Jensen surveyed a selection of 19th-century American newspapers and concluded that they contained only a handful of NINA ads. He argued that a popular 1862 song entitled 'No Irish Need Apply' was more responsible for the continued 'memory' of this form of discrimination than actual ads or signs.[10]

British historian Don MacRaild then investigated NINA ads in 19th-century UK newspapers. He argued that the term originated early in the century in the wake of the 1798 Rebellion and fears of further Catholic Irish rebellions.[11] But MacRaild agreed with some of Jensen's conclusions, finding relatively few NINA ads for male workers, with the majority of them being for female domestic servants in cities with large Irish immigrant populations. He also found that there was an upswing in ads using variants such as 'Protestant Only' or 'English Only' from the 1860s onwards. Overall, MacRaild found far more job advertisements in Britain specifying that Irish were not welcome to apply than did Jensen in his analysis of the US. MacRaild also found significant numbers of ads for housing and accommodation specifying NINA, a category that Jensen had not investigated for the US.[12] Jensen's findings were widely accepted until 2015 when Rebecca Fried researched very much larger data sets of newspapers then available to test Jensen's analysis.[13] She discovered that there were in fact a number of such ads for male workers. These ads appeared mainly in papers aimed at working-class readers. Such papers have not been fully digitised and Jensen had not used them in his research.

The work of MacRaild and Fried has demonstrated that there is a collection of these advertisements for both male and female workers in UK and US newspapers, as well as popular commentary referring to them, particularly in the song 'No Irish

Need Apply' and its variants. This song, initially in the voice of an Irish servant girl, was originally performed in Britain by Kathleen O'Neill in about 1861. It was rewritten by John F Poole in the voice of a male worker in the US in 1862.[14] The music for the song was available in Sydney in that same year.[15] However, the phrase NINA was known in job advertisements in the colonies well before this and, indeed, was sufficiently familiar that *Melbourne Punch* could state in 1857 that: 'No Irish Need Apply ... is a pretty constant addendum to advertisements for servants of various kinds'.[16]

'No Irish Need Apply' in Australia

To investigate how widespread such advertising was in Australia, we searched for the term in digitised Australian newspaper databases.[17] We used the National Library of Australia's website, Trove, which hosts digital copies of thousands of newspapers dating from the early 19th century up until the mid-20th century. We found over 1000 uses of the term in the digitised Australian newspapers before 1920. However, this alone is not very revealing, so we used more analysis to break that number down into three broad categories. There were firstly job advertisements for employees; secondly, there were malicious uses of the term obviously aimed at damaging commercial interests; and thirdly, the phrase was used as a shorthand way of indicating and then arguing against discrimination based on Irishness. We will discuss the second and third of these uses later in the chapter. For the moment, we will concentrate on the job advertisements.

There are some caveats about using digital searches for newspaper employment advertising. Firstly, while advertisements for domestic servants dominated newspaper classifieds until at least the 1930s, there were other avenues for contact between potential employers and employees.[18] These included signs in windows, labour-hire agencies, personal recruitment through word-of-mouth or through work gangs. It is difficult, if not impossible, to find historical traces of the use of signs in windows. Labour-hire agencies were common in colonial Australian cities and serviced both urban and rural employers seeking employees. In January 1865, for example, the Melbourne *Argus* carried ads for at least six domestic-hire agencies, announcing that they had positions for all varieties of domestic labourers and servants.[19] These did not usually advertise specific positions; more often they had general ads.[20] Some agencies explicitly publicised the characteristics of the employees they were seeking. In Sydney, Mr and Mrs Craggs ran a Protestant Servants' Agency in Castlereagh Street and advertised for Protestant housekeepers, cooks and needlewomen and, in November 1879, for a general servant for a household in Wagga, New South Wales (NSW), as well as for grooms and coachmen in March and June 1880.[21] In 1920, Mrs McClusky was advertising in the *Sydney Stock and Station Journal* on behalf of the Federal Protestant Governess and Servants' Registry, which specialised in servants for outback stations.[22] Another way for prospective employees, especially domestic servants, to find work was to place notices advertising their services in newspapers themselves. In addition to the above caveats, we also need to remember that to date Trove's coverage of all newspapers that were ever published in Australia is not complete. Also, the employment ads usually appear in small crowded print that does not always allow for accurate data mining by search engines. Our survey results are necessarily underestimates. However, these surveys and searches did result in data sets of many Australian ads published during the 19th and early 20th centuries specifying that the Irish or Catholics were not welcome.[23] These are worth investigating in detail.

There were three common phrases used in these advertisements signalling that Catholic Irish immigrants and Irish Australians would not be considered for a job. The most obvious was 'No Irish Need Apply', followed by 'English Only' or 'English or Scotch Only'. Another phrase used was 'Protestant Preferred'. We will take each of these phrases in turn and analyse their frequency over the period from the 1830s until 1919. After 1919, although job ads continued to use the phrase 'Protestant Preferred', it was more often used in accommodation and personal ads.

As the table (opposite) demonstrates, although NINA ads were never numerous in Australia, they can be found scattered through newspapers from the 1830s up until 1919. The table also suggests that the frequency of ads was influenced by spatial and temporal factors: in other words, ads clustered according to place and time. As Table 1 shows, NINA ads were most likely to be published in metropolitan newspapers, rather than in the rural and regional press.

The first NINA employment ad in our survey appeared in a Launceston newspaper, the *Cornwall Chronicle*, in February 1838. It specified: 'Wanted: a housemaid of middle age, having a knowledge of plain cooking. No Irish woman need apply.'[25] The style of the ad was similar to one published 70 years later in the Perth *West Australian* in 1908: 'Wanted: Housemaid accustomed to first class business. References required. No Irish need apply.'[26] The latest ad we found was in the Adelaide *Advertiser* in 1916. It was rather ambiguous in its wording as to whether the 'respectable girl over 16' required was to be a companion or an adopted daughter. Either way, 'no Irish need apply'.[27]

Table 1: Number of NINA newspaper ads in cities and towns, 1830–1919[24]

CITY/TOWN	1830-9	1840-9	1850-9	1860-9	1870-9	1880-9	1890-9	1900-9	1910-9	TOTAL
Sydney	2		13	2		5				22
Melbourne			32		1	10				43
Brisbane				2						2
Adelaide		1	6			3	1		1	12
Perth				1				1		2
Ballarat (VIC)				3						3
Bendigo (VIC)			1	1	1					3
Castlemaine (VIC)				1						1
Geelong (VIC)						1				1
Kyneton (VIC)					1					1
Launceston (TAS)	1			1						2
Maryborough (QLD)					1					1
Rockhampton (QLD)				1						1
Totals	**3**	**1**	**52**	**12**	**4**	**19**	**1**	**1**	**1**	**94**

Our survey of Australian newspaper employment ads is broadly in line with the results of MacRaild's research on UK newspapers, and the chronological range of the UK ads is also similar: the earliest that MacRaild discovered was in 1828 and the latest were published during the 1880s.[28] As in the UK, most Australian NINA ads were seeking female domestic servants. Out of the 94 ads we found in Australian newspapers, 77 (82 per cent) were for female domestic servants. A further two ads were for married couples to work on country properties, with the woman employed in the house and the man out-of-doors, and there was one ad for a female office worker. The 12 ads for male employees that specified NINA were seeking a variety of workers, including woodcutters, farm labourers, general tradesmen, a groom, an apprentice bootmaker, navvies, drivers and pilots. A larger number of different occupations were available for working-class men than for women, and it would seem that even employers of unskilled labour sometimes chose to exclude the Irish. An 1858 ad in the Sydney *Empire*, placed by the proprietor of the Kentish Brewery, not only wanted Kentish brewers, but also specifically stated that 'no Irish should apply'.[29]

The largest number of NINA ads appeared during the 1850s and they were most common in Melbourne. The city's population grew enormously due to the gold rushes – from 23 000 in 1851 to 125 000 in 1861 – as did its citizens' prosperity.[30] These changes massively boosted the demand for domestic servants. Irish women were the largest proportion (48.6 per cent) of female assisted migrants arriving in NSW and Victoria at the time. These women, like almost all other female assisted migrants, had listed their occupation on arrival as 'domestic servant'.[31] But at the same time, anti-Irish and anti-Catholic sentiment was strong in Melbourne, with young

Catholic Irish female immigrants – just the sort of women likely to seek work as domestic servants – being prime targets for hostility. This hostility continued throughout the 1850s, but was particularly intense in 1848–50 due to the so-called 'Famine orphans' scheme: the dispatch of around 4100 teenage girls from overcrowded Irish workhouses to Sydney, Melbourne and Adelaide.[32] The Melbourne press was especially outspoken in its opposition. In a leading article in January 1850, the *Argus* described the girls as 'coarse, useless creatures', whose household knowledge 'barely reaches to distinguishing the inside from the outside of a potato' and whose previous 'intellectual occupation' consisted of little more than 'occasionally trotting across a bog to fetch back a runaway pig'. The paper was especially alarmed at the prospect of intermarriage between Irish female domestic servants and the colony's British working-class males. The 'squat, stunted figures, thick waists, and clumsy ankles' of these Irish immigrants, claimed the *Argus*, constituted a serious threat to the 'physique of the future colonists of Victoria'. An even more serious threat was religion. In the 1850s there were many newspaper warnings of the dangers ahead for the Protestant colonies if large numbers of Catholic Irish women were allowed to subvert the family through 'mixed marriages'.[33] The *Argus* claimed in 1850 that if these Irish women married 'shepherds, hutkeepers, stockman, &c.', who were themselves mostly 'little better than heathens', the children of such unions would almost certainly be raised as Catholics, thus diluting the Protestant British character of the workforce and threatening the colony's future 'liberty ... public happiness [and] progress'.[34] Given such fears, it is little wonder that during the gold-rush decade some of Melbourne's inhabitants preferred not to employ Catholic Irish servants in their homes.

Irish and Irish-Australian job-seekers needed to take note not only of NINA ads, but also ads that specified 'English or Scotch Only or Preferred'. As with NINA ads, these were particularly prevalent in Melbourne during the 1850s and 1860s.

Table 2: 'English or Scottish Only' and 'English or Scotch Preferred' in employment ads, 1840–1919

NEWSPAPER TITLE	CITY/ TOWN	STATE	1840–9	1850–9	1860–9	1870–9	1880–9	1890–9	1900–9	1910–9
Sydney Morning Herald (1842–)	Sydney	NSW	34	291	295	35	59	29	10	71
Daily Telegraph (1883–)	Sydney	NSW					4	53	47	8
Argus (1848–1957)	Melbourne	VIC		988	1692	372	41	4	1	28
Age (1854–)	Melbourne	VIC		40	54	45	86	41	7	33
Star/ Ballarat Star (1855–1924)	Ballarat	VIC		12	252	14		1		
Brisbane Courier (1864–1922)	Brisbane	QLD			44	2	4	19	14	3
Telegraph (1872–1947)	Brisbane	QLD				2	12	41	9	21
South Australian Register (1839–1900)	Adelaide	SA		133	55	18	3			
South Australian Advertiser (1858–89)	Adelaide	SA		43	13	4	9			

Again these types of ads were mainly for female domestic servants, such as the ad in the *Argus* in January 1854 for a 'competent Housemaid, Scotch or English preferred', with the address at the offices of Messrs Jacob Montefiore in Collins Street. Jacob Montefiore was one of the wealthiest Jewish merchants in the colonies and his brother Eliezer ran the Melbourne branch of the firm.[35]

English or Scottish servants were considered to be the best trained and the most dependable and deferential, while the Irish and colonials – the latter possibly of Irish parentage – were viewed as ignorant, unreliable and likely to be impertinent. The demand for domestic servants always outstripped supply for most of the 19th century, meaning that even though a hopeful housewife might advertise for an 'English or Scotch' housemaid, she was likely to be disappointed.[36] Experienced servants were also in demand in England and could usually find employment without emigrating. For those who did wish to emigrate, they were also in demand in other destinations, such as in Canada, South Africa and the US, so far fewer of them were likely to have made the long, expensive journey to Australia.[37] Richard Twopeny claimed in 1883 that the shortage of good English servants was a 'plague' on the lives of many middle-class colonial families – including his own.[38] The search for superior English domestic servants continued into the 1920s, with an advertisement for a cook for a household in the Blue Mountains appearing in the *Sydney Morning Herald* specifying: 'COOK-GENERAL, experienced, wanted immediately, for Leura, Blue Mountains, English preferred, Protestant, help given, no washing, liberal outings.'[39] Government-funded immigration schemes during the 1920s specifically targeted what they called the 'British Domestic Girl' in the largely unrealised hope of persuading young Protestant

English and Scottish women to come to Australia to work as servants.[40]

The servants who were available then for Australian colonial households were often Irish – much to the disappointment and frustration of householders. The fact that even 'Irish convicts, against whom strong prejudices are usually held here, find ready hirers' was the main proof of the great need for more servants, according to the lieutenant-governor of Van Diemen's Land, Sir William Denison, in 1853.[41] Many, if not nearly all, of the Irish women who arrived as domestic servants found work. Analysis of census data by historian Chris McConville shows that from 1871 to 1901 there were clusters of single Irish-born women living in the upper-class suburbs of Hunters Hill in Sydney and Kew in Melbourne, indicating that many Irish women were employed as servants in these wealthy homes.[42] Some Irish women remained in service for life. Ann McIntyre, a Catholic woman from King's County (now County Offaly), arrived in Melbourne in 1868 and moved to the mining town of Stawell in western Victoria shortly afterwards. There she worked until her death in 1917 in the households of the successful County Wexford Scallan and Kinsella families.[43] Others went in and out of service as their circumstances changed. Ellen Real, for example, was widowed on a journey to Queensland in 1850, leaving her as sole support for her children. She worked as a domestic servant in Ipswich until her son, the future barrister and judge Sir Patrick Real, was old enough to get a job.[44]

Even though large numbers of Irish women were available to work as domestic servants, some employers continued to try and avoid hiring them. It is likely that readers of newspaper employment ads interpreted the other popular discriminatory phrases in these ads, 'English Only' or 'English or Scotch

Preferred', as virtually identical to 'No Irish Need Apply'. In 1859, 'An Irish Girl' wrote an indignant letter to the editor of the *Bendigo Advertiser*, complaining about the 'No Irish Need Apply' strictures in two ads published the day before. In fact, both these ads for servants specified 'English or Scotch only'.[45] Clearly 'An Irish Girl' saw this as a rejection of Irish servants, writing: 'Surely these intolerant bigots must see in every Irish servant, either an emissary from the Pope or the d—1 direct, or a "White Boy" in petticoats, that they shut their doors against them as they would against a pestilence.'[46] 'An Irish Girl' believed that Irish servants were rejected because of fears that they would contaminate the respectable Protestant colonial home with their links to 'Popery' and 'Whiteboys', that is to Irish secret societies.[47]

Irish Australians were very aware of employment discrimination in these various ads and, like 'An Irish Girl', they were often quick to condemn them. When ads were placed specifying that no Irish servants would be employed in commercial businesses or by owners of shops, Catholic newspapers sometimes ran campaigns urging the Irish to withdraw their patronage from such establishments. In this they were copying a similar campaign that took place in London in the early 1840s. A meeting of a London branch of O'Connell's Repeal Association had resolved in 1841 to confront the widespread use of NINA in London ads by keeping lists of tradespeople who used it, with a view to avoiding doing business with them.[48] That such tactics proved successful in Australia is suggested by a series of retractions of NINA ads. In Sydney, in early 1840, a number of ads were placed over several weeks withdrawing an ad that had appeared the previous November seeking a nursery maid for the household of a confectioner, Mr Dunsdon. The November ad had included the phrase 'No Irish Need Apply'. The subsequent apology, headlined 'To the Sons and Daughters of Hibernia', stated that the ad had been placed in error. The public retraction was seemingly necessary because Dunsdon's business was being hurt by the Irish reaction.[49] In 1850, a Sydney hairdresser was moved to publish a personal retraction and apology for an ad that appeared under his name seeking two hairdressers and including that 'No Irish Need Apply'.[50] In 1855, in Adelaide, a series of advertisements were placed by 'An Irishman' in the form of a letter outlining how several members of a prominent business family had advertised for domestic servants specifying 'No Irish'. The letter urged Irish customers to shop elsewhere.[51] The practice of publicising these ads and then organising campaigns against them was also evident in Queensland. In 1863, an Irishman, who had applied for a position in a Brisbane shop only to be told that 'they did not engage Irish hands', quickly wrote to the *North Australian*. His letter, headed 'No Irish Need Apply', reported that he and his friends no longer purchased goods at the shop and he urged other readers also to avoid it.[52] Such measures may perhaps have had an effect locally, since NINA ads were not as common in Brisbane and Adelaide as they were in Melbourne.

The anger felt at the occasional use of NINA in employment ads clearly led to an Irish community backlash against some advertisers. Irish and Irish-Australian servants who did secure employment could also make use of legal protections offered under the various colonial masters and servants Acts if they experienced abuse or poor treatment. In 1870, a squatter family on a station about 40 miles from Deniliquin in southern NSW hired an Irish married couple to work on their property, probably through a city agency. The husband was engaged to work in an outdoor capacity and the wife as a domestic servant. On their first morning on the job, the Irish servant, Mrs O'Brien, met with her employer, Mrs Turnbull, who reportedly said: '[s]he did not think she was going to have any "dirty Irish" there and called Mrs O'Brien a vagrant'. After a few days of this treatment, Mrs O'Brien walked off the property to the nearest town, about 17 miles away. The Turnbulls then sued the O'Briens for breach of contract under the 1828 *NSW Masters and Servants Act*. But the case was dismissed by a magistrate and the O'Briens won a separate legal action against the Turnbulls.[53]

While legal measures such as those used by the O'Briens were an option, Irish servants could easily take advantage of the general shortage of servants to demand better conditions with the real threat of leaving one household for another. Many cartoons and comic verses expressed anxiety and a pained awareness of the power that female servants could wield over mistresses who desperately needed their services. Perhaps the most striking of this type of cartoon was one drawn by Hop, entitled 'A domestic matter' (see page 182) and published in the *Bulletin* in 1883.[54] Hop had only arrived in Sydney a few months earlier, but having previously lived in New York City for many years, he would have been very familiar with Irish domestic servants.[55] In the cartoon a giant Bridget towers, like Gulliver, over a Lilliputian world. She has a heavy jaw, wide mouth and small nose, while her folded arms are very muscular; and with one enormous foot she holds down the squirming bodies of her master and mistress. Around this frightful figure appear a series of vignettes illustrating aspects of household life, all of which attest to Bridget's dictatorial control of the family. This is an Irish woman who almost matches the Fenian in terms of her ferocious presence and implied menace.

Many far less fierce Bridgets featured in other cartoons that nevertheless testified to their economic bargaining power. The title of a *Melbourne Punch* cartoon, 'Antipodean', reflected,

A DOMESTIC MATTER.

The vignettes surrounding this powerful female figure illustrate the anxieties felt by Australian middle-class families when confronted by demanding Irish domestic servants. With markedly racialised facial features and muscular arms, this Irish servant crushes her puny master and mistress beneath one gigantic foot.
Source: 'A domestic matter', *Bulletin*, 26 May 1883, p. 16.

not the Australian location of the scene, but a world turned upside down. It shows a plump, well-dressed Bridget seated in a comfortable chair as she interviews a potential mistress who stands meekly before her. Satisfied with the mistress's appearance and the wages that she is offering, Bridget then asks the woman for a reference from her previous servant. When this is not forthcoming, Bridget contemptuously dismisses her potential employer with: 'I couldn't think of accepting the appointment.'[56]

The popular stereotypes appearing in these cartoons underlined the widespread view that Irish domestic servants were troublesome on a number of levels, and it would be best if prudent housewives could avoid employing them. Specifically adding 'No Irish Need Apply' to employment ads was one way of doing that. However, these ads were used less frequently after the 1880s. One reason was that the cohort of young Irish-born immigrants of the 1840s, 1850s and 1860s were aging and were less likely to be seeking employment as domestic servants. Another reason for the decline in NINA ads was that the term's meaning was shifting because the Catholic Irish themselves were increasingly using it as shorthand to highlight anti-Irish discrimination. In this they were following their compatriots in Ireland, Britain and the US who, throughout the 1850s and 1860s, protested at the use of NINA in job ads and in music-hall acts.[57] Using NINA to refer to wider anti-Irish discrimination started early in the Australian colonies, with writers in Hobart in the 1840s employing the term when protesting at Irish exclusion from political power.[58] There are many examples of later uses of NINA to protest anti-Irish measures. A letter writer employed it when alleging that anti-Irish prejudice had meant that John O'Shanassy, the first Catholic Irish premier of Victoria, had been unable to hold together a stable government in April 1857.

According to this writer: '"No Irish need apply!" That cry, of which respectable Englishmen are now ashamed, has been revived in Australia – the new home of all nations.'[59] Catholic Irish political commentators used the phrase liberally when they wanted to call out what they saw as overt discrimination. In 1899, the Sydney *Catholic Press* reported a speech by Cardinal Moran in which he listed the numbers of Protestant men who held high office in the colony, as judges, senior public servants, members of parliament and editors of major newspapers, finishing with: 'We are heavily taxed, yet we are excluded from the Legislature and all the big State positions. We support public companies, and yet when there is a vacancy worth filling "No Irish need apply"'.[60] NINA was losing its usefulness by the 1880s: it had increasingly limited value in winnowing out undesirable employees and the Irish had converted it into an effective tool to protest against discriminatory employment and other practices.

'Protestant Preferred' in Australia

If 'No Irish Need Apply' or 'English Only' ads declined from the 1880s, the phrase 'Protestant Preferred' became more common and endured far longer. We found over 10 000 'hits' for 'Protestant Preferred' in the advertising sections of the Trove database of Australian newspapers published between 1840 and 1919. The widespread use of the phrase signals that Australian-born Catholic job-seekers continued to face the sort of discrimination that had confronted their Irish-immigrant parents when they were subjected to NINA ads.

In investigating 'Protestant Preferred' ads, we looked at all 56 newspapers that published more than five advertisements

Table 3: Consolidated metropolitan newspapers with 'Protestant Preferred' ads by 10-year intervals, 1840–1919[61]

CITY	1840-9	1850-9	1860-9	1870-9	1880-9	1890-9	1900-9	1910-9
Sydney	6	160	286	133	377	447	504	293
Brisbane			10	22	72	124	251	162
Melbourne		18	99	128	223	369	206	211
Adelaide				20	83	75	78	85
Perth					7	6	26	11
Hobart		2	5	1		3	8	1
Total	**6**	**180**	**400**	**304**	**762**	**1024**	**1073**	**763**

Table 4: Consolidated rural and regional newspapers with 'Protestant Preferred' ads by 10-year intervals, 1860–1919[62]

REGION	NO. OF NEWSPAPER TITLES	1860-9	1870-9	1880-9	1890-9	1900-9	1910-9
NSW regional	18[63]	3	12	48	31	37	84
Queensland regional	4[64]		5	23	1	6	36
Victoria regional	8[65]	14	28	5	32	17	22
Tasmania regional	2[66]		4	2	1	1	7
Total	**32**	**17**	**49**	**78**	**65**	**61**	**149**

using the words between 1840 and 1919. These included the metropolitan daily newspapers in each colony or state, as well as smaller regional and rural papers, some of which were only in operation for part of the period surveyed. It is likely that a number of non-employment ads are among this count, as included in the same columns were ads for 'matrimony', ads in which babies and small children were sought or offered for adoption, and also accommodation ads. Advertisements for board and lodging in single rooms that specified 'Protestant Preferred' became more common after the First World War.

As with the NINA ads, the use of the phrase 'Protestant Preferred' changed over time under the influence of political events. Irish-Australian sources, in commenting upon discriminatory employment practices, certainly believed that they tended to increase during periods of heightened political or religious tension.[67] The marked upswing in the use of the term in employment ads in Sydney during the 1870s coincided with a rise in anti-Irish feeling in the wake of the attempted assassination of Prince Alfred by an alleged Fenian in March 1868. Irish Australians certainly saw a direct link between the prevalence of these ads and general discrimination. 'Erigena' wrote to the Sydney *Freeman's Journal* in June 1868 stating that the 'consequence flowing from this horrible bigotry is that many Irish and Catholic laborers, mechanics and others are leaving the colony.' Protestant employers using these terms, he claimed, 'may at some future day find their stations thinned of servants, their now sleek horses ungroomed'.[68] Anti-Irish sentiment increased again in the Australian colonies in the early 1880s during violent Fenian campaigns in both Ireland and Britain. In Victoria especially, there was a marked rise in 'Protestant Preferred' advertising. Local events also probably contributed here, as the

Victorian premier from 1881 to 1883 was Sir Bryan O'Loghlen, an Irish Catholic with a history of supporting Irish nationalism and who, as we have seen in the previous chapter, was subjected to relentless anti-Irish caricaturing in the press.

Although 'Erigena' saw fears of Irish political violence as associated with male workers, more employers seemed to fear that their female Irish servants were contaminated with violent Irish politics. Bridget's loyalty was questioned in a number of cartoons,[69] but perhaps most vividly in 1885 when the NSW government controversially dispatched a small contingent to support Britain's disastrous Sudan invasion. *Melbourne Punch* mocked the fact that American Fenians had offered to fight the British on behalf of the charismatic Muslim leader, the Mahdi. In doing so, it reproduced an American cartoon commenting on Fenian fundraising among Irish servants, 'What they will soon be if they go' (see page 188).[70] The cartoon's Fenian character, in typical Irish peasant garb and grandly calling himself 'The O'Brien', confronts a broom-wielding Bridget on the doorstep. In response to his request, 'Faix, then, Bridget, me darlint, I've come for yer subscription to the cause', Bridget rebukes him: 'not another saxpince from me till there's more ixploshuns in London. It's nothing at all, at all, yez are after doing now.' The O'Brien attempts to reassure her, though his unwitting use of 'corpse' instead of 'corps' actually foreshadows disaster: 'Isn't it the *corpse* of a thousand min we're after sending from Chicago to help the Mahdi in Egypt, good luck to him.' Both figures are heavily physically caricatured, with prognathous jaws, receding foreheads, small noses and large ears. Bridget had rarely been simianised in Australian cartoons and by the mid 1880s the simianised Fenian was also going out of fashion, but it is clear that this type of caricature remained understood by Australian

WHAT THEY WILL SOON BE IF THEY GO.

The O'Brien (collecting).—" FAIX, THEN, BRIDGET, ME DARLINT, I'VE COME FOR YER SUBSCRIPTION TO THE CAUSE."

Bridget.—" LOOK HERE, NOW, JUDGE, NOT ANOTHER SAXPINCE FROM ME TILL THERE'S MORE IXPLOSHUNS IN LONDON. IT'S NOTHING AT ALL, AT ALL, YEZ ARE AFTHER DOING NOW."

The O'Brien.—AH ! SURE AND DON'T SAY THAT, ME ANGEL. ISN'T IT THE *corpse* OF A THOUSAND MIN WE'RE AFTHER SENDING FROM CHICAGO TO HELP THE MAHDI IN EGYPT, GOOD LUCK TO HIM."

Bridget's heavily caricatured facial features match those of the Fenian collecting funds to send Irish Americans to fight against the British in north Africa. This American cartoon, in portraying Bridget's preference for more bombing campaigns in England, highlights fears about the political allegiances of Irish domestic servants.

Source: 'What they will soon be if they go', *Melbourne Punch*, 5 March 1885, p. 100.

audiences.[71] And fear of Bridget as a funder of violent Irish nationalist causes was common to both countries.

Again, it is interesting to compare our Australian ad survey with MacRaild's results for the UK. He too found far more 'Protestant Only' ads than NINA ads, but not on the same scale as in Australia: he collected 1734 'Protestant Only' ads compared to 625 NINA ads.[72] He also suggested that the rise in the use of 'Protestant Only' after 1860 may have been intended as a less confrontational way of ensuring that the Catholic Irish did not breach the boundaries of middle-class Protestant homes. While this may have been the case in Britain, in Australia there was much greater use of 'Protestant Preferred' generally, as well as a marked rise in them from the 1880s onwards. In this instance, Australian employers appear to have been much more likely to attempt to discriminate against the Catholic Irish and their offspring than did employers in either Britain or the US. In contrast to these countries, however, Catholics were a much larger proportion of the population in Australia. Throughout the 19th and early 20th centuries, the proportion of Catholics of either Irish birth or descent hovered between 20 and 25 per cent. This sizable minority meant that Irish Catholics were more numerous and more visible in the working population than they were in Britain or the US.

'Catholic Preferred' in Australia

While many Catholic Irish Australians were working class and sought employment as servants or labourers, there were also Catholic Irish households that employed servants. This mirrored practices in 19th-century Ireland, where it was not only

middle-class families but upper working-class and successful
farming families who employed domestic servants. In smaller
Irish farming households, the single servant was often a young
girl of a similar class background who worked temporarily
in service prior to her own marriage.[73] This meant that many
women who employed servants had themselves worked earlier
in service. There is evidence of similar patterns among Irish-
headed households in the Australian colonies from the mid
19th century into the first half of the 20th century.[74] One such
household was that of Honora Jenkins, who had emigrated from
Limerick and who, in the 1860s, employed a 13-year-old nurse to
help her with her children and in running a busy hotel in the
small township of Glenorchy in western Victoria. Honora had
previously worked in the same household as a servant herself
and had married her employer after the death of his wife. As well
as the young girl, Honora also employed another Catholic Irish
woman as a housekeeper.[75] The roles of servant and mistress in
such households were thus differentiated by age and marital
status, rather than by class. There were other differentials of class
and race within these households, though, as Irish-Australian
women were as likely as other white women to employ Aboriginal
women as domestic servants.[76] Mary O'Brien employed 'native
girls' to help in her Queensland household, while she herself
had worked as domestic help in the household of a pastoralist
family when she first arrived in the Rockhampton district as a
newlywed immigrant.[77]

Some of these Irish mistresses sought out Catholic servants,
by specifying 'Catholic Preferred' when they advertised for staff.
In Melbourne, they could also use the services of domestic servant
agencies run specifically for Catholic households and employees,
such as the domestic training school attached to the Convent

Table 5: 'Catholic Preferred' in classified ads in Metropolitan newspapers, 1850–1919

NEWSPAPER	1850–9	1860–9	1870–9	1880–9	1890–9	1900–9	1910–9	TOTAL
Sydney Morning Herald	14	15	23	43	32	13	43	183
Age (Melbourne)	1	7	16	162	249	199	67	701
Argus (Melbourne)	14	42	44	26	24	29	57	236
Advertiser (Adelaide)				3	39	64	67	173
Express and Telegraph (Adelaide)			4	35	82	62	93	276
Telegraph (Brisbane)	14	42	44	26	24	29	57	236
West Australian (Perth)					31	24	15	70
Total	**43**	**106**	**131**	**295**	**481**	**420**	**399**	**1875**

of Mercy in Fitzroy in the 1880s.[78] We also analysed 'Catholic Preferred' ads in the same range of Australian newspapers as before and found that most were for governesses, servants and, increasingly towards the end of our survey period, they were also for accommodation.

A sample of the classified ads in Table 5 shows that the majority of these ads were for female domestic servants and governesses. A family from Geelong, for example, advertised in the *Age* in 1870 for a nursery governess: 'Wanted, a well-educated, middle aged, Roman Catholic nursery governess, must teach music and sewing.'[79] Some of these ads were for staff to work in hotels which probably had an Irish clientele. In Adelaide in 1877, Mr Morcom's Temperance Hotel in Hindley Street advertised for two female servants, 'Irish Catholics Preferred'.[80] Some of the classified ads were for situations wanted, as Catholic Irish servants sought positions and stated a preference for a Catholic employer. Thus in the Perth *West Australian* in 1895, a Miss O'Keefe advertised: 'Housekeeper and Housemaid wishes situation in the country, Catholic preferred, good references, experienced.'[81] Analysis of the 18 ads using 'Catholic Preferred' in the Melbourne *Age* in 1890 and of 23 ads in 1899 reveals that all the employment ads specifying 'Catholic Only' were for female domestic servants. There were nine such ads in 1880 and a further 19 in 1889. In those sample years, there were also a small number (five) of accommodation ads, two ads for adoptive parents to care for Catholic babies and two seeking Catholic marriage partners. By the early decades of the 20th century, most of the classified ads that used 'Catholic Preferred' were for accommodation either wanted or offered. An ad in the Adelaide *Express and Telegraph* in 1910, for example, read: 'Board wanted by Young Man, Norwood, Catholic family preferred.'[82]

Concentrating our attention on 'No Irish Need Apply', 'English Only' or 'Protestant Preferred' employment ads is not to suggest that the majority of employment advertisements in Australia made distinctions on the basis of Irishness, Englishness or religion. They did not, and there were many days, weeks and even months when the dedicated job-hunter in the major cities would not have seen one. However, at other times and in some newspapers there were many. On 12 January 1865, the Melbourne *Argus*, which often published conservative and anti-Irish commentary, ran a total of 14 advertisements for male servants, grooms or messenger boys and 67 for female servants, cooks, nursery girls or washwomen. Nine (13 per cent) of the latter specified that they wanted either English or Protestant female servants.[83] Bridget, if she was looking for work on that day, would know she had to be careful to avoid being turned away before she even had a chance to speak to a prospective employer.

'No Irish Need Apply' advertisements were expressions of stereotyped and gendered anti-Irish attitudes. Such prejudices were reinforced by caricatures in the popular press appearing in cartoons, jokes and anecdotes emphasising Irish servants' racial and religious 'otherness' when compared with idealised English servants. Irish-Australian political commentators and newspaper letter writers used the catchcry 'No Irish Need Apply' to refer to the exclusion of Catholics from the masculine world of politics, business and public affairs. This use, along with demographic changes, contributed to a shift in advertising practices. With NINA now more associated with complaints about discrimination by increasingly vocal Catholic Irish-Australian men, its use in job ads declined and it was replaced by other terms, such as 'Protestant Preferred'. The fact remained, though, that throughout the 19th century and the early years of the 20th century, a minority of employers actively sought to avoid hiring Irish or Irish-Australian Catholics, especially for work within their own homes.

CHAPTER 7

Crime and the Irish: from vagrancy to the gallows

Irish men figure only fleetingly in many general works of Australian history, but when they do appear it is usually as participants in a series of well-known violent events. They are prominent in all accounts of the 1804 convict rebellion at Castle Hill near Sydney; in most histories of the 1854 miners' revolt at the Eureka Stockade in Ballarat; and in books dealing with bushranging, especially the 1878–80 Kelly outbreak in north-east Victoria. Even in terms of religious history, which defines the Irish as Catholics, sectarianism is normally highlighted, with violent words, if not deeds, to the fore.[1]

Irish men emerge from this body of work as a thoroughly belligerent lot: very willing, when thwarted, to take the law into their own hands. Left-wing Australian historians have tended to romanticise the Irish as perennial rebels, always ready to defy authority and resist oppression, and major contributors to an enduring dissident tradition.[2] Manning Clark sought to explain – perhaps even to excuse – Irish violence. Yet he only succeeded in reinforcing the Irish reputation for lawlessness. According to him, the Irish, 'believing there was no justice for a Catholic in a court presided over by Protestants', concluded that any means was 'permissible' to 'outwit [their] traditional enemy', including 'lying, informing, treachery, arson, theft, outrage and even murder'.[3] In 1988, in a wide-ranging study of the Irish diaspora, historian DH Akenson, after looking at such accounts felt compelled to deplore what he called '[this] misleading, contumacious image of the Australian Irish' as a 'mélange of people from prison ships, of Irish rebels, of Ned Kelly, and of wild colonial boys' – although he excepted from his critique Patrick O'Farrell's recently published history of the Irish in Australia.[4]

More conservative commentators, by contrast, have tended to downplay the violence of the colonial past and to portray events such as those of 1804, 1854 and 1878–80 as not truly representative of Australia's mainstream 'British' settler history, thus rendering the Irish atypical and marginal. In 2014, historian John Hirst conceded that the Irish had been 'prominent' in the outbreaks of 1804 and 1854, but, according to him, these were isolated events. Moreover, he argued that the role of the Irish in creating 'Australian anti-authoritarianism' had been exaggerated by the likes of Russel Ward and Patrick O'Farrell. Being 'more communal and tribal' and 'less interested in independence', the Irish, although given to outbursts of political violence, were actually 'pleased to find a patron who would protect them: "God bless you, your honour"'. It would appear that, in Hirst's flippant analysis, what the violent, 'tribal' Irish basically craved was strong – in other words, British – leadership.[5] But, in truth, neither of these approaches is particularly accurate or very helpful. Both types of historian simplify in prosecuting their respective agendas, wilfully ignoring the fact that, for one thing, in all these violent incidents there were Irish on both sides. The Irish convicts and miners killed in 1804 and 1854 were in some instances shot down by Irish soldiers, while the Kelly gang was pursued by numerous Irish policemen, three of whom Ned Kelly killed. Even many bitter sectarian debates and clashes saw Irish Protestants pitted against Irish Catholics. The Irish role in Australian outbreaks of violence is far more multifaceted than is usually represented.

Yet there is no doubt that the British, whether in Britain or in Australia, believed that the Irish were more prone than they themselves to disloyalty, political unrest and also to violent crime.[6] O'Farrell too accepted the widely held belief that, probably more than most other nations, the Irish were addicted to violence. Although he mocked apologists who claimed that Irish convicts transported to Australia were not really criminals at all, but 'exiles' or 'martyrs', the innocent victims of English political and religious persecution, O'Farrell also pointed out that, among free immigrants, there was 'considerable Irish overrepresentation in the statistics for crime, drunkenness and insanity'. This he interpreted as a 'legacy' of the 'frantic, troubled countryside' from which most had come.[7] But was O'Farrell right: is this widely accepted portrayal of the Irish as a characteristically violent people, whether in Ireland or Australia, correct? In seeking answers to this question, we will first consider recent studies of historic crime rates in Ireland and then examine rates in the Australian colonies. In addition to petty crime, we will also investigate capital crime and why numbers of Irish-born men ended up on the gallows. Case studies will allow us to see to what extent popular stereotypes of the Irish as violent and lawless affected the way in which they were treated by the Australian criminal justice system.

Irish crime in Ireland and England

In recent years, historians of crime in 19th-century Ireland have called into question representations of the country as exceptionally violent. Richard McMahon, in a detailed study of homicide during the 1830s and 1840s, demonstrated that if infanticide is removed from the figures, then homicide rates in Ireland were 'broadly similar' to those prevailing in England and Wales at the time.[8] Studies by Ian O'Donnell have shown that after 1850 Irish homicide rates fluctuated somewhat, but declined steeply from the 1890s, reaching a record low during the 1950s and early 1960s – an era described by one Irish historian as 'a policeman's paradise' – before a sustained increase set in.[9] The incidence of violent crime in 20th-century Ireland followed a pattern similar to many other countries, including Britain, large parts of Europe, and Australia. McMahon went on to suggest that there was a 'certain political utility' to be gained during the 19th century from portraying Ireland as unusually violent. On the one hand, for Irish and British unionists, violence in Ireland offered a powerful justification for Westminster rule to continue; conversely, Irish nationalists used outbreaks of violence and crime to argue that the country was being seriously misgoverned by the British.[10] In other words, the issue of crime was highly politicised in Ireland; and in colonial Australia too allegations of Irish lawlessness proved useful to groups promoting a variety of different agendas.

In many parts of the Irish diaspora, 19th-century contemporaries were convinced of a strong link between the Irish and crime. Yet, as crime historian Roger Swift has pointed out for England, the extent of Irish criminality remains unclear and explanations are largely tentative, since the statistical analysis carried out so far has been selective and simplistic.[11] As in the Australian colonies, many of the English policemen arresting Irish immigrants and their offspring were themselves Irish immigrants or the sons of immigrants, although this topic too is under-researched.[12] Swift and others have identified certain characteristics that bear marked similarities to the Irish experience of crime in Australia. Crimes committed by Irish immigrants in England were 'overwhelmingly concentrated in less-serious or petty categories rather than serious, particularly violent, crime'. Irish offences fell mainly into the 'interrelated categories of drunkenness, disorderly behaviour, assault (including assaults on police) and, to a lesser extent, petty theft and vagrancy'. Drunken brawling by Irish labourers, prostitution by Irish women, and petty theft or gang-related violence by Irish youngsters – these were the crimes particularly associated with the Irish in England.[13] It was often for vagrancy, though, that the Irish were arrested and imprisoned. Irish navvies and rural labourers, migrating annually in search of seasonal work in Britain, as well as Famine refugees of the 1840s and 1850s, were especially vulnerable to the *Vagrancy Act 1824*, which had been passed in England partly in response to fears about growing Irish immigration.[14] It was a flexible act, providing police and magistrates with wide discretionary powers aimed essentially against the homeless, the unemployed, beggars and prostitutes: in other words, against the mobile poor. The Australian colonies were quick to appreciate the advantages of such a useful Act, many of them passing similar legislation from the 1840s onwards. In England and Wales perhaps around 40 per cent of those arrested for vagrancy during the 1850s were Irish; and, moreover, some of the Irish convicted under the act were transported to Australia.[15]

Irish men were associated in urban England – and in Australia too – with brawling, mainly on weekends. After being paid on a Saturday afternoon or evening, it was not uncommon for labourers and tradesmen to embark upon bouts of binge drinking. For many of the English working class, it was not so much that they disapproved of the Irish fighting, it was how the Irish fought that showed them to be uncivilised and unmanly. A London rubbish carter summed up the situation for the journalist and social researcher Henry Mayhew when he said: 'why, the Irishes don't stand up to you like men. They don't fight like Christians, sir; not a bit of it. They kick and scratch, and bite and tear, like devils, or cats or women.'[16] As for Irish women, the question of whether so many of them were arrested under the vagrancy Act because they were prostitutes was hotly debated at the time – as it was in Australia. Most Irish-born Catholic clergy working in England flatly denied the allegation, insisting that Irish women were renowned for their chastity.[17] But a study of Liverpool, based on the report of a Catholic prison chaplain, has suggested that in the early 1860s around 60 per cent of prostitutes serving prison sentences in the port city were Irish-born, while a broader study of Lancashire towns found Irish women 'disproportionately involved in prostitution during the mid-nineteenth century'.[18] In colonial Australia, like England, the Irish were to feature in debates about crime especially as vagrants, prostitutes, drunkards and juvenile delinquents.

Irish crime in colonial Australia: Victoria

DH Akenson, in an influential 1993 survey history of the Irish diaspora, noted that crime was a 'theme' that ran 'throughout the literature' devoted to Irish migration. There was widespread agreement, he wrote, that the Irish were 'disproportionately represented in criminal statistics' through the 19th and 20th centuries. In support of this claim, Akenson cited New South Wales (NSW) figures from the 1860s and 1880s.[19] O'Farrell, as noted, was also convinced that Irish immigrants were 'overrepresented' amongst those convicted of crime in Australia, citing contemporary official statistics for Victoria as well as NSW.[20] But the way in which Akenson, O'Farrell and many 19th-century commentators presented and interpreted these figures was faulty, because they do not in fact prove that the Irish were 'overrepresented' amongst criminals, especially violent criminals.

One of the most outspoken critics of the Irish in late 19th-century Australia was, as we have already seen, the English-born businessman, AM Topp, who for nearly 30 years worked as a leader-writer on Melbourne's conservative *Argus* newspaper.[21] In the second of two articles attacking the Irish, published in the *Melbourne Review* in 1881, Topp drew attention to violence and crime, providing recent Victorian statistics in support of his argument that the Irish were vastly overrepresented amongst the colony's criminals. Topp's figures are set out in Tables 1 and 2 opposite.

These statistics had originally been compiled and published by the Victorian government statistician, English-born HH Hayter; and they included figures that O'Farrell himself would later use. Topp confidently informed his readers that data on executions and arrests confirmed the well-known fact that the 'Catholic Irish ... contributed ... a large proportion of our criminal class'. During the period 1865–79, the Irish-born and Catholics formed the largest ethnic and religious cohorts amongst those executed

Table 1: Executions in Victoria by birthplace and religion, 1865–79[22]

BIRTHPLACE	NUMBER (PERCENTAGE)	RELIGION	NUMBER (PERCENTAGE)
Ireland	18 (41.7)	Catholic	22 (51.2)
England	10 (23.3)	Anglican	13 (30.2)
China	4 (9.3)	Wesleyan	3 (7.0)
Scotland	2 (4.7)	Pagan	3 (7.0)
Australia (not VIC.)	2 (4.7)	Presbyterian	2 (4.6)
Other	7 (16.3)		
Total	43 (100)	Total	43 (100)

Table 2: Arrests in Victoria by birthplace and religion, 1879[23]

BIRTHPLACE	NUMBER	PER 1000 OF ETHNIC POPULATION	RELIGION	NUMBER	PER 1000 OF RELIGIOUS POPULATION
Ireland	7754	80.30	Protestant	13 331	20.76
England & Wales	6653	26.72	Catholic	10 813	51.05
Victoria	5450	11.18			
Scotland	2166	40.23			

in Victoria, while in the year 1879, they were the largest groups amongst those arrested by the police. Topp went on to warn, 'how deeply implanted even in the more educated' of the Irish 'is the tendency to resort to personal violence instead of calling in the aid of the law or of public opinion'. For Topp, physical violence was a defining facet of the racial character of the Celtic Irish: 'their tendency to acts of violence' being 'an obvious characteristic of an imperfectly civilized race ... one that has never been taught to respect the law, but only to yield to brute force'.[24] To test Topp's racial analysis, we need to take a closer look at his Victorian data and then at statistics for NSW and Queensland as well.

Topp's article offers a very good example in fact of how crime figures can be manipulated and distorted to apparently prove what is actually a fallacious argument. In the tables on page 201, Topp did accurately reproduce statistics from Hayter's 1879–80 *Victorian Year Book*. However, he selected only certain figures, overlooking others that were equally relevant but that did not support his anti-Irish case. He also selectively quoted from Hayter's commentary on the figures, reproducing for instance Hayter's remark that, in 'proportion to their numbers in the community, Roman Catholics supplied more than twice as many arrested persons as the Protestants'.[25] But Topp ignored other aspects of Hayter's analysis that presented the Irish and Catholics in a far less damning light.

Statistics for executions and arrests made the Irish appear especially addicted to violent crime. This is of course why Topp employed them selectively to support his theory about the innately lawless and uncivilised character of the Celtic Irish race. But Hayter had actually pointed out that most Irish and Catholic arrests were for non-violent offences against public order, often involving drunkenness, not for violent crimes against the person. By the 1880s, Victoria had at least 15 major public order offences, which criminalised many aspects of traditional working-class culture and leisure.[26] Offences against public order consisted chiefly of drunkenness, but also included riotous or offensive behaviour, abusive language, having no visible means of support, begging, cruelty to animals and illegal gambling – and lunacy. As in England, the police used vagrancy legislation to clear the streets of unwanted characters, such as drunks, beggars, prostitutes, the homeless, hawkers and often the poor and indigent generally.

Hayter's figures show that, in 1879, of Catholics arrested in Victoria, fully 71 per cent were taken into police custody for public order or minor property offences, including 46 per cent for drunkenness. And this pattern of Catholic crime was not so very different from that for Protestants, because 68 per cent of them were also arrested for non-violent or minor offences, including 44 per cent for drunkenness.[27]

Hayter, alongside data on arrests, also provided information on the fates of those arrested. Of the Irish arrested, few were committed to stand trial before a criminal court charged with a serious offence; the majority appeared in magistrates' courts and were either released, fined or imprisoned for relatively short periods of time. And even committal did not necessarily mean conviction, for in 1879 a little over one-third (37 per cent) of those committed by magistrates to a higher court were either not ultimately prosecuted or, if tried, they were acquitted. In comparing arrests and committals for trial, Hayter remarked that Irish offences were 'not ... as a whole ... [of] so serious a nature as those ... [for] which the English were arrested'. This was very evident in the fact that, although in 1879 more Irish (7754) than English and Welsh immigrants (6653) were arrested, in percentage terms, twice as many of the English and Welsh (183 or 2.8 per cent) were committed to stand trial than were the Irish (108 or 1.4 per cent).[28]

On the following page is a table compiled by Hayter, which includes both arrest and committal rates for 1879. It reveals that, while the Irish made up 31.5 per cent of those arrested, they formed only 17.2 per cent of those committed to stand trial for a serious offence. Topp reproduced the arrest column of this table – see Table 2 on page 201 – ignoring committals because they did not support his argument that the Irish were far more prone to violent crime than were the English.

Table 3: Arrests and committals to trial in Victoria by birthplace and religion, 1879[29]

BIRTHPLACE	ARRESTS PER 1000 OF ETHNIC POPULATION	COMMITTALS PER 1000 OF ETHNIC POPULATION
Victoria	11.18	3.70
Other Australian colonies	26.72	10.61
England & Wales	40.23	11.06
Scotland	39.91	5.34
Ireland	80.30	11.18
China	12.64	4.51
Other	—	—
Total	27.72	7.07
RELIGION	Arrests per 1000 of religious population	Committals per 1000 of religious population
Protestants	20.76	5.67
Catholics	51.05	11.09
Jews	14.90	11.29
Pagans	10.10	3.67
Other	—	—

Another significant point Hayter made, and which Topp also ignored, was that serious and violent offences were declining sharply in Victoria during the 1870s. Committals to trial fell by 25.4 per cent between 1869 and 1879. Male arrests also fell slightly overall (by 3.3 per cent), although female arrests rose (by 10.5 per cent). But this latter figure reflected the continuing, and indeed growing, prominence of public order offences that targeted female prostitution.

Hayter was also keen to draw attention to the important point that the age profiles of different populations could have a dramatic impact on per capita rates of offending. This explained, in large part, why those born in Victoria appeared to have much lower crime rates than did those born overseas, or even those born elsewhere in the Australian colonies. Most crime was committed by adults. In 1879, 68 per cent of those arrested in Victoria were aged between 20 and 50, yet the Victorian-born population was a youthful one, with nearly one half being under 15 years of age. This demographic structure inevitably produced lower per capita crime rates amongst the locally born, but higher rates amongst immigrant populations, which, like the Irish, were overwhelmingly composed of adults. However, as the young Victorian-born population aged, so crime amongst them quickly increased. Hayter gave figures showing that arrests of people born in Victoria had jumped a huge 157 per cent in just the eight years from 1871 to 1879.[30]

The pattern of crime in Victoria over a longer period of time is revealed in the table below. As is apparent, public order offences, especially drunkenness, consistently formed the bulk of arrests, and their proportion increased significantly between the 1870s and 1910s, whereas other types of crime, especially violent crime, declined. By 1911, fully two-thirds of all arrests by police in Victoria were for drunkenness, with arrest rates for Catholics and Protestants being similar.[31]

Hayter wrote in 1885–86 that drunkenness and other breaches of public order, along with some property offences like trespass, could be 'considered as, comparatively speaking, minor offences, hardly amounting to crimes' at all. Noting that in 1885 arrests for such offences made up around 90 per cent of total arrests, he concluded that only about 10 per cent of arrests in the colony 'were for crimes in the strict sense of the word'.[33]

In terms of female Irish offenders, historian Sharon Morgan

Table 4: Types of charges against persons arrested in Victoria by percentage, 1871, 1891, 1911[32]

TYPES OF CHARGES	1871 PERCENTAGE	1891 PERCENTAGE	1911 PERCENTAGE
Crimes against the person	6.2	4.8	3.4
Crimes against property	18.1	12.5	9.8
Crimes against public order (drunkenness figures in brackets)	69.2 (46.4)	79.6 (52.9)	83.8 (65.3)
Other (perjury, desertion, etc)	6.5	3.1	3.0
Total	100	100	100

pointed out in a 1989 study that Irish women were the largest single female ethnic group in Victoria's gaols during the 1850s.[34] In 1857, for example, Irish-born women formed 43 per cent of the colony's female prison population; 66 per cent of these women had been convicted of public order offences under the colony's 1852 vagrancy Act; 90 per cent were Catholic; 59 per cent were illiterate in English; and 45 per cent were former convicts.[35] Clearly, many Irish ex-convicts filled the colony's gaols during the gold-rush decade. As for the free young Irish women who arrived on government-assisted passages, like the Famine orphan scheme of 1848–50, they were often greeted with intense suspicion by male colonists. We saw in the previous chapter the hostility that 'Bridget', the stereotypical Irish servant, faced. Given the prevalence of 'No Irish Need Apply' ads in Melbourne during the 1850s, it must have been difficult at times to find employment. Yet most female Irish immigrants did get jobs and later started families, although a minority certainly fell into vagrancy, public drunkenness and prostitution.[36] A March 1850 official survey of 621 Famine orphans sent to Adelaide in 1848–49 found that

7 per cent had become 'common prostitutes', but it also found that nearly 70 per cent were working as domestic servants and a further 16 per cent had already married.[37] But more research, like Morgan's study, is needed on other colonies and other decades before we have an accurate picture of Irish women's experience of the courts and gaols of mid and late 19th-century Australia.[38]

What emerges from these Victorian statistics is not a 'race' of uncivilised Irish brutes addicted to violent crime, as imagined by AM Topp and others, but rather a significant number of Irish men and women who by their behaviour in public places managed to attract the attention of vigilant constables and were then arrested for public order offences that even the colony's official statistician admitted were not crimes 'in the strict sense of the word'.

Irish crime in colonial Australia: NSW and Queensland

There were similar patterns of offending in NSW and Queensland. By 1894, for example, offences against public order in NSW accounted for 72.3 per cent of all arrests, with drunkenness alone accounting for 47.6 per cent.[39] Women figured particularly prominently in arrests for drunkenness. In NSW in 1894, only 7.2 per cent of offences against the person were committed by women, but 18.5 per cent of those arrested for drunkenness were women. In fact, of total female arrests, a majority (55.6 per cent) were for drunkenness, whereas, amongst men, drunkenness made up 46.1 per cent of all arrests. Therefore, roughly half of all offending involved drunkenness, with the police exercising their considerable powers of discretion under the vagrancy statutes and showing a marked inclination to arrest women they suspected of being drunk in public. It is likely of course that the police thought many of these women were prostitutes, but it was easier to arrest them for drunkenness.[40]

As the table below shows, arrests of Irish immigrants and Catholics in NSW in 1894 were in line with the general colonial pattern: that is, the majority – 84 per cent of Irish arrests and 75.5 per cent of Catholic arrests – were for public order offences.

Table 5: Types of charges against the Irish-born and Catholics arrested in NSW by percentage, 1894[41]

TYPES OF CHARGES	IRISH-BORN PERCENTAGE	CATHOLIC PERCENTAGE
Crimes against the person	4.4	6.9
Crimes against property	7.9	12.9
Crimes against public order	84.0	75.5
Forgery	0.2	0.3
Other	3.5	4.4
Total	100	100

TA Coghlan, the NSW government statistician who compiled these statistics, was the son of Irish immigrant parents and, perhaps for this reason, he was particularly careful in how he handled Irish and Catholic crime figures.[42] In discussing the religion of offenders, he took pains to point out that the 'religious profession' entered by police on charge-sheets should be considered in many cases merely 'nominal'. Because an offender was Irish-born or had Catholic parents did not necessarily make him or her automatically a Catholic.[43] But, in looking at the apparently 'large excess of Roman Catholic offenders' who made up 45.4 per cent of those arrested, even though Catholics were only 25.5 per cent of the total NSW population, Coghlan speculated in 1896 that this situation, which had 'obtained for many years', had 'in all probability been due to the lower social condition of the members of the Roman Catholic community'.[44] In other words, Coghlan believed there was a link between poverty and arrests for crime, although, unfortunately, he did not spell out what this link consisted of exactly.

Coghlan went further than Hayter by seeking to compare crime rates with the adult male population rather than the whole male population. He also analysed committals to stand trial, rather than arrests, because increasingly police were summonsing people rather than arresting them, while large numbers of those arrested were either never prosecuted or were acquitted. Committals, Coghlan believed, were a more accurate indicator of levels of crime than arrests. Below are comparative figures he published for NSW adult male per capita committal rates in 1894, according to place of birth.

Table 6: Males committed to stand trial in NSW by birthplace per 1000 adult males, 1894[45]

BIRTHPLACE	COMMITTALS PER 1000 ADULT MALES	BIRTHPLACE	COMMITTALS PER 1000 ADULT MALES
Queensland	67	Ireland	25
United States	63	New South Wales	23
New Zealand	44	Scotland	21
Sweden/Norway	40	South Australia	19
France	30	England	18
Tasmania	28	Germany	16
Victoria	27	China	10
Denmark	26		

It is obvious from the figures in Table 6 that in NSW during the early 1890s Irish-born men did not have a higher rate of criminal offending than adult males from other ethnic or racial backgrounds. Coghlan's findings have been confirmed by later local studies, such as migration and crime scholar RD Francis's analysis of prisoners held in Wollongong gaol during 1901. He discovered that of 121 prisoners, 15 per cent were Irish-born. They included 16 men and two women, with 75 per cent of them having been convicted of public-order offences. Using adult populations as the basis for his calculations, Francis found that the Irish rate of imprisonment ranked fifth from the top among the eight groups in his sample, behind those born in Europe, New Zealand, the United States and Scotland.[46] As the work of Coghlan and Francis on NSW clearly demonstrates, when committal, conviction or imprisonment – rather than arrest – rates are calculated on the basis of the adult population, then it is apparent that Irish rates of offending were far from disproportionate or excessive.

Police historian Mark Finnane's study of the Irish and crime, focusing largely on Queensland, revealed a pattern of Irish offending in that colony similar to that evident in both Victoria and NSW. He found crimes against public order were the offences for which the Irish were most commonly arrested and prosecuted. But the same was true for other immigrant groups, including the English and the Scots. Like Victoria, among the various public order offences, the Irish were most frequently charged with drunkenness. Finnane, however, pursued the matter further by examining court cases, seeking to discover what proportion of Irish defendants were convicted and what penalties they suffered. Research in other parts of the Irish diaspora had suggested that prejudice against the Irish might have affected the decisions of courts.[47] Finnane sampled court records between 1871 and 1911 in four towns: Dalby, Bundaberg, Charters Towers and Brisbane. His conclusion was that 'no great disparity' existed between the conviction rates for the Irish and for other ethnic groups; nor was sentencing of the Irish much different either. Across all groups, 50 to 66 per cent of charges heard did not result in any sentence and in only about 10 per cent of cases was a sentence of more than one month's imprisonment imposed.[48] This dearth of significant penalties underlines the unreliability of arrest statistics as a measure of genuine crime and suggests that the police took public order offences, like drunkenness, far more seriously than did local courts.

How many Irish men were executed?

The Irish were therefore no more likely to be convicted of serious crimes than other groups – indeed, in some instances they were less likely – yet much was made during the late 19th century of supposed links between the Irish and violence. In his 1881 article, Topp not only quoted figures for Irish and Catholic arrests, but also for executions. And, once again, his data though largely accurate is at the same time misleading. In the period 1865–79, there were 43 executions in Victoria and, according to Topp, 18 of those executed were Irish (41.8 per cent), while 22 were Catholic (51.2 per cent). Topp assumed that all the Irish-born executed were Catholics and that the Catholics executed, who were not Irish-born, were the offspring of Irish immigrants. But this was not in fact the case: only 15 of the 43 executed (34.9 per cent) in 1865–79 were Catholic Irish-born immigrants, three of the Irish-born were Protestants and of the 22 Catholics, seven were not from Ireland.[49] Still, one-third does seem a substantial figure.

Yet, by arbitrarily selecting figures for just a 14-year period, Topp significantly inflated the proportion of the Catholic Irish amongst those executed in colonial Victoria. Executions began in what was then the Port Phillip District of NSW in 1842, with the first Irish immigrant being hanged in that year, while the last execution of an Irish-born man in Victoria took place in 1891. For a more accurate indication of the proportion of the Catholic Irish amongst those executed, we need to focus on the half century 1842–91, during which time a total of 152 people – including one woman – were hanged. Table 7 opposite, which summarises these statistics as they appeared in the 1892 *Victorian Year Book*, demonstrates that, of those executed up to 1891, around 90 per cent were born overseas. This figure would suggest that the Irish formed part of a bigger picture of immigrant overrepresentation among those hanged. Only adults were executed and immigrant ethnic groups, as already noted, contained far more adults than did the Victorian-born population. This marked demographic difference renders comparisons across foreign- and native-born groups and between ethnic groups and the general population highly dubious exercises.

As we saw with Topp's 1865–79 figures, not all the Irish executed were Catholics and not all the Catholics executed were of Irish birth or descent. If we remove the Protestants from the Irish-born group listed in Table 7, we get a figure of 24.3 per cent for the proportion of those executed during 1842–91 who were both Irish-born and at least nominally Catholic: that is around one-quarter, which is not hugely out of line with the number of the Irish in the general Victorian population. But, in order to better understand why these nearly 40 Irish male immigrants were hanged, we need to examine individual cases and particular circumstances.

Table 7: Executions in Victoria by percentages of birthplace and religion, 1842–91[50]

BIRTHPLACE	PERCENTAGE
England & Wales	41.4
Ireland	27.6
Australia	9.9
Scotland	5.3
China	5.3
United States	3.3
West Indies	1.3
Other	5.9
RELIGION	PERCENTAGE
Protestant	55.9
Catholic	36.2
Buddhist, Confucian, etc.	4.6
Other (Aboriginal people)	3.3

Firstly, though, it is important to bear in mind that the majority of those convicted of capital crimes by juries and sentenced to death by judges were not ultimately executed. Capital punishment was a highly selective business.[51] One study of the history of executions in Victoria concluded that capital punishment amounted to 'death by lottery'.[52] During 1842–91, for example, only one woman was executed. Yet between 1860 and 1887, at least 11 women, six of whom were Irish immigrants, were sentenced to death. Three of the Irish women had been convicted of murder – one in 1871 of her brothel-keeper, one in 1884 of her husband and one in 1887 of her sister – while the other three had been convicted of infanticide. Yet all were reprieved.[53] There was an obvious reluctance on the part of successive colonial governments to execute women: one historian has termed this a policy of 'arbitrary chivalry'.[54] The only woman executed before the early 1890s was 23-year-old English immigrant Elizabeth Scott, who in 1863 was implicated when her alcoholic husband was murdered by her young lover and another man. It was widespread public disapproval of this reputed affair that helped send Scott to the gallows, whereas many other women who had actually committed murder were and continued to be reprieved.[55] The Scott case provides a salutary reminder of just how arbitrary a punishment execution was. Gender could obviously play a determining role in whether it was carried out or not, but could race, ethnicity and religion as well?[56]

The *Argus* journalist JS James, who wrote under the pen-name 'The Vagabond', certainly thought that they could. In 1877, in a series of articles about life in Melbourne's Pentridge penitentiary, he claimed that prisoners with the right political connections were able both to escape the noose and to secure remission of their sentences. He mentioned by name John O'Shanassy, the Catholic Irish-born former premier of the colony, as one politician who, when in power, had used his influence to save convicted Irish murderers from the gallows.[57] Critics of Irish politicians, such as AM Topp and the *Argus*, routinely accused them of corruption and nepotism; above all else, the 'tribal' Catholic Irish were allegedly bent upon protecting and furthering the interests of members of their own race and religion. But whether James's allegations against O'Shanassy were true or not remains something of a moot point for, during O'Shanassy's three premierships in the late 1850s and early 1860s, at least seven Irish men were executed in Victoria. So, even if O'Shanassy saved some, he did not save them all.[58]

Irish men on the scaffold, 1842–91

Who were these Irish men and what were the crimes for which they went to the gallows? Most were executed for murder while three were hanged for shooting with intent, two for rape, one for sodomy and one for robbery.[59] Whereas the United Kingdom had drastically reduced the number of its capital crimes so that by 1861 there were only four, the Australian colonies had shown a greater inclination to maintain a 'bloody code'. A major criminal law Act passed in Victoria in 1864 retained hanging as a punishment for certain forms of the following crimes: attempted murder, rape, carnal knowledge, sodomy, robbery, burglary and arson – as well as for murder and treason. Indeed, a statistical analysis of the use of the death penalty in Victoria found that defendants convicted of robbery or burglary with wounding were more likely to be executed than those convicted of actual murder.[60]

The first Irish man to be hanged in Melbourne, in June 1842, was bushranger Martin Fogarty, one of three members of a gang convicted of shooting with intent to murder.[61] All three were sentenced to death and executed. Driven through the streets of Melbourne in an open cart, seated on their coffins, they were publicly hanged before an 'immense' crowd near Swanston Street, where two Indigenous men had been executed earlier in the same year.[62] Two of the three died quickly, whereas Fogarty was slowly strangled by the noose. According to a later report, he had cried on the scaffold, but was quick to explain that he did not cry out of 'fear', rather it was for 'his friends at home'.[63]

William Armstrong, one of at least five Irish Protestants executed during 1842–91, was another man hanged for shooting with intent. During the 1858 holdup of a group of travellers carrying a large amount of gold, one man was killed and two were wounded. Armstrong and his accomplice, Chamberlain, were first tried for murder, but after a jury acquitted them, they were put on trial again, this time for shooting with intent to murder. The evidence against them was largely circumstantial. One of the crown's two main witnesses was an Irish miner named James McMahon. Dr Sewell, the barrister defending Armstrong and Chamberlain, made clear his opinion of this witness when he referred to him as the 'very dregs of society'. McMahon, according to Sewell, had, 'throughout the whole of his examination ... displayed that low cunning in fencing with the questions ... for which the lower orders of his countrymen were proverbial'.[64] Sewell obviously subscribed to the common view that the Irish were a 'cunning' lot and inveterate liars. Nevertheless, McMahon's evidence helped hang both defendants.

In another case that may or may not have been murder, Dublin-born Edward Feeney was executed in May 1872 for the shooting of Charles Marks. Feeney was said by police to have had a good Catholic education before, in 1859, joining the British army. After leaving the army in 1870, he moved to Melbourne and worked for 18 months as a wardsman at Melbourne Hospital. There he met fellow wardsman Charles Marks, a 28-year-old former sailor. Letters between the two men discovered by the police suggested a close relationship, with Marks writing: 'I love you as a brother and perhaps more.' On 5 March 1872, after drinking heavily, the two men went to the Treasury Gardens in the city centre. Bystanders heard a shot and discovered Marks dead from a bullet wound to his chest and a drunken Feeney lying on the grass nearby 'coolly' smoking a cigar. When questioned, he maintained they had come to the gardens to die together and that Marks had shot himself. The medical evidence offered in court contradicted this account and, after deliberating for only 15 minutes, the jury returned a verdict of guilty. The judge, in imposing the death penalty, told Feeney that he was a 'traitor and a coward', who had entered into a suicide pact with Marks, but at the last moment had shot Marks instead of himself. The judge believed Feeney, who feared Marks and was dominated by him, had intended all along not to honour the pact but to commit a premeditated murder and claim it was a suicide.[65] The *Argus* initially appeared bewildered by the whole affair, referring to the two men as a 'strange couple'.[66] But, at the same time, readers were given unmistakable clues as to the likely nature of the relationship between them. One mutual friend was reported as saying: 'there was an unusual fondness on the part of Marks towards Feeney'.[67] According to JB Castieau, the governor of Melbourne Gaol, where Feeney was held prior to his execution, Feeney strongly denied there was anything between himself and Marks beyond 'ordinary friendship'. Castieau passed this information on to the press and was reported as saying that he believed Feeney since, in his experience, Catholics facing execution were unlikely to lie. However, after Feeney's execution, in the privacy of his diary, Castieau came to a rather different conclusion. He had attended the post-mortem required immediately after a hanging and noted that the coroner found Feeney's body exhibited evidence of 'vicious indulgence'.[68]

An Irish man who did appear to have committed murder was Clare-born James Cusick (or Cusack) who was tried in 1870 for killing his wife. He was known to have often beaten her when drunk and was apparently also motivated by jealousy since he suspected his Tipperary-born wife, Ann, was having an affair with a neighbour. The violence that had been inflicted upon Ann Cusick shocked those who saw her body. According to the Sydney

Freeman's Journal: 'The corpse did not look like that of a white woman in any way. The face was black ... and the whole body was one mass of bruises.'[69] Cusick was tried before the Irish judge Redmond Barry and defended by an Irish barrister, Richard Ireland. His defence amounted to a further assault upon his now dead wife, as Ireland maintained that Ann Cusick was a promiscuous drunkard who 'cruelly' neglected her family. The jury were obviously swayed by Ireland's renowned skill as an advocate for, although they convicted Cusick of murder, they made a strong plea for mercy. But Judge Barry was having none of it. He sentenced Cusick to death and rebuked the jury for recommending mercy on the basis of a suspicion of adultery; a suspicion was not evidence, he tartly pointed out.[70]

Yet drunken Irish men convicted of fatally assaulting their wives or partners did sometimes cheat the gallows. In a well-known case, Richard Heraghty, who battered his 'paramour' Rose Malone to death in 1878, leaving her body covered in at least 50 injuries, was also sentenced to death by Redmond Barry. But the executive council – the governor in consultation with the premier and cabinet – which could exercise the royal prerogative of mercy in capital cases, commuted his sentence to life imprisonment. One is left wondering if the sentence would have been commuted had Malone been Heraghty's legal wife rather than his *de facto* wife. *Melbourne Punch* protested strongly against the outcome and, in seeking an explanation, it suggested that Irish members of the radical Berry government had played a part in securing the reprieve. Certainly, at the executive council meeting that considered the case, Irish-born attorney-general Sir Bryan O'Loghlen voted for Heraghty's sentence to be commuted.[71] The *Argus* too disapproved of the decision, lamenting that, as regards capital punishment, there was 'little consistency in this land and less justice'.[72] This view has been endorsed by later legal historians, who have pointed out that leaving the ultimate life-and-death decision to political appointees rather than the courts – to the governor, premier and ministers representing the crown, not the trial judge and jury – made a 'mockery of traditional valued ideas such as rule of law and the separation of powers doctrine'.[73]

The murder of John Price, 1857

One notorious case, which saw five Irish men charged with murder and three executed, is worth exploring in some detail. Francis Brennigan, a Catholic labourer, born in 1814 in King's County (now County Offaly), was transported to Van Diemen's Land in 1842 for 14 years, probably because he had deserted from the British army. In 1854, he arrived in Melbourne under the alias 'Frank Bragan'. Soon, though, he was back in custody because in April 1855 he, along with fellow Irish man Daniel Donovan, was sentenced to 15 years' hard labour, the first three to be served in irons, by Irish-born judge Arthur Wrixon for 'robbery in company', that is for bushranging.[74] Brennigan began his sentence on the hulk *Success* moored at Williamstown on Hobson's Bay, one of several hulks used to relieve pressure on the colony's overcrowded gaols and stockades. Hard labour for the nearly 90 prisoners on the *Success* involved quarrying stone and building defensive fortifications on the bay while shackled in irons. Brennigan had not submitted quietly to his sentence and was punished a number of times with solitary confinement in a cramped box fixed to the side of the ship.[75]

In March 1857, a group of between 20 and 30 hulk prisoners working at the Williamstown quarry attacked and killed

Cornish-born John Price, the inspector general of Victorian prisons. Price had gone to the quarry in response to threats by prisoners to stop work if their complaints about poor conditions and ill-treatment were not addressed. Price had acquired a fearsome reputation for brutality when he was governor of Norfolk Island. In reporting his murder, the Melbourne *Age*, a vocal critic of his policies, claimed that many people saw him as a 'monster of cruelty' and so would probably regard his bloody end as entirely in keeping with the manner of his life.[76] The inquest into Price's death delivered a verdict of wilful murder against 15 prisoners, at least five of whom were Irish: Francis Brennigan, Daniel Donovan, Henry Smith, Thomas Maloney and James Kelly.[77] In April 1857, the men faced separate trials in four groups before Judge Redmond Barry; seven of them were convicted, sentenced to death and executed, including Brennigan, Smith and Maloney.[78]

Newspaper accounts of the trials are revealing of attitudes towards the Irish and of the way in which the law was applied to disadvantage the prisoners accused of Price's murder. The *Age* chose to introduce Francis Brennigan to its readers in the following manner: 'The prisoner Brennigan is an Irishman, and certainly the most unfavourable specimen of the lowest class of his countrymen we have seen.' By contrast, one of Brennigan's fellow accused, 20-year-old William Brown, was described as 'quite a youth' and 'as harmless as a schoolboy'. The third accused, Richard Bryant, was 'a fine athletic man, with a countenance which, if the rules laid down by Lavater can be relied upon, indicates the possession by him of a powerful intellect'.[79] In the eyes of the *Age* reporter, influenced by the theories of physiognomy fashionable at the time, which taught that character could be discovered by analysing physical appearance,

Brennigan was a very 'unfavourable' Irish 'specimen', lacking the youthful innocence or the impressive body and mind of his two English co-defendants.

Only Bryant was represented by a barrister, GM Stephen, while Brennigan and Brown conducted their own defences.[80] No evidence was presented at the trial to prove conclusively that any of the three men had struck Price. In summing up his defence, Brannigan was brief: 'All he had to say was, he was innocent of this charge, and no one had sworn to his striking a blow'.[81] Why then was he convicted of murder? His conviction hinged upon a legal point that the prosecution and Judge Barry repeatedly drew to the jury's attention and Bryant's barrister tried hard to refute. Brennigan and the others could be convicted of murder even though they had not planned the crime nor participated directly in killing Price. In directing the jury, Barry told them it was not necessary that the death of Price should have been 'originally contemplated' because the prisoners, in attempting to press their complaints upon him, had become a 'riotous and insubordinate assembly' united in a 'common unlawful purpose'. Under the law, all those in the crowd, whether they had struck Price or not, were considered equally responsible for his death.[82] The jury brought in guilty verdicts against all three prisoners, but they were not happy about Brennigan's conviction, as they strongly recommended mercy for him: that is, he should be spared the death penalty. When Barry enquired why they wanted mercy for Brennigan, the jury foreman replied that 'they believed he had not struck a blow'. But Barry dismissed this plea, remarking that 'no hope could be held out for him'.[83]

In addition to the jury's plea for mercy, a petition was presented to Charles Gavan Duffy requesting that the executive council reprieve Brennigan, as well as Henry Smith, another Irish prisoner convicted at one of the earlier trials. The petitioners argued that the two men should not be executed on the basis of 'questionable evidence', for some of the witnesses against them were 'twice and thrice convicted felons'. But, with Barry strongly opposed to commuting the death sentences he had passed, there was indeed 'no hope'. The executive council, which included three Irish-born ministers – John O'Shanassy as premier, Gavan Duffy as public works commissioner and John Leslie Fitzgerald Vesey Foster as treasurer – declined to reprieve either of these two Irish prisoners and both were hanged.[84] Yet the verdicts of the various trials were inconsistent. Despite witnesses claiming to have seen Kelly and Donovan physically attack Price, both were acquitted; yet Brennigan and Smith were convicted, although no witnesses had testified that they were involved in assaulting Price. As JV Barry, a judge himself, argued in his analysis, the trials were really about vengeance and retribution, as well as a desire to intimidate the remaining large and discontented prison population.[85]

Brennigan was hanged for essentially the same legal reason that Elizabeth Scott would be hanged six years later. It was not because it had been proved conclusively he had committed murder, but because he was considered a member of a group with an 'unlawful purpose' and murder was the outcome of the actions of some members of this group. Gender obviously played an important role in Scott's execution, but whether race or ethnicity did in Brennigan's is harder to determine. As noted, there were attempts to have his sentence commuted, though they failed, which was unusual. Recommendations by juries for mercy in capital cases were rare, but normally they resulted in the commutation of the death sentences; not, however, in Brennigan's case, nor in Smith's either.[86]

The *Age*'s description of Brennigan, as a 'most unfavourable specimen of the lowest class' of Irish man points to the existence of anti-Irish sentiment in connection with the case. And we know from the strong opposition to Irish immigration evident in Victoria during the 1850s that anti-Irish attitudes were widespread. Comments made by the *Argus*, then under the editorship of Dublin-born Protestant barrister George Higinbotham, later chief justice of Victoria, are interesting in this context. Thomas Maloney was executed for Price's murder with fellow Catholics Henry Smith and Thomas Williams. On the scaffold, the *Argus* reported that all expressed 'sincere contrition' for their past crimes and showed 'patient resignation to their fate'. But, unlike the other two, Maloney 'declared himself innocent to the last' of the murder of Price. The *Argus* warned its readers against believing Maloney's protestations of innocence in the face of imminent death. The 'notorious and habitual cunning' of such a 'criminal character', it went on, should not shake public faith in the jury verdicts. It tried to explain away Maloney's final words by claiming, rather unconvincingly, that he 'cherished to the last some faint hope that the penalty would be commuted'.[87] The *Argus* seemed anxious to have those convicted of Price's murder confess their guilt, repent and be reconciled to their respective churches before execution. Obviously, such an outcome would uphold the criminal justice system that Higinbotham supported and prove that the verdicts of the dubious trials were correct. Maloney failed to oblige, so had to be discredited as a typically 'cunning' Irish criminal, but Francis Brennigan complied, or at least the *Argus* claimed that he did. It reported that just before his execution, he admitted to having pushed Price over, although he maintained that it was Thomas Williams who actually hit him over the head with a shovel. The *Argus* was quick to interpret this as a confession of guilt. Yet it hardly amounted to a confession of murder, while at the same time Brennigan insisted that a number of the others convicted were innocent, including the young man William Brown who was hanged with him.[88]

Brennigan and other Irish prisoners were probably unlucky in being tried before their Irish countryman Redmond Barry. In his long career on the Victorian bench from 1852 to 1880, Barry heard a remarkable 358 capital cases, and statistics show that, of those he sentenced to death, 53 per cent were executed. This was a higher proportion than that of any other contemporary Victorian judge.[89] As with the Scott case in 1863, the Price case in 1857 demonstrates very clearly how arbitrary the death penalty could be. And this fact inevitably calls into question attempts, like that made in 1881 by AM Topp, to use execution statistics as evidence of an innate propensity towards violent crime on the part of the Irish.

An Irish hangman

Topp's narrow focus on the Irish in the dock and on the scaffold ignores the many other Irish people involved in the criminal justice system, whether as judges, lawyers, policemen, prison warders, complainants or witnesses. If the Irish suffered unfairly under this justice system – as some of those executed for the murder of John Price obviously did – at the same time, they also participated in the system and helped to operate it. A good example of this is provided by the Armstrong trial in 1859. As we have seen, Irish-born William Armstrong and an accomplice were sentenced to death after being convicted of shooting with intent to kill. The judge who sentenced them was Irish-born Robert Molesworth; the prosecution at the trial was led by Irish-born barrister Richard Ireland; one of the crown's main witnesses was Irish-born miner James McMahon; while the doctor who gave evidence about the wounds inflicted on the victims was Irish-born Robert James Fisher. Many of Victoria's early judges and barristers were Protestant Irish men and, at the lower levels of the justice system, amongst police constables and prison warders especially, Catholic Irish men abounded.[90] Even some of the Irish men executed in Victoria during this period were executed by an Irish hangman.

The journalist JS James, when intending to write about Pentridge in 1877, went undercover and organised employment for himself in the prison's hospital as a general assistant to the prison doctor. On his first day in the job, he was asked by warders if he could extract a rotten tooth from a complaining prisoner. James confidently agreed, although he had no previous experience of dentistry. The prisoner with toothache was a man named Michael Gately, known in the prison as 'Balleyram', or perhaps 'Balla Ram'. He was an 'old hand', having been transported in 1841 to Van Diemen's Land and having later served prison sentences in NSW and Victoria. Below is James's very revealing description of him.

> A frightful animal – the immense head, powerful protruding
> jaw, narrow receding forehead and deficient brain space,
> seemed fitly joined to tremendous shoulders and long, strong
> arms, like those of a gorilla, which he resembles more than a
> man. All the evil passions appeared to have their home behind
> that repellent, revolting countenance ... a natural brute.[91]

Despite his intimidating appearance, in James's account, Gately proves to be a coward, crying out 'don't hurt me' and roaring loudly as the journalist struggled, using the strongest forceps he could find, to extract the 'tusk' from the 'foul jaws' of this 'brute'. James was quick to inform his readers that Gately was an 'Irishman' and a 'Roman Catholic', or at least he had been a Catholic. Finding it hard 'to gammon the priest' in the confessional, James claimed that Gately had converted to Judaism. But even if he was now a Jew, Gately emerges from James's pen portrait as a vivid example of the Catholic Irish man stereotyped as a 'natural brute', a 'frightful animal', more like a gorilla than a man. Gately had once saved the life of an overseer being attacked by another prisoner, and for this intervention he was rewarded in 1873 with the job of official hangman, the previous incumbent having died suddenly. But warders told James that Gately's behaviour had only deteriorated since he had become the colony's executioner.[92]

Among Gately's 'customers' during the late 1870s were several fellow Irish men. In June 1879, for example, though still a prisoner himself, Gately travelled to Beechworth in north-east Victoria to hang Thomas Hogan, a 34-year-old Catholic selector from County Tipperary who had been convicted of murdering his younger brother, James, with whom he was in dispute about money. Thomas shot his brother outside his house one night in February after they and their other brother, William, another selector, had spent much of the day drinking at Mackinnon's Hotel in Bundalong. Thomas was drinking whiskey and the others beer. One press report claimed that all three brothers were 'men of a violent temper': William had once attacked a relative with an axe and Thomas had already served a prison sentence in NSW for assault. Witnesses also reported that while drinking, the brothers had argued about the Kelly gang, with Thomas heatedly defending them and threatening to shoot anyone who criticised them. Thomas Hogan's barrister defended him in court by claiming that he suffered from *delirium tremens* and was 'temporarily insane' when he shot his brother, but the judge rejected this argument and the jury brought in a guilty verdict. In his report to the governor-in-council, the judge concluded that the 'case was clearly proved'. Among the government ministers who signed off on Hogan's death sentence were at least two Catholic Irish men: the attorney-general, Sir Bryan O'Loghlen, and the postmaster-general and the former Eureka Stockade leader, Peter Lalor.[93]

In the local community, which contained many struggling Irish selectors, feelings about Hogan's execution were mixed. An editorial published after the trial in the *Ovens and Murray Advertiser* supported a reprieve for Hogan. The paper deplored the effects of the excessive consumption of 'ardent spirits', arguing that Hogan's killing of his brother was not premeditated, being the act of a 'madman' in the grip of alcoholism. It also pointed out that large numbers of death sentences were commuted: at least 40 per cent, it claimed, including sentences for murders as bloody as that committed by Heraghty in the previous year. An unnecessary hanging, the paper went on, was nothing short of 'legalised murder'. But the sentence was not commuted and, in the end, the press generally agreed that Hogan met his end with 'no signs of trepidation'.[94]

The last Irish man hanged
in Victoria, 1891

The last Irish-born man hanged in Victoria was 69-year-old
Cornelius Bourke, executed in April 1891. In this case too, questions around a lack of premeditation and the possibility that he
might be insane were to the fore. Bourke had at least two things
in common with Francis Brennigan, executed nearly 35 years
earlier, aside from the fact that they were both Irish. Bourke was
also a former convict, while George Higinbotham, who had written about the 1857 executions when working as a newspaper editor, was in 1891 the judge who presided over Bourke's trial.

According to newspaper accounts, Cork-born Bourke turned
to crime after migrating to England and in 1841 was transported
for theft to Van Diemen's Land, where he proved insubordinate,
was flogged and ended up at Port Arthur. A later newspaper
report described his back as 'covered in scars'.[95] He arrived on the
mainland in 1850 and, after gold was discovered, he worked as a
miner. Initially he made money, but squandered it on drink and
'dissipation', eventually becoming a vagrant picking up casual
rural labouring jobs and spending his meagre wages on drink.[96]
From 1875 onwards, Bourke accumulated at least 11 convictions
for vagrancy and two for larceny. The Melbourne Catholic
Advocate described him as 'an old gaol bird, who has spent a great
part of his life in prison', while, in the opinion of the *Ballarat
Star*, he had lived a 'wretched life'. But Bourke's life did reflect
the experience of many aging disappointed diggers after the gold
rushes of the 1850s and 1860s.[97]

In February 1891 in south-west Victoria, Bourke and a
77-year-old man named Charles Stewart were sentenced by
Warrnambool magistrates to six months' imprisonment for

vagrancy. Stewart, who also had numerous vagrancy convictions, was in extremely poor health. Housed for a night in the same cell at the Hamilton lock-up, en route to gaol in Portland, Bourke beat the ailing Stewart to death, apparently in an argument about boots, and he also attacked Constable JJ Curtain, who tried to come to Stewart's aid. A local newspaper painted a very unattractive physical picture of Bourke as the quintessentially brutish Irish man. According to the *Hamilton Spectator*, he was a 'short, stout man with grey hair, [an] iron-grey beard and hard features', which included 'bright shifty eyes and a prominent crooked nose'; his jaws were 'heavy', his forehead receded, and 'the back of the head, being very largely developed, [gave] a peculiarly ferocious expression to his face'. Constable Curtain believed Bourke had only kicked or hit Stewart three or four times, but, given the old man's precarious physical condition, this was sufficient to cause his death.[98]

At Bourke's trial in Ballarat before Chief Justice Higinbotham, the defence entered a plea of not guilty by reason of insanity, arguing that Bourke suffered from 'senile dementia'. But the jury found him guilty, although with a strong recommendation for mercy. When Higinbotham came to pass sentence of death, Bourke constantly interrupted him, loudly repeating some of his words. As the judge concluded with, 'And may God have mercy on your soul', Bourke responded: 'Have mercy on your own, never mind God.' Although the insanity defence had failed at the trial, both the prison doctor and chaplain, who spent time with Bourke, became convinced that he was not responsible for his actions. The government agreed to postpone the execution to allow time for a panel of four doctors to examine Bourke. They decided that he was sane enough to understand the crime he had committed and the inevitable penalty for it.[99] Bourke went to the gallows, while prayers were said for him in some Catholic churches.[100]

If these varied cases illustrate one thing, it is how arbitrary the death penalty could be: a lottery seems an apt metaphor for it. People convicted of very similar crimes might or might not be executed. Even at the time there were frequent complaints about contradictory verdicts, inconsistent sentencing and inexplicable reprieves. Reprieves especially were a source of discontent, largely because, as we have seen, there was a strong suspicion that decisions about capital punishment made by the colony's executive council, which involved senior politicians, were swayed by political considerations. Therefore, statistics on the numbers and types of people executed in colonial Victoria must be treated with considerable caution. The figures do certainly suggest a reluctance to execute women and perhaps also a greater willingness to execute people who had not been born in Victoria, but, despite AM Topp's assertions, they do not offer reliable quantifiable data proving that the Irish were overrepresented among violent criminals.

The stories of those executed are, nevertheless, of considerable interest because they provide us with graphic snapshots of a range of Irish men in extreme circumstances: ex-convicts turned bushrangers incarcerated on prison hulks; violent drunkards brutally beating their wives to death; gay lovers embarked upon failed suicide pacts; indebted selectors involved in bitter family disputes over money; elderly, demented diggers reduced to a life of impoverished vagrancy; and, last but not least, Irish prisoners employed as state executioners. A diverse array of situations and imperatives, and often pure chance, sent Irish men to their deaths on the gallows. When cases are looked at closely, there is little indication of any innate racial or tribal propensity to violence amongst them, while even many contemporaries considered capital punishment in certain cases to have been unwarranted and unfair.

Much that has been asserted about the Irish and crime in Australia is inaccurate and misleading. It is easy to see how hostile stereotypes about the violence and lawlessness of the Irish shaped the views of 19th-century commentators, but it is harder to understand why historians have continued to offer interpretations unsupported by solid evidence. We have focused here largely on late 19th-century eastern Australia: Victoria especially, with consideration of NSW and Queensland as well, where similar patterns of Irish criminality were evident. But a more substantial, longer-term national study of offences ranging from vagrancy to murder among Irish immigrants and, if possible, among their children also, is required before we can hope to provide a reliable and truly definitive answer to the perennial question of how lawless and violent the Irish really were.

CHAPTER 8
Madness and the Irish

Nineteenth-century commentators and more recent historians have not only drawn a connection between the Irish and crime, but one between the Irish and madness as well. Patrick O'Farrell remarked upon the large numbers of the Catholic Irish in lunatic asylums. He calculated that, in New South Wales (NSW) in 1881, the rate of committal for Irish-born men and women was in per capita terms roughly eight times that of the Australian-born population. Yet, while we certainly need to consider why so many Irish immigrants ended up in institutions for the mentally ill, we also need to ask if their numbers have in fact been exaggerated, both at the time and since. Is O'Farrell's calculation that Irish committal rates were vastly in excess of Australian-born rates accurate? In pondering the matter, O'Farrell recognised that there was 'no simple explanation' for the apparently high Irish committal rates, but he speculated that some Irish immigrants 'must have been isolated, friendless and unable to cope'. He also suspected that, just as families sent physically ill members to the Antipodes in hopes that warmer climes would prove therapeutic, some may have 'deliberately despatched ... relatives with mental problems, to relieve themselves of the burden'. But he made clear that, 'in the absence of research findings', his attempts to find an explanation could only be tentative.[1]

Much important research has been done since O'Farrell wrote this over 30 years ago, but more work is still needed before we have a reliable picture of the historical relationship between the Irish and Australian mental health services. As a step towards creating that picture, this chapter will first explore statistics on rates of Irish psychiatric committal. But as well as understanding the statistics on committal, we also need an appreciation of how and why patients entered psychiatric institutions. We need to know who these people were and how they were viewed by asylum staff, especially doctors. And, in order to grasp the Australian situation, we need to set it against a broader transnational background. The picture that then emerges is rather different from the one O'Farrell painted a generation ago, but it does illustrate his comment that there is 'no simple explanation' for Irish psychiatric institutionalisation.

The Irish in Australian asylums, 1880–1910: the statistics

The apparently disproportionate number of Irish-born immigrants committed to lunatic asylums was widely viewed as a problem during the late 19th century. O'Farrell focused on NSW, but concern was expressed throughout the Australian colonies and much of the rest of the Irish diaspora as well. We need to begin therefore with a survey of some of the statistical data. But, as we shall soon see, contemporary statistics cannot be accepted at face value. Statistics collected during the early 1880s in NSW certainly pointed to a significant overrepresentation of the Irish-born in psychiatric institutions. In 1881, across the six NSW asylums, Irish immigrants made up around 30 per cent of total patients.[2] They were the largest single ethnic cohort, followed by people born in Australia, and in England and Wales (combined), each being around 27 per cent of the total. Yet, according to the 1881 census, only 9.2 per cent of the NSW population were immigrants from Ireland.[3] In his 1882 and 1885 reports, the NSW inspector-general of the insane, Dr Frederick Norton Manning, drew attention to such numbers, describing the overrepresentation of the Irish as 'perhaps the most remarkable fact shown by these returns'.[4] Comments such as this were made frequently at the time because the statistical evidence appeared clear – and yet it is not.

Colonists of British birth or descent, often already convinced that the Irish were by nature an irrational and mentally unstable people, were quick to believe figures pointing to large numbers of Irish immigrants filling NSW lunatic asylums, especially when these figures appeared in reports authored by respected medical experts. Yet characteristics of the immigrant population that had little to do with its mental health predisposed the Irish both to higher committal rates and to statistical exaggeration of those rates. Australian asylums, although not exclusively pauper institutions, catered mostly for working-class adult patients. Irish immigrants were largely working class and most had arrived as young adults. The Australian-born population, on the other hand, reflected a wider class spectrum and, moreover, it was very youthful. In most colonies during the second half of the 19th century, from 40 to 50 per cent of the Australian-born were children. These demographic characteristics, which set Irish immigrants clearly apart from the Australian-born population, meant that working-class Irish adults were more likely to make use of asylums, just as they were more likely to be arrested for the public order offences than were the Australian-born, as was noted in the previous chapter. On top of this, calculating rates of committal based on total population figures, which include children, as Manning did in his reports, inevitably exaggerates Irish numbers. Therefore, comparisons between Irish immigrants and the Australian-born, such as O'Farrell made, that do not factor in age and class differences are not valid because they are simply not comparing like with like.[5]

As Table 1 below demonstrates, beginning in the late 1880s, there was a marked shift in the ethnic composition of the NSW asylum population. By 1891, the Australian-born had overtaken the Irish-born to become the largest single group and, during the next two decades, Australian numbers continued to increase markedly, while the Irish-born cohort dwindled.

Table 1: Ethnic cohorts as percentages of NSW lunatic asylum inmates, 1881–1910[6]

YEAR	PERCENTAGE BORN IN IRELAND	PERCENTAGE BORN IN ENGLAND & WALES	PERCENTAGE BORN IN AUSTRALIA
1881	29.9	26.7	26.9
1891	25.9	22.8	35.7
1910	11.9	15.9	59.8

While catering mainly for immigrants before 1880, by the early years of the 20th century NSW's mental hospitals were housing patient populations that were substantially Australian-born. Inspector-General Manning was very aware of these developments and drew attention to them in his annual reports to the NSW parliament, writing in his 1887 report that the 'most noticeable fact is that *for the first time* the natives of NSW were the most numerous' amongst asylum inmates. Yet Manning, who advocated for restricting immigration on mental health grounds, continued to argue that the 'proportion of those born in Ireland is still much larger than it should be, considering the number of Irish nationality among the general population'.[7]

The phenomenon of Irish overrepresentation was recognised throughout colonial Australia. Manning, in an address to the Intercolonial Medical Congress held in Melbourne in 1888, cited figures demonstrating that the Irish-born, at 26.7 per cent of all patients, were the largest ethnic cohort in the Australian asylum population as a whole. He also remarked that this figure was probably an underestimate since case records, which included patients' countries of birth, were poorly maintained in Victoria and Tasmania.[8] But the figures he gave for each colony, which are reproduced below, certainly seemed to confirm claims of an excess number of Irish immigrants among asylum inmates.

Table 2: Irish-born as percentage of general and lunatic asylum populations in Australian colonies, 1887–91[9]

STATE	IRISH-BORN PERCENTAGE OF GENERAL POPULATION, 1891	IRISH-BORN PERCENTAGE OF ASYLUM POPULATION, 1887
Western Australia	7.0	33.8
Queensland	10.9	33.4
New South Wales	6.6	28.1
Victoria	7.3	25.2
South Australia	4.5	25.0
Tasmania	3.9	15.7

During the 19th and early 20th centuries, Australian censuses did not record the ethnic ancestry of the population. Therefore, historians have been forced to use the numbers of Australian

Catholics before 1945 as a proxy measure of Irish ancestry. In the annual reports on NSW psychiatric institutions between 1880 and 1910, tables listing religion should mean we can begin to detect the emergence of an Irish-Australian cohort of patients. Admittedly, this cohort cannot be measured with a high degree of accuracy; nevertheless, we can at least gain a general impression of its size.

Table 3: Percentages of Irish-born, Catholic and Australian-born Catholic patients in NSW lunatic asylums, 1881–1910[10]

YEAR	PERCENTAGE IRISH-BORN	PERCENTAGE CATHOLIC	PERCENTAGE AUSTRALIAN-BORN CATHOLIC
1881	29.9	37.6	7.7
1910	11.9	35.1	23.2

As Table 3 shows, while the percentage of Irish-born patients fell by nearly two-thirds between 1881 and 1910, the percentage of Catholics remained relatively stable. It is probable that most of the Catholic patients in 1910 who were not actually Irish-born were the children of Irish immigrants, since there were few other Catholic patients in these hospitals.[11] In other words, as aging Irish-born Catholic inmates began to die out, they were being replaced – to an extent – by some of their offspring. But to what extent? In 1910, around 23 per cent of NSW patients not born in Ireland were Catholic and, according to the 1911 census, Catholics made up 25 per cent of NSW's total white population. Thus, in 1910–11, the offspring of Catholic Irish immigrants were not overrepresented in NSW's mental institutions.[12] It would seem then that, in NSW at least, whatever combination of factors propelled large numbers of Catholic Irish immigrants into lunatic asylums – even if their rates of committal have been exaggerated – the same factors do not appear to have affected their descendants to anything like the same extent.

The Irish in asylums in Ireland and the diaspora, 1840–2000

Before looking more closely at Australian psychiatric institutions and their Irish inmates, we need to understand what was happening elsewhere, both in Ireland and other parts of the Irish diaspora. This is because a similar picture of apparent over-representation was evident in virtually all other places and sometimes this did extend to the children of the immigrants.[13] We need to understand attitudes towards mental illness and psychiatric institutions among Irish rural communities from where most Irish immigrants came, because it is certain that those departing Ireland drew upon such attitudes when confronted by mental health problems in Australia.

Medical sociologist Damien Brennan has recently highlighted that the growth in psychiatric patients in Ireland in the 19th century was, by any standard, extreme.[14] During the period 1851–1911 there was a four-fold increase in mental asylum patient numbers whereas at the same time the population of the island of Ireland fell by one-third. This growth in numbers continued uninterrupted in the south after the country was partitioned in 1921–22. By the 1930s the Irish Free State (later Irish Republic) had the highest committal rates in Europe, but rates did not peak until 1956.[15] By then, according to figures published by the World Health Organization (WHO) and covering 84 countries, the Irish Republic had the highest rate of psychiatric institutionalisation in the world. Northern Ireland came fourth on the WHO's list, with Australia in twelfth place.[16]

This extraordinary reliance by the Irish upon mental hospitals has puzzled scholars.[17] At least part of the answer to the puzzle is to be found in the legal framework under which asylums operated – a framework that is relevant to Australia as well.[18] Under the union with Britain, Ireland was provided with an extensive network of large public psychiatric institutions.[19] But the regulations governing committal to these institutions were lax. Irish asylum records show parents initiating the committals of disobedient children; brothers of financially dependent unmarried sisters; wives of drunken husbands; and children of elderly demented parents. Under the more common of the two methods for committal, the *Dangerous Lunatics Act 1838* (1 Vic., c. 27), once a family or family member had instituted committal proceedings, the alleged 'lunatic' was taken into police custody and brought before a petty sessions court presided over by part-time magistrates. If two of these magistrates – men without any medical or legal training – decided that the person was indeed mad, then up until 1867 they would have been sent to gaol, from where they might be transferred to an asylum when a bed became available. While this could mean months of imprisonment, one important advantage of this system for families was that, once a relative was legally declared a 'dangerous lunatic', the families were relieved of the costs of care.[20]

Under an amended Act in 1867 (30 & 31 Vic., c. 118), which operated in the south of Ireland until 1945, magistrates required a medical certificate from at least one government-employed doctor in order to declare someone mad; also, the person now had to be sent directly to an asylum. The police played a major role in taking alleged lunatics into custody, bringing them before magistrates and transporting them to an asylum.[21] There was no right of appeal under these two Acts and, even if the asylum authorities decided that a person was not insane or had later recovered, their families were not obliged to take them back. In that event, they might well be kept in the asylum for an extended period or be transferred to a pauper workhouse.[22] Irish lunatic asylums and mental hospitals thus housed many people who today would not be classed as mentally ill. From the mid 19th century onwards, Irish families clearly found in these institutions an effective means of solving problems created by difficult relatives.[23]

High rates of psychiatric institutionalisation were also found throughout the Irish diaspora: in the United States (US), Britain, Canada and New Zealand, as well as Australia.[24] This suggests that, while factors peculiar to Irish society are important, we also need to take account of how Irish immigrants were received and how they fared in their new homelands. In the US, complaints about the numbers of Irish immigrants committed to lunatic asylums became common from the 1850s onwards, and high Irish committal rates continued well into the 20th century.[25] These complaints have been substantiated by research in New York state that shows Irish-born immigrants had significantly higher committal rates than the white American-born popu-lation, while Irish immigrants' children too had higher rates, although not quite as high as those of their parents.[26] There was a similar picture in England starting in the 1840s and extending up until recent decades. Studies in 1971 and 1981, for example, showed that the Irish-born had the 'highest rates of mental hos-pitalisation' of any ethnic group in England and Wales. Irish rates were more than twice those of the native-born and 'far higher' than those of other major immigrant minorities. Irish over-representation was apparent in most diagnostic categories, but especially with regard to depression and alcoholism.[27]

As we have seen, O'Farrell stressed poverty as a key causal factor in Irish committals in Australia. Other scholars too have argued that the fact the Irish were poor – often very poor – was far more important than that they were Irish: in other words, class is more significant than ethnicity or race.[28] New studies are, however, calling this earlier judgment into question. A 2009 investigation of a group of Irish immigrants admitted during 1843–53 to a London asylum, the Bethlem Royal Hospital, compared them to a control group of non-Irish patients. This was not a pauper asylum as 39 per cent of the Irish were in professional or skilled jobs and 30 per cent of them were Protestants. Yet the study found significant differences between the illnesses ascribed by asylum doctors to the two groups. The Irish, even well-off Protestants, were far more likely to be diagnosed as suffering from mania than were the non-Irish; and the Irish were also more likely to be confined for longer periods.[29] The study's authors, both psychiatrists, after considering possible reasons for these marked differences, concluded that they 'reflect the possibility of a "cultural bias" on the part of the treating physicians'. If they are right, then some Irish may have ended up – and remained for long periods – in asylums, diagnosed with essentially incurable mania, not necessarily because they were poor or even Catholic, but because they were Irish. For, as these authors have also pointed out, character traits that 19th-century English race theorists ascribed to the Irish, like mental excitability and erratic behaviour, exhibited a 'noticeable overlap with mania symptoms' as doctors understood them at the time.[30]

The sample used in this London study was small, but research on a much larger sample of Irish immigrants committed to

Lancashire's four main asylums during 1856–1906 has confirmed some of its key findings. Lancashire, and the city of Liverpool in particular, received vast numbers of Irish immigrants during and immediately after the Great Famine.[31] After opening in 1851, Liverpool's Rainhill Asylum found itself struggling to cope with an Irish inmate population that was overwhelmingly poor.[32] By 1871, when the Irish-born had fallen to 16 per cent of Liverpool's total population, they still made up 46 per cent of Rainhill's patients. And, as at Bethlem, the Irish were far more likely to be diagnosed as suffering from mania than were non-Irish patients and were also more likely to remain in the asylum for lengthy periods. The authors of this study, like those of the London study, concluded that 'racial stereotyping' on the part of the asylum medical staff was a significant influence on how the Irish were diagnosed and treated. They quoted the example of an 1873 medical report commenting that an Irish male patient 'resembles more a monkey than a human being'.[33] And it was apparent that this stereotyping applied to the second-generation Irish as well. Rainhill's superintendent wrote in 1870 that children born in England to Irish immigrants were 'essentially Irish in everything but their accidental birth place'. For him Irishness denoted an innate tendency towards 'immorality, intemperance, violence and recklessness', which left the Irish, particularly when stressed, highly susceptible to mania.[34]

These studies of Ireland and of parts of the Irish diaspora suggest that in considering the Irish inmates of Australian asylums we need to pay particular attention to several factors. One is the role of families and the criminal justice system in the committal process. Alongside this we also need to try and detect any prejudices exhibited by asylum medical staff towards Irish-born patients that might have influenced both diagnosis and prognosis.

The police and the 'Dangerous Lunatics' Acts in Australia

The committal procedure in most Australian colonies was more like the Irish one than the English one: that is, those suspected of being mentally ill were dealt with under the criminal justice system, not the poor law.[35] In Australia, like Ireland, alleged lunatics were taken into custody by the police as potential criminals threatening public order; they appeared before magistrates for sentencing; they could spend time in prison before reaching an asylum; and it was the police who delivered them to the prison and the asylum.[36] The basic committal procedure was set out in 1843, in NSW's first major lunacy statute, the *Dangerous Lunatics Act 1843*, and the procedure remained remarkably similar when the colony's lunacy laws were consolidated in 1898. The title of the 1843 Act made plain that it was intended, firstly, to prevent 'offences by persons dangerously Insane' and only secondly to provide 'care'.[37]

The 1843 act stated that in order to prevent 'persons insane' from committing crimes, including suicide, suspected 'lunatics' and 'idiots' were to be 'apprehended' and brought before two justices of the peace (JPs). The JPs were to 'call to their assistance any two legally qualified medical practitioners'. If, 'on oath', the doctors agreed that the person was a 'dangerous' lunatic or idiot, then the JPs could issue a warrant for their committal 'to some gaol house of correction or public hospital', where they were 'to be kept in strict custody' until such time as the JPs decided they could be released. A new lunacy Act passed in 1867 amended the committal process so as to allow JPs to send the insane person to a lunatic reception house, rather than a prison or general hospital.[38] Reception houses, initially established in Sydney, later spread to other parts of NSW and to Victoria and Queensland. They acted as transit facilities where alleged lunatics could be observed and assessed, where committals could occur, or where paperwork could be finalised.[39] Further major lunacy acts in 1878 and 1898 in NSW, and parallel Acts in Victoria and Queenland, specified in more detail the role and powers of the police in the committal process.[40] Any police constable who found a person he suspected of being insane was empowered to 'apprehend' that person and take them before two magistrates who would, with medical advice, determine whether the accused was insane or not. Under the lunacy laws, the police clearly had wide powers to arrest anyone they decided, for whatever reason, was acting suspiciously.[41]

Although not mentioned in the NSW legislation, as well as holding the alleged lunatic for up to two weeks, it was also the police who in most colonies conveyed those convicted of lunacy by magistrates to a reception house or asylum. If the committal was ordered by JPs in rural or outback areas, then this might involve not only incarcerating the lunatic in a police lock-up or town gaol, but also transporting him or her to the nearest asylum, which could involve a lengthy journey. Criticisms, especially by asylum doctors, of how the police handled lunatics in their custody were not uncommon, as were allegations that police and JPs colluded to rid themselves of troublemakers, such as 'habitual drunkards', by attempting to have them committed to asylums as insane.[42] Yet while the police had the power to arrest suspected lunatics in public places, it appears that many police committals were instigated by families requesting police aid. In 1882, for example, 73 per cent of committals to Victorian asylums were the result of police action. But by 1892 the figure was down to 50 per cent, and in 1907 it was 46 per cent. The asylum and police authorities in

Victoria had actively sought to diminish the role of constables in the apprehension, incarceration and transportation of lunatics. But as the police themselves admitted, families often approached them for help, insisting that they take violent or threatening relatives into custody and put them before magistrates for committal. While this public demand existed, the police were unable to divorce themselves entirely from involvement in the committal process.[43]

Another key factor that needs to be introduced at this stage of the discussion is that, in most Australian colonies, the police forces were composed of large numbers of Irish-born immigrants. Some forces were modelled on the Royal Irish Constabulary (RIC); they were governed according to Irish-style regulations; and they were led by officers who had actually served in the constabulary in Ireland.[44] But many ordinary constables – the sort of constables who apprehended alleged lunatics – were Irish-born too, and some had been policemen in Ireland. This was especially true in Victoria, where, in 1874, fully 82 per cent of the colony's police force was Irish-born; 46 per cent had seen previous service in the RIC; and two-thirds of those with RIC experience were Catholic.[45] Numbers of Irish policemen were high in virtually all the Australian colonies.[46]

One question that this information prompts is: did the fact that policemen were so frequently Irish-born have an impact on the numbers of Irish-born immigrants taken into police custody as alleged lunatics? As we have seen, psychiatric institutionalisation appears to have been normalised amongst the Irish during the course of the 19th century in a way that was not the case with the English and the Scots. And, presumably, immigrants brought such attitudes to Australia.[47] While the police played an important role in committals in Ireland, we know that many of these committals arose out of family conflicts. When Irish families in Australia were faced with difficult relatives, did they turn to local Irish-born constables for help? This is certainly what they would have done in Ireland. And were Irish policemen particularly obliging because they too were familiar with the Irish practice of the police helping families rid themselves of lunatic relatives? Unfortunately, much of this discussion can only be speculative at present since little research has been done. Nonetheless, one thing is clear: it would be a mistake to focus only on the Irish as asylum inmates and to ignore their broader involvement in the mental health system. Most importantly, we need to bear in mind that it was the Irish who initiated many committals, whether as relatives or as policemen.

The Irish as asylum attendants

Another related issue, the significance of which also remains obscure at present, is the employment of the Irish in the asylums.[48] In June and July 1876, the English-born journalist JS James worked for a month as an attendant in Victoria's two largest asylums, at Kew and Yarra Bend in Melbourne, at the same time that a government inquiry was investigating allegations that patients were being mistreated. Under the pen-name, 'The Vagabond', James published six articles in the *Argus* newspaper that were very critical of the Kew 'barracks', although less so of the cottage-style Yarra Bend Asylum. James was convinced that families were using asylums to rid themselves of troublesome members. It is certainly true that Victoria had high committal rates: according to a leading English asylum expert, insanity appeared 'more general' in Victoria than in any other Australasian colony.[49] It is interesting that, in support of his argument, James chose to use the example of 'an honest old Irishman', Peter Carley from Geelong. All the attendants said he 'should be let out', and James thought him 'sane enough', even if 'a little weak-minded'; however, his family had insisted that he stay in Kew.[50] Using an Irish patient as an example of wrongful committal was certainly appropriate since, from the 1850s into the 1880s, the Irish-born were the largest ethnic cohort in Victoria's asylums.[51]

There were also many Irish amongst the staff. James wrote that, except for four English men, the 50 male attendants at Kew were all Irish: 'sons of the sod' or 'the boys', as he mockingly called them. James routinely resorted to stereotypes in his writings about the Irish. Most were 'R.C.s', he went on, but there were also some 'Orangemen', which, given the Irish love of a 'row', made for 'some lively times in the [attendants'] mess room'.[52] James's anecdotes were backed up by the report of the inquiry into Kew, which found that, of the nearly 90 male and female attendants, 'a very large majority ... are Irish and Roman Catholic'.[53] James claimed that some of the attendants were former prison warders and policemen. Certainly, when Irish-born William French applied for an attendant's job in 1860, he listed among his qualifications his service in the Irish constabulary, which he said had afforded him plenty of experience in dealing with 'violent' lunatics.[54]

Asylum medical records and female patients

In studying asylum patients, medical records are essential windows onto patient care, but the view they offer is by no means a clear one. Asylum admission registers and case books vary considerably in the amounts of information that they contain.[55] Dr FN Manning and his successors as superintendents of Sydney's Gladesville Asylum endeavoured to keep detailed notes on both the mental and physical conditions of their patients; other asylum superintendents, struggling to manage overcrowded institutions on inadequate budgets, were not nearly so scrupulous. Manning was right in 1888 when he complained about Victoria's asylum patient records: the surviving ones are often less detailed and complete than are those of NSW.[56] In reading any of these records, however, it is important to always bear in mind that they are highly mediated sources. In them the patient's voice goes essentially unheard. Instead, we hear the voice of the asylum doctor. Doctors also often recorded some of what appeared in the admission documentation, which may have represented the opinions of family, friends, police, magistrates and the certifying physicians. In addition, doctors may have reported things allegedly said by patients, but there is no way of knowing how accurate this data is as the information could possibly originate from attendants rather than the patients themselves. All in all, case documents generally tell us more about the attitudes and values of asylum staff, and sometimes of relatives and police, than they do about patients and what, if anything, was wrong with them. But, even given all these limitations, asylum records are still valuable and sometimes extremely revealing sources.[57]

During the late 19th century and into the early 20th century, men made up the majority of patients in Australian asylums; not until the 1930s did women come to predominate. This in part reflected the fact that the general population contained more men than women, with the imbalance being most pronounced in all immigrant groups, except for the Irish. In 1881, for example, nearly two-thirds (65.4 per cent) of NSW's asylum inmates were men. Amongst Irish inmates, though, the proportion of the sexes was markedly different. In NSW, Irish men were more numerous than Irish women in the asylums, but only narrowly so – in 1881, men were 55.6 per cent of all Irish inmates.[58] Elsewhere in the colonies, however, the balance tipped the other way. In all colonies, except NSW and Tasmania, women formed a majority amongst Irish asylum inmates. Overall, as Table 4 below demonstrates, while men formed a clear majority of Australian asylum inmates in 1887, amongst the Irish-born, the number of women slightly exceeded the number of men.

Table 4: Women as percentages of Australian asylum inmates by place of birth, 1887[59]

PLACE OF BIRTH	PERCENTAGE OF FEMALE INMATES IN DIFFERENT ETHNIC COHORTS
Ireland	50.6
Others[60]	43.9
Scotland	43.0
Australia	42.5
England and Wales	36.3
Germany	29.5
France	16.7
China	0.0
Total female percentage of Australian asylum population	42.0

This means that doctors employed in colonial Australian lunatic asylums, most of whom were English- or Scottish-born and trained, would have found themselves face to face with many Irish-born working-class women. Doctors were thus dealing with patients who differed from them in fundamental ways: not just in terms of gender, but also ethnicity, culture, religion and class, and sometimes language as well. How these men viewed such women can be explored by studying the case notes of a sample of Irish women committed to Sydney's Gladesville Asylum during the second half of the 19th century.

Irish women in Gladesville Asylum, Sydney, 1860s–1880s

English-born Dr FN Manning was medical superintendent of Gladesville Asylum from 1868 to 1878, before being appointed NSW inspector-general of the insane; in 1883 Scottish-born Dr Eric Sinclair followed him in the Gladesville position and, in 1898, succeeded him as inspector-general. Gladesville housed a total of 1048 patients in 1881, of whom almost one-third (31.7 per cent) were Irish-born. The Irish-born comprised 24.6 per cent of the 533 male patients, but 39 per cent of the 515 female patients.[61] Random samples of patient records from the late 1860s through into the late 1880s throw some light on who these many Irish women were and why they were committed, but, more especially, on how medical staff like Manning and Sinclair viewed them.

Winifred Sharkey, aged 46, and Catherine Dobson, aged 35, were both Catholic Irish immigrants.[62] Sharkey was living with her labourer husband at Maitland in the Hunter Valley region north of Sydney, while Dobson and her sailor husband lived in Sydney. Both women were committed to Gladesville in early 1878: Sharkey remaining there for nearly four years, whereas Dobson was discharged after only two months. Sharkey was diagnosed with delusional mania and Dobson with melancholia, and both were ultimately released into the care of their husbands. Winifred Sharkey had been in Gladesville previously and was discharged as recovered. But her husband gave evidence that, within a week of her return home, she 'broke out again', threatening to shoot him and having 'delusions' about the 'improper conduct' of a priest and others. Yet, once back in the hospital, she denied she had been violent. We can only wonder if marital conflict was an issue here, and had the parish priest intervened on the side of Sharkey's husband?

Sharkey's medical notes commented that she exhibited 'numerous strange fancies', believing that there was 'a devil inside her' and that 'fairies drop lice on her'. Sharkey's conviction that she was being tormented by a 'devil' and 'fairies' may well have seemed strange to the English-born asylum doctor and a symptom of madness, but in light of her Irish cultural background such notions were not strange at all. During the 1830s, when Sharkey would have been growing up in rural Ireland, belief in malevolent supernatural creatures was widespread. Such ideas were part of a vibrant popular religious culture that existed alongside the formal structures of the Catholic Church. Belief in demons or fairies would not necessarily have denoted lunacy in rural Ireland, even though it clearly did in the mind of Sharkey's English-born doctor.[63] Sharkey's medical notes become sparse after this initial information, but they do gradually shift from negative in tone to generally positive. At first, Sharkey was said to be 'very insane', as well as 'idle', but gradually over time she became 'quiet', gave 'no trouble' and proved 'useful', once she began working in the 'sewing room'. In June 1881, the doctor commented that there 'seems no reason why she should not be again tried at home', adding the proviso, 'if her husband will take her'. But it was not until six months later, in December, that she was finally discharged into her husband's care. Whether the delay was due to any reluctance on his part is unclear from the surviving documentation.

Catherine Dobson too had been committed to Gladesville on a previous occasion. Since her discharge, she had been in 'three situations', or jobs. The case notes assumed this meant she had 'not been very settled in mind', although, as we have seen, frequent changes in employment were common among Irish domestic servants in Australia. Dobson was committed in 1878 because she had threatened 'some of her friends' and had to be restrained from 'running undressed into the street'.[64] When taken into police custody, she had refused to eat or sleep, but the asylum 'had the effect of steadying her', the doctor thought, for, when she reached Gladesville she began to eat and sleep well and was 'obedient to direction'. Nevertheless, on occasion she was 'flighty and peculiar'. The case notes amplified these remarks by explaining that she spent long periods reading her 'prayer book' and sometimes laughed quietly to herself. When questioned, she flatly denied behaving 'strangely'. The doctor, though, clearly considered her enjoyment of devotional literature a symptom of a disordered mind. As Dobson was a Catholic and the doctor almost certainly a Protestant, different religious sensibilities may well have been operating here. The doctor believed that 'in all probability' she suffered from 'religious delusions and possibly hallucinations of hearing'. But Dobson frustrated the Gladesville doctors by her behaviour. The case notes describe her as 'an odd, silent reserved peculiar woman who has however the cunning to conceal her delusions and thoughts'. In this case, the doctor was convinced that Dobson was deluded, but her Irish craftiness enabled her to conceal her state of mind from him.

Since her suspected 'delusions' remained obscure, her 'bodily health' was improving, she was working 'well in the sewing room' and her husband was willing to take her back, she was discharged in June 1878 after only two months in Gladesville.

Whereas some female patients went in and out of the asylum on more than one occasion, others who entered never left. Hannah McCarthy, aged 22, a single, Irish-born Catholic servant working in suburban Sydney, was committed to Gladesville in early 1878, diagnosed with sub-acute mania.[65] She had only been 'out from Ireland' for about two years and had two unmarried sisters living in the colony. She was taken into custody at Ashfield railway station, having just left her employer's house. It was noted that the police at the train station thought her 'excited and peculiar' and so arrested her as a suspected lunatic. The case notes show that the doctors were puzzled by her condition. McCarthy's employment had always been in 'respectable places', and the 'attack' she suffered was 'sudden' and, according to her sisters, 'completely unaccounted for'. She was described as a 'tall, dark, well-formed woman ... in good health', but she was diagnosed as 'maniacal'. Her behaviour was characterised as 'restless, flighty and occasionally noisy'; she also made 'random and absurd statements' and was 'mischievous'. This mischief seems to have consisted of her singing, dancing and acting 'absurdly' on occasion. Yet at other times she could be perfectly calm and rational; 'quiet and manageable' were the words used in the case notes, signifying that asylum staff considered her under their control. Nevertheless, she was 'always idle'.

Unlike Sharkey and Dobson, McCarthy, even when considered 'manageable', refused to undertake domestic chores. The male medical staff viewed this rejection of asylum authority and of traditional female tasks as a sure sign of madness. In addition, unlike married inmates, McCarthy did not have a husband willing – even if reluctantly – to offer her a home on release. Presumably her unmarried sisters, who may well have been working as servants themselves, were not in a position to care for her. Thus, after five years in Gladesville, McCarthy was consigned to Parramatta Asylum, judged a 'chronic' case. It is difficult to determine her mental condition from these brief case notes. But Hannah McCarthy's experience certainly highlights how vulnerable young, single, working-class Irish women, recently arrived in the colony and without strong family support networks, could be. If their public behaviour attracted the attention of the police and they defied the gendered expectations of the medical profession, then they might find themselves facing a very bleak future indeed.

Words like 'peculiar', 'odd' and 'strange' appear frequently in the case notes of Gladesville's Irish female patients. It is apparent that their states of mind puzzled the non-Irish male medical staff observing them. The doctors were also not prepared to necessarily believe what these women told them. If patients insisted, for instance, that they were not subject to delusions or hallucinations, doctors suspected them of being 'cunning' and of attempting to conceal their madness. This attitude is very clear in the case of Joanna Herlihy, a 50-year-old Irish Catholic widow from Albury on the NSW-Victoria border, who was committed in September 1887, diagnosed with acute mania, and who eventually died in July 1910 while being boarded out by the hospital.[66] Her medical certificate delivered to the hospital by the police claimed that she was 'excitable' and had accused her neighbours of trying to 'injure her character', as well as those of her husband and daughter. The Gladesville doctor admitting her – possibly Eric Sinclair – noted that she had a 'dogged contrary expression of face'. He clearly did not like the look of her. She was, he went on, 'troublesome' and 'spiteful' and 'as a rule silent, refusing to answer questions'. From her silence, he concluded that she 'has no doubt many prominent delusions and hallucinations ... but at present will not talk of them'.

Not answering questions was interpreted as a sure sign of a disturbed mind. When faced with silent patients, doctors sought a better understanding through observing women's bodies and behaviour. If a woman was eating and sleeping well and was clean and neat in appearance, obeying orders and working at traditional household tasks like sewing and washing, she was thought to be improving. But women who persistently talked or talked loudly, who laughed and sang, read for long periods, were untidy in their dress, or who refused to undertake domestic work, were likely to be diagnosed as victims of a 'chronic' mental illness. In that case, they might well have found themselves transferred from Gladesville to Parramatta, where cases considered 'chronic' were warehoused.

Gender stereotypes obviously played a major role in how male doctors assessed the mental health of their female patients, but ethnic and racial stereotypes were influential as well. There is certainly plenty of evidence of racial stereotypes operating with regard to Chinese and Indigenous Australian asylum inmates, but the Irish too were not immune from doctors' ethnic or racial preconceptions.[67] There are hints of prejudice in criticisms of Irish women for being 'peculiar', for singing and dancing, for talking 'absurdly' – perhaps in Irish or employing Hiberno-English idioms – for refusing to wear shoes and for insisting on reading Catholic devotional literature. In her comparative study of the inmates of Melbourne's Yarra Bend Asylum and the Auckland Asylum between 1873 and 1910, medical historian Catharine

Coleborne found evidence of what she termed a 'heightened awareness' of Irish ethnicity among the medical staff, with Irish women especially criticised for being 'too talkative' and 'troublesome'.[68] But comments on women's bodies – and men's too – are even more revealing.

Johanna Flynn, a 57-year-old Irish Catholic widow, working as a servant at Milton south of Sydney, was committed to Gladesville in October 1887, before being transferred in February 1889 to a benevolent asylum.[69] The medical certificate that came with her indicated she had expressed a wish to be dead and had 'refused to perform any household duties' for her employer, instead lying in bed 'in a filthy state', displaying 'obscene habits', and alleging that her food and drink were being poisoned. Yet at the Darlinghurst reception house and in Gladesville Asylum, she was 'quiet and clean'. This suggests that her committal may have been the result of a quarrel with her employer. The asylum doctor was clearly unsure what to make of her mental state. He therefore turned to her physical appearance and her behaviour. She had, he noted, 'a Celtic type of face' and 'black hair commencing grey, dark eyes and a straight short broad nose, good teeth and a ruddy complexion'. The 'short broad nose' and 'ruddy complexion' the doctor saw in Flynn were both characteristic of the Irish physical stereotype evident in cartoons of the period. Many doctors, like cartoonists, relied heavily upon physiognomy, which, as we have seen, taught that a person's character, intelligence and even mental health could be determined by a study of their facial features.[70] In addition, because Flynn answered the doctor's questions 'indifferently', he concluded that she was 'not very intelligent'. Laziness and superstition were other typical Irish traits that this doctor discovered in Flynn. She was 'idle and listless', he noted. She claimed to be 'too weak to do anything' and said that this weakness, which she had suffered from for six years, was the 'will of God'. The doctor clearly did not take this explanation seriously, convinced instead that she was 'really strong' physically and simply lazy. Flynn was eventually transferred to a pauper institution, which suggests that the medical staff did not consider her mentally ill. But she was an aging widow, who claimed to be no longer physically able to undertake the demanding work of a domestic servant. Without a family to support her, the Gladesville doctors had little option but to send her to one of NSW's benevolent asylums.

We have seen already how pervasive and persistent were hostile stereotypes depicting the personal characteristics, appearance and behaviour of the Irish. It is hardly surprising then that English and Scottish doctors, when faced with Irish patients in Australian lunatic asylums, resorted to such stereotypes in order to make sense of the people they were confronted with. If their Irish patients happened to be women, then expectations of appropriate female behaviour also came heavily into play. Research in the records of late 19th-century asylums in England and New Zealand, as well as Australia, has already uncovered evidence of such ethnic stereotyping, but transnational studies are still lacking. Comparisons between the medical records compiled in Australasian, British and North American institutions have the potential to throw much light on differences and similarities in perceptions of the Irish in the major diaspora countries.

Irish men in Gladesville Asylum, Sydney, 1860s–1880s

Ethnic stereotyping is similarly apparent in the asylum case notes on male Irish patients. A few examples will suffice to illustrate how the Gladesville doctors saw the Irish men committed to their care. James Ryan, a 45-year-old, unmarried, Irish-born labourer from Tenterfield in northern NSW, was committed to Gladesville in May 1878 diagnosed as suffering from dementia.[71] The medical certificate authorising his committal noted that for many years his neighbours had thought him 'silly and queer', but of late he had begun to wander about in the bush wearing only a shirt. The police were called and Ryan was arrested. On his medical certificate, he was described as 'incoherent', 'dirty', 'sleepless', 'threatening' and subject to 'delusions about being poisoned'. In Gladesville, the doctor summed him up succinctly as: 'a fair complexioned ugly specimen of a drunken old Irishman'. That Ryan was described as an 'ugly' example of the typical alcoholic Irish labourer suggests that the doctor found him especially difficult and offensive. The notes go on to record that he 'mumbles continually to himself', 'his gait is extremely tottering', and his 'mental faculties are blank'. Unsurprisingly, after six months in Gladesville, Ryan was dispatched to join the chronic cases in Parramatta Asylum.

There is an almost palpable sense of disgust in the doctor's notes on James Ryan. Another Irish-born inmate who produced a somewhat similar reaction in Gladesville's doctors was Thomas Cahill.[72] Like Ryan, Cahill was an unmarried Catholic labourer diagnosed with dementia. At 60, he was considerably older than Ryan and, in November 1887, had been transferred from the Liverpool asylum for male paupers. Cahill's medical certificate described him as 'violent' and 'filthy'; he 'wandered aimlessly about' and was unable to care for himself'. The Gladesville doctor – possibly Eric Sinclair – noted that Cahill was 'ill nourished' and in 'very poor health'. He had 'bleary' blue eyes, 'iron grey hair and beard', and his teeth were 'scarce'. His complexion was 'dusty' and 'earthy'; moreover, 'all expression [had been] wiped out of his face as if with a sponge'; and he had 'no memory at all and no idea of time or place'. The doctor here, as in Ryan's case, portrayed him as primitive to the point of being scarcely human: a product of the 'dusty' earth, lacking in facial expressiveness and in temporal and spatial awareness. Cahill died in Gladesville only seven months after he was committed.

Whereas alcoholic or demented Irish labourers might elicit a degree of revulsion from doctors, comic Irish men, even if maniacal, could prompt a superficially more positive response. John Larkin was a 45-year-old unmarried Catholic quarryman from Taralga, south-west of Sydney, committed to Gladesville in August 1887, having been diagnosed with sub-acute mania.[73] His medical certificate described him as 'restless, excitable, sleepless and incoherent'. Yet, the Gladesville doctor – again, possibly Eric Sinclair – took a very different view of Larkin. He was, the doctor wrote, a man 'with a very jocular, happy-go-lucky expression of face'. He had red hair and a red beard, blue eyes, 'good' teeth, a 'large Roman nose', and a 'florid complexion'. He displayed a 'happy manner', the notes went on, and was intelligent; he worked 'well', gave 'no trouble', ate and slept 'well' and answered questions 'well'. The only critical remarks made were that Larkin was prone to 'flightiness' and was 'extremely garrulous'.

Irish women patients, as we have seen, were also sometimes criticised for being flighty and talkative. The word 'flighty' seems to have meant not being as serious about their circumstances as the doctor expected a patient committed to a lunatic asylum should be. Again, one can only speculate that, due to cultural differences, aspects of the demeanour and behaviour of the Irish must have seemed 'peculiar' to non-Irish medical staff. While silence was certainly not acceptable, garrulousness was equally frowned upon. In the case of John Larkin, though, everything was not as 'well' with him as his doctor imagined, for only two weeks after he was committed Larkin contracted pneumonia and four days later he was dead.

The 'typical lunatic' in colonial Australia: British or Irish, male or female?

The notes made by English and Scottish doctors on their Irish patients, while seldom blatantly anti-Irish, nevertheless do contain clear evidence of the influence of negative ethnic, racial and religious stereotypes. The same can be said of the medical notes compiled by doctors about patients from other groups. Indigenous Australian, Chinese and Jewish patients were also assessed in terms of contemporary stereotypes. Yet studies of Australian asylum populations usually follow the practice – common to Australian history more generally – of lumping the Irish into the category 'British', alongside the English, Scots and Welsh. This means that important aspects of the Irish asylum experience are inevitably lost. In investigating late 19th-century asylums, Australian historians have highlighted the fact that the majority of the 'British' inmate population were male, middle aged, poor and unskilled, and frequently from rural backgrounds. Medical historian Stephen Garton concluded his pioneering history of NSW lunatic asylums by arguing that the 'typical lunatic' of the period 1850–1900, in addition to being between 25 and 55 years of age, was 'a single, male, rural, itinerant labourer' who had caused a public disturbance through drunkenness or violence and was usually diagnosed with mania.[74] Religious historian Anne O'Brien, in an important study of NSW poverty during 1880–1918, highlighted a similar cohort of men as especially vulnerable to institutionalisation. These were unmarried, unskilled immigrants, who had arrived in search of gold in the 1850s or 1860s usually without any existing family connections in NSW. But towards the end of the century, they were 'ageing, rootless' and 'semi-debilitated'.[75] Large numbers of such men ended up in benevolent asylums for paupers or in lunatic asylums.

Both Garton and O'Brien illustrate their arguments on lunacy and poverty in colonial NSW with examples of individual Irish immigrants, yet when it comes to the broader picture, they both employ the term 'British'. Garton, for instance, describes his 'typical lunatic' as being a male of 'British descent'. Elsewhere in his book, he does accept the 'overrepresentation of Irish Catholics in the patient population', but here he follows the common Australian practice by classing the Irish as 'Catholics' – that is, as a group defined essentially by their religion – while categorising their ethnicity as 'British'.[76] However, by employing the term 'British' loosely in this manner, Garton only succeeds in obscuring the fact that it was those born in Ireland, not in Britain, who were the largest ethnic group in late 19th-century NSW asylums.

Middle-aged, Irish rural labourers like James Ryan, Thomas Cahill and John Larkin largely fit Garton's profile of the 'typical lunatic', though Winifred Sharkey, Catherine Dobson, Hannah McCarthy, Joanna Herlihy and Johanna Flynn obviously do not. The distinctive gender balance among the Irish is lost with the use of the category 'British'. Garton says that by the 1930s women had come to form the majority of the NSW mental hospital population.[77] But among the Irish-born patient population, women were a majority or a near majority 50 years earlier. In addition, equating Irish with Catholic overlooks the many Protestant Irish who were inmates of Australian asylums and about whom we still know little. A study of Melbourne's Yarra Bend Asylum during the 1850s and 1860s has suggested that as many as 20–25 per cent of Irish patients may have been Protestant.[78]

Research on poverty, ill-health and isolation in colonial Victoria has produced a similar picture to that of NSW in terms of vulnerable unmarried, unskilled male immigrants who had typically arrived during the gold-rush era.[79] In a study of death certificates, social historian Janet McCalman has pointed out that, of those aged 12 and over who died in Victoria between 1836 and 1888, one-third died without anyone present knowing their father's name. And, according to McCalman, this was especially true in the case of Irish immigrants, who were more likely than the English or Scots to have arrived in the colony as single young adults, not as members of family groups.[80] The doctors' notes on Irish patients in Melbourne's Yarra Bend Asylum certainly do yield many examples of comments like 'no friends' or 'no family' and, occasionally, 'solitary life'. There is the case, for instance, of Margaret Cuthbert, a 45-year-old Irish woman committed to Yarra Bend in May 1897. In his notes, the asylum doctor dismissed her simply as 'stupid', writing that she had been 'brought by police' and that 'nothing else [was] known' about her.[81] FN Manning thought that 'isolation and nostalgia' were among the causes of insanity in NSW in 1880. Non-English speaking immigrants, itinerant rural workers and those with no family in the colony were especially prone, Manning wrote, to a lonely life and the pangs of homesickness that inevitably accompanied it, which could over time result in madness.[82]

We need to be careful, though, not to exaggerate the isolation of Irish migrants. As migration and medical historian Angela McCarthy discovered in her study of the Irish-born inmates of a New Zealand asylum between 1864 and 1909, while often unmarried and with their parents left behind in Ireland, these immigrants were frequently part of 'alternative family networks', composed of siblings, cousins, nephews and nieces, uncles and aunts, and sometimes even of childhood friends from the same parish or townland in Ireland. Migration historian David Fitzpatrick has demonstrated the significance of siblings and cousins in Irish chain migration to Australia by showing that in 1861, of assisted Irish immigrants to Victoria, about half (51.4 per cent) were sponsored by siblings already in the colony and nearly another quarter (23 per cent) by cousins; spouses sponsored only 8 per cent of immigrants and parents a mere 3.2 per cent.[83] So, while many Irish in the Antipodes lacked parents and spouses, significant numbers still had other relatives in the colonies, at least at the time of arrival. But, as we saw earlier, family, however it is defined, occupies an ambiguous position in terms of Irish committals. In many instances, it was relatives who instigated the committal process. At the same time, though, lack of a strong family support network could leave immigrants vulnerable, not just to committal, but to spending the remainder of their lives in a lunatic asylum.

In Ireland and large parts of the diaspora including Australia, the Irish were committed to psychiatric institutions in substantial numbers. Nonetheless, contemporary official figures on Irish committal rates, especially when compared to rates for the

Australian-born, need to be treated sceptically as the statistical methodology often employed in calculating them was faulty. Patrick O'Farrell was right when he acknowledged that there is 'no simple explanation' for the large numbers of Irish immigrants committed to colonial Australian lunatic asylums. Over the past 30 years, much research has been done on Australian asylums and mental hospitals, their patients and their staff. Overseas, the topic of asylums and the Irish has attracted a good deal of attention, notably in Ireland itself, but in the US, Britain, Canada and New Zealand as well. Less attention has, however, been paid to the Irish in Australian asylums.

In this chapter, while we have looked at more research data than O'Farrell had available to him in the 1980s, at the same time, we have raised many questions that only further research can hope to answer. The relationship between the Irish and asylums was a multifaceted one. It did not involve only Irish patients, but also Irish families, Irish policemen and Irish attendants, and on occasion Irish doctors. Distinctive attitudes towards asylums and asylum committal developed in Ireland: attitudes that were different from those prevailing in England. Irish immigrants brought these attitudes with them to the colonies, where they found a committal process very similar to the one they had been familiar with in Ireland. Thus, while the fact that Irish immigrants were mostly unmarried working-class adults predisposed them to committal – more so certainly than the youthful Australian-born population – their cultural background in terms of their familiarity with and acceptance of lunatic asylums probably also played a part in precipitating many of them into Australian asylums.

A close reading of medical case notes also makes clear that asylum doctors – most of whom were of English or Scottish birth and education – approached their Irish-born patients with pre-conceptions regarding Irish character, behaviour, even the face and body. The fact of being Irish could therefore have an impact on diagnosis and length of time in the asylum. Although during the 19th and early 20th centuries, most inmates of Australian asylums were male, the Irish always had substantial numbers of women amongst them: by the 1880s on an Australia-wide basis women constituted the majority of Irish asylum inmates. Therefore, explanations for burgeoning asylum populations that focus largely on the problems of specific groups of men, like itinerant rural labourers or ex-miners, do not account for the many Irish women found in asylums. These distinctive features of the Irish asylum experience mean that it is a serious mistake to subsume the Irish into the ethnic category 'British', for the Irish relationship with institutions for the mentally ill was markedly different from that of patients and staff born in Britain.

SECTION THREE:
POLITICS

CHAPTER 9

Colonial politics: Daniel O'Connell's 'Tail' and the Catholic Irish premiers

Fears expressed in Australia about the arrival of large numbers of Irish convicts, and later of Irish immigrants, almost invariably raised the spectre of violence and rebellion. In other words, the Irish were considered potential political players from the outset, but their aims and tactics were widely perceived as threatening British and imperial interests. It was therefore essential that they be defeated or at least contained.[1] During the 1790s, Ireland experienced an upsurge in popular unrest as Catholic and Protestant members of the urban middle and working classes, inspired by the French Revolution, sought to overthrow British rule. The British government responded with a crackdown on dissent, aimed to cow the population into submission and prevent a rebellion. There were mass arrests, with many either transported to the new penal colony in New South Wales (NSW) or pressed into the British navy. These extreme measures were not successful in preventing rebellion, although the 1798 and

1803 rebellions, which included a major French invasion in 1798, were poorly organised and ill-coordinated affairs. Nonetheless, untold thousands of people died in large-scale pitched battles, guerrilla campaigns and sectarian massacres.[2] Many Irish convicts, dispatched to Sydney directly from Ireland after 1791, had been involved in these bloody political upheavals, which together constituted the most serious threat to British rule in Ireland in over a century.[3]

It is hardly surprising then that when the Irish arrived in NSW the British initially reacted with fear, combined with more than a little loathing. These two emotions would set the tone for Irish involvement in Australian politics for many decades to come. To understand the considerable hostility that Catholic Irish political activities – even peaceful ones – generated, we need to bear in mind this Irish background and how the British perceived the Irish when it came to politics. Political and economic unrest, along with threats of rebellion, persisted in Ireland up until the early 1920s; and from the late 1850s, well-funded Irish-American revolutionary organisations emerged dedicated to overthrowing British rule in Ireland. Sectarianism was another deeply divisive factor, with Catholic Irish immigration widely perceived as heralding a concerted effort by Rome to expand its power into new territories. These ongoing threats helped fuel anxiety among Australians of Protestant British descent about Catholic Irish politicians and politics. Understanding this Irish background is essential, as without it reactions to Irish politicians in Australia can sometimes appear exaggerated and even inexplicable.

Daniel O'Connell and his 'Tail' in Australia

If rebellion in Ireland during the 1790s helped shape initial responses to the arrival of Irish convicts in colonial Australia, responses to free Irish immigrants after the 1820s were shaped by the campaigns of County Kerry lawyer, landowner and politician, Daniel O'Connell. During the 1820s and again in the early 1840s, O'Connell created mass popular movements in Ireland with the support of Catholic parish clergy. His first, successful, movement was aimed to force a reluctant British Tory government into allowing Catholic men to take up seats in the House of Commons, from which they had been barred since the late 17th century, while his second, unsuccessful, movement aimed to repeal the 1801 act of union between Britain and Ireland and restore a self-governing Irish parliament.[4]

O'Connell's use of extra-parliamentary political tactics was innovative and influential well beyond Ireland's shores. He publicly rejected political violence and instead relied upon mass mobilisation. This involved creating a national self-funding organisation, staging large-scale demonstrations and organising voters – all intended to pressure hostile governments into agreeing to his demands. During his repeal campaign of the early 1840s, he also staged 'monster meetings' throughout the south of Ireland, at which he delivered stirring speeches, attracting audiences numbering in the tens, if not hundreds, of thousands.[5] Yet, whereas O'Connell consistently advocated peaceful tactics, his mobilisation of vast numbers of working-class people meant his opponents considered he was threatening them with rebellion if they did not concede his demands. O'Connell also insisted that his campaigns were non-sectarian, but the fact that he recruited parish priests to help him win and maintain mass Catholic support alienated many Protestants, who saw him as promoting the Catholic Church to a position of political dominance. O'Connell was widely admired for his democratic methods by radicals and liberals throughout Europe and the Americas, but, in the eyes of British Protestant conservatives and many of their kin in Australia, he was a dangerous demagogue who aspired to undermine both the United Kingdom (UK) and the British Empire by establishing an independent Ireland with himself as dictator, his authority underwritten by the Catholic Church.[6]

O'Connell had many admirers and friends in NSW, but also enemies. In 1831, a reforming British Whig government had appointed Irish-born General Richard Bourke as governor of the colony. Bourke arrived to find a society split between successful free immigrants, many of whom had prospered as pastoralists and merchants and were known as 'Exclusives', and former convicts, some of whom had been equally economically successful, and were known as 'Emancipists'. The new governor soon attracted the ire of the Exclusives, who claimed that he favoured Emancipists, especially those who were Irish and Catholic. Under Bourke's administration, Catholic Irish lawyers like John Hubert Plunkett and Roger Therry served in senior government legal positions. Therry was related to O'Connell, as well as being a friend, while Plunkett was also an O'Connell family friend. Both men had actively supported the Catholic emancipation cause in Ireland during the 1820s. O'Connell helped Plunkett secure the position of NSW solicitor-general in 1832 and the two remained in contact, with Plunkett supplying O'Connell with information about the colony that enabled the Irish leader to make well-informed interventions in House of Commons debates during the 1830s on issues like convict transportation and colonial governance.[7]

O'Connell praised Bourke's appointment as governor and later his 1836 church act, which introduced equivalent government funding for the major Christian churches. But state funding of Catholicism outraged NSW's Protestant Exclusive faction.[8] In January 1836, the conservative *Sydney Herald* editorialised under the heading 'The Whigs in New South Wales' warning that 'respectable … Gentlemen' were in danger of becoming 'slaves' to the 'O'Connell Tail faction'.[9] The 'O'Connell Tail' was a term used by the English Tory press to disparage Irish nationalist members of parliament (MPs) for their subservience to O'Connell. It was intended to reinforce the notion that he was a dictator. The colonial press picked up the term and used it to attack Bourke and his Irish and Emancipist supporters.[10] Indeed, into the 1850s, the 'O'Connell Tail' continued to be employed in the Australian colonies as a term of political abuse even in non-Irish contexts.[11]

Despite intense hostility, however, O'Connell and his 'Tail' did exercise considerable influence on British and colonial politics, especially in the mid to late 1830s. During most of Bourke's governorship (1831–37), the UK was ruled by progressive Whig/Liberal administrations led by Lords Grey and Melbourne. And from 1835, the Melbourne government increasingly relied upon the votes of O'Connell and his Irish MPs to stay in power. As well as concessions to Catholics in NSW, major concessions were also made to Catholics in Ireland in the areas of official appointments, policing, church tithes, local government and education.[12]

During the 1830s, along with state aid to the Catholic Church, increased government-assisted Irish immigration emerged as a controversial issue. In September 1840, the *Sydney Gazette* attacked the arrival of growing numbers of assisted Irish immigrants or what the paper termed 'Papistical Immigrants'. The *Sydney Gazette*'s editor, George William Robertson, an

Irish-born Protestant, warned his readers against the demands for 'equality' O'Connell and his Catholic clerical friends were making in both Ireland and Australia. By equality, he said, they really meant 'papistical ascendancy' as Rome had determined on the 'establishment of Popery in this Colony' via Irish immigration.[13] Five weeks later, Robertson issued an even more dire warning, arguing that, if assisted Irish immigration continued at existing levels, within 10 to 12 years there would be 'few, if any, Protestants left' in NSW. He appealed to the government to fund instead the importation of 'Coolie labour' as, 'in a moral and religious sense', Indian 'coolies' were 'less evil' than the Catholic Irish. Indians might be 'Pagans' or members of the 'Mahomedan Church', but adherents of the 'Church of Rome' constituted a much more serious threat than did 'simple ... coolies'. Catholics threatened a 'second St Bartholomew Massacre' – that is, a surprise attack on Protestants with the aim of exterminating them. Robertson went on to urge his readers to form an 'Anti-papistical Association' whose members would pledge themselves to employ 'None But Protestants'.[14]

The return to office in 1841 of a British Tory government under Sir Robert Peel was unsurprisingly hailed by conservative colonial newspapers. In 1844, Peel's government put O'Connell on trial in Dublin for conspiracy to incite political disaffection. Alongside him in the dock was 28-year-old Charles Gavan Duffy, then editor of the Young Ireland newspaper, the *Nation*. The trial was followed closely by the Australian press with the *Sydney Morning Herald*, in reports headed 'English News', gloating when O'Connell was sentenced to 12 months in prison.[15] Duffy received a nine-month sentence. By contrast, Sydney's Catholic *Morning Chronicle*, edited by Irish-born Archdeacon John McEncroe and his nephew Michael D'Arcy, under the heading

'Irish News', lamented that an 'illustrious … patriot' had been convicted after an unfair trial merely for 'advocating the cause of Ireland and the well-being of her people'.[16]

One of O'Connell's biographers, Oliver MacDonagh, has written that a 'line of leading colonial politicians … first trained in O'Connell's "school"' had an 'unquestionably immense' influence on Australia's emerging democratic system of government.[17] This may well be true, but Patrick O'Farrell was also right when he characterised O'Connell as a divisive figure in Australia.[18] Protestant critics of the Catholic Irish distrusted O'Connell and those trained in his 'school'. In their eyes, he was an unscrupulous populist bent upon manipulating gullible people to advance his own interests, as well as those of the detested Catholic Church. Election-rigging, bribery, intimidation, jobbery, perjury and fraud were all crucial items in his political toolkit. And, if all else failed, then violent rebellion and sectarian massacre were options he might well resort to, since his pacifist rhetoric was an obvious sham. Many later Irish and Catholic colonial politicians were to be tarred with the same brush, that is portrayed as members of the 'O'Connell Tail': products of a distinctively Catholic Irish school of democratic politics of which O'Connell was the founder and exemplar.

Irish-born and Irish-Australian colonial premiers, 1855–1900

Irish immigrants and Catholic clergy, as MacDonagh pointed out, were active in colonial politics during the mid and late 19th century.[19] Catholic clergy campaigned tirelessly to have state aid restored to their schools. First introduced during the late 1830s in NSW by Governor Bourke, from the early 1870s onwards state funding was progressively withdrawn from church schools in most colonies. In reaction against Catholic lobbying, which continued up until the 1960s, some Protestants joined organisations like the Orange Order and various Protestant defence associations. These fiercely opposed what they saw as unwarranted Catholic demands for state subsidies as well as church interference in politics.[20] A Catholic Church historian has described the struggle over state aid as a full-scale 'religious war', while for one Labor Party historian it constituted the 'oldest, deepest, most poisonous debate in Australian history'.[21] For the better part of a century, any Catholic man or woman aspiring to pursue a political career in Australia had to grapple with the dilemma of state aid. Should they support it and please the Catholic Church, though at the risk of alienating many Protestant voters; or should they oppose it, which might cost them much-needed Catholic votes as well as giving offence to their priests and perhaps their families and friends too? Most 20th-century Labor Party leaders, whether Catholic or Protestant, came to regard the state aid question as 'political poison'.[22]

The Australian Irish also followed events in Ireland. From the 1840s, immigrants were helped to keep in touch with Ireland through the proliferation of newspapers aimed specifically at Catholic audiences. These provided more coverage of Irish happenings than did the mainstream press, which often relied for its Irish news on hostile English Tory papers.[23] From the mid 1860s through into the early 1920s, politics in Ireland were dominated by a series of campaigns and movements aiming to bring about major change in the political relationship between Britain and Ireland. These 60 years transformed Ireland in fundamental ways, but they also witnessed much violence and, after a series of rebellions and wars, the country emerged in the early 1920s partitioned into two antagonistic political entities: one independent and the other still part of the UK. All these movements and events found eager audiences of both supporters and opponents in Australia.[24]

The Fenians or Irish Republican Brotherhood attracted some adherents in the colonies from the early 1860s onwards, but Fenianism was never as popular among the Irish in Australia as it was in the United States or even in Britain. Nevertheless, the attempted assassination of one of Queen Victoria's sons in Sydney in 1868 by an Irish man claiming to be a Fenian, as well as the spectacular rescue of six Irish military convicts from Fremantle in 1876 by Irish-American Fenians, convinced many colonists that Fenianism was a significant menace.[25] Yet it was the campaign for a devolved Irish parliament, known as 'home rule', pursued in conjunction with land reform, that captured the loyalty of most Catholic Irish Australians from the late 1870s up until 1916. Supporters of home rule posed the question: since the young Australian colonies had been granted self-government with their own parliaments, why should not the ancient Irish nation enjoy the same privilege? But many Protestant Australians, including most of those of Irish descent, were strongly opposed to home rule, seeing it as calculated to weaken the UK and by extension the empire at a time of growing European great power rivalry. They believed that the Australian colonies, whose populations were largely of Protestant British descent, could be trusted to exercise self-government wisely, whereas the same could certainly not be said of the Catholic Irish.[26]

The Irish were politically active within the Australian parliamentary system as well as lobbying for change outside it.[27] Self-government, granted by the British between 1855 and 1890, allowed Irish men to stand for election to the six colonial parliaments. Some were successful and a handful even became heads of government or premiers.[28] A focus on premiers, although it does not capture the full extent of Irish involvement in Australian colonial governance, does permit a revealing comparison between the Catholic Irish and other groups along both ethnic and religious lines. Table 1 below lists the numbers of men who served as premiers between the beginning of self-government in each colony and 1900.[29] It shows how many of these men were of Irish birth or had at least one Irish-born parent and how many were Catholics.

Table 1: Number of colonial premiers of Irish and Catholic birth or parentage, 1855–1900[30]

COLONY	TOTAL NUMBER OF PREMIERS	IRISH BIRTH	CATHOLIC	IRISH PARENTAGE	CATHOLIC
NSW	13	2	1	1	0
Victoria	19	4	3	0	0
Queensland	15	1	0	1	1
Tasmania	19	1	0	1	0
South Australia	21	1	0	1	0
Western Australia	1	0	0	0	0
Total	88	9	4	4	1

As Table 1 shows, 13 out of 88 premiers (15 per cent) were of Irish birth or parentage, and of these 13, only five were Catholic. A clear majority (62 per cent) of Irish-born and Irish-Australian colonial premiers were Protestant, although Protestants were a minority within the Australian-Irish community as a whole, probably never exceeding around 25 per cent.[31] When it came to high political office during the late 19th century, however, the Protestant Irish obviously enjoyed distinct advantages over their Catholic fellow countrymen.[32] The historian Colm Kiernan was wrong therefore when he claimed that: 'Irish-Protestant Australians have not played as prominent a role in Australian politics as Irish-Catholic Australians'. During the colonial period at least, the reverse was true.[33]

Table 2 below expresses the number of premiers of Irish birth or parentage in each colony in percentage terms and compares these proportions to the corresponding figures for those of English, Scottish and Welsh birth or parentage.

Table 2: Ethnic backgrounds of colonial premiers by percentages, 1855–1900

COLONY	PERCENTAGE WITH IRISH BIRTH OR PARENTAGE	PERCENTAGE WITH ENGLISH BIRTH OR PARENTAGE	PERCENTAGE WITH SCOTTISH BIRTH OR PARENTAGE	PERCENTAGE WITH WELSH BIRTH OR PARENTAGE
NSW	23.1	61.5	15.4	0.0
Victoria	21.0	47.4	31.6	0.0
Queensland	13.3	40.0	40.0	6.7
Tasmania	10.5	73.7	15.8	0.0
South Australia	9.5	85.7	4.8	0.0
Western Australia	0.0	0.0	100.0	0.0
Total	14.8	62.5	21.6	1.1

If it was difficult for the Catholic Irish to achieve high political office in colonial Australia, Table 2 suggests that the Protestant Irish may have faced hurdles as well. Irish immigrants had always significantly outnumbered Scottish immigrants during the 19th century: in 1881, for example, the Irish-born made up 9.5 per cent of Australia's total settler population, whereas the Scottish-born were only 4.4 per cent. Yet 22 per cent of colonial premiers were of Scottish birth or parentage compared with only 15 per cent who had an Irish background.[34] So Irish origins may well have been a handicap for aspiring colonial politicians regardless of whether they were Protestant or Catholic, even though Protestants obviously enjoyed more success than did Catholics.

Of the five colonial premiers who were Catholics, four were Irish-born, and the other had Irish parents. Three were premiers of Victoria, while one served in NSW and the other in Queensland. Victoria's three Catholic Irish-born premiers – John O'Shanassy, Charles Gavan Duffy and Bryan O'Loghlen – first came to power in 1857, 1871 and 1881 respectively, while NSW did not have its only Catholic Irish-born premier – Patrick Jennings – until 1886. Queensland had no premiers of Catholic Irish birth, but one of Catholic Irish parentage – Thomas J Byrnes – who served briefly as premier in 1898. Tasmania had one premier of Irish birth – James Agnew – in 1886–87 and one of Irish parentage – Richard Dry – in 1866–69, both of whom were Protestants. The same was true for South Australia: it had a premier of Protestant Irish birth – Robert Torrens – in 1857 and one of Protestant Irish parentage – Charles Cameron Kingston – in 1893–99.[35] Western Australia only had one premier before 1900 and he was the son of Scottish immigrants, but its second premier, George Throssell, who lasted for only three months in 1901, was a Protestant from County Cork.

These statistics generate as many questions as answers. For instance, what were the main barriers to Catholic Irish success in colonial Australian politics? Were these barriers breached more successfully in Victoria than elsewhere? We will examine the careers of the five Catholic premiers of Victoria, NSW and

Queensland, as well as one NSW acting premier, to help shed light on these questions.

Victoria: O'Shanassy, Duffy and O'Loghlen, mid-1850s to early 1880s

Victoria had a substantial Irish-born and Catholic population, although so did NSW and Queensland.[36] The 'Catholic vote' was recognised as an influential factor in Victoria's politics, but the electorate still contained a substantial majority of Protestant men of British birth or descent.[37] The emergence of Catholic Irish political leaders in such circumstances was unusual. By comparison, New York City did not have its first Catholic Irish-American mayor until 1880, Boston until 1886 and Chicago until 1893.[38] When Tipperary-born John O'Shanassy first occupied the office of premier in 1857 – even though his government lasted only seven weeks – Charles Gavan Duffy pointed out that: '[n]obody had ever seen Irish Catholics in Cabinet office under the British Crown' before, not since the 17th century.[39]

The apparent successes of the Catholic Irish in Victoria came, however, at a high price in terms of a ferocious anti-Irish and anti-Catholic backlash that damaged the political careers of the three premiers. In his study of sectarianism in Australia, religious and political historian Michael Hogan suggested that after the Orange riots in Melbourne in 1846, sectarianism decreased during the gold-rush decade of the 1850s, but with the election of Catholics like O'Shanassy and Duffy, the emergence of the state aid question and the threat of Fenianism, sectarianism revived in the 1860s.[40] A comparison of newspaper reports dealing with Victoria's Catholic Irish premiers with reports on the Catholic premiers of NSW and Queensland certainly indicates that the rhetoric of the press in the southern colony was far more ferociously hostile.[41] Thus, rather than being a mark of substantial and secure achievement, the premierships of O'Shanassy, Duffy and O'Loghlen simply underlined the considerable barriers to lasting political influence that the Catholic Irish faced in colonial Australia.

As we saw when discussing male stereotypes in a previous chapter, critics of the three premiers drew freely upon anti-Irish tropes in their attacks, as well as upon negative readings of O'Connell's political style. O'Shanassy was depicted as an ignorant Irish peasant in thrall to the Catholic Church or, alternately, as the chieftain of a primitive tribe; Duffy was a dangerous republican rebel; and O'Loghlen was an unscrupulous corrupter of British justice and colonial democracy. Victoria under self-government was characterised by frequent changes of government: 29 ministries held office between 1855 and 1900. Unstable factions organised around specific issues or individuals heaped abuse upon one another relentlessly, abetted by a highly partisan press. In this febrile atmosphere, all politicians were subject to sometimes scurrilous attack. Yet those of Protestant British birth or parentage were rarely assailed on the basis of their ethnicity, race or religion, and their right to participate in colonial governance was unquestioned.[42]

Future Australian prime minister Alfred Deakin grew up in the 1860s and early 1870s amid scares about Fenian assassinations and rebellions and claims that 'priestcraft' – his own term – was on the march.[43] While at Melbourne Grammar School in 1871, he took the role of crown prosecutor in the mock trial for high treason of three Irish pupils. The Irish boys were accused of plotting to take over the colony with the intention of massacring the Protestants, declaring war on Britain and establishing an Irish republic.[44] When the fastidious Deakin later encountered John O'Shanassy in parliament, he found him 'uncouth in manner', being a 'peasant in build, gait and habit'. Like Daniel O'Connell, O'Shanassy, who held the premiership in 1857, 1858–59 and 1861–63, was an 'impatient intriguer'. He had an 'ungovernable appetite for power' and a 'disposition for jobbery in the interests of his countrymen', plus a 'marked subservience to his Church'.[45] In Deakin's eyes, O'Shanassy, despite having considerable 'brain-power', displayed all the flaws characteristic of his race, religion and class. Taken together, these should have disqualified him from high public office.[46]

Deakin's critique was mild, however, compared to that emanating from liberal and conservative newspapers, which were united in little else save their intense dislike of the Catholic Irish. When O'Shanassy was premier in 1861–63, the liberal *Age* described him as a 'low, scheming short-sighted peasant', with the 'shallow cunning' typical of the Irish lower orders. The paper was confident, though, that he would soon 'sink to his own proper low level, as a boor and ignoramus', when challenged by the 'varied intelligence, the superior manners and education and the broad political views' of men 'belonging to the middle classes of the United Kingdom'.[47]

The historian Stuart Macintyre has remarked that, in England, the Liberal Party had generally been sympathetic to O'Connell's campaign for Catholic emancipation during the 1820s and later supported Irish home rule, whereas the Tories tended to remain more doggedly anti-Catholic and anti-Irish. But in Victoria, liberalism had Scottish non-conformist and Irish Protestant roots, steeped in centuries of hatred for 'popery'.[48] Scottish-born Presbyterian David Syme, proprietor of the *Age* from 1860 until his death in 1908 and Deakin's mentor, typified this brand of liberalism. He championed the values of freedom and tolerance, while at the same time taking every opportunity, according to his biographer, to launch 'relentlessly fierce, often vicious attacks' against the Catholic Church and its Irish adherents.[49]

Charles Gavan Duffy and Bryan O'Loghlen were harder to caricature as Irish peasants or tribal chieftains, although some cartoonists did attempt to do so.[50] Duffy came from a prosperous Ulster farming family and was a journalist before being elected to the British House of Commons in 1852. Dublin-born O'Loghlen was both a barrister and a baronet. The title had been conferred by the crown upon his father, Michael, who served as a government law officer and judge under the Whigs during the 1830s, making him the first Catholic since the 1680s to hold such positions in either Ireland or England. Michael O'Loghlen was a close friend of O'Connell, while his eldest son, Colman, also a barrister, had helped defend O'Connell and Duffy in court in 1844.[51] Charles Gavan Duffy and Bryan O'Loghlen were both Irish nationalists and Catholics like the 'peasant' O'Shanassy, but, unlike him, they were unquestionably middle-class professional men.

In terms of colonial politics, Duffy's Achilles heel was his radical nationalist past. His involvement with the Young Ireland movement, supporters of which had staged the 1848 Rebellion, and his own unsuccessful prosecutions for treason-felony in 1848–49, provided his opponents with an inexhaustible supply of ammunition. In Victoria, his enemies believed that his past record disqualified him for political office in any British territory. At a public dinner of welcome in 1856, the newly arrived Duffy, presumably ignorant of the strength of anti-Irish sentiment in the colony, made an unfortunate speech that was to haunt him. He informed his audience that he had no intention 'to repudiate or apologise for any part of my past life'. 'I am still', he insisted, 'an Irish rebel to the backbone and to the spinal marrow.'[52] This last sentence would be thrown back at Duffy by opponents for the remainder of his 24 years in Victoria. In his autobiography, written during the 1890s, a sadder and wiser Duffy acknowledged that in leaving the northern hemisphere, he had naively hoped to get away from rancorous sectarian politics, but he had discovered to his cost that they flourished as strongly in the southern hemisphere. Stuart Macintyre has gone further, arguing that antagonism between the Catholic Irish and the Protestant Irish, English, Scots and Welsh was 'even more virulent' in settler colonies like Victoria than in the UK, because the greater freedom enjoyed by 'transplanted communities merely enabled their enmity to run unchecked'.[53]

Historians have generally judged Duffy's political career in Victoria a failure.[54] His championing of federation from the 1850s onwards, alongside O'Shanassy, is sometimes praised, but his seriously flawed *Land Act 1862* is invariably held against him.[55] Historian of colonial Victoria, Geoffrey Serle, thought 'he never fulfilled his great promise'. This was partly due, Serle felt, to his personality, for he was prone to 'pettiness, petulance and egotism'. Yet Serle also recognised the strength of the opposition that Duffy faced: 'his Irish background condemned him to fight battle after battle against prejudice which could never be borne down'.[56] Serle acknowledged that in such circumstances, it was almost impossible for Catholic Irish politicians to have a major impact.[57]

More recently, though, political historian Sean Scalmer has suggested that Duffy had more impact than previously recognised. Duffy's attitude to Daniel O'Connell was deeply ambivalent as, like many Young Irelanders, he blamed O'Connell for the failure of the repeal campaign. However, in an 1880 history of the Young Ireland movement, Duffy had nothing but praise for the series of 'monster meetings' that O'Connell had staged in 1843 at sites of Irish historic importance.[58] During his brief premiership in 1871–72, Duffy used the long summer parliamentary recess to embark with his Cabinet on a series of speaking tours through rural and regional Victoria, visiting more than a dozen townships and settlements, trying to whip up popular support for the government and its policies. As Scalmer demonstrates, Duffy's visits were carefully orchestrated performances, which included formal invitations, travel by special trains, elaborate processions, the laying of foundation stones, civic openings and inspections, and grand banquets with numerous toasts and lengthy speeches. Duffy told audiences that governments were 'strong only so long as the tramp of the people is heard on the same highway marching to the same goal', united under an 'Australian banner'.[59] The Melbourne press reacted with horror to these visits, accusing Duffy of bypassing parliament and attempting, like O'Connell, to establish an extra-parliamentary movement answerable only to himself. His tours were portrayed as an attack on British constitutional conventions and colonial responsible government by a man with an Irish revolutionary past.[60] Scalmer sees Duffy's visits as politically innovative and considers that O'Connell's 1843 meetings were his most likely inspiration.[61]

After these tours, Duffy was confident of victory at the next election. Thus, when in June 1872 his government lost its majority in the lower house amid accusations of jobbery, he asked the governor to dissolve parliament so that an election could be held. But the governor flatly refused, instead calling upon the Opposition, led by London-born James G Francis, to form a government, which it promptly did. *Melbourne Punch* satirised Duffy in the character of a pig-tailed Chinese gambler, 'That Haythen Duf-fee', exposed as a cheat, with cards labelled 'bribes' cascading out of the sleeves of his exotic gown.[62] The Francis government proceeded to pass a new education Act introducing, for the first time in colonial Australia, free, compulsory, secular elementary education and ending state financial support for Catholic schools. After serving as speaker of the lower house, the by-then Sir Charles Gavan Duffy eventually retired in 1880, settling in the south of France. In his autobiography, he wrote that he might have continued in Victorian politics, except that he 'loathed the task of answering again and again the insensate inventions of religious bigotry'.[63]

Like O'Shanassy and Duffy, Bryan O'Loghlen has been judged a failure by historians of Victorian colonial politics. Serle dismissed him as a 'stop-gap' premier, heading a 'minority ministry of Catholics, party rebels and opportunists, dominated by "Tommy" Bent'.[64] Deakin, who campaigned with O'Loghlen in elections aimed at winning the 'Catholic vote', summed him up as 'genial, gentle, indolent, lethargic, procrastinating, improvident and impoverished'. At the same time, Deakin disapproved of O'Loghlen's Irish nationalism, or what Deakin called his deplorable tendency to see 'his opponents as Saxon oppressors due to suffer for their past sins against his country'. Deakin implied that it was O'Loghlen's lack of character that made him susceptible to the influence of the 'degraded' and 'untrustworthy' half-Irish convict's son, Thomas Bent, a man Deakin considered to be devoid of all morals and principles.[65] The conservative Bent was happy for the more liberal O'Loghlen to occupy the premiership in 1881–83 while he controlled the railways portfolio, since this allowed him to speculate freely in railway construction for his own personal financial gain.[66]

Circumstances also conspired against O'Loghlen, as we saw in an earlier chapter. He had been attorney-general in the Berry government at the time of the Kelly outbreak in 1878–80. The conservative press relished portraying him then as 'Bryan O'Larrikin', the 'larrikin son of old and respectable Micky O'Loghlen', who after fleeing Ireland to escape his creditors was given a crown prosecutor's job in Victoria in 1863 during the premiership of the corrupt O'Shanassy.[67] The allegation that O'Loghlen was somehow in league with Ned Kelly appeared vindicated when the Kelly gang was finally apprehended shortly after Berry and O'Loghlen lost office.[68] In 1879, a Catholic Education Defence League was established to campaign at elections to restore state aid to church schools. Whereas O'Shanassy strongly supported the organisation, O'Loghlen opposed it, arguing – rightly as it turned out – that it would be counterproductive and only promote a sectarian backlash.[69] Serle certainly thought that Victoria, in the decade after the *Education Act 1872*, suffered its 'worst period of sectarian antagonism' before 1916.[70]

The *Leader*, a weekly linked to the daily *Age*, believed that the 'whole secret' of O'Loghlen's method of government was to spend lots of money on railways and public works, to give 'large orders' to manufacturers and importers, to cram the civil service with 'Flynns and Flannagans' and, for 'every difficulty', to set up a committee of inquiry.[71] Lacking a stable majority in parliament, O'Loghlen did attempt to defer divisive issues like education and Aboriginal affairs by establishing inquiries. But when his royal commission on education produced conflicting reports,

O'Loghlen called a snap election in February 1883. This proved a disastrous decision. With the *Age* orchestrating a ferocious defence of the 1872 education Act against alleged Catholic attack, the government was soundly defeated.[72] O'Loghlen lost his seat, as did at least half the Catholic members of the Legislative Assembly, including O'Shanassy, who died three months later.[73]

Victoria had six premiers of Protestant Irish birth or parentage between 1883 and 1914, including in 1913 its first Labor premier, George Elmslie.[74] But the colony's experiment with Catholic Irish-born premiers ended in 1883. A Catholic Scottish-born premier governed briefly in 1899–1900, but there were no further premiers of Irish Catholic background until Labor's Edmond J Hogan took office for the first time in 1927.[75]

NSW: Jennings and Dalley, mid 1880s

Patrick Jennings served briefly as premier of NSW from February 1886 until January 1887, the only Irish-born Catholic to do so.[76] Jennings was from a middle-class Ulster family and had trained as a civil engineer in England, before immigrating to Victoria in 1852, where he made money running a general store on the goldfields. He then invested in land during the 1860s, acquiring a string of pastoral properties in NSW and Queensland. After moving to NSW, he served several terms in the colony's parliament, although he was generally considered a rather reluctant politician. He supported the Irish home rule movement when it emerged during the 1870s and, unlike O'Loghlen in Victoria, he welcomed John and William Redmond on their fundraising tour in 1883. But like many of his fellow Catholic Irish immigrants who had prospered in the Australian colonies, he was an

THE LESSON OF THE ELECTIONS.

[See preceding page.

A loyal Victoria shows Premier O'Loghlen out the door after his defeat.
O'Loghlen, in Irish peasant dress, takes with him objects that had ensured
his downfall, including a Fenian and a Catholic bishop, a knife dripping
with blood labelled 'Redmond Mission' and a paper marked 'Grattan
Address'. A tethered pig, branded with a mitre symbolising the church,
follows him out.

Source: 'The lesson of the elections', *Melbourne Punch*, 1 March 1883, pp. 4–5.

imperialist, convinced that Irish home rule would strengthen rather than weaken the ties of empire. As well as receiving a papal knighthood in 1874, Jennings accepted a British knighthood in 1879.[77]

Politics in colonial NSW, as in Victoria, were faction-ridden, acrimonious and often chaotic, with frequent changes of government. In 1885 alone, three men occupied the position of premier, while a fourth served for a time as acting premier. Revenue from land, which the government depended heavily upon, was in decline and the deficit was mounting alarmingly. In a move aimed to tap new sources of finance, Jennings, who had previously supported free trade, proposed a duty on imported goods.[78] Free traders in parliament and even in his own ministry bitterly opposed the measure, although he did manage to get it through. Even economic issues could become clouded by anti-Irish sentiment, for Catholics in NSW were widely seen as supporters of protection. The *Bulletin* argued that this was due to 'race' not class, since the Irish blamed free trade for the Great Famine of the 1840s.[79] In January 1887, however, Jennings abruptly resigned. It was suggested that his health was suffering under the strain of trying to maintain order among his 'unruly' team of ministers, with his deputy George Dibbs – one of the four 1885 premiers – being especially obstructive. In these trying circumstances, Jennings had simply lost his appetite for politics.[80]

But another explanation offered in the press for Jennings' resignation concerned the notorious Mount Rennie rape case. In September 1886, a 16-year-old domestic servant named Mary Jane Hicks was raped by a gang of youths at Moore Park in Sydney. Most of the young men, described as 'larrikins' by newspapers, came from a part of the nearby working-class suburb of Waterloo known as 'Irish Town'. Eleven of them were tried in November and nine convicted, six of whom were Catholics of Irish parentage. In 1886 rape was still a capital crime in NSW and, despite the jury recommending mercy, the judge sentenced all nine to death. Amid intense public debate about the fairness of the trial and the appropriateness of the death penalty for rape, it was then up to the executive council, composed of the governor, premier and Cabinet, to decide if the executions should proceed.[81] Newspapers reported that the Cabinet was split, four ministers supporting execution and four reprieve, with Dibbs among the former group and Jennings leading the latter. The *Daily Telegraph* speculated that Jennings's resignation was a ploy to get rid of Dibbs, so the premier could reconstitute his Cabinet creating a majority in favour of a reprieve.[82] If Jennings' resignation was tactical, aimed to remove Dibbs and save the Mount Rennie rapists, then it failed.

The press fulminated against larrikins, but there were sectarian and racist undertones to some of the commentary. In an article entitled 'Our Larrikins', the *Sydney Mail* announced that the 'source' of the problem was a 'want of self-control' among young men. Most of the convicted rapists had attended a 'denominational school', by which the article meant a Catholic school. Such schools, instead of teaching religion and morality, were far too concerned with questions of 'theology'. Further anti-Irish tropes were invoked in describing the appearance and behaviour of larrikins. These youths were clannish, congregating in small groups on street corners and in parks. A 'certain type of larrikin face' had developed, the article alleged, which made larrikins very difficult to tell apart, just like the Chinese. Most had 'thick lips' and a 'sensual self-asserting' manner; their eyes were always on the 'look-out for opportunity', though with an 'expression of mental vacuity'.[83] Characteristics often ascribed to the Irish, like clannishness, violence, cunning, laziness, immorality and ugliness were all deployed in 'Our Larrikins' to condemn the Catholic teenagers convicted of the Mount Rennie rape.

After a protracted executive council meeting in mid December 1886, a decision was taken to reprieve three of those convicted. But public campaigns both for and against the execution of the remaining six continued. Heading the anti-execution forces were Catholic clergy and politicians and the *Bulletin* magazine. Jennings held lengthy meetings with the governor, Lord Carrington, urging further reprieves, while Archbishop Patrick Moran of Sydney, in a letter to Carrington, stressed the 'youth and ignorance of the culprits' and warned against the 'frenzy for blood' that the affair had unleashed.[84] With the executions scheduled for 7 January 1887, a deputation composed of Moran, former premier Henry Parkes, Anglican bishop Alfred Barry and WB Dalley, acting premier in 1885, saw the governor in person on 5 January to plead for mercy for all six youths. But the next day Carrington announced that he would reprieve only two. Ultimately, four went to the gallows in Darlinghurst Gaol before a large audience in a botched hanging that saw three of them strangled to death. Of the four, three were Catholics.[85] After visiting Australia in 1895, Michael Davitt, who was a penal reformer as well as an Irish nationalist, expressed outrage at the Mount Rennie case, though he commended WB Dalley, a barrister connected with the defence, who had spoken out in the strongest possible terms against the sentences, comparing them to 'some of the darkest pages of a very dark period of Irish history'.[86]

William Bede Dalley, a close friend of Jennings, has not been included in the lists of NSW premiers of Irish birth or parentage in Tables 1 and 2. This is because he was only acting NSW premier from October 1884 to May 1885 during the illness of Premier Alexander Stuart; otherwise, Dalley had served in several governments as attorney-general. Yet in many respects his brief premiership was more significant than that of Jennings, because Dalley was, as discussed in a previous chapter, responsible for the Sudan contingent: the dispatch of a military force to fight beyond Australasian shores for the first time. The contingent was intended to help the British recapture Khartoum from Muslim fundamentalists and avenge the death of General Charles Gordon. Some historians have portrayed the initiative as a 'rehearsal' for Australia's participation in future 'unnecessary' overseas wars.[87]

The Catholic Dalley, a successful barrister, journalist and politician, was, like Jennings, a supporter of both Irish home rule and the British Empire. Dalley favoured imperial federation: strengthening the ties of empire by giving the settler colonies and Ireland a larger say in imperial policy. But to earn their place at the table of empire, Australians had to be willing to fight for Britain. Dalley envisaged the colonies as the 'camps and barracks of Imperial forces ready to die for the Empire'.[88] A man noted for his sense of humour, he also enjoyed confounding the expectations of Orangemen. It was ironic, Dalley noted, that having been labelled 'plotting Papists and Fenian rebels' for so many years, it was now a 'Paddy and a Holy Roman' who was sending nearly 800 Australians, one-quarter of them Catholics, overseas to 'serve the Queen on the field of battle' for the first time.[89]

Journalist JF Hogan, in his celebratory 1887 book *The Irish in Australia*, hailed Dalley as the foremost 'Australian Patriot' of the day, a worthy successor to WC Wentworth, another NSW statesman of Irish parentage. Hogan saw the Sudan contingent as signalling that 'a new nation was beginning to put forth its strength in the antipodes' in support of the empire.[90] The English historian JA Froude, who was noted for his anti-Irish opinions, happened to be visiting Sydney at the time and spoke at length with Dalley. He later wrote that the NSW colonists 'cared nothing about the Soudan', rather they were 'making a demonstration in favour of national identity'.[91] The historian Ken Inglis generally agreed with the assessments of Hogan and Froude, arguing that the contingent amounted to an attempt by those of convict or Catholic Irish ancestry – or, like Dalley, both – to erase their past. As one contemporary NSW politician grandly put it, the contingent would wash away the disgrace of Botany Bay in the waters of the Nile.[92]

Before the contingent's departure, newly arrived Archbishop Moran said mass for the Catholic soldiers. Unlike the imperialist Dalley, however, the archbishop made no mention of Britain or the empire. According to him, the contingent, under an 'Australian banner', was destined to help Christianise and civilise Africa.[93] Critics, with the *Bulletin* and Henry Parkes in the vanguard, mocked Dalley's bravado. The critics considered themselves vindicated when, before the contingent even reached Africa, the British decided to abandon their plans to conquer the Sudan. Within less than four months, the contingent was back in Sydney, having seen little action and sustained a handful of casualties due mainly to disease.[94]

Queensland: Byrnes and the rise of labour, 1890s

If, during the 1880s, NSW Catholic politicians like Jennings and Dalley were imagining a future for their colony fighting to extend imperial frontiers, while helping to determine policy in London alongside a home rule in Ireland, by the 1890s expectations had changed significantly. In Ireland, the home rule movement fractured in 1890-91 over the O'Shea divorce scandal into two mutually hostile parties, while at the same time home rule was beginning to face challenges from more radical political and cultural causes. Meanwhile, in the midst of a serious economic depression in colonial Australia, conservative and liberal politicians were thrown together to combat the emerging threat of political labour.

Thomas Joseph Byrnes, the son of poor Catholic Irish immigrant parents, became premier of Queensland in 1898 at the relatively young age of 38. But his premiership was cut short: assuming office in April, Byrnes was dead by September, a victim of measles and pneumonia. He achieved little as premier, yet his political career is nevertheless revealing of the challenges Catholic politicians still faced at the end of the century.[95] Byrnes's Irish-born father died young, plunging the family into poverty. But, recognised as an extremely bright pupil at his north Queensland state primary school, Byrnes won a scholarship to Brisbane Grammar School and then another to Melbourne University, where he studied law. After returning to Brisbane in 1890 he entered politics, initially in the upper house before winning a lower house seat in 1893. He was appointed attorney-general in a conservative administration. At the next election in 1896, he was defeated in North Brisbane, but captured the seat of Warwick on the Darling Downs, which had a significant Catholic population. Supporters of secular education and opponents of the Labor Party were later to put him forward as an example - albeit a rare one - of a poor Catholic boy who had reached the top of public life via the state school system and non-labour politics.[96]

As Byrnes was entering the Queensland political arena from the right, Irish immigrants were entering it from the left. The first man elected to the colony's parliament representing the interests of labour was miner and trade unionist Thomas Glassey, an Ulster Presbyterian. His election in 1888 was followed in 1890 by that of Tipperary-born John Hoolan, a former carpenter and miner who owned radical newspapers. But not until 1892 was a formally endorsed Labor candidate returned at a by-election. He was shearer and unionist Thomas J Ryan, born to Irish immigrant parents during their voyage to Australia in 1852. Another who played an important role in labour politics outside parliament was Charles Seymour, a Dublin-born seaman and journalist, who was secretary of the Queensland branch of the Seamen's Union. He was also a sub-editor and later editor of the Brisbane *Worker*, one of the most influential labour newspapers in the country. Throughout most of the 1890s, either Glassey or Hoolan led the growing number of Labor members elected to the Legislative Assembly (MLAs). When Irish nationalist leader Michael Davitt visited Brisbane in 1895, he spoke to all the Labor MLAs and, although he acknowledged that they were 'inexperienced ... in Parliamentary tactics', he predicted that 'within the next few years' there will be 'a Labour-ruled Queensland'.[97] But both Glassey and Hoolan had been displaced by December 1899, when, in the wake of the political disruption caused by Byrnes's death, the Queensland Labor Party first took office. Although Labor rule lasted a mere six days, it marked a milestone in being the first Labor government that Australia had ever seen.[98]

The battle between left and right in Queensland during the depression of the 1890s was hard fought and bitter. As a senior government law officer, Byrnes used his formidable skills to combat labour interests and protect those of the colony's employers, pastoralists and plantation owners. After TJ Ryan was elected to the Legislative Assembly in 1892, Byrnes helped amend the 1885 electoral Act to include stricter residential requirements and to halve parliamentary salaries, thus depriving many itinerant workers of the vote and making it harder for working-class men to pursue parliamentary careers. In 1894, during a shearers' strike, Byrnes championed a peace preservation Act that the *Worker*, using Irish terminology, labelled a 'coercion act'.[99] This measure allowed the executive council to imprison people without trial. Davitt, touring Queensland in 1895, found himself constantly asked how Queensland's 'Coercion Act' compared with those imposed on Ireland.[100]

Although he served the non-labour cause loyally and effectively, Byrnes could not escape the fact that he came from a Catholic Irish background when most on his side of politics were of Protestant British birth or descent and therefore deeply suspicious of the Catholic Irish. As in Victoria and NSW, sectarianism was ingrained in Queensland society and was reflected in its politics as well.[101] For many, a Catholic Irish-Australian conservative like Byrnes was a political anomaly. Sectarianism featured prominently in both the 1893 and 1896 Queensland elections.[102] In 1896, before successfully contesting Warwick, Byrnes had been soundly defeated in the seat of North Brisbane amid a sectarian campaign. As well as attacks from the *Worker* on the left, Byrnes also faced attacks from the Brisbane *Telegraph* on the right. The *Worker* accused him of hypocrisy and arrogance. He came of 'poor parents', which was 'no disgrace', and had been educated through scholarships, which was 'to his credit'. But why then, the paper asked, did he oppose socialism, for where would he be without state schools and universities? Whereas Byrnes was eloquent in his 'denunciations of the English landlord's oppression of the Irish peasant', the paper went on, at the same time, he was 'white hot ... in advocating the oppression of the Queensland bushman by the squatter'.[103] The *Worker* obviously thought that Byrnes's Catholic Irish background fitted him for labour rather than conservative politics.[104] From his own side of politics, Byrnes's support for Irish causes and for state aid to Catholic schools attracted the ire of elements in the conservative press. During the 1896 campaigns in both North Brisbane and Warwick, anti-Catholic leaflets attacking him personally were distributed to voters.[105] He claimed in speeches that the Brisbane *Telegraph* was responsible for mounting a sectarian campaign against him.[106] The *Telegraph* hit back by insisting that, as he was a Catholic, Byrnes's assurances he would not attempt to amend the education Act to allow the restoration of state aid could not be trusted.[107]

Colonial Australia's Catholic premiers of Irish birth or descent, regardless of their political complexion, suffered fierce attacks based on their race, ethnicity and religion. Even Dalley in NSW, who sent troops overseas for the first time to fight for the British Empire, and Byrnes in Queensland, who successfully championed employers against labour, did not escape racial and sectarian vilification. And, as a new century opened with Federation in 1901, such abuse only became more entrenched in the country's political culture.

CHAPTER 10

Catholic Irish Australians in the political arena after 1900: from sectarianism to the split

The first half of the 20th century was in many ways the heyday of Catholic Irish-Australian political activism. The Australian Labor Party (ALP) provided an avenue, at both state and federal level, for many more Catholics of Irish descent – mostly but not exclusively working class – to become involved in politics.[1] But, just as Catholic Irish politicians in colonial Australia sparked a backlash based on race, ethnicity and religion, so too did Catholic prominence in the ALP. After 1900, while Catholics mainly aligned themselves to Labor, Protestants mostly supported a variety of non-Labor parties. But, within the ALP itself, clashes along religious lines also occurred. In the 40 years between 1915 and 1955, the Labor Party underwent major splits on three occasions, with particularly the first and third of these splits pitting large numbers of Catholic members of the party against their non-Catholic fellow members.[2] The splits were not about religion as such, but they did reflect aspects of Catholic

Irish-Australian culture that continued to set it apart from the values held by Australians of Protestant British descent. This chapter will examine events surrounding the first split over conscription during the First World War, while also looking briefly at the third split in the mid 1950s. It will consider the extent of Catholic Irish-Australian involvement in the ALP; what impact political events in Ireland between 1900 and 1923 had on the Australian Catholic community; and the bitterly divisive nature of sectarianism in early 20th-century Australia.

Catholic Irish Australians and the ALP

Catholics joined the Labor Party in all states, but particularly in the eastern states, where most Irish immigrants had settled during the 19th century.[3] Historian Celia Hamilton's work on turn-of-the-century New South Wales (NSW) politics demonstrated that, whereas in 1891 only 8 per cent of the first Labor members of the NSW Legislative Assembly were Catholic, by 1910–11 this proportion had jumped to around 36 per cent.[4] Both Sydney's Catholic newspapers, the *Freeman's Journal* and the *Catholic Press*, threw their support behind the ALP, as did the city's archbishop, Cardinal Patrick Moran. When Labor representatives were first elected in NSW in 1891, even though few were Catholic at that stage, Moran nevertheless hailed their success in no uncertain terms, calling it a 'glory' and a 'triumph'. Basing his statements on the authority of Pope Leo XIII's recent encyclical on workers' rights, *Rerum Novarum*, Moran upheld the 'just claim of labour' to safe working conditions and fair wages. But at the same time, he also warned workers against the evils of socialism, anarchism and nihilism. Indeed, he was keen to see Catholic workers join the ALP in large numbers to combat socialist influence within the party.[5]

William Redmond MP, brother of the leader of the Irish home rule party, was impressed on a visit to Australia in 1905 by the power of the new federal Labor Party, writing that, although not then in government, it was still able to ensure that the 'interests of labour' were 'hedged around and safeguarded in every way'. Redmond thought that the strength of the ALP lay in the fact that it had 'largely acted on the model of the Irish party in the House of Commons'. Like the home rule party, but unlike any other British or Australian party, the ALP was 'pledge bound', which meant that members were obliged to sign a statement pledging themselves to advocate and vote exclusively for the party's agreed platform.[6] Colm Kiernan has argued that the ALP acquired the pledge via former members of the Irish National League, an organisation established in Ireland in 1882 and introduced into Australia by the Redmond brothers during their 1883 tour. The League, which constituted the extra-parliamentary lobbying and fundraising arm of the home rule party, went into decline when the Irish party split in 1890–91 over the O'Shea divorce.[7] This prompted some of the League's most active Irish-Australian members to transfer their allegiance to the emerging Labor Party.[8]

Catholic Irish-Australian support for the ALP is often explained in straightforward economic terms. As they were predominantly working class, Catholics naturally backed the party that best represented their class interests. While this is undoubtedly true, it should be borne in mind that during the late 19th century significant numbers of Irish Australians were upwardly mobile and men from poor backgrounds could achieve middle-class status, as demonstrated by the careers of politicians like O'Shanassy, Dalley and Byrnes. The 1933 federal census, which was the first to correlate religion with income, offers a valuable snapshot of economic and social stratification within the Australian Catholic community. The census revealed that Catholic male workers, who made up 19 per cent of the total male workforce, were spread widely through all income brackets.[9] However, at 15 per cent, they were under-represented among top earners; whereas, at 21 per cent, they were overrepresented among low-income earners; and, at 24 per cent, they made up nearly a quarter of the many unemployed. A significant Catholic middle class obviously existed by the 1930s, but Catholics continued to be dogged by low pay and unemployment, as compared to the non-Catholic working class.[10]

Chris McConville's study of the residential distribution of Catholics in Sydney and Melbourne between the 1850s and the 1930s showed that they were slower to move out of inner-city, working-class suburbs than were non-Catholics. Even in 1933, there remained clusters of Catholic Irish-Australian households within these poorer suburbs that appear to have maintained a distinctive sub-culture, centred on the church and the pub.[11] In socio-economic terms, Catholics were clearly on the rise, but, even during the 1930s, they still had some way to go to catch up with non-Catholic Australians. That large numbers of them were conscious of their disadvantage and looked to the Labor Party and the trade union movement to help them bridge the gap is perhaps not surprising.[12]

But, as Patrick O'Farrell argued, it was not only economic factors that created the Catholic alliance with Labor. With the non-Labor parties being 'increasingly identified with Protestantism, even militant Protestantism, Catholics were not only ... pulled towards Labor by their self-interest as workers, but pushed towards it by the anti-Catholicism of non-Labor'. Non-Labor parties simply did not welcome Catholic members and, for politically ambitious Catholics, the chances of being selected to stand for parliament as a non-Labor candidate were small. Catholics really had few other political options than to join or vote for the ALP.[13]

Irish-Australian premiers and prime ministers, 1901–45

A comparison between state premiers with Irish family backgrounds during the years 1901-45 and premiers from the colonial period helps to highlight the Irish-Australian contribution to the leadership of the ALP.

Table 1: State premiers with Irish family backgrounds, 1901–45[14]

STATE	TOTAL NUMBER OF PREMIERS	NUMBER FROM IRISH FAMILIES	PERCENTAGE FROM IRISH FAMILIES	PERCENTAGE OF IRISH PREMIERS / ALP MEMBERS
NSW	14	4	28.6	50.0
Victoria	17	8	47.0	50.0
Queensland	11	5	45.4	80.0
Tasmania	12	5	41.7	100.0
South Australia	13	0	0.0	0.0
Western Australia	15	3	20.0	33.3
Total	82	25	30.5	64.0

Whereas during 1855-1900 only 15 per cent of all premiers came from an Irish immigrant family, Table 1 shows that during 1901-45 this proportion had doubled to 30 per cent. Moreover,

nearly two-thirds (64 per cent) of this latter group were members
of the ALP, while most ALP premiers with Irish ancestry appear
to have grown up in Catholic families (81 per cent). These figures
underline the very significant role that the ALP played in the rise
of Catholic politicians during the first half of the 20th century.
There were other notable changes from the colonial period
as well. We saw in the previous chapter that a clear majority
(61.5 per cent) of the pre-1900 Irish-Australian premiers were
Protestants. Although it is not always easy to identify the
religious affiliations of the 1901–45 Irish-Australian premiers,
it appears that around 56 per cent were either Catholics or had
at least come from a Catholic family background. So, although
many Irish Australians of Protestant descent remained involved
in state politics, as they had been during the colonial era, they
were now outnumbered by those of Catholic descent.

Irish Australians also figured prominently in federal politics
and, again, most were members of the ALP. In his study of federal Labor, political scientist LF Crisp found that those with an
Irish family background made up 11 per cent of the delegates
elected to the party's first policy-making federal conference held
in 1900; by 1905 they were 30 per cent; in 1915, the figure was
33 per cent; in 1921, after the party split over conscription, it
had jumped to 56 per cent; and, in 1939, on the eve of war, Irish
Australians comprised 61 per cent of federal ALP conference delegates.[15] Clearly, Catholic involvement and influence in the ALP
had increased substantially in the five decades after 1900.

Of the 16 men who held the office of prime minister between
1901 and 1945, eight were of Irish ancestry, and in five cases, both
parents had been born in Ireland.

Table 2: Australian prime ministers with Irish family backgrounds, 1901–49[16]

NAME	DATES IN OFFICE	PARTY	FAMILY RELIGION	IRISH LINK
JC Watson	1904	ALP	Protestant	Mother[17]
SM Bruce	1923–9	Non-Labor	Protestant	Father
JH Scullin	1929–32	ALP	Catholic	Parents
JA Lyons	1932–9	Non-Labor	Catholic	Parents
AW Fadden	1941	Non-Labor	Protestant	Parents
John Curtin	1941–5	ALP	Catholic	Parents
FM Forde	1945	ALP	Catholic	Parents
JB Chifley	1945–9	ALP	Catholic	Mother

Of the eight prime ministers with an Irish family background, five represented the ALP. Four of these five (Scullin, Curtin, Forde and Chifley) came from Catholic families, although some later abandoned their faith altogether or switched to other denominations. Of the three non-Labor prime ministers of Irish parentage, two were Protestants (Bruce and Fadden), while one was a Catholic (Lyons), although he had begun his political career in the ALP, leaving the party in the split that occurred during the Depression.

Sectarianism before 1914

The entry of more Catholics into politics via the Labor Party unleashed, perhaps inevitably, a sectarian backlash.[18] John Rickard has argued that with the ALP being 'recognised as a permanent part of the political scene' from 1900 onwards, 'a more pervasive form of political sectarianism emerged', not tied, as it had been in the colonial past, to specific issues or politicians.[19] Other divisive forces were at work from the 1890s up until the First World War as well. Cardinal Moran's decision to stand for election to the 1897 federal convention ignited what O'Farrell has termed a 'sectarian explosion', with many Protestants seeing it as a blatant political power grab by the country's most senior Catholic cleric.[20] Moran's candidature failed and, indeed, of the 50 delegates elected to the convention, only two were Catholic and only one represented the labour movement.[21] The participation of colonial contingents in the second South African (Boer) War in 1899–1902 also sparked tensions since, although many Catholic men volunteered, both Moran in Sydney and Archbishop Thomas Carr in Melbourne expressed grave doubts as to whether the war was a just one.[22] Anti-Catholic sentiment was further inflamed in 1908 by Rome's *Ne Temere* decree against 'mixed' Catholic-Protestant marriages.[23] As the state considered such marriages valid, the decree appeared to Protestants to be yet another instance of the church putting itself above the law.[24]

Events in Ireland also affected Australian politics before the outbreak of war. In 1906, the return to power of a strong reforming British Liberal government revived both expectations and fears in Australia that Irish home rule was imminent. The new federal Labor Party showed it was generally in favour of Irish self-government, supporting pro–home rule parliamentary resolutions in 1905 and again in 1914. By contrast, the non-Labor parties remained, as they had been since the 1880s, strongly opposed to allowing the Irish to govern their domestic affairs.[25] Another important Irish development, although little remarked upon in Australia at the time, was the emergence in Dublin in 1905 of a newspaper called *Sinn Féin*.[26] The success of the paper and the movement it spawned was a sign that some Irish people, the young in particular, were turning away from the home rule party towards groups offering more radical remedies for Ireland's discontents.[27] This trend would have serious repercussions in Australia in 1916–17.

Before 1914, Catholic and anti-Catholic forces also became better politically organised. In 1901, the Reverend William Dill Macky, Ulster-born Presbyterian minister and grand chaplain of the NSW Orange Order, established the Australian Protestant Defence Association (APDA) in Sydney, with a branch inaugurated in Melbourne in 1902.[28] The aim of the association was to 'combat the tyranny of Romanism in a Protestant country', by, among other things, supporting Protestant candidates in elections and ensuring Protestants were appointed to the public service.[29] In 1911, the Catholic Federation was established in Melbourne, and it too expanded quickly: to Sydney in 1913 and later to South Australia and Tasmania.[30] The federation, like the APDA, was essentially a lobbying organisation, aiming to promote Catholic interests, especially to gain the support of politicians and electoral candidates for the restoration of state aid to church schools.[31] These developments were all symptomatic of deep political and religious divisions, while at the same time they served to widen and harden these divisions. Sectarianism, long a feature of colonial life, was being institutionalised in the new Australian Commonwealth's political culture.

Events during the First World War, notably another Irish rebellion at Easter 1916 and the conscription crisis in Australia during 1916–17, further deepened Catholic-Protestant divisions, with the years from 1919 into the mid 1920s proving among the most bitterly sectarian in Australia's history.

Conscription and home rule in Australia and Ireland, 1914–18

In the months before hostilities commenced in August 1914, tensions over Irish politics were running high in Australia. A Liberal government bill to introduce home rule for Ireland was proceeding slowly through the United Kingdom (UK) parliament during 1912–14, amid fierce opposition from Ulster unionists and the British Conservative Party.[32] In 1914, large pro–home rule rallies were held in Melbourne, Sydney and Adelaide, but these were met by counter-rallies organised by the Orange Order. Both the Australian Liberal prime minister, Joseph Cook, and the new governor-general, Sir Ronald Munro Ferguson, expressed concern at how divisive Irish politics were proving to be in Australia. Scottish-born Munro Ferguson, a committed imperialist whose wife came from a leading Ulster unionist family, warned the British government in June that home rule was exciting 'great interest' in Australia and, since the 'Catholic Irish' were 'nearly a quarter of the population', there was substantial support for it. In the event of war, Munro Ferguson considered that the loyalty of Catholic Irish Australians could not be relied upon.[33]

When war was declared in August 1914, Protestant Australians overwhelmingly supported the government's decision to commit Australian troops to the British war effort and, in 1916–17, many also accepted the need for conscription. Among Catholic Irish Australians, views about the war and conscription were mixed and they sometimes changed across the years between 1914 and 1918. As strong supporters of Irish home rule, most were delighted in September 1914 when the home rule bill was finally passed by the UK parliament, even though the act was immediately suspended for the duration of the war. They also endorsed the decision of the home rule party leader, John Redmond, to call on Irish men to enlist in the British army, since supporting the British war effort was regarded as a way of guaranteeing home rule. But serious obstacles remained. The home rule act did not address the desire of most Irish and British unionists for six of the nine Ulster counties to continue to be governed by the British parliament in London, not by an Irish parliament in Dublin.[34]

Australia and Ireland were among the few combatant nations on either side in 1914-18 not to rely upon conscription. Thus, their enlistment figures offer an opportunity to measure shifting support for the war. Australia and Ireland were also comparable in that their military-aged male populations were of a similar size.[35] David Fitzpatrick has estimated that approximately 210 000 Irish men fought in the war.[36] In Australia, the figure was nearly 417 000 men. That is, 21 per cent of Irish males aged 15-44 volunteered, as compared to 37 per cent of Australian males in the same age bracket. Australians clearly enlisted in significantly greater numbers than did the Irish. But, in the initial months of the war enlistments in the two countries were comparable: 52 000 in Australia compared to 44 000 in Ireland. It was in 1915 that numbers diverged dramatically, with nearly 166 000 Australians volunteering compared to only 46 000 Irish. The Gallipoli disaster certainly had an impact in discouraging recruitment in Ireland, but, as we shall soon see, the changing political situation regarding home rule did as well. In 1916, Australian enlistments declined to 124 000, while Irish enlistments collapsed to a mere 19 000. It appears that the Irish started to have serious doubts about the war during 1915, before the Easter Rising in April 1916, whereas Australian doubts emerged somewhat later: beginning in 1916, but becoming much more pronounced in 1917, when Australian enlistments fell to 45 100.[37]

We know that about 6600 Irish-born men enlisted in Australia, but the rate at which Catholic Irish Australians enlisted has proved rather more difficult to determine.[38] Historian LL Robson, in his pioneering study of First World War recruitment, found that 19.7 per cent of his small sample of volunteers were Catholics, which he said was about the same as the proportion of Catholic men in the general population. This is not altogether accurate, however, for if we focus on the Australian adult male population, rather than the total male population, we find that 21.4 per cent of them were Catholic.[39] Contemporary critics who labelled Catholics 'shirkers' may have been exaggerating, but there does appear to have been a slight under-representation of Catholic military-aged men in the Australian Imperial Force (AIF). Larger samples than Robson used are needed to investigate the issue further. Robson also noted that Catholics were significantly under-represented among AIF officers, with only 9.5 per cent of the officers in his sample whose religion was recorded being Catholic.[40] So, while Catholic soldiers were slightly under-represented among the rank-and-file of the AIF, the force's officer corps was overwhelmingly Protestant. In this respect, though, the AIF was like the British regular army, which had long contained a large proportion of Catholic Irish soldiers, but very few Catholic Irish officers.[41]

Many of the sons of the Catholic Irish-Australian middle class enlisted eagerly. Motives varied, with some young men caught up in the intense patriotism of the time, while others were convinced that small nations, like Catholic Belgium, had to be protected from German militarism. One of these young Irish Australians was 19-year-old John Davitt Jageurs, son of Melbourne home rule activist, Morgan Jageurs, and godson of the Irish nationalist leader, Michael Davitt. In February 1915, John wrote to his father requesting permission to enlist. He pointed out that Irish home rule had at last been secured. As a 'staunch Irishman', his father had objected earlier to him 'fighting for England', but now, it was 'not England alone, Papa, we are fighting for, but for ourselves. Australia is sending its own separate unit ... and young Ireland is prepared to send John Redmond's Brigade'. Morgan Jageurs was Irish-born, but his family had originally come to Ireland from Germany. Yet for John, the name 'Jageurs' was just that, a name. He summed up his identity by saying: 'I am of true Irish blood descent, German only in name and Irish Australian to the backbone.'[42] When his father approved his request, John Davitt Jageurs enlisted and was killed in France in July 1916.[43]

Young Irish-Australian men like Jageurs saw themselves as fighting for Australia and a home rule Ireland, not primarily for England. Therefore, when the prospect of home rule began suddenly to recede, the Irish both in Ireland and Australia started to question what they were really fighting for – and whether they should be fighting at all. In May 1915, in the wake of the disastrous Gallipoli landings, a British coalition government was formed to prosecute the war. As well as Liberals, it included leading Tories and Ulster unionists in Cabinet positions along with one member of the British Labour Party.[44] Among the new Cabinet members was Irish-born Sir Edward Carson who, less than 12 months earlier had, with the backing of leaders of the Tory Party, been threatening civil war in Ireland if the Liberals imposed home rule on Ulster.[45] It seemed unlikely that a government led by such men would ever put home rule into effect; or, if it did, then only at the cost of the partition of Ireland by excluding most of Ulster. An Irish bishop, who was a strong supporter of the home rule party, lamented at the time: 'Home Rule is dead and buried.'[46]

Historians have often portrayed the Easter Rising of April 1916, and especially the 15 executions that quickly followed it, as a turning point in terms of Irish-Australian attitudes to the war. For some, like Archbishop Daniel Mannix of Melbourne, it undoubtedly was, but unease and concern had been mounting for nearly 12 months before the Rising.[47] The Australian Catholic press condemned the appointment of Carson, the rebel unionist leader of 1914, as attorney-general in the 1915 coalition. The Melbourne *Advocate* summed up its opinion when it headlined the news: 'A Deplorable Scandal'.[48] On the other hand, the president of the NSW Loyal Orange Institution expressed 'profound satisfaction' at the news.[49] When criticising the executions of the republicans who led the 1916 Rising, labour newspapers took a similar line to the Catholic press, arguing that the two sides in Ireland – nationalists and unionists – were not being treated equally. In May 1916, the Brisbane *Worker* commented bluntly that the 'rebel leaders of the recent revolt were not raised to Cabinet rank ... they were shot'.[50] Labour papers called upon the British government to introduce home rule for the whole of Ireland immediately since that was obviously the democratically expressed wish of the Irish people.[51]

In August 1916, faced with mounting casualties and declining voluntary enlistments, Labor prime minister WM Hughes announced that conscription for overseas military service would be introduced.[52] Britain had begun conscripting men for its army in January 1916, enlarging the scheme substantially in May.[53] Conscription was not extended to Ireland at that time for fear it would destabilise the already fragile political situation, but there was an expectation that it might in the future. New Zealand, Canada and the United States (US) all introduced conscription during the war. But whereas the British Labour Party supported conscription, albeit reluctantly, Hughes knew that many in the ALP did not.[54] Similarly, there was widespread opposition to conscription in Ireland, not only from the Irish Labour Party and republicans, but from the home rule party and the Catholic Church as well.[55]

Conscription had been previously introduced for military service only within Australia. To send troops overseas, Hughes needed specific enabling legislation. Aware that most of his own party were unlikely to agree to this, he put the issue to Australian voters.[56] The unexpected and narrow defeat of conscription at the October 1916 poll had major political ramifications. Hughes and his supporters split from the Labor Party and, in coalition with Liberals, they won the May 1917 federal election. Buoyed by his election success, Hughes went ahead with another conscription plebiscite in December 1917, only again to be defeated and this time by a larger majority.[57] Against the backdrop of ever mounting casualties – over 42 000 killed or wounded in 1916 and a further 77 000 in 1917 – the two conscription campaigns, barely a year apart, were hard-fought and bruising experiences, not just for the politicians involved but for the whole country.[58]

The results of the conscription votes were hotly disputed at the time and have continued to be debated by historians ever since. Which group swung the balance against conscription: was it rural voters or female voters; was it urban workers or farmers or soldiers; or was it perhaps Catholic Irish Australians? While progress has been made in answering such questions, there is still much about individual voting intentions that remains obscure.[59] Yet Hughes himself was in no doubt as to who was to blame for his defeat.[60] He identified the main 'disloyal' groups in Australia as sympathisers with an assortment of radical foreign causes: the 'IWWers', members of the American-based syndicalist International Workers of the World, and the 'Sinn Feiners', supporters of Irish republicanism. The latter comprised Catholic Irish Australians, led by Archbishop Daniel Mannix. In late 1917, Hughes added to his list of anti-Australian villains supporters of the Bolsheviks, who had just seized power in Russia and were determined to make peace with Germany.[61] Hughes, however, held the Catholic Church largely responsible for the higher 'no' vote in the second plebiscite. He told British prime minister David Lloyd George that it was the Catholic Church that had 'killed conscription', but, by the Catholic Church, Hughes seems to have meant Mannix.[62]

Yet there were prominent Catholic Irish-Australian politicians, like senators Patrick Lynch from Western Australia and Thomas Bakhap from Tasmania, who had long called for conscription and who campaigned energetically in their states for a 'yes' vote.[63] Mannix in his speeches in 1916–17 appealed more to working-class Irish Australians than to men like Lynch and Bakhap. Many of Mannix's arguments were economic rather than patriotic.[64] In a February 1917 speech, he claimed that the war was not really about the rights of small nations. Like 'most wars', it was a 'trade' or economic war, the result of British and French 'jealousy' at the growing imperial might of Germany. He also argued that the burden of the war was being shared unequally, with the working class suffering wage cuts or losing their jobs, while many businessmen were making handsome profits.[65] Echoing the arguments of the labour movement, Mannix also claimed that, should conscription be introduced, employers would replace their departed 'white' working men with 'cheaper' female workers and imported 'coloured' labour. Recent studies have confirmed that economic issues played a significant role in determining how people voted, so Mannix's claims about the economic motives behind the war, and especially its economic costs for the working class, were likely to have had wide appeal.[66] In November 1917, when campaigning during the second plebiscite, he told audiences that they should put 'Australia ... first and the Empire second'.[67] Mannix argued that in defying Britain and excluding 'coloured' British subjects under the white Australia policy, Australia was doing what Irish republicans wanted to do. 'You here in Australia are Sinn Feiners', he said, 'though you do not call yourselves by that name.' This was because Australians, like the Irish, had put their national interests before those of imperial Britain.[68]

Mannix's opposition to conscription in Australia in 1916–17 was in line with the stance taken by the Catholic Church over conscription in Ireland. Whereas the threat of conscription proved hugely divisive in Australia, in Ireland it had the opposite effect, uniting opposing parties and groups – albeit temporarily. The British government had contemplated extending conscription to Ireland in 1916, but it was not until a major German offensive in March and April 1918 that an Irish conscription bill was introduced into the House of Commons. The Catholic hierarchy spoke out forcefully against conscription, opposing it just as strongly as Mannix had done in Australia only a few months earlier. The bishops issued a declaration warning that if an attempt was made to enforce conscription 'against the will of the Irish nation', the Irish people would 'have a right to resist by all means that are consonant with the law of God'. The British government responded with mass arrests of Sinn Féin leaders, but was obliged to abandon its Irish conscription plans when the army concluded that forcing conscription on Ireland would likely tie up more troops than conscription would produce. The outcome of British mismanagement of Irish affairs became apparent seven months later when, in the December 1918 general election, republican Sinn Féin won a landslide victory in Ireland and the Irish home rule party was all but annihilated.[69]

In attempting to resolve the problem of unionist opposition to home rule, in May 1916 British prime minister HH Asquith had put the crafty David Lloyd George in charge of negotiations with Redmond's home rule party and Carson's Ulster unionists. By June, Lloyd George had succeeded in persuading Redmond to accept temporary exclusion of six Ulster counties and, in July, he went much further, announcing that exclusion would be permanent. Thus, when Lloyd George replaced Asquith as prime minister in December 1916, it was clear to Irish nationalists, both in Ireland and Australia, that the British government was committed to the partition of Ireland. For Irish Australians, the conscription campaigns in late 1916 and late 1917 were fought against the backdrop of what they saw as continuing British duplicity in Ireland. The implementation of home rule would still have to await the end of the war, but it would now have to be paid for with partition – a price many Irish nationalists considered too high. In a powerful metaphor Mannix protested in November 1917 that 'Ireland should not be thrown on the dissecting-table of the British Parliament' to be 'hacked and cut up into sections ... to please the unworthy and disloyal faction in the North of Ireland'.[70]

If the situation in Ireland continued to deteriorate during 1917–18, in Australia the conscription plebiscites stirred up intense religious animosity. Mannix insisted in June 1917 that he supported the Australian war effort, but it was very difficult for 'loyal' Catholics to appear on recruiting platforms because they and their religion were regularly 'insulted' by other speakers.[71]

He identified one of the main abusers as Frank Critchley Parker, the journalist son of English immigrants. Parker was editor and publisher of the *Australian Statesman and Mining Standard*, a Melbourne weekly combining analysis of current events with information for the mining industry.[72] Parker described his paper as: 'Anti-pro-German-Sinn Fein-I.W.W.-Pacifist-and-paid-agents' of the anti-conscription cause.[73] A February 1917 article weighed up whether Catholic Irish 'disloyalty' was due to race or religion, before concluding that 'deplorable weaknesses' in the Irish character were 'fostered by the RC priesthood for its own purposes'.[74] In an attempt to reach a wider audience, between 1915 and 1918, Parker published a series of 31 *Patriotic Pamphlets* for circulation throughout the country.[75] The first 14 in the series were conventionally pro-British and anti-German, but when the October 1916 conscription plebiscite was defeated, Parker used the remainder of the series to argue that Catholic Irish Australians, and particularly Daniel Mannix, were treacherously supporting Germany.[76]

Cartoons were used with great effect during the hard-fought conscription campaigns, and Parker included some in his pamphlets. But instead of contemporary works, he reproduced anti-Irish and anti-Catholic caricatures originally published in London *Punch* as early as the 1850s and 1870s. Parker obviously believed that their racial and sectarian messages were still relevant to the Australian situation during the First World War.[77]

Simianised caricatures of Irish men and women had virtually disappeared in Australia after the 1880s, but they made a modest comeback in the wake of the Easter Rising. In May 1916, *Melbourne Punch* published a cartoon claiming that Sinn Féin was delivering Ireland into the hands of Germany, illustrated with animal-like Irish and German characters.[78] In April 1918,

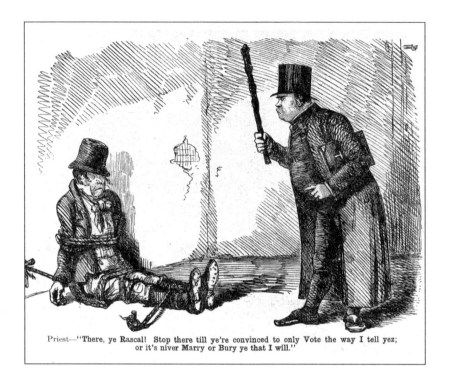

Priest—"There, ye Rascal! Stop there till ye're convinced to only Vote the way I tell yez; or it's niver Marry or Bury ye that I will."

This cartoon, originally published in London *Punch* in 1852, reflected fears during a UK election campaign of both increased Irish immigration to Britain and a resurgent Catholic Church. By republishing it in the context of the 1917 Australian federal election, Critchley Parker was suggesting that Irish Catholics had always voted the way their priests ordered them to.

Source: 'Astounding discovery by P.L.L. – All roads lead to Rome'. *Australian Statesman and Mining Standard*, 8 March 1917, insert.

the Sydney *Bulletin* featured on its cover a striking cartoon by Norman Lindsay, whose father was an Ulster Protestant. It showed a simianised Irish peasant couple, 'brooding' over their 'wrongs' and 'too miserable' to answer the call of Britannia who warns them that 'our' home is burning down (see page 320).[79] While the cartoon was published in the context of the Irish conscription crisis of April–May 1918, the *Bulletin*'s readers must have viewed it with the recent defeat of the 1917 plebiscite in mind as well. In criticising the cartoon, the Sydney *Catholic Press*, which had been a staunch opponent of conscription, drew an explicit connection between the 'low, dirty, yahoo type of mind' that enjoyed 'slandering the Irish' in English cartoons and its Australian 'mouthpiece' Critchley Parker, lamenting that the 'once chivalrous *Bulletin*' had now fallen to a similarly low level.[80]

While the Catholic anti-conscription vote may not have been as decisive as has sometimes been claimed, studies of rural areas with large Catholic populations have suggested that they did return high 'no' votes in the conscription plebiscites.[81] Equally, there is evidence that areas with large Protestant populations of Irish descent returned high 'yes' votes. Groups of Ulster Protestant immigrants, originally from counties Fermanagh, Tyrone and Donegal, had settled dairy-farming regions on the NSW south coast during the mid-19th century. Members of some of these families later relocated to the Northern Rivers district, without severing their ties to friends and relatives who remained on the south coast.[82] Intense loyalty to Britain and the empire, a strong evangelical Protestant faith and membership of the Orange Order were hallmarks of both these communities. Indeed, between the 1880s and the 1920s, the NSW south coast and Northern Rivers areas boasted some of the highest number of Orange lodges in the country.[83] If Protestant Irish Australians

TOO MISERABLE.

THE SPIRIT: "It is our own home that is on fire. Come and help to save it."
THE DISPIRITED: "Och, sure, let it burn. 'Tis us will stay here broodin' over our wrongs."

In the context of a new German offensive on the Western Front and continuing Irish opposition to conscription, the cartoonist Norman Lindsay berates the Irish people, portrayed as a 'dispirited' peasant couple – the man with markedly ape-like facial features. They would rather brood miserably over 'our wrongs' than defend their home against enemy attack.

Source: 'Too miserable', *Bulletin*, 18 April 1918, cover.

voted strongly in favour of conscription, the evidence should be found in these regions.

The electoral division of Richmond, including the Northern Rivers area and the town of Lismore, was the only NSW rural district to vote 'yes' in both plebiscites. In other rural parts of NSW, farmers tended to vote 'no', mainly due to fear of rural labour shortages.[84] Kiama and its hinterland of rich dairy country was in the electoral division of Illawarra. That division also took in the heavily unionised coalmining region around Wollongong. In both conscription plebiscites, Illawarra voted 'no' by a clear majority. But, when Illawarra is compared with Newcastle to the north, the other NSW electoral division whose economy was dominated by coal, it is apparent that there was a surprisingly high 'yes' vote on the south coast.

Table 3: Percentages of 'yes' and 'no' votes in selected NSW electoral divisions in the conscription plebiscites of October 1916 and December 1917[85]

NSW ELECTORAL DIVISION	1916 'YES' PERCENTAGE	1916 'NO' PERCENTAGE	1917 'YES' PERCENTAGE	1917 'NO' PERCENTAGE
Richmond	60.50	39.50	56.66	43.01
Illawarra	43.54	53.96	41.00	58.00
Newcastle	32.86	67.14	28.57	71.43

Table 3 shows that both the northern division of Richmond, with a largely rural population, and the southern division of Illawarra, with a mixed farming and mining population, recorded higher 'yes' votes than similar electoral divisions elsewhere in NSW. In terms of their inhabitants at the time, the most striking similarity between the two regions was their substantial farming communities of Ulster Protestant descent. In analysing the role of Irish Australians in the bitter conscription campaigns, historians have focused largely, if not exclusively, on Catholics. Yet Richmond and Illawarra point to there being a Protestant Irish-Australian story to tell as well.

Without public opinion polls it is difficult, if not impossible, to offer a definitive assessment of how significant either the Catholic or the Protestant Irish-Australian vote was in the conscription plebiscites. Nevertheless, it is important to bear in mind that Hughes and many of his supporters believed at the time, and continued to believe for many years afterwards, that Catholic Irish Australians led by Daniel Mannix had played a decisive role in defeating conscription.[86] Malcolm Fraser, Liberal Party prime minister of Australia in 1975–83, recalled how his father, who served with the British army in France in 1916–17, had accepted Hughes's claims and always believed that the Irish had been 'treacherous' during the war. Robert Menzies, another Liberal Party prime minister (1949–66), was a Melbourne law student in 1916–17 and shared Fraser senior's opinion. In a 1917 letter to a Catholic friend, he railed against Mannix's hypocrisy and disloyalty, labelling him 'cunning, sinister, and a national menace!'[87] This widely shared viewpoint helped shape intense hostility towards Catholics, and particularly Mannix, during the post-war years – an 'era of rabid sectarianism' as one NSW ALP leader called the 1920s.[88] Fraser, born in Melbourne in 1930 into a prominent pastoral family of Scottish ancestry, testified that bigotry and discrimination against Catholics were 'commonplace' during his childhood.[89] Later he would become a critic of sectarianism, but Menzies never abandoned his hostility to Catholic Irish republicanism and the federal Liberal Party did not have a Catholic deputy leader until 1972 nor its first Catholic leader until 2009.[90]

Irish Australians and the Irish War of Independence, 1919–22

Many in the Catholic Irish-Australian generation born during the 1860s and 1870s to immigrant parents had embraced the cause of Irish home rule, hoping to see Ireland become, like the Australian colonies, a self-governing political entity within the British Empire. Home rule advocates tried, with limited success, to persuade their fellow Australians of Protestant British ancestry that Irish self-government would strengthen rather than weaken Britain and the empire. Yet, after apparently triumphing at the start of the war in late 1914, by the end of the war in late 1918, Irish home rule was dead. With the political consensus around home rule shattered, a younger generation, born to Irish or Irish-Australian parents during the 1880s and 1890s and radicalised by the labour movement, the war, the conscription crisis in Australia and the Easter Rising in Ireland, was obliged to seek for a different answer to what the British insisted on calling the 'Irish question'.[91]

The political direction in which some Irish Australians were heading became clear during the St Patrick's Day parade in Melbourne in March 1918. This, according to one of Archbishop Mannix's admiring biographers, was 'something of a victory march', intended to celebrate the defeat of conscription in the December 1917 plebiscite.[92] With Mannix taking the salute, groups of marchers openly proclaimed their support for an Irish republic. There were banners and floats commemorating the 1916 Rising and about 100 members of the republican Irish National Association (INA) marched behind a Sinn Féin banner. Mannix removed his biretta as a mark of respect for a depiction of the 'martyrs of Easter week', but did not remove it when a band played the national anthem, 'God Save the King'. A furious reaction from the city's Protestant elite quickly followed. Mannix was accused of treason, while loyalist groups called for him to be deported as an enemy alien under the *War Precautions Act 1914*.[93] After a large protest meeting in the town hall, businessman Herbert Brookes, whose mother was Ulster-born and who had married a daughter of Alfred Deakin, led a deputation to lobby Prime Minister Hughes personally. As a result, Sinn Féin was added to the list of organisations banned under the act.[94] But before the ban was made public, detectives raided the offices and homes of members of the INA in Sydney, Melbourne and Brisbane, the organisation being considered the principal representative of Sinn Féin in Australia.[95]

Always small, the INA was founded in Sydney in 1915 by Albert Dryer, the Australian-born son of an Irish mother and a father of German descent.[96] Although he never visited Ireland, Dryer was a passionate advocate of Irish causes from 1914 until his death nearly half a century later in 1963.[97] Branches of the INA were established in Melbourne, Brisbane and Adelaide, and Dryer made contact with radical cultural and political groups, like the Gaelic League in Ireland and the Fenians in the US. He modelled the INA on the League by promoting the Irish language in tandem with fundraising for Irish-American Fenianism and running paramilitary training at camps in the Blue Mountains west of Sydney.[98] After the police raids in March and further raids in May, seven prominent INA members, including Dryer, were arrested in June 1918 and interned in Sydney's Darlinghurst Gaol, accused of being members of an illegal organisation. Most were released in December 1918 after the end of the war, although Dryer was held until February 1919.[99] The INA hardly constituted a serious threat to the Australian war effort, but in moving against it in 1918 the authorities had hoped to gain evidence of Mannix's association with the now-banned Sinn Féin. In the wake of the defeat of conscription, deporting or at least discrediting Mannix had become a priority, viewed as a way of undermining Irish republican sentiment in Australia.

Meanwhile, in Ireland, the 73 Sinn Féin members elected in December 1918 to the British parliament refused to take their seats and instead convened in Dublin as the first Dáil Éireann, or Irish parliament. On the same day in January 1919, the killing of two Irish policemen by republicans in County Tipperary was seen, in retrospect, as marking the beginning of what has come to be called the Irish War of Independence. The volunteers of the Irish Republican Army (IRA) fought a guerrilla campaign, mainly in the south and east of the country, against the British army and the Royal Irish Constabulary, reinforced with British war veterans known as the Black-and-Tans and Auxiliaries. As with most guerrilla wars, the fighting was brutal, with civilians frequently caught up in the conflict: a recent estimate of fatalities has suggested that around 48 per cent were non-combatants.[100] A truce was finally agreed in July 1921, but this left most of the main political problems unresolved.

Catholic Irish Australians were appalled by British violence in Ireland and especially the exploits of the Black-and-Tans and Auxiliaries, who appeared to indulge in revenge attacks and reprisals against civilians, unrestrained and perhaps even encouraged by their superiors.[101] Large protest meetings were held, supported by the ALP, demanding that British troops be withdrawn from Ireland.[102] But Protestant Anglo-Australian politicians and newspapers were equally outraged by the 'Sinn Feiners', who they believed were intent upon destroying the UK, if not the empire. Australian papers relied heavily for information about the Irish war on the reporting of the English Tory press. Thus, the Melbourne *Age* reprinted an account from the conservative London *Morning Post* describing the looting and burning of nearly 90 premises in Cork city centre in December 1920. 'It is evident', the article stated, 'that the fires are due to an Anarchist element which is only concerned with the breakup of the Empire.'[103] Later it emerged that it was a group of Auxiliaries who had carried out the attack in reprisal for an IRA ambush.[104]

It was against this background of war in Ireland and polarised public opinion in Australia that another St Patrick's Day parade took place in Melbourne in March 1920, permission for a march having been refused in 1919. The 1920 event was preceded by months of argument and negotiation, with pro-British groups demanding that 'disloyal' flags and emblems be banned and the Union Jack displayed prominently.[105] In a carefully choreographed display, the 1920 parade featured some 6000 returned soldiers and sailors in uniform. They included 14 Victoria Cross winners mounted on white horses, who formed a guard of honour around Mannix's car. The inclusion of so many war veterans was intended to disprove accusations of Catholic Irish-Australian 'shirking' or disloyalty during the war. The parade was organised, paid for and filmed by John Wren, a wealthy businessman of Irish parentage, a supporter of Mannix and an ALP powerbroker, who had made a fortune in illegal gambling, as well as in horse racing, boxing and other sports.[106] Loyalists, however, were deeply offended when the Union Jack was not displayed as the organisers had promised, the parade being led instead by two returned servicemen carrying large Australian flags.[107] While Mannix was overseas for more than 12 months in 1920–21, the film of the parade, now entitled *Ireland Will Be Free* and containing additional

THE HEIGHT OF IMPOSSIBILITY— No. 3.

Barred by the British government from landing in Ireland during the Irish War of Independence in late 1920, Archbishop Mannix spent several months in England publicly denouncing British policy in Ireland. Cartoonists liked to mock Mannix as a trickster: an impish figure who deliberately provoked his enemies, revelling in their angry responses. Here, in a satirical reversal, he skips along flourishing a Union Jack: a flag he had banished from St Patrick's Day parades in Melbourne in favour of the Australian flag.

Source: 'The height of impossibility – no. 3', *Melbourne Punch*, 23 December 1920, p. 5.

republican propaganda, was shown widely at venues in Victoria, Tasmania, South Australia, NSW and Queensland.[108]

Sectarianism after 1918

Mannix's 1918 and 1920 parades in Melbourne, and Wren's film of the latter parade, employed emotive symbols, such as flags, music and marching soldiers, to celebrate the heroism of Catholic Irish-Australian volunteers in war and the defeat of conscription. Through their banners, the parades also promoted the cause of Irish independence. Critics saw such displays not only as expressing opposition to Britain, but as menacing Australia too. Other events compounded this sense of menace. The Catholic Federation, founded in 1911 to lobby politicians to restore state aid to church schools, having grown tired of unfulfilled ALP promises, created its own political party in late 1919, the Democratic Party, and stood candidates at the March 1920 NSW state election. But the party failed to win any seats, as most Catholic voters stayed loyal to Labor. In the face of staunch ALP opposition, the Democratic Party soon disappeared and the Catholic Federation quietly ceased operations in 1924, but membership of Protestant defence associations soared.[109]

The early 1920s witnessed a resurgence of the Orange Order in Australia. Additional lodges appeared in many areas, including north-eastern NSW and southern Queensland.[110] In South Australia there was a steady increase in Orange Order membership, with 1927 recording the highest numbers since 1909.[111] Energised Protestant groups actively opposed the ALP, which they perceived as now dominated by Catholics and the Irish. In Tasmania, a Loyalty League was established and candidates fielded at elections. As a result, in the December 1919 federal election, all ALP Tasmanian candidates were defeated and three Loyalty League senate candidates were elected. One of the new senators, JD Millen, an Ulster-born Presbyterian and former president of the state's Protestant Defence Association, told a Loyalty League meeting that they were fighting a conspiracy against British Australia: a conspiracy involving Mannix, the pope, Irish republican revolutionaries and Bolshevism.[112]

Pamphlets circulated in NSW in 1921–22 claiming that the Catholic Federation was a church front seeking to take control of politics in Australia.[113] In the bitterly contested 1922 NSW state election, the Protestant Federation aggressively lobbied non-Labor parties, alleging disproportionate Catholic influence in the ALP, the public service and other areas of governance. This scare campaign appears to have succeeded because Labor was heavily defeated. The new government under Sir George Fuller, who had been born in Kiama on the NSW south coast to a Protestant Irish father, held office until 1925 with the support of the Protestant Federation. It was openly anti-Catholic, passing legislation aimed to make the Catholic Church's 1908 *Ne Temere* decree against mixed marriages illegal.[114]

The Irish Civil War and the republican envoys of 1923 and 1924

Given heightened sectarian tensions in Australia and continuing political violence in Ireland, the arrival in 1923 and 1924 of two Irish republican fundraising missions was bound to create controversy. Following the July 1921 truce in Ireland, a treaty was negotiated in London in December between Irish and British representatives which created a new British dominion, modelled on Canada, to be called the Irish Free State. It would enjoy self-government within the empire, the British monarch continuing as head of state. But the Free State was composed of only 26 of the 32 counties of Ireland; six of the Ulster counties, to be known as Northern Ireland, were to remain within the UK, their local affairs managed by a devolved parliament based in Belfast. When, in January 1922, Dáil Éireann voted narrowly to accept the treaty, the Irish republican movement split. Hardliners, under the leadership of Éamon de Valera, rejected the treaty, plunging the country into a bitter civil war that lasted from June 1922 until de Valera's surrender in April 1923.[115]

During the Irish War of Independence, most Catholic Irish Australians had supported Irish republicans in their struggle against British rule, as had most of the clergy. The Irish Civil War, however, proved divisive. The 1921 treaty, although it provided for dominion status, not a republic, and entailed partition, was generally, if sometimes reluctantly, accepted by the Catholic community and church in Australia. Yet there were those who, like de Valera and his followers in Ireland, remained vehemently opposed to the treaty. An INA-affiliated member of the Irish Foresters in Adelaide wrote privately in 1925 that: 'The mixed state affairs in Ireland has split national opinion here in twain, in our National association some are Free Staters and others like myself Republicans.'[116] Daniel Mannix, who had met and befriended de Valera while both were touring the US in 1920, was steadfast in his opposition to the treaty. But Mannix was isolated within the church, as most other Australian bishops, like the Irish bishops, threw their support behind the Free State government.[117]

De Valera drew upon his friendship with Mannix in 1923 and again in 1924, when he dispatched two separate delegations to

Australia to raise much-needed funds and to whip up opposition to the Free State. Both delegations established contact with the INA in Sydney and with former INA members in Brisbane and Melbourne, as well as with Mannix.[118] The first delegation in 1923 was composed of Father Michael O'Flanagan and JJ O'Kelly. These 'Irish envoys', as they were called, were deported five months after their arrival under the *Immigration Act 1920*, which allowed the Commonwealth to expel those accused of advocating the overthrow of any 'civilized' government.[119] Although their meetings drew large crowds in Sydney and Brisbane, O'Flanagan and O'Kelly did not have the support of the Catholic press or of archbishops Kelly in Sydney and Duhig in Brisbane.[120] This partly explains why their fundraising was less successful than they had hoped.[121] Their confrontational style, which included fierce denunciations not only of the Free State and the British government but also of the Australian bishops, was probably another factor contributing to their lack of success. The envoys' rhetoric raised the ire of Protestant British Australians and the anti-Catholic Fuller government in NSW played an important role in persuading the Commonwealth to deport them.[122]

In 1924, after the end of the Civil War, de Valera dispatched another rather more successful fundraising delegation, composed of Linda Kearns and Kathleen Barry.[123] Between November 1924 and March 1925, with better organisational skills and more political subtlety than O'Flanagan and O'Kelly, Kearns and Barry raised over £8000 for the support of the families of republican prisoners, who numbered nearly 12000 at the end of the Civil War.[124] The women were careful not to comment on Irish or Australian politics. Instead, they tapped into conventional gender stereotypes by presenting themselves as charitable women providing economic aid to the innocent wives and children of political prisoners. Both were in fact seasoned activists, having been imprisoned for their roles in fighting in Dublin.[125] Their appeals for money were less successful in Fuller's NSW than in Mannix's Victoria or in Queensland, where the Labor government of Premier EG Theodore welcomed them. Kearns addressed pupils at Queensland Catholic schools, where she was presented with books by CJ Dennis, including *The Moods of Ginger Mick*.[126] The two women spent less time in NSW, in part due to rumours that they too might soon be deported for sedition.[127] Although Prime Minister Stanley M Bruce, whose father was an Irish Protestant, rejected NSW government requests for their deportation, Kathleen Barry told her husband in a letter that she was convinced the intelligence services were 'after her'.[128]

With the release of the last of the republican prisoners in Ireland by the end of 1924 and the departure of Kearns and Barry in early 1925, many of the Australian organisations that had sprung up to support the Irish struggle for independence faded. The INA in Sydney continued, but societies in other states closed. During the 1920s, immigration from Ireland was running at low levels as, with Irish loyalty to empire deeply suspect, the Australian authorities gave preference to assisting British rather than Irish migrants.[129] Nevertheless, small numbers of republicans, faced with discrimination and bleak employment prospects in the Free State, did make their way to Australia.[130] A recent study of a sample of 338 IRA veterans who left Ireland during the late 1920s found that the majority went to the US, with only 2 per cent moving to Australia, mostly to Victoria and Queensland.[131] Small groups followed Irish news in the Catholic press, while they continued to hope for the realisation of their dream of an all-Ireland republic: a dream they shared with Daniel Mannix.

Mannix, the Movement and the ALP split

Mannix died, aged 99, in November 1963. Towards the end of his long life, he saw his dream of an Irish republic realised. The Irish Republic was formally established in 1948–49, although, ironically, it was brought into being peacefully by the successors of the Free Staters of the 1920s, not by their republican enemies. Partition remained though, with Northern Ireland continuing as part of the UK. On his deathbed, Mannix was informed by his protege, BA Santamaria, that after a near century-long campaign, state aid to Catholic schools was to be restored.[132] Yet, here too, there was irony. Rather than having the Catholic-dominated Labor Party to thank for this measure, the church owed its gratitude to a conservative coalition government headed by Sir Robert Menzies, a man not noted for his Irish or Catholic sympathies.[133] By the time of Mannix's death, the alliance between Labor and the Catholic community was crumbling. The ALP was out of power everywhere in Australia, except for NSW and Tasmania, and those governments too fell in 1965 and 1969 respectively.

Whereas, during the late 1890s, Cardinal Moran of Sydney had urged Catholic workers and voters to support the fledgling Labor Party, in part to curb socialist influence within it, during the late 1950s Mannix in Melbourne was urging them to do the very opposite: neither to join nor vote Labor because, he claimed, the party was now little more than a front for communism.[134] As Australian Catholics of Irish descent became more prosperous during the mid 20th century, they tended to switch their political allegiance from Labor to the non-Labor parties.[135] Nevertheless, in the late 1940s and early 1950s, many Catholics still belonged to or voted for the ALP; around 55 per cent of delegates to the federal conference had Irish backgrounds, while 60 per cent of federal Labor parliamentarians were Catholics.[136] But that situation sustained a major shock in the mid 1950s. In October 1954, having been defeated in an election earlier in the year, the federal ALP leader HV Evatt publicly alleged that a 'small minority' of 'disloyal' Labor members existed within the party, who were 'largely directed from outside the Labor Movement'. This group, he went on, was located mainly in Victoria and, since 1949, it had adopted tactics resembling 'Communist and Fascist infiltration of larger groups', with the aim of subverting both the ALP's policies and its leadership.[137] Evatt was referring to a secret organisation called the Catholic Social Studies Movement – known usually as just 'The Movement' – established by Santamaria in the early 1940s, with Mannix's encouragement, and funded from 1945 by the Catholic hierarchy.[138] The Movement was tasked by the bishops with destroying communist power in the trade unions, but Mannix and Santamaria also aimed to use the organisation to enhance Catholic power within the ALP.[139] When Evatt began expelling Movement members from the party, Santamaria responded by helping to create a new anti-communist Democratic Labor Party. Mannix then called on Catholic voters to support it rather than the ALP.[140]

The split damaged Labor's electoral fortunes in several states, as well as contributing to the party's long period in opposition at the federal level, which extended from 1949 to 1972. Many historians studying the Movement and the ALP split have argued that Mannix must bear some responsibility for what occurred: firstly, because he encouraged Santamaria's secret political ambitions and then, when they were exposed, he used his ecclesiastical authority to try to destroy Catholic support for the ALP.[141]

O'Farrell, who was a critic of both men, acknowledged that the ALP split in the mid 1950s was '[l]amentable and deeply wounding as civil wars are'. Yet, at the same time, he thought that it also 'cleared the air – not least because it revealed that Catholics were seriously divided among themselves'. They could no longer be seen, as they had often been since the 19th century, as a monolithic political group, blindly following the orders of their priests. Even more importantly, the split signalled the end of over half a century of Catholic Irish-Australian 'slavish attachment' to the ALP. From the mid 1950s onwards, O'Farrell wrote, Catholic votes now had to be seriously fought for – by all sides of politics.[142]

Epilogue: Irish Australia in the 21st century

Irish Australia was undergoing major change at the time of Archbishop Daniel Mannix's death in Melbourne in 1963. In the wake of the split in the mid 1950s and the resolution of the long-standing state aid question in the early 1960s, the Australian Labor Party could no longer lay confident claim to the support of Catholic Irish-Australian voters. Equally importantly, from the late 1940s onwards, the pews of Catholic churches were no longer the almost exclusive preserve of the offspring of Irish immigrants. Southern and eastern European Catholics, fleeing economic devastation and political upheaval in the aftermath of the Second World War, began to make their presence felt in Australia's churches, while their children later filled Catholic classrooms as well. The Australian Catholic world was rapidly ceasing to be an overwhelmingly Irish one. The distinctiveness of Catholic Irishness, which had been so apparent to 19th- and early 20th-century observers, was fading as new and more obviously different groups of immigrants arrived in the country after 1945.

Changing stories: the Irish-born
in Australia after 1945

Immigrants from Ireland did continue to settle in Australia during the late 20th and early 21st centuries, although over time the character of these immigrants changed markedly. After independence in 1922, the economy of the south of Ireland did not prosper, remaining heavily dependent upon small-scale farming for decades. Thus emigration from the 26 counties continued at high levels. Most of those departing now took the short and inexpensive trip across the Irish Sea to Britain. Irish immigration to the United States (US) declined, while immigration to Australia remained at low levels in part because it was no longer subsidised. In England after 1945, Irish men found plentiful employment opportunities in the construction industry as post-war rebuilding got underway, while Irish women worked in the new National Health Service as nursing and ancillary staff or in schools, which were expanding to cope with the post-war baby boom.[1] Yet, despite the attractions of Britain, and of the US as well, small numbers of Irish immigrants continued to come to Australia. And, as in the 19th century, previous generations of older relatives or friends, who had immigrated earlier, often smoothed the way for young new arrivals by helping them to find accommodation and employment.

But by 1954, the Irish-born constituted only 0.6 per cent of the total Australian population. Unlike the mid and late 19th century when many Irish women were assisted to make the long and expensive journey to Australia, the majority of the post-war Irish arrivals were men, with the sex ratio of immigrants being 132 males to 100 females. And, as in England at the time, these men usually sought employment in the construction and transport industries. During the late 1960s and early 1970s, how-ever, in response to the onset of the Troubles, there was a spike in arrivals from Northern Ireland, including many family groups.[2] The 1980s witnessed another notable shift in the pattern of Irish immigration when, due to the federal government's introduc-tion of new entry requirements, immigrants became increasingly highly trained and educated, finding employment now mainly in skilled and professional areas of the Australian economy.[3]

By 1981, there were a little over 67000 Irish-born people in Australia. As in the 19th century, they continued to settle largely in the eastern states. Just over 30 per cent were living in New South Wales, 22 per cent in Victoria and 12 per cent in Queensland, with smaller proportions in the other states and territories. Most were city dwellers. For many new arrivals, Irish clubs and societies played an important role in their lives, as had been the case since the late 19th century. In Sydney, for example, young Irish immigrants arriving during the 1980s joined social networks based around Irish clubs and other organisations. On the other hand, older immigrants, who had lived longer in Australia, tended to drift away from specifically Irish groups, preferring instead to socialise more informally with workmates and in pubs.[4]

However, such broad patterns inevitably obscure important individual stories. Some immigrants continued to be active in Irish cultural or political groups for decades after their arrival. Seamus McGettigan, for instance, who emigrated from County Donegal in 1954, was initially employed on the Snowy Mountains hydroelectric scheme. Later he trained as an engineer and worked as a teacher and shopkeeper. In an interview in 1996, shortly before his death, he explained that he had not involved himself in any Irish social organisations on arrival since many met in pubs and he did not drink. But he did become a political activist, joining the socialist Connolly Association in Melbourne, and for many years he helped organise annual commemorations of the 1916 Easter Rising and led Irish contingents at May Day and St Patrick's Day festivities.[5]

Melbourne by 1996 was home to just over 10 000 Irish-born immigrants, some 4000 of them having arrived since 1981. Most came between 1985 and 1989, years when the Irish Republic experienced a serious economic recession leading to an upsurge in emigration. The majority of these Melbourne immigrants were young single adults or childless couples and they took up mainly professional and managerial jobs in Australia. Most initially did not intend to settle permanently; they expected to return to Ireland once the economy had recovered. Migration was for them about travel and adventure and the chance to do an interesting and well-paid, albeit temporary, job: in other words, they saw living in Australia as something of a working holiday. Some did indeed return when Irish economic conditions began to improve from the early 1990s.[6] But many others decided to stay, often because they had started families.[7] County Offaly–born Aileen Garry was fairly typical of this late 1980s immigrant generation in that she had trained as a nurse in Ireland and immigrated to Tasmania in 1987 shortly after her marriage. She found work, had children and she and her husband, like many of the 1980s Irish, eventually settled permanently in Melbourne.[8]

Oral histories, like those provided by Seamus McGettigan and Aileen Garry, are a vital supplement to census and immigration data. They show that while the lives of many immigrants certainly did accord with the general patterns evident in the statistics, others did not. They also reveal that in major ways the immigrants of the 1980s were different from those who had arrived a generation earlier at mid-century: the difference reflecting, among other things, significant socio-economic changes that had occurred in Ireland since the 1960s. Historians are currently working on several oral history projects that include post-war Irish immigrants and, as these come to fruition, a more detailed understanding of the variety of immigrants' lives should emerge. One especially important ongoing interview series is the Irish National Association Centenary Oral History Project, which started in October 2013 and is hosted by the National Library of Australia.[9]

Irish-Australian connections and disconnections since 1945

It is not really possible, unfortunately, to determine with any certainty how many of the descendants of 19th-century Irish immigrants continued to feel a connection to Ireland a century or more after their ancestors' arrival in Australia. An important link was certainly maintained while large numbers of Irish-born priests and nuns staffed the Catholic Church. Generations of Australia's Catholic children were exposed to Irish accents, viewpoints and values in their local schools and churches, while Catholic schools also often took part in St Patrick's Day celebrations.[10]

Denis Walker, a descendant of Irish immigrants who had arrived from County Cork about 1860, grew up in a working-class Melbourne suburb during the 1950s. He attended a state school, but received an hour's religious instruction each week from an Irish priest, who made very clear to his young audience that England had always treated Ireland 'badly'. Walker's father, though, was rather ambivalent about his Irish ancestry. He considered himself only 'half Irish', viewing Irish culture and language as 'primitive' and abhorring 'stereotyped wakes and leprechauns'. Denis too had perceived Ireland as a 'declining small place' that could not compare with 'our modernist country Australia'. Yet an Irish-born friend of his father named Christopher O'Kelly, who was both a Marxist and an Irish republican, made a powerful impression on young Denis during the mid 1950s. Although he spoke little about Ireland, O'Kelly 'radiated ... Irishness' in Walker's words. This Irishness was essentially all about difference. O'Kelly contradicted the 'concrete Anglo verities of Menzies-era newspapers'; his views were very unlike those of 'ordinary Australians'; and he 'warned us we might have to think for ourselves in life'. O'Kelly's Irishness revealed to young Denis that 'there might be plural truths'. Walker thought that, during the 1950s, working-class Irish Australians, although 'their ethos had been watered down by the Anglo-Australian culture and ideas flowing all around them', still 'orally transmitted their own critical perspectives on Britain ... and on power structures in Australia', as O'Kelly had obviously done in his own case.[11]

Some Irish Australians maintained a sense of Irish identity through their membership of Irish clubs and societies, such as the Celtic Club in Melbourne, the Irish National Association in Sydney and the Queensland Irish Association, or through participation in Irish dancing and music.[12] But Denis Walker in his recollections said that he had been struck, especially during the 1970s when he became involved in Irish groups, by the differences and sometimes antagonism between Irish Australians and recently arrived Irish immigrants. The latter tended to look down on the former as 'just vague atomistic "friends" who were not part of the Irish Nation'.[13] And such tensions were only accentuated by the deteriorating political situation in Ireland.[14]

During the late 1960s and throughout the 1970s, as the conflict in Northern Ireland first began and then showed no signs of ending soon, not only did the Australian media turn their attention to Irish affairs for the first time in decades, but some Irish Australians started to rethink their Irish heritage in the context of the contemporary violence. The 1981 republican hunger strike in Belfast's Maze Prison, during which ten men died over a four-month period, had a particularly powerful impact in Australia. When the hunger-strike leader, Bobby Sands, died in May, a mass for the repose of his soul was celebrated before a large congregation in Melbourne's St Patrick's Cathedral.[15] Social historian Val Noone has argued that events such as the death of Sands, combined with the apparently intractable nature of the Troubles, were instrumental in prompting some Irish Australians to begin studying Irish history, language and culture in a more serious and systematic fashion than ever before.[16]

A regular series of Irish studies conferences began in Canberra in 1980, which continues to this day. The conferences produced numerous books of proceedings, while in 2000 an Irish studies journal was established in Perth, and in 2006 transferred to Melbourne. There was also a marked upsurge of interest in the Irish language, with classes and summer schools held in Sydney, Melbourne and elsewhere from the 1980s onwards. During the 1990s, the 150th anniversary of the Great Famine, as well as the bicentenary of the 1798 Rebellion, saw an outpouring of books, numerous conferences and the erection of commemorative monuments in various parts of Australia. Academic chairs of Irish studies appeared in universities in Melbourne and Sydney during the first decade of the new century. And, at the same time, genealogical research into Irish family history was flourishing, with Australians more interested than ever in discovering if they had Irish ancestry, even Irish convict ancestry.[17]

By the late 1990s, optimism about Ireland's future was on the rise. The 1998 Belfast Good Friday Agreement seemed to finally mark the end of the 30-year-long Troubles in Northern Ireland, while the Celtic Tiger economy boomed in the Republic, apparently promising an end too to large-scale emigration from Ireland. Yet peace in the North has proved fragile, while in the South the economy went spectacularly from boom to bust in 2008, ushering in years of austerity, high unemployment and deteriorating social services. In the wake of economic collapse, a new wave of Irish immigrants began arriving in Australia in search of jobs that were suddenly no longer available for them in Ireland. As in the past, many were young and single, although there were young families among them as well. But this 21st-century generation of immigrants, unlike those who came before them, had access to relatively cheap airfares, the internet and social media, which allowed them to stay in close touch with their families in Ireland and with fellow Irish immigrants.[18] Their experiences of migration and settlement, as they navigate an increasingly globalised world, are therefore likely to be markedly different from the experiences of the many previous generations of Irish immigrants to Australia.

The Irish as 'Anglo-Celtic', 'white' or 'Australo-British'

From the despised convicts of the late 18th century to the globalised citizens of the early 21st century, the Irish-born have always been a vital element in the story of modern Australia. Yet, as this study has amply demonstrated, for many decades the Catholic Irish were perceived by the Protestant Anglo-Australian majority not just as a different ethnic group, but often as an inferior race. In addition, they were adherents of a foreign church, widely regarded as aggressive and believed to harbour authoritarian political ambitions. In both roles, the Irish appeared to threaten Australian harmony, stability and prosperity. Their politics too were suspect, since the Catholic Irish had a centuries-long history of violent opposition to British rule. They had proved themselves an innately rebellious people, repeatedly threatening the integrity of the British Empire. On top of all these negative attributes, Irish immigrants, being in the main young, unskilled and from poor rural backgrounds, swelled the ranks of the working class. But not only were many of them poor, they were frequently looked upon as the 'undeserving poor' in terms of charity, having a reputation for drunkenness, crime and general fecklessness. Race, ethnicity, religion, history, culture, politics and class all differentiated the Irish in the eyes of British Australians. The perceived differences seemed readily identifiable.

Yet, as we have also demonstrated, there have been persistent attempts – that are still ongoing – to subsume the Irish into larger categories and thereby to efface their multiple differences. In the Introduction, we saw how Irish immigrants, stripped of their ethnic and cultural distinctiveness, were often included by both 19th- and 20th-century commentators in the category 'British', their children being consigned to the exclusively religious category, 'Catholics', again with significant aspects of their ethnic background obscured. In recent decades the category 'Anglo-Celts' and the designation 'white', both first used in the late 19th century, have become increasingly popular.[19] However, the growing reliance on the term 'Anglo-Celtic' in both academic and popular discourse requires critical investigation and challenge because it ignores major fault lines clearly visible in Australian society prior to 1945.

Even writers who employ the term 'Anglo-Celtic' have struggled to make sense of it. In 1997, for example, a book about Federation characterised its supporters during the 1890s as aspiring to maintain an 'Anglo-Celtic monoculture' and 'Anglo-Celtic racial purity'. Yet, elsewhere in the book, the authors recognised that 'Irish-Australians, especially those who were Roman Catholic, always had an ambivalent relationship' with notions of a cohesive 'British-Australian identity'.[20] Clearly, such ambivalence contradicts the notion of an 'Anglo-Celtic monoculture'. A somewhat similar contradiction can be detected in Miriam Dixson's controversial 1999 book, *The Imaginary Australian: Anglo-Celts and Identity*. In that she expressed concern about the rise of multiculturalism and the erosion of what she called Australia's 'Anglo-Celtic core culture'. Yet she too highlighted British and Irish difference, remarking that 'in Australia, for a long time, the divide between the world's first modernisers, the English, and the partly-premodern, partly-clan Irish ran deep and bitter'.[21] Dixson made no attempt, though, to reconcile this 'deep and bitter' divide with her assertion of a monolithic 'Anglo-Celtic core culture'.

Others have been far more critical. Ann Curthoys, a historian of British descent and one very conscious of Irish difference, wrote in 1997 that she certainly 'did not feel Anglo-Celtic' and in fact considered that 'Anglo-Celtic was scarcely an identity at all'.[22] Anthropologist Ghassan Hage, in his influential 1998 critique of multiculturalism, entitled *White Nation*, explicitly confronted the problem of terminology when he asked: what should the descendants of immigrants from Britain and Ireland who had arrived in Australia before the 1940s be called? He recognised that the category 'Anglo-Celtic', while it tells us 'something about the dominant culture, mystifies the struggles of valorisation between Englishness and Irishness which characterise Australian history'. Therefore, he opted to use the word 'white', partly because he believed it was a more common form of 'self-perception', even if 'largely an unconscious one'.[23] Yet Hage admitted that 'white' too had its problems, since, like 'Anglo-Celtic', it obscured significant Anglo-Irish divisions. So, instead, he invented the ungainly term 'Australo-Britishness' to try and describe the emergence of a 'culturally classless' Australian identity during the late 19th century based on the concept of mateship, which was, he claimed, the product of 'a partly working class, partly Irish encounter with the "Australian" natural environment'.[24]

Writing shortly after 2000, in one of his last papers, Patrick O'Farrell was characteristically far more forthright in his assessment of 'Anglo-Celtic'. According to him, the term was a 'grossly misleading, false and patronising contemporary convenience, one crassly present-centred.'[25] In other words, 'Anglo-Celtic' is simply not an accurate or useful term, for it obfuscates major differences, tensions and conflicts that characterised pre-1945 Australia and significantly affected the lives of countless Australians, whether their origins were Irish or British.

The anti-Irish joke in 21st-century Australia

Ironically, towards the end of the 20th century, when Irish-born immigrants and Irish Australians were being homogenised with British Australians under the name 'Anglo-Celts', negative Irish stereotypes that had held sway throughout the 19th century were continuing to be recycled in Australia via anti-Irish jokes and caricatures. This study has discussed many racial and ethnic jokes, cartoons, poems and stories satirising the Irish. Such representations were brought to Australia largely by English immigrants and they reflected England's long and fraught relationship with Ireland. They were then adapted to comment upon Australian events and circumstances involving the Irish. Such satires were ubiquitous, particularly during the late 19th century when the Irish-born population was at its height. But comic portrayals of the Irish persisted even as the number of Irish-born people living in Australia fell to relatively low levels during the mid 20th century, and they have continued to be popular into the 21st century, readily recognised and embraced by non-Irish Australian audiences.

As during the 19th century, many of the current jokes and stories revolve around the presumed ignorance and stupidity of the Irish. In mid 2015, for example, after same-sex marriage was approved by referendum in the Irish Republic, Grahame Morris, a senior advisor to the conservative Australian Liberal Party, rejected the idea that Australia should follow Ireland's example. 'I love the Irish and half the [Australian federal] parliament's full of Irishmen', he said in a newspaper interview, 'but these are people who can't grow potatoes, they've got a mutant lawn weed as their national symbol and they can't verbalise the difference between a tree and the number three.'[26] The specific charges Morris levelled against the Irish were all incorrect, but the general sentiment expressed – that the Irish, though somehow 'lovable', were at the same time a decidedly stupid people and thus not to be emulated – is one that informs numerous past and current anti-Irish jokes.[27]

More recently, in early 2018, a series of frauds and scams committed in Queensland by people allegedly speaking with Irish accents elicited a satirical article in the *Brisbane Times* from the writer John Birmingham. While the immigration authorities were focusing on crimes in Melbourne said to be committed by 'imaginary' gangs of Africans, complained Birmingham, 'Shifty McGintys and Slippery O'Tooles' and other 'bog-dwelling fiends' and 'brassy Irish scrubbers' were left free to defraud the citizens of Brisbane. In addition, these 'scheming boyos', with their diet of unwashed potatoes, were clogging up the 'innocent' toilets of Australia. Birmingham seemed to want to attack the racial policies of the 'blacksuits', as he called the country's new border police force. They were, he claimed, 'targeting the wrong foreigners'.[28] But, in defending one group of immigrants, Africans, against racial slurs, he chose instead to slur a different group of immigrants, the Irish.

Anti-Irish jokes have not been confined to newspaper articles, however; they have also recently been recycled extensively in books. The popular accounts of Australia's history published in comedy writer David Hunt's *Girt* in 2013 and *True Girt* in 2016 were obviously intended to be light and amusing. Both volumes proved successful, attracting favourable reviews, being nominated for book prizes and selling well.[29] Some examples of Hunt's humour need to be cited here to illustrate the deeply anti-Irish nature of his work. In volume 1, for example, in a section entitled 'Fookin Eejits', Hunt decided that English jokes about the 'Irish peasantry being a bit dim' were well founded, because Catholic priests had been banned from educating the 'little tykes' and 'malnutrition resulted in high levels of mental retardation'. In another section entitled 'Paddymonium', Hunt agreed that English settlers' fears about Irish violence were justified: 'The

Irish were into violence in a big way – and the more sectarian the better', he wrote.[30] In volume 2, readers were informed in relation to Ned Kelly's armour that: '[o]nly a person of proud Irish stock could design' such hopelessly inadequate protection for himself. The thousands of teenage girls sent from famine-racked Ireland to Australia during the late 1840s were, according to Hunt, 'short, ugly and mostly Catholic', and 'many … forged successful careers in the exciting prostitution and vagrancy industries'. Due to this 'Orphangate' scandal, few could find respectable husbands and so they were forced to marry Chinese gold prospectors.[31]

Nearly all the classic anti-Irish stereotypes that had circulated in past centuries were resurrected and rehearsed in these two volumes: the Irish were stupid, violent, drunken, ugly, corrupt, impoverished and sectarian. The success of these books, as well as the anti-Irish remarks of Morris in 2015 and Birmingham in 2018, demonstrate that an undercurrent of prejudice continues to thrive, reflected in what its proponents often like to defend as harmless fun. But racially or ethnically based stereotypes and caricatures are not the stuff of innocent good humour; they reflect real contemporary or historic prejudice and discrimination – usually a bit of both. The challenge then is to recognise what these stereotypes meant in the past and to try to understand why they remain comprehensible and potent in 21st-century Australia, more than a century after the end of large-scale Irish immigration. A nation of immigrants, like Australia was in the 19th century and is today, cannot afford to take such humour lightly: jokes, and the negative stereotypes they perpetuate, are a serious matter.

Bibliography

PRIMARY SOURCES

Manuscripts

Capital Cases Files, Public Record Office Victoria [PROV], Melbourne, VPRS 0264 - P/0000, Boxes 6, 7, 9.

Central Register for Male Prisoners, vol. 4 (1855), PROV, VPRS 515 - P0000.

Central Register of Female Prisoners, vol. 1 (1855–61), nos 1-750, PROV, VPRS 516-P1 Microfiche.

Deportations 1920–30, National Archives of Australia [NAA], Canberra, A1, 1927/19900.

Dillon, J, Memorandum from the Assistant Secretary, Department of Home Affairs, Canberra, 9 May 1930, NAA, B13, 1930/9443.

Dryer, A, documents, Irish Bureau of Military History, Dublin, W.S. 957 and W.S. 1526, <www.bureauofmilitaryhistory.ie/>.

Examination of persons under the Immigration Act. Reports by collectors of customs regarding practice in vogue. Guidance to officers, 1911, NAA, A1, 1911/10657.

Gladesville Hospital for the Insane, Sydney, Admissions Registers and Case Books, 1868–88 State Records New South Wales, Sydney, NRS 5031/4/8163.

Haddon, AC, papers, University of Cambridge Library, Cambridge, MS 22, MS 3058.

Hunt, A, Melbourne, to Captain R Collins, London, 20 June 1906, Department of External Affairs, NAA, A2910.417/4/2.

McCarthy, J, Deportations 1920-30, NAA, B13, 1929/6049.

Maloney, K Barry, Papers, University College Dublin Archives, Dublin, P94.

Morrissey, G, witness statement, Irish Bureau of Military History, Dublin, W.S. 874, <www.bureauofmilitaryhistory.ie/>.

NSW Inspector-General of the Insane Reports, 1881–1910, Mitchell Library, Sydney, Q362.2/N.

O'Farrell, P, Bibliography, unpublished writings on sectarianism, <www.patrickofarrell.com>.

——, Manuscripts (MS 6265), photographs (P 2215), pamphlets and personal papers (prefix OFA), National Library of Australia, Canberra.

Walsh, T, Papers relating to deportation attempts, NAA, 1925, A467, SF12/2-28.

Yarra Bend Asylum, Melbourne, Admission Registers and Case Books, 1848–1905, PROV, VA2839, VPRS 7400/12/9.

Websites

Australian Bureau of Statistics, 'Table 8.1: Population (a), sex and country of birth, NSW census years 1846–1891', *Australian Historical Population Statistics 2014*, 3105.0.65.001, <www.ausstats.abs.gov.au>.

Australian Dictionary of Biography (ADB), online edition, <adb.anu.edu.au/>.

Australian Psychiatric Care website, <www.ahpi.esrc.unimelb.edu.au/index.html>.

Census of the Commonwealth of Australia taken on 2 and 3 April 1911, Australian Bureau of Statistics, <www.ausstats.abs.gov.au>.

Census of the Commonwealth of Australia, 30 June 1933, Australian Bureau of Statistics, 2110.0, <www.ausstats.abs.gov.au>.

2016 Commonwealth of Australia Census: 2024.0 Census of Population and Housing, Australian Bureau of Statistics, <www.abs.gov.au>.

Irish Anzacs Project, database, University of NSW, <www.repository.arts.unsw.edu.au>.

Victorian Year Books, Australian Bureau of Statistics, 1301.2, <www.abs.com.au>.

Audio-visual

Kehoe, P (director), *An Dubh ina Gheal: Assimilation*, A Saoi Media Production for TG4/BAI television, Dublin, 2015.

Printed sources

Ackland, M (ed.), *The Penguin Book of 19th-Century Australian Literature*, Penguin Books, Melbourne, 1993.

Approved Readers for the Catholic Schools of Australasia. Book 4, Brooks, Sydney, 1908.

Australian Electoral Commission, *Australian Referendums, 1906–99*, CD ROM, Commonwealth of Australia, Canberra, 2000.

Avery, JG, 'Civilisation; with especial reference to the so-called Celtic inhabitants of Ireland', *Journal of the Anthropological Society of London*, vol. 7, 1869, pp. 221–37.

Banton, M, *Race Relations*, Basic Books, New York, 1967, p. 8.

Bates, D, *The Passing of the Aborigines: A Lifetime Spent Among the Natives of Australia*, 1938, John Murray, London, 1966.

Beddoe, J, 'Colour and race', *Journal of the Anthropological Institute of Great Britain and Ireland*, vol. 35, 1901, pp. 219–50.

——, *Memories of 80 Years*, JW Arrowsmith, Bristol, 1910.

——, *The Races of Britain: A Contribution to the Anthropology of Western Europe*, JW Arrowsmith, Bristol, 1885.

Bonwick, J, *The Wild White Man and the Blacks of Victoria*, Ferguson & Moore, Melbourne, 1863.

Burdett, HC, *Hospitals and Asylums of the World*, vol. 1, J & A Churchill, London, 1891.

Calwell, AA, *Be Just and Fear Not*, Rigby, Melbourne, 1972.

Castieau, JB, *'The Difficulties of My Position': The Diaries of Prison Governor John Buckley Castieau, 1855–84*, M Finnane (ed.), National Library of Australia, Canberra, 2004.

Coghlan, TA, *The Wealth and Progress of New South Wales*, 1894, vol. 2, Charles Potter, Government Printer, Sydney, 1896.

Collins, D, *An Account of the English Colony in New South Wales from Its First Settlement, in January 1788, to August 1801*, 2 vols, T Cardell Jr and W Davies, London, 1802.

Commission on Emigration and Other Population Problems, 1948–54: Reports, Stationery Office, Dublin, [1954].

Croly, DG & Wakeman, G, *Miscegenation; The Theory of the Blending of the Races, Applied to the American White Man and Negro*, H. Dexter, Hamilton and Co., New York, 1864.

Cunningham, DJ & Haddon, AC, 'The Anthropometric Laboratory of Ireland', *Journal of the Anthropological Institute of Great Britain and Ireland*, vol. 21, 1892, pp. 35–39.

Dampier, A & Walch, G, *Robbery Under Arms*, R Fotheringham (ed.), Currency Press, Sydney, 1985.

Davitt, M, *Life and Progress in Australasia*, Methuen, London, 1898.

Deakin, A, *The Crisis in Victorian Politics, 1879–81: A Personal Retrospective*, JA La Nauze & RM Crawford (eds), Melbourne University Press, Melbourne, 1957.

——, *The Federal Story: The Inner History of the Federal Cause*, Robertson and Mullens, Melbourne, 1944.

Deeny, J, *Tuberculosis in Ireland: Report of the National Tuberculosis Survey, 1950–53*, Medical Research Council of Ireland, Dublin, 1954.

Denham, A, 'The Kelly Gang' (1899), in R Fotheringham (ed.), *Australian Plays for the Colonial Stage, 1834–99*, University of Queensland Press, Brisbane, 2006.

Denison, TS, 'Patsy O'Wang: An Irish farce with a Chinese mix-up', in *Lively Plays for Live People*, T.S. Denison, Chicago, 1895, pp. 77–106.

Dennis, CJ, *The Moods of Ginger Mick*, Angus and Robertson, Sydney, 1916.

Dilke, CW, *Greater Britain: A Record of Travel in English-Speaking Countries During 1866 and 1867*, 1869, Cosimo Classics, New York, 2005.

Duffy, CG, *My Life in Two Hemispheres*, 2 vols, T. Fisher Unwin, London, 1898.

——, *Young Ireland: A Fragment of Irish History, 1840–45*, new ed., M.H. Gill and Son, Dublin, 1884.

Durack, M, *Kings in Grass Castles*, 1959, O'Neil, Melbourne, 1974.

Edgeworth, M, *An Essay on Irish Bulls*, J Desmarais & M Butler (eds), University College Dublin Press, Dublin, 1999.

Franklin, J, Nolan, GO & Gilchrist, M (eds), *The Real Archbishop Mannix from the Sources*, Connor Court Publishing, Ballarat, VIC, 2015.

Franklin, M, *My Brilliant Career*, 1901, Folio Society, London, 1983.

Froude, JA, *Oceana or England and Her Colonies*, Longmans, Green & Co., London, 1886.

'Garryowen' [E Finn], *The Chronicles of Early Melbourne, 1835 to 1852*, 2 vols, Fergusson & Mitchell, Melbourne, 1888.

Gelder, K & Weaver, R (eds), *The Colonial Journals and the Emergence of Australian Literary Culture*, UWA Publishing, Perth, 2014.

Grattan, J, 'On the importance, to the archæologist and ethnologist, of an accurate mode of measuring human crania, and of recording the results; With the description of a new craniometer', *Ulster Journal of Archaeology*, 1st Series, vol. 1, 1853, pp. 198-208.

Haddon, AC, *History of Anthropology*, G.B. Putnam, New York, 1910.

——, *The Races of Man and Their Distribution*, F.A. Stokes, New York, 1909.

——, 'Studies in Irish craniology: The Aran Islands, County Galway', *Proceedings of the Royal Irish Academy*, vol. 2, 1891-93, pp. 759-67.

Haddon, AC & Browne, C, 'The ethnography of the Aran Islands, County Galway', *Proceedings of the Royal Irish Academy*, vol. 2, 1891-93, pp. 768-830.

Hogan, E, *The Irish People, Their Height, Form and Strength*, Sealy, Bryers and Walker, Dublin, 1899.

Hogan, JF, *The Irish in Australia*, Ward & Downey, London, 1887.

Horne, D, *The Education of Young Donald*, Angus and Robertson, Sydney, 1967.

Huxley JS & Haddon, AC, *We Europeans: A Survey of 'Racial' Problems*, Jonathan Cape, London, 1935.

Jordan, RD & Pierce, P (eds), *The Poets' Discovery: Nineteenth-Century Australia in Verse*, Melbourne University Press, Melbourne, 1990.

Just, P, *Australia; or, Notes Taken during a Residence in the Colonies from the Discovery of Gold in 1851 till 1857*, Durham and Thomson, Dundee, 1859.

Kingsley, F (ed.), *Charles Kingsley: His Letters and Memories of His Life*, 2 vols, Macmillan, London, 1891.

Knox, R, *The Races of Men: A Fragment*, Lea and Blanchard, Philadelphia, 1850.

'Knox on the Celtic race', *Anthropological Review*, vol. 6, no. 21, 1868, pp. 175-91.

'Kodak' [E O'Farrell], 'And the singer was Irish', in Ethel Turner (ed.), *The Australian Soldiers' Gift Book*, Voluntary Workers' Association, Sydney, 1918, pp. 91-93.

Lang, JD, *Reminiscences of My Life and Times*, DWA Baker (ed.), Heinemann, Melbourne, 1972.

Lang, JT, *I Remember*, Invincible Press, Sydney, 1956.

Laughlin, AM & Hall, TS (eds), *Handbook to Victoria*, A.J. Mullett, Government Printer, Melbourne, 1914.

Lindsay, J, *Life Rarely Tells: An Autobiographical Account Ending in the Year 1921 and Situated Mostly in Brisbane, Queensland*, Bodley Head, London, 1958.

Lyng, J, *Non-Britishers in Australia: Influence on Population and Progress*, 2nd ed., Melbourne University Press, Melbourne, 1935.

McGinness, J, *Son of Alyandabu: My Fight for Aboriginal Rights*, University of Queensland Press, Brisbane, 1971.

Manning, FN, 'Address in psychological medicine, delivered at the Intercolonial Medical Congress in Melbourne on 11 January 1888', *Journal of Mental Science*, vol. 35, no. 150, 1889, pp.149–78.

——, *The Causation of Insanity*, Thomas Richards, Government Printer, Sydney, 1880.

Martin, AP, *Australia and the Empire*, David Douglas, Edinburgh, 1889.

Martin, EA (ed.), *The Life and Speeches of Daniel Henry Deniehy*, 1884, Sydney University Press, Sydney, 1998.

Maxwell, WH, *History of the Irish Rebellion in 1798; With Memoirs of the Union and Emmett's Insurrection in 1803*, 1845, Bell and Daldy, London, 1866.

'Miscegenation', *Anthropological Review*, vol. 2, no. 5, 1864, pp. 116–21.

Moran, HM, *Viewless Winds: Being the Recollections and Digressions of an Australian Surgeon*, Peter Davies, London, 1939.

Morgan, P (ed.), *B.A. Santamaria: Your Most Obedient Servant. Selected Letters, 1938–96*, Miegunyah Press, Melbourne, 2007.

Mudie, J, *The Felonry of New South Wales, with Anecdotes of Botany Bay Society*, 1837, W Stone (ed.), Lansdowne Press, Melbourne, 1964.

Mulvaney, J, Morphy, H & Petch, A (eds), *'My Dear Spencer': The Letters of F.J. Gillen to Baldwin Spencer*, Hyland House, Melbourne, 1997.

Neville, AO, *Australia's Coloured Minority: Its Place in the Community*, Currawong Press, Sydney, 1947.

Noone, V (ed.), *Nicholas O'Donnell's Autobiography*, Ballarat Heritage Services, Ballarat, VIC, 2017.

O'Brien, J, 'The agrarian agitation in Ireland: A reply', *Victorian Review*, vol. 1, 1880, pp. 902–14.

——, 'English institutions and the Irish race: A reply', *Melbourne Review*, vol. 6, 1881, pp. 111–30.

O'Farrell, P (ed.), *Letters from Irish Australia, 1825–1929*, UNSW Press and Ulster Historical Foundation, Sydney and Belfast, 1984.

O'Farrell, P & O'Farrell, D (eds), *Documents in Australian Catholic History*, 2 vols, Geoffrey Chapman, London, 1969.

Osborne, J, 'Nine Crowded Years', in Michael Hogan (ed.), *The First New South Wales Labor Government, 1910–1916*, UNSW Press, Sydney, 2005.

Osborne, WA, *What We Owe to Ireland*, Lothian Book Publishing, Melbourne, 1918.

Paterson, AB, *An Outback Marriage*, Angus & Robertson, Sydney, 1906.

Redmond, W, *Through the New Commonwealth*, Sealy, Bryers and Walker, Dublin, [1906].

Rudd, S, *On Our Selection*, Bulletin Newspaper, Sydney, 1899.

——, *Our New Selection*, Bulletin Newspaper, Sydney, 1903.

Sinclair, E, 'Presidential address in the section of neurology and psychiatry of the Australasian Medical Congress held at Melbourne, October 1908', *Journal of Mental Science*, vol. 55, no. 229, 1909, pp. 213–43.

St Ledger, A, *Thomas Joseph Byrnes 1860–98: Sketches and Impressions*, Alex Muir & Co., Brisbane, 1902.

Topp, AM, 'English institutions and the Irish race', *Melbourne Review*, vol. 6, no. 21, 1881, pp. 9–27.

——, 'A few more words on the Irish question', *Melbourne Review*, vol. 6, no. 22, 1881, pp. 194–214.

Tucker, GA, *Lunacy in Many Lands*, Charles Potter, Government Printer, Sydney, 1887.

Turner, HG, *A History of the Colony of Victoria*, 2 vols, 1904, Heritage Publications, Melbourne, 1973.

Urquhart, AR, 'Three Australian asylums', *Journal of Mental Science*, vol. 25, no. 112, 1880, pp. 480–89.

Vamplew, W (ed.), *Australians: Historical Statistics*, Fairfax, Syme & Weldon Associates, Sydney, 1987.

Walker, D, 'Memories of a 1950s Irish leftie in St Kilda, Melbourne', *Tinteán*, 6 June 2016, <tintean.org.au>.

Wood, GT, *Royal Commission of Inquiry into Alleged Killings and Burning of Bodies of Aborigines in East Kimberley*, Government Printer, Perth, 1927.

York, B (ed.), *Immigration Restriction, 1901–57: Annual Returns as Required under the Australian Immigration Act between 1901 and 1957 on Persons Refused Admission*, 3rd ed., Victoria University of Technology, Melbourne, 1997.

SECONDARY SOURCES

Aan de Wiel, J, *The Catholic Church in Ireland, 1914–18: War and Politics*, Irish Academic Press, Dublin and Portland, OR, 2003.

Adam-Smith, P, *Heart of Exile: Ireland, 1848, and the Seven Patriots Banished*, Nelson, Melbourne, 1986.

Akenson, DH, *Small Differences: Irish Catholics and Irish Protestants, 1815–1922: An International Perspective*, McGill-Queen's University Press, Montreal and Kingston, 1988.

——, *The Irish Diaspora: A Primer*, P.D. Meany and Queen's University, Toronto and Belfast, 1993.

Allen, TW, *The Invention of the White Race*, 2 vols, Verso, London, 1994, 1997.

Amos, K, *The Fenians in Australia, 1865–80*, UNSW Press, Sydney, 1988.

Anderson, H, *The Poet Militant: Bernard O'Dowd*, Hill of Content, Melbourne, 1968.

Anderson, W, *The Cultivation of Whiteness: Science, Health and Racial Destiny in Australia*, Melbourne University Press, Melbourne, 2002.

Andreon, H, 'Olive or white? The colour of Italians in Australia', *Journal of Australian Studies*, vol. 77, 2003, pp. 81–92.

Archer, R, 'Labour and liberty: The origins of the conscription referendum', in R Archer, J Damousi, M Goot & S Scalmer (eds), *The Conscription Conflict and the Great War*, Monash University Publishing, Melbourne, 2016, pp. 37–66.

——, 'Stopping war and stopping conscription: Australian labour's response to World War I in comparative perspective', *Labour History*, no. 106, 2014, pp. 43–67.

Atkinson, A, *The Europeans in Australia. Volume 2: Democracy*, 2nd ed., UNSW Press, Sydney, 2016.

——, *The Europeans in Australia. Volume 3: Nation*, UNSW Press, Sydney, 2014.

——, 'Four patterns of convict protest', *Labour History*, no. 37, 1979, pp. 28–51.

Australians: The Guide and Index, Fairfax, Syme & Weldon Associates, Sydney, 1987.

Auty, K, 'Patrick Bernard O'Leary and the Forrest River massacres, Western Australia: Examining "wodgil" and the significance of 8 June 1926', *Aboriginal History*, vol. 28, 2004, pp. 122–55.

Ayres, P, *Prince of the Church: Patrick Francis Moran, 1830–1911*, Miegunyah Press, Melbourne, 2007.

Bagnall, K, 'Across the threshold: White women and Chinese hawkers in the white colonial imaginary', *Hecate*, vol. 28, no. 2, 2002, pp. 9–32.

——, 'Golden Shadows on a White Land: An Exploration of the Lives of White Women Who Partnered Chinese Men and their Children in Southern Australia, 1855–1915', PhD thesis, University of Sydney, 2007.

——, 'Rewriting the history of Chinese families in nineteenth-century Australia', *Australian Historical Studies*, vol. 42, no. 1, 2011, pp. 62–77.

Bagot, A, *Coppin the Great: Father of the Australian Theatre*, Melbourne University Press, Melbourne, 1965.

Baker, D, '"Men to monsters": Civility, barbarism, and "race" in early modern Ireland', in P Beidler & G Taylor (eds), *Writing Race Across the Atlantic World*, Palgrave Macmillan, New York, 2005, pp. 153–69.

Ballantyne, G & Burke, L, '"People live in their heads a lot": Polymedia, life course, and meanings of home among Melbourne's older Irish community', *Transnational Social Review*, vol. 7, no. 1, 2017, pp. 10–24.

Ballantyne, T, *Orientalism and Race: Aryanism in the British Empire*, Palgrave Macmillan, Basingstoke, Hampshire, 2006.

Banta, M, *Barbaric Intercourse: Caricature and the Culture of Conduct, 1841–1936*, University of Chicago Press, Chicago, 2003.

Banton, M, *Race Relations*, Basic Books, New York, 1967. 'The vertical and horizontal dimensions of the word race', *Ethnicities*, vol. 10, 2010, pp. 127–40.

——, *What We Now Know About Race and Ethnicity*, Berghahn, New York, 2015.

Barkan, E, *The Retreat of Scientific Racism: Changing Concepts of Race in Britain and the United States between the World Wars*, Cambridge University Press, Cambridge, 1994.

Barrett, JR, *The Irish Way: Becoming American in the Multiethnic City*, Penguin Books, New York, 2012.

Barry, JV, *The Life and Death of John Price: A Study of the Exercise of Naked Power*, Melbourne University Press, Melbourne, 1964.

Bartlett, P, *The Poor Law of Lunacy: The Administration of Pauper Lunatics in Mid-Nineteenth Century England*, Leicester University Press, London, 1999.

Bashford, A, *Global Population: History, Geopolitics and Life on Earth*, Columbia University Press, New York, 2014.

——, 'Insanity and immigration restriction', in C Cox & H Marland (eds), *Migration, Health and Ethnicity in the Modern World*, Palgrave Macmillan, Basingstoke, Hampshire, 2013, pp. 14–35.

Bashford, A & Macintyre, S (eds), *The Cambridge History of Australia*, 2 vols, Cambridge University Press, Cambridge, 2013.

Bavin-Mizzi, J, *Ravished: Sexual Crime in Victorian Australia*, UNSW Press, Sydney, 1995.

Beaumont, J, *Broken Nation: Australians in the Great War*, Allen and Unwin, Sydney, 2013.

Belchem, J, *Irish, Catholic and Scouse: The History of the Liverpool Irish, 1800–1939*, Liverpool University Press, Liverpool, 2007.

Bellanta, M, *Larrikins: A History*, University of Queensland Press, Brisbane, 2012.

Berryman, J 'The concept of civilization in Manning Clark's "History of Australia"', *History Australia*, vol. 14, no. 1, 2017, pp. 82–98.

Bew, P, 'The politics of war', in J Horne (ed.), *Our War: Ireland and the Great War*, Royal Irish Academy, Dublin, 2008, pp. 95–107.

Bhabha, H, *The Location of Culture*, Routledge, London and New York, 1994.

Bhavsar, V & Bhugra, D, 'Bethlem's Irish: Migration and distress in nineteenth-century London', *History of Psychiatry*, vol. 20, no. 2, 2009, pp. 184–98.

Biddiss, MD, 'The politics of anatomy: Dr Robert Knox and Victorian racism', *Proceedings of the Royal Society of Medicine*, vol. 69, no. 4, 1976, pp. 245–50.

Bielenberg, A, 'Fatalities in the Irish revolution', in J Crowley, D Ó Drisceoil & M Murphy (eds), *Atlas of the Irish Revolution*, Cork University Press, Cork, 2017, pp. 758–59.

——, 'Irish emigration to the British Empire, 1700–1914', in A Bielenberg (ed.), *The Irish Diaspora*, Longman, Harlow, Essex, 2000, pp. 215–34.

Blainey, G, *A History of Victoria*, rev. ed., Cambridge University Press, Cambridge and Melbourne, 2006.

Bollard, R, 'Economic conscription and Irish discontent: The possible resolution of a conundrum', in P Deery & J Kimber (eds), *Fighting against War: Peace Activism in the Twentieth Century*, LeftBank Publications, Melbourne, 2015, pp. 139–56.

Bolton, G, 'The Irish in Australian historiography', in C Kiernan (ed.), *Australia and Ireland, 1788–1988: Bicentenary Essays*, Gill and Macmillan, Dublin, 1986, pp. 5–19.

Bongiorno, F, 'Bernard O'Dowd's socialism', *Labour History*, no. 77, 1999, pp. 97–116.

——, *The People's Party: Victorian Labor and the Radical Tradition, 1875–1914*, Melbourne University Press, Melbourne, 1996.

——, *The Sex Lives of Australians: A History*, Black Inc., Melbourne, 2012.

Bonnett, A, *White Identities: Historical and International Perspectives*, Prentice Hall, Harlow, Essex, and New York, 2000.

Bornstein, G, *The Colors of Zion: Blacks, Jews, and Irish from 1845 to 1945*, Harvard University Press, Cambridge, Mass., 2011.

Borrie, WD, *The European Peopling of Australasia: A Demographic History, 1788–1988*, Australian National University, Canberra, 1994.

Bourke, A, *'The Visitation of God': The Potato and the Great Irish Famine*, J Hill & C Ó Gràda (eds), Lilliput Press, Dublin, 1993.

Bowman, T, 'The Ulster Volunteer Force, 1910–20: New perspectives', in DG Boyce & A O'Day (eds), *The Ulster Crisis, 1885–1921*, Palgrave Macmillan, Basingstoke, Hampshire, 2006, pp. 247–58.

Bracken, PJ, Greenslade, L, Griffin, B & Smyth, M, 'Mental health and ethnicity: An Irish dimension', *British Journal of Psychiatry*, vol. 172, no. 2, 1998, pp. 103–105.

Brady, C (ed.), *Interpreting Irish History: The Debate on Historical Revisionism*, Irish Academic Press, Dublin, 1994.

Breen, F, 'Emigration in the age of electronic media: Personal perspectives of Irish migrants to Australia, 1969–2013', in A McCarthy (ed.), *Ireland in the World: Comparative, Transnational and Personal Perspectives*, Routledge, New York, 2015, pp. 198–233.

Brennan, D, *Irish Insanity, 1800–2000*, Routledge, London and New York, 2014.

Brennan, N, *John Wren, Gambler: His Life and Times*, Hill of Content, Melbourne, 1971.

Brett, J, 'Class, religion and the foundation of the Australian party system: A revisionist interpretation', *Australian Journal of Political Science*, vol. 37, no. 1, 2002, pp. 39–56.

——, *The Enigma of Mr Deakin*, Text Publishing, Melbourne, 2017.

Broad, R, *Volunteers and Pressed Men: How Britain and Its Empire Raised Its Forces in Two World Wars*, Fonthill, Oxford, 2016.

Broinowski, A, *The Yellow Lady: Australian Impressions of Asia*, Oxford University Press, Oxford, 1992.

Brooks, R, 'The Melbourne tailoresses' strike, 1882–1883: An assessment', *Labour History*, no. 44, 1983, pp. 27–38.

Broome, R, *Aboriginal Australians: A History since 1788*, 4th ed., Allen & Unwin, Sydney, 2010.

——, *Aboriginal Victorians: A History since 1800*, Allen & Unwin, Sydney, 2005.

Bryan, H, 'John Murtagh Macrossan and the genesis of the white Australia policy', *Journal of the Royal Historical Society of Queensland*, vol. 5, no. 2, 1954, pp. 885–906.

——, *John Murtagh Macrossan: His Life and Career*, University of Queensland Press, Brisbane, 1958.

Buckridge, P, 'Two Irish poets in colonial Brisbane: Eva O'Doherty and Cornelius Moynihan', in J Wooding (ed.), *Old Myths and New Lights*, Queensland Irish Association, Brisbane, 1991, pp. 16–26.

Burgmann, V, 'Revolutionaries and Racists: Australian Socialism and the Problem of Racism, 1887–1917', PhD thesis, Australian National University, Canberra, 1980.

Cage, RA, *Poverty Abounding, Charity Aplenty: The Charity Network in Colonial Victoria*, Hale & Iremonger, Sydney, 1992.

Cahill, AE, 'Cardinal Moran's politics', *Journal of Religious History*, vol. 15, no. 4, 1989, pp. 525–31.

Cain, F, *The Australian Security Intelligence Organization: An Unofficial History*, Frank Cass, Abingdon, Oxon, 1994.

Cameron, J, 'George Fletcher Moore' in B Reece (ed.), *The Irish in Western Australia*, University of Western Australia, Perth, 2000, pp. 21–34.

Camm, JCR & McQuilton, J (eds), *Australians: A Historical Atlas*, Fairfax, Syme and Weldon Associates, Sydney, 1987.

Campbell, M, *Ireland's New Worlds: Immigrants, Politics and Society in the United States and Australia*, University of Wisconsin Press, Madison, WN, 2008.

——, 'Irish women in nineteenth-century Australia: A more hidden Ireland', in P Bull, C McConville & N McLachlan (eds), *Irish-Australian Studies: Papers Delivered at the Sixth Irish-Australian Conference, July 1990*, La Trobe University, Melbourne, 1991, pp. 25–38.

Campion, E, *Australian Catholics: The Contribution of Catholics to the Development of Australian Society*, Penguin Books, Melbourne, 1987.

Cannon, M, *The Land Boomers*, Melbourne University Press, Melbourne, 1966.

Canny, N, *The Elizabethan Conquest of Ireland: A Pattern Established, 1565–76*, Harvester Press, Hassocks, Sussex, 1976.

——, *Making Ireland British 1580–1650*, Oxford University Press, Oxford, 2001.

——, 'Protestants, planters and apartheid in early modern Ireland', *Irish Historical Studies*, vol. 25, no. 98, 1986, pp. 105–15.

Carew, M, *The Quest for the Irish Celt: The Harvard Archaeological Mission to Ireland, 1932–36*, Irish Academic Press, Newbridge, County Kildare, 2018.

Carey, H, 'Australian religious culture from Federation to the new pluralism', in L Jayasurya, D Walker & J Gothard (eds), *Legacies of White Australia: Race, Culture and Nation*, University of Western Australian Press, Perth, 2003, p. 70–92.

——, 'Companions in the wilderness? Missionary wives in colonial Australia, 1788–1900', *Journal of Religious History*, vol. 19, no. 2, 1995, pp. 227–48.

—— (ed.), 'Special issue: Religion and memory', *Journal of Religious History*, vol. 31, no. 1, 2007, pp. 1–58.

——, 'Subordination, invisibility and chosen work: Missionary nuns and Australian Aborigines, c. 1900–1949', *Australian Feminist Studies*, vol. 13, no. 28, 1998, pp. 251–67.

Carlson, EA, *The Unfit: A History of a Bad Idea*, Cold Spring Harbor Laboratory Press, Cold Spring Harbor, New York, 2001.

Carroll, C, 'Barbarous slaves and civil cannibals: Translating civility in early modern Ireland', in C Carroll & P King (eds), *Ireland and Postcolonial Theory*, Cork University Press, Cork, 2003, pp. 63–80.

Carville, J, 'Resisting vision: Photography, anthropology and the production of race in Ireland', in C Breathnach & C Lawless (eds), *Visual, Material and Print Culture in Nineteenth-Century Ireland*, Four Courts Press, Dublin, 2010, pp. 158–75.

Cato, N, *Mister Maloga*, University of Queensland Press, Brisbane, 1976.

Chetkovich, J, 'The New Irish in Australia: A Western Australian Perspective', PhD thesis, University of Western Australia, Perth, 2005.

Chisholm, A, *The Life and Times of C.J. Dennis*, Angus and Robertson, Sydney, 1982.

Choi, CY, *Chinese Migration and Settlement in Australia*, Sydney University Press, Sydney, 1975.

Clark, M, *A Short History of Australia*, 2nd ed., New American Library, New York, 1980.

Cleary, PS, *Australia's Debt to Irish Nation-Builders*, Angus and Robertson, Sydney, 1933.

Coleborne, C, '"His brain was wrong, his mind astray": Families and the language of insanity in New South Wales, Queensland and New Zealand, 1880s–1910', *Journal of Family History*, vol. 31, no. 1, 2006, pp. 45–65.

——, *Insanity, Identity and Empire: Immigrants and Institutional Confinement in Australia and New Zealand, 1873–1910*, Manchester University Press, Manchester, 2015.

——, 'Passage to the asylum: The role of the police in committals of the insane in Victoria, Australia, 1848–1900', in R Porter & D Wright (eds), *The Confinement of the Insane: International Perspectives, 1800–1965*, Cambridge University Press, Cambridge, 2003, pp. 129–48.

——, 'Pursuing families for maintenance payments to hospitals for the insane in Australia and New Zealand, 1860s–1914', *Australian Historical Studies*, vol. 40, no. 3, 2009, pp. 308–22.

Collins, V, '"A one-battalioned mind": Albert Thomas Dryer (1888–1963). Identity, Culture and Politics', MA thesis, University of Melbourne, 2013.

Connolly, CN, 'Class, birthplace, loyalty: Australian attitudes to the Boer War', *Historical Studies*, vol. 18, no. 71, 1978, pp. 210–32.

——, 'Miners' rights: Explaining the "Lambing Flat" riots of 1860–61', in A Curthoys & A Markus (eds), *Who Are Our Enemies? Racism and the Australian Working Class*, Hale & Iremonger, Sydney, 1978, pp. 35–47.

Connolly, SJ, *Priests and People in Pre-Famine Ireland, 1780–1845*, Gill and Macmillan, Dublin, 1982.

Connor, J, 'Why was it easier to introduce and implement conscription in some English-speaking countries than in others?', in R Archer, J Damousi, M Goot & S Scalmer (eds), *The Conscription Conflict and the Great War*, Monash University Publishing, Melbourne, 2016, pp. 148–68.

Connors, L & Turner, B, '"I cannot do any more": Resistance, respectability and ruin—Recapturing the Irish orphan girls in the Moreton Bay districts', in T McClaughlin (ed.), *Irish Women in Colonial Australia*, Allen & Unwin, Sydney, 1998, pp. 105–22.

Conor, L, *Skin Deep: Settler Impressions of Aboriginal Women*, UWA Publishing, Perth, 2016.

Coolahan, J, 'The Irish and others in Irish nineteenth-century textbooks', in JA Mangan (ed.), *The Imperial Curriculum: Racial Images and Education in the British Colonial Experience*, Routledge, London, 1993, pp. 54–63.

Couchman, S, 'Introduction', in K Bagnall & S Couchman (eds), *Chinese Australians: Politics, Engagement and Resistance*, Brill, Leiden, 2015, pp. 1–21.

Coughlan, N, 'The coming of the Irish to Victoria', *Historical Studies*, vol. 12, no. 45, 1965, pp. 68–86.

Cowling, M, *The Artist as Anthropologist: Representation of Type and Character in Victorian Art*, Cambridge University Press, Cambridge, 1989.

Cox, C, *Negotiating Insanity in the Southeast of Ireland, 1820–1900*, Manchester University Press, Manchester, 2012.

Cox, C, Marland, H & York, S, 'Emaciated, exhausted and excited: The bodies of the Irish in late nineteenth-century Lancashire asylums', *Journal of Social History*, vol. 46, no. 2, 2012, pp. 500–524.

Crisp, LF, *The Australian Federal Labour Party, 1901–51*, Longmans, Green and Co., London, 1955.

Cronin, K, *Colonial Casualties: Chinese in Early Victoria*, Melbourne University Press, Melbourne, 1982.

Cronin, M & Adair, D, *The Wearing of the Green: A History of St Patrick's Day*, Routledge, London and New York, 2002.

Crowther, A, 'Administration and the asylum in Victoria, 1860s–1880s', in C Coleborne & D MacKinnon (eds), *'Madness' in Australia: Histories, Heritage and the Asylum*, University of Queensland Press, Brisbane, 2003, pp. 85–95.

Cunningham, AE, *The Price of a Wife? The Priest and the Divorce Trial*, Anchor Books Australia, Sydney, 2013.

Curthoys, A, 'History and identity', in W Hudson & G Bolton (eds), *Creating Australia: Changing Australian History*, Allen & Unwin, Sydney, 1997, pp. 23–28.

——, '"Men of all nations, except Chinamen": Europeans and Chinese on the goldfields of New South Wales', in I McCalman, A Cook & A Reeves (eds), *Gold: Forgotten Histories and Lost Objects of Australia*, Cambridge University Press, Cambridge, 2001, pp. 103–23.

——, 'Race and Ethnicity: A Study of the Response of British Colonists to Aborigines, Chinese and Non-British Europeans in N.S.W., 1856–1881', PhD thesis, Macquarie University, Sydney, 1973.

——, 'White, British and European: Historicising identity in settler societies', in J Carey & C McLisky (eds), *Creating White Australia*, Sydney University Press, Sydney, 2009, pp. 3–24.

Curtis Jr, LP, *Apes and Angels: The Irishman in Victorian Caricature*, rev. ed., Smithsonian Institution, Washington DC, 1997.

Cusack, D, *With an Olive Branch and a Shillelagh: The Life and Times of Senator Patrick Lynch*, Hesperian Press, Perth, 2004.

Daly, ME, 'Death and disease in independent Ireland, c. 1920–70: A research agenda', in C Cox & M Luddy (eds), *Cultures of Care in Irish Medical History, 1750–1970*, Palgrave Macmillan, Basingstoke, Hampshire, 2010, pp. 229–50.

Damousi, J, *Colonial Voices: A Cultural History of English in Australia, 1840–1940*, Cambridge University Press, Cambridge and New York, 2010.

——, 'Universities and conscription: The "yes" campaign and the University of Melbourne', in R Archer, J Damousi, M Goot & S Scalmer (eds), *The Conscription Conflict and the Great War*, Monash University Publishing, Melbourne, 2016, pp. 92–110.

Davies, S, 'Aborigines, murder and the criminal law in early Port Phillip, 1841–51', *Historical Studies*, vol. 22, no. 88, 1987, pp. 315–20.

Davis, RP, *Arthur Griffith and Non-violent Sinn Fein*, Anvil Books, Dublin, 1974.

——, *Orangeism in Tasmania, 1832–1967*, Ulster University, Newtownabbey, Co. Antrim, 2010.

Davison, G, Dunstan, D & McConville, C (eds), *The Outcasts of Melbourne: Essays in Social History*, Allen & Unwin, Sydney, 1985.

Day, C, 'Magnificence, Misery and Madness: A History of the Kew Asylum', PhD thesis, University of Melbourne, 1998.

De Mórdha, D & Walsh, C, *The Irish Headhunter: The Photograph Albums of Charles R. Browne*, Stationery Office, Dublin, 2012.

De Nie, M, *The Eternal Paddy: Irish Identity and the British Press, 1798–1882*, University of Wisconsin Press, Madison, WN, 2004.

De Serville, P, *Pounds and Pedigrees: The Upper Class in Victoria, 1850–80*, Oxford University Press, Melbourne, 1991.

——, *Rolf Boldrewood: A Life*, Miegunyah Press, Melbourne, 2000.

De Vries, S, *Desert Queen: The Many Lives and Loves of Daisy Bates*, HarperCollins, Sydney, 2008.

Delaney, E, *The Irish in Post-war Britain*, Oxford University Press, New York, 2007.

Delaney, E, Kenny, K & MacRaild, DM, 'Symposium: Perspectives on the Irish diaspora', *Irish Economic and Social History*, vol. 33, 2006, pp. 35–58.

Devlin-Glass, F, 'The Irish in grass castles: Re-reading the victim tropes in an iconic pioneering text,' in LM Geary & AJ McCarthy (eds), *Ireland, Australia and New Zealand: History, Politics and Culture*, Irish Academic Press, Dublin and Portland, OR, 2008, pp. 104–18.

Dick, W, '"Vigorous-minded and independent": Ellen Mulcahy as a labour leader,' *Labour History*, no. 104, 2013, pp. 31–48.

Dixson, M, *The Imaginary Australian: Anglo-Celts and Identity—1788 to the Present*, UNSW Press, Sydney, 1999.

——, *The Real Matilda: Women and Identity in Australia, 1788 to the Present*, 3rd ed., Penguin Books, Melbourne, 1994.

Dodson, P, 'Resonance: Irish Australians and Aboriginal Australians', in P Gray (ed.), *Passing the Torch: The Aisling Society of Sydney, 1955–2005*, The Aisling Society of Sydney, Sydney, 2005, pp. 264–76.

Dolan, TP (ed.), *A Dictionary of Hiberno-English: The Irish Use of English*, Gill and Macmillan, Dublin, 1999.

Donnelly Jr, JS, 'The construction of the memory of the Famine in Ireland and the Irish diaspora, 1850–1900', *Eire-Ireland*, vol. 31, nos 1–2, 1996, pp. 26–61.

Dormandy, T, *The White Death: A History of Tuberculosis*, Hambledon Press, London, 1999.

Douglas, R, Harte, L & O'Hara, J, *Drawing Conclusions: A Cartoon History of Anglo-Irish Relations, 1798–1998*, Blackstaff Press, Belfast, 1998.

Douglas, R & Laster, K, 'A matter of life and death: The Victorian executive and the decision to execute, 1842–1967', *Australian and New Zealand Journal of Criminology*, vol. 24, no. 2, 1991, pp. 144–60.

Doyle, AM, RSM *Mercy, Mater and Me: A Tale of Compassion and Determination*, University of Queensland Press, Brisbane, 2010.

Doyle, DN, 'The Irish in Australia and the United States: Some comparisons, 1800–1939', *Irish Economic and Social History*, vol. 16, 1989, pp. 73–94.

Doyle, E, 'Sir Charles Gavan Duffy's land act, 1862: Victoria through Irish eyes', in C Kiernan (ed.), *Australia and Ireland: Bicentenary Essays*, Gill and Macmillan Dublin, 1986, pp. 145–55.

Doyle, H, 'Allegations of disloyalty at Koroit during World War I', in P Bull, F Devlin-Glass & H Doyle (eds), *Ireland and Australia 1798–1998. Studies in Culture, Identity and Migration*, Crossing Press, Sydney, 2000, pp. 165–76.

Duggan, GC, *The Stage Irishman: A History of the Irish Play and Stage Characters from the Earliest Times*, Longmans Green, London, 1937.

Duncan, B, *Crusade or Conspiracy? Catholics and the Anti-Communist Struggle in Australia*, UNSW Press, Sydney, 2001.

Dutton, D, 'The Commonwealth Investigation Branch and the political construction of the Australian citizenry, 1920–40', *Labour History*, no. 75, 1998, pp. 155–74.

Dyrenfurth, N, *Heroes and Villains: The Rise and Fall of the Early Australian Labor Party*, Australian Scholarly Publishing, Melbourne, 2011.

——, *Mateship: A Very Australian History*, Scribe, Melbourne and London, 2015.

Eagan, CM, 'Still "black" and "proud": Irish Americans and the racial politics of Hibernia', in D Negra (ed.), *The Irish in Us: Irishness, Performativity and Popular Culture*, Duke University Press, Durham, NC, 2006, pp. 20–63.

——, '"White" if "not quite": Irish whiteness in the nineteenth-century Irish-American novel', in K Kenny (ed.), *New Directions in Irish-American History*, University of Wisconsin Press, Madison, WN, 2003, pp. 140–55.

Earls, B, 'Bulls, blunders and bloothers: An examination of the Irish bull', *Béaloideas*, vol. 56, 1988, pp. 1–92.

Earls, T, '"The opportunity of being useful": Daniel O'Connell's influence on John Hubert Plunkett', in LM Geary & AJ McCarthy (eds), *Ireland, Australia and New Zealand: History, Politics and Culture*, Irish Academic Press, Dublin and Portland, OR, 2008, pp. 170–82.

——, *Plunkett's Legacy: An Irishman's Contribution to the Rule of Law in New South Wales*, Australian Scholarly Publishing, Melbourne, 2009.

Ebsworth, W, *Pioneer Catholic Victoria*, Polding Press, Melbourne, 1973.

Ellinghaus, K, 'Absorbing the "Aboriginal problem": Controlling interracial marriage in Australia in the late 19th and early 20th centuries', *Aboriginal History*, vol. 27, 2003, pp. 183–207.

——, *Taking Assimilation to Heart: Marriages of White Women and Indigenous Men in the United States and Australia, 1887–1937*, University of Nebraska Press, Lincoln, NA, and London, 2006.

Evans, R, Moore, C, Saunders, K & Jamison, B, *1901 – Our Future's Past: Documenting Australia's Federation*, Macmillan, Sydney, 1997.

Evans, T, *Fractured Families: Life on the Margins in Colonial New South Wales*, UNSW Press, Sydney, 2015.

Fabian, S (ed.), *Mr Punch Down Under: A Social History of the Colony from 1856 to 1900 Via Cartoons and Extracts from* Melbourne Punch, Greenhouse Landmark, Melbourne, 1982.

Fahey, C, '"Abusing the horses and exploiting the labourer": The Victorian agricultural and pastoral labourer, 1871-1911', *Labour History*, no. 65, 1993, pp. 96–114.

Fedorowich, K, 'The problems of disbandment: The Royal Irish Constabulary and imperial migration, 1919–29', *Irish Historical Studies*, vol. 30, no. 117, 1996, pp. 88–110.

Fennell, P & King, M (eds), *John Devoy's 'Catalpa' Expedition*, New York University Press, New York, 2006.

Field, L, *The Forgotten War: Australia and the Boer War*, 1979, Melbourne University Press, Melbourne, 1995.

Fielding, S, *Class and Ethnicity: Irish Catholics in England, 1880–1939*, Open University Press, Buckingham, 1993.

Finnane, M, 'Asylums, families and the state', *History Workshop*, no. 20, 1985, pp. 134–48.

——, 'Deporting the Irish envoys: Domestic and national security in 1920s Australia', *Journal of Imperial and Commonwealth History*, vol. 41, no. 3, 2013, pp. 403–25.

——, '"Habeas corpus Mongols" – Chinese litigants and the politics of immigration in 1888', *Australian Historical Studies*, vol. 45, no. 2, 2014, pp. 165–83.

——, *Insanity and the Insane in Post-Famine Ireland*, Croom Helm, London, 1981.

——, 'Introduction: Writing about police in Australia', in M Finnane (ed.), *Policing in Australia: Historical Perspectives*, UNSW Press, Sydney, 1987, pp. 1–14.

——, 'The Irish and crime in the late nineteenth century: A statistical inquiry', in O MacDonagh & WF Mandle (eds), *Irish-Australian Studies: Papers Delivered at the Fifth Irish-Australian Conference*, Australian National University, Canberra, 1989, pp. 77–98.

——, 'Law as politics: Chinese litigants in Australian colonial courts', in S Couchman & K Bagnall (eds), *Chinese Australians: Politics, Engagement and Resistance*, Brill, Leiden, 2015, pp. 117–36.

——, *Police and Government: Histories of Policing in Australia*, Oxford University Press, Melbourne, 1994.

——, 'The politics of police powers: The making of police offences acts', in M Finnane (ed.), *Policing in Australia: Historical Perspectives*, University of New South Wales Press, Sydney, 1987, pp. 88–113.

Finnane, M & O'Donnell, I, 'Crime and punishment', in EF Biagini & ME Daly (eds), *The Cambridge Social History of Modern Ireland*, Cambridge University Press, Cambridge, 2017, pp. 363–82.

Firth, S, & Darlington, R, 'Racial stereotypes in the Australian curriculum: The case-study of New South Wales', in JA Mangan (ed.), *The Imperial Curriculum: Racial Images and Education in the British Colonial Experience*, Routledge, London, 1993, pp. 123–59.

Fitzgerald, B, '"Blood on the saddle": The Forrest River massacre, 1926', *Studies in Western Australian History*, vol. 8, 1984, pp. 7–15.

Fitzgerald, J, *Big White Lie: Chinese Australians in White Australia*, University of New South Wales Press, Sydney, 2007.

Fitzhardinge, LF, *The Little Digger 1914–1952. William Morris Hughes. A Political Biography, Volume II*, Angus and Robertson, Sydney, 1979.

Fitzpatrick, D, 'Emigration, 1801-70', in WE Vaughan (ed.), *A New History of Ireland. Volume V. Ireland under the Union I: 1801–70*, Clarendon Press, Oxford, 1989, pp. 562–622.

——, 'Exporting brotherhood: Orangeism in South Australia', *Immigrants & Minorities*, vol. 23, nos 2–3, 2005, pp. 277–310.

——, 'Ireland and the empire', in A Porter (ed.), *The Oxford History of the British Empire. Volume 3 Nineteenth-Century*, Oxford University Press, Oxford, 1999, pp. 495–521.

——, 'Irish emigration in the later nineteenth century', *Irish Historical Studies*, vol. 22, no. 86, 1980, pp. 126–43.

——, 'Militarism in Ireland, 1900-22', in T Bartlett & K Jeffery (eds), *A Military History of Ireland*, Cambridge University Press, Cambridge, 1996, pp. 379–406.

——, *Oceans of Consolation: Personal Accounts of Irish Migration to Australia*, Cork University Press, Cork, 1994.

Foord, P, 'The three promises: story of the Lew Shing family', 27 February 2009, <arrow.latrobe.edu.au/store/3/4/5/5/1/public/stories/lewshing.htm>.

Ford, P, *Cardinal Moran and the A.L.P.: A Study in the Encounter between Moran and Socialism, 1890–1907*, Melbourne University Press, Melbourne, 1966.

Foster, G, 'Locating the "Lost Legion": IRA emigration and settlement after the Civil War', in J Crowley, D Ó Drisceoil & M Murphy (eds), *Atlas of the Irish Revolution*, Cork University Press, Cork, 2017, pp. 744–47.

Foster, RF, *Vivid Faces: The Revolutionary Generation in Ireland, 1890–1923*, Allen Lane, London, 2014.

Fotheringham, R, *In Search of Steele Rudd, Author of the Classic Dad and Dave Stories*, University of Queensland Press, Brisbane, 1995.

Fox, C & Scates, B, 'The beat of weary feet', in V Burgmann & J Lee (eds), *Staining the Wattle: A People's History of Australia since 1788*, McPhee Gribble and Penguin Books, Melbourne, 1988, pp. 132–49.

Fox, JW, 'Irish immigrants, pauperism and insanity in 1854 Massachusetts', *Social Science History*, vol. 15, no. 3, 1991, pp. 315–36.

Frances, R, 'Authentic leaders: Women and leadership in Australian unions before World War II', *Labour History*, no. 104, 2013, pp. 9–30.

Francis, RD, *Migrant Crime in Australia*, University of Queensland Press, Brisbane, 1981.

Frankenberg, R, *Displacing Whiteness: Essays in Social and Cultural Criticism*, Duke University Press, Durham, NC, and London, 1997.

Franklin, J, 'Catholic missions to Aboriginal Australia: An evaluation of their overall effect', *Journal of the Australian Catholic Historical Society*, vol 37, no. 1, 2016, pp. 45–68.

French, M, 'Roman Catholics and the Labor Party: An early conflict in South Australia', *Labour History*, no. 32, 1977, pp. 55–65.

Freudenberg, G, *A Certain Grandeur: Gough Whitlam in Politics*, Sun Books, Melbourne, 1978.

Fried, RA, 'No Irish need deny: Evidence for the historicity of NINA restrictions in advertisements and signs', *Journal of Social History*, vol. 49, no. 4, 2016, pp. 829–54.

Galbally, A, *Redmond Barry: An Anglo-Irish Australian*, Melbourne University Press, Melbourne, 1995.

Gallman, JM, *Receiving Erin's Children: Philadelphia, Liverpool and the Irish Famine Migration, 1845–55*, University of North Carolina Press, Chapel Hill, NC, and London, 2000.

Gantt, J, *Irish Terrorism in the Atlantic Community, 1865–1922*, Palgrave Macmillan, Basingstoke, Hampshire, 2010.

Garner, S, *Racism in the Irish Experience*, Pluto Press, London, 2004.

Garton, S, 'Bad or mad? Developments in incarceration in NSW, 1880–1920', in Sydney Labour History Group (eds), *What Rough Beast? The State and Social Order in Australian History*, George Allen & Unwin, Sydney, 1982, pp. 89–110.

——, 'Eugenics in Australia and New Zealand: Laboratories of racial science', in A Bashford & P Levine (eds), *The Oxford Handbook of the History of Eugenics*, Oxford University Press, Oxford, 2012, pp. 243–57.

——, *Medicine and Madness: A Social History of Insanity in New South Wales, 1880–1940*, UNSW Press, Sydney, 1988.

——, 'Policing the dangerous lunatic: Lunacy incarceration in New South Wales, 1843–1914', in M Finnane (ed.), *Policing in Australia: Historical Perspectives*, UNSW Press, Sydney, 1987, pp. 74–87.

——, 'Sound minds and healthy bodies: Reconsidering eugenics in Australia, 1914–40', *Australian Historical Studies*, vol. 26, no. 103, 1994, pp. 163–81.

Gatrell, VAC, *The Hanging Tree: Execution and the English People, 1770–1868*, Oxford University Press, Oxford, 1994.

Geoghegan, P, *King Dan: The Rise of Daniel O'Connell, 1775–1829*, Gill and Macmillan, Dublin, 2008.

——, *Liberator: The Life and Death of Daniel O'Connell, 1830–47*, Gill and Macmillan, Dublin, 2010.

Gifford, P, 'Murder and "the execution of the law" on the Nullarbor', *Aboriginal History*, vol. 18, 1994, pp. 103–22.

Gilbert, A, 'The conscription referenda, 1916–17: The impact of the Irish crisis', *Historical Studies*, vol. 14, no. 53, 1969, pp. 54–72.

Glass, M, *Charles Cameron Kingston: Federation Father*, Melbourne University Press, Melbourne, 1997.

——, *Tommy Bent: 'Bent by name, Bent by nature'*, Melbourne University Press, Melbourne, 1993.

Golway, T, *Irish Rebel: John Devoy and America's Fight for Irish Freedom*, St Martin's Griffin, New York, 1998.

Goodman, D, *Gold Seeking: Victoria and California in the 1850s*, Allen & Unwin, Sydney, 1994.

Goot, M, 'The results of the 1916 and 1917 conscription referendums re-examined', in R Archer, J Damousi, M Goot & S Scalmer (eds), *The Conscription Conflict and the Great War*, Monash University Publishing, Melbourne, 2016, pp. 111–46.

Gothard, J, *Blue China: Single Female Migration to Colonial Australia*, Melbourne University Press, Melbourne, 2001.

——, 'Wives or workers? Single British female migration to colonial Australia', in P Sharpe (ed.), *Women, Gender and Labour Migration: Historical and Global Perspectives*, Routledge, London and New York, 2001, pp. 145–62.

Gould, SJ, *The Mismeasure of Man*, rev. ed., W.W. Norton & Co., New York and London, 1981.

Grainger, E, *Martin of Martin Place: A Biography of Sir James Martin, 1820–86*, Alpha Books, Sydney, 1970.

Greenslade, L, Madden, M & Pearson, M, 'From visible to invisible: The "problem" of the health of Irish people in Britain', in L Marks & M Worboys (eds), *Migrants, Minorities and Health: Historical and Contemporary Studies*, Routledge, London and New York, 1997, pp. 147–78.

Griffin, J, *John Wren: A Life Reconsidered*, Scribe Publications, Melbourne, 2004.

Griffiths, P, 'The Coolie labour crisis in colonial Queensland', *Labour History*, no. 113, 2017, pp. 53–78.

——, 'The "necessity" of a socially homogeneous population: The ruling class embraces racial exclusion', *Labour History*, no. 108, 2015, pp. 123–44.

Grimes, S, 'Irish immigration after 1945', in J Jupp (ed.) *The Australian People: An Encyclopedia of the Nation, Its People and Their Origins*, 2nd ed., Cambridge University Press, Cambridge, 2001, pp. 480–84.

——, 'Postwar Irish immigrants: The Sydney experience', in S Grimes & GÓ Tuathaigh (eds), *The Irish-Australian Connection*, University College Galway, Galway, 1988, pp. 137–59.

Grimshaw, P, 'Faith, missionary life and the family', in P Levine (ed.), *Gender and Empire*, Oxford University Press, Oxford, 2004, pp. 260–80.

Grimshaw, P, McConville, C, & McEwen, E (eds), *Families in Colonial Australia*, George Allen & Unwin, Sydney, 1985.

Haebich, A, *For Their Own Good: Aborigines and Government in the Southwest of Western Australia, 1900–1940*, University of Western Australia Press, Perth, 1988.

Hage, G, *White Nation: Fantasies of White Supremacy in a Multicultural Society*, 1998, Routledge, New York and London, 2000.

Haldane, R, *The People's Force: A History of the Victoria Police*, Melbourne University Press, Melbourne, 1986.

Hall, C, *Civilising Subjects: Metropole and Colony in the English Imagination 1830–1867*, Polity, London, 2002.

Hall, D, 'Defending the faith: Orangeism and Ulster Protestant identities in colonial New South Wales', *Journal of Religious History*, vol. 38, no. 2, 2014, pp. 207–23.

——, '"God sent me here to raise a society": Irishness, Protestantism and colonial identity', in HM Carey & C Barr (eds), *Religion and Greater Ireland*, McGill-Queen's University Press, Kingston and Montreal, 2015, pp. 319–39.

——, 'Irish Republican women on tour: Kathleen Barry and Linda Kearns in Australia 1924–25', *Irish Historical Studies*, forthcoming 2019.

——, 'Irishness, gender and "an up-country township"', in L Proudfoot & MM Roche (eds), *(Dis)Placing Empire: Renegotiating British Colonial Geographies*, Ashgate, Aldershot, Hampshire, 2005, pp. 81–97.

——, '"Now him white man": Images of the Irish in colonial Australia', *History Australia*, vol. 11, no. 2, 2014, pp. 167–95.

Hall, D & Malcolm, E, 'Diaspora, gender and the Irish', *Australasian Journal of Irish Studies*, vol. 8, 2008/9, pp. 3–29.

——, 'English institutions and the Irish race: Race and politics in late nineteenth-century Australia', *Australian Journal of Politics and History*, vol. 62, no. 1, 2016, pp. 1–15.

Hall, S, 'The multi-cultural question', in B Hesse (ed.), *Un/Settled Multiculturalisms. Diasporas, Entanglements, Disruptions*, Zed, London, 2001, pp. 209–41.

Hamilton C, 'Catholic interests and the Labor Party: Organised Catholic action in Victoria and New South Wales, 1910-16', *Historical Studies*, vol. 9, no. 33, 1959, pp. 62–73.

——, 'Irish-Catholics of New South Wales and the Labor Party, 1890–1910', *Historical Studies*, vol. 8, no. 31, 1958, pp. 254–67.

Hamilton, P, 'Domestic dilemmas: Representations of servants and employers in the popular press', in S Sheridan (ed.), *Debutante Nation: Feminism Contests the 1890s*, Allen & Unwin, Sydney, 1993, pp. 71–90.

——, *'No Irish Need Apply': Aspects of the Employer-Employee Relationship in Australian Domestic Service, 1860–1900*, Australian Studies Centre, University of London, London, 1985.

——, 'The "servant class": Poor female migration to Australia in the nineteenth century', in E Richards (ed.), *Poor Australian Immigrants in the Nineteenth Century*, Australian National University, Canberra, 1991, pp. 117–32.

——, '"Tipperarifying the moral atmosphere": Irish Catholic immigration and the state, 1840-1860', in Sydney Labour History Group (eds), *What Rough Beast:*

The State and Social Order in Australian History, George Allen & Unwin, Sydney, 1982, pp. 13–30.

Hannaford, I, *Race: The History of an Idea in the West*, Johns Hopkins University Press, Baltimore, MD, 1996.

Hansord, K, 'Eliza Hamilton Dunlop's "The Aboriginal Mother": Romanticism, anti-slavery and imperial feminism in the nineteenth century', *Journal of the Association for the Study of Australian Literature*, vol. 11, no. 1, 2011, pp. 1–12.

Harris, S, *The Prince and the Assassin: Australia's First Royal Tour and Portent of World Terror*, Melbourne Books, Melbourne, 2017.

Hart, PR, 'J.A. Lyons, Tasmanian Labour Leader', *Labour History*, no. 9, 1965, pp. 33–42.

Haskins, V and Maynard, J, 'Sex, race and power: Aboriginal men and white women in Australian history', *Australian Historical Studies*, vol. 126, 2005, pp. 191–216.

Hayton, D, 'From barbarian to burlesque: English images of the Irish, c. 1660–1750', *Irish Economic and Social History*, vol. 15, 1998, pp. 5–31.

Healy, D, 'Irish psychiatry in the twentieth century', in H Freeman & GE Berrios (eds), *150 Years of British Psychiatry. Volume II: The Aftermath*, Athlone Press, London, 1996, pp. 268–91.

Hennessey, T, *Dividing Ireland: World War I and Partition*, Routledge, London and New York, 1998.

Hickman, MJ, 'Reconstructing deconstructing "race": British political discourses about the Irish in Britain', *Ethnic and Racial Studies*, vol. 21, no. 2, 1998, pp. 288–307.

Higman, B, *Domestic Service in Australia*, Melbourne University Press, Melbourne, 2002.

Hirst, J, *Australian History in 7 Questions*, Black Inc., Melbourne, 2014.

Hocking, G, *The Rebel Chorus: Dissenting Voices in Australian History*, Five Mile Press, Melbourne, 2007.

Hogan, M, *The New South Wales State Election, 1922*, New South Wales Parliamentary Library and University of Sydney, Sydney, 1995.

——, *The Sectarian Strand: Religion in Australian History*, Penguin Books, Melbourne, 1987.

——, 'The Sydney style: New South Wales Labor and the Catholic Church', *Labour History*, no. 36, 1979, pp. 39–46.

Holst, H, 'Equal before the law? The Chinese in the nineteenth-century Castlemaine police courts', *Journal of Australian Colonial History*, vol. 6, 2004, pp. 113–36.

Hopkins, DJ, *Hop of the* Bulletin, Angus and Robertson, Sydney, 1929.

Hopkinson, M, *Green Against Green: The Irish Civil War*, Gill and Macmillan, Dublin, 1988.

Hoppen, TK, *Governing Hibernia: British Politicians and Ireland 1800–1921*, Oxford University Press, Oxford, 2016.

Howe, S, 'Historiography' in Kenny, K (ed.), *Ireland and the British Empire*, Oxford University Press, Oxford, 2004, pp. 220–50.

Hunt, D, *Girt: The Unauthorised History of Australia*, Black Inc., Melbourne, 2013.

——, *True Girt: The Unauthorised History of Australia*, Volume 2, Black Inc., Melbourne, 2016.

Ignatiev, N, *How the Irish Became White*, Routledge, New York, 1995.

Inglis, K, *Australian Colonists: An Exploration of Social History, 1788–1870*, Melbourne University Press, Melbourne, 1993.

——, 'Conscription in peace and war, 1911–45', in R Forward & B Reece (eds), *Conscription in Australia*, University of Queensland Press, Brisbane, 1968, pp. 34–45.

——, *The Rehearsal: Australians at War in the Sudan, 1885*, Rigby, Adelaide, 1985.

Irvin, E, *Gentleman George, King of Melodrama: The Theatrical Life and Times of George Darrell, 1841–1921*, University of Queensland Press, Brisbane, 1980.

Irving, H, 'Making the federal Commonwealth, 1890–1901', in A Bashford & S Macintyre (eds), *The Cambridge History of Australia. Volume 1: Indigenous and Colonial Australia*, Cambridge University Press, Melbourne, 2013, pp. 242–66.

Jackson, A, *Home Rule: An Irish History, 1800–2000*, Weidenfeld and Nicolson, London, 2003.

James, S, '"From beyond the sea": The Irish Catholic press in the southern hemisphere', in A McCarthy (ed.), *Ireland in the World: Comparative, Transnational and Personal Perspectives*, Routledge, New York and London, 2015, pp. 81–109.

Jeffery, K, *Ireland and the Great War*, Cambridge University Press, Cambridge, 2000.

Jenkins, B, *The Fenian Problem: Insurgency and Terrorism in a Liberal State, 1858–74*, Liverpool University Press, Liverpool, 2008.

Jensen, RJ, '"No Irish need apply": A myth of victimization', *Journal of Social History*, vol. 36, no. 2, 2002, pp. 405–29.

Jones, D, *Crime, Protest, Community and Police in Nineteenth-century Britain*, Routledge & Kegan Paul, London, 1982.

Jones, G, *'Captain of all these men of death': The History of Tuberculosis in Nineteenth- and Twentieth-Century Ireland*, Editions Rodopi B.V., Amsterdam and New York, 2001.

Jones, I, *Ned Kelly: A Short Life*, Lothian Books, Melbourne, 1995.

Jones, JL, 'The master potter and the rejected pots: Eugenic legislation in Victoria, 1918–39', *Australian Historical Studies*, vol. 30, no. 113, 1999, pp. 319–42.

Jupp, J, *The English in Australia*, Cambridge University Press, Cambridge, 2004.

Kain, JS, 'Preventing "Unsound Minds" from Populating the British World: Australasian Immigration Control and Mental Illness, 1830s–1920s', PhD thesis, University of Northumbria, Newcastle, UK, 2015.

Kamp, A, 'Formative geographies of belonging in white Australia: Constructing the national self and other in parliamentary debate, 1901', *Geographical Research*, vol. 48, no. 4, 2010, pp. 411–26.

Kaplan, C, 'White, black and green: Racialising Irishness in Victorian England', in P Gray (ed.), *Victoria's Ireland? Irishness and Britishness*, Four Courts Press, Dublin, 2004, pp. 51–68.

Kavanagh, J & Snowden, D, *Van Diemen's Women: A History of Transportation to Tasmania*, History Press Ireland, Dublin, 2015.

Kelly, B, *Hearing Voices: The History of Psychiatry in Ireland*, Irish Academic Press, Newbridge, Co. Kildare, 2016.

Kelly, J, '"We were all to be massacred": Irish Protestants and the experience of rebellion', in T Bartlett, D Dickson, D Keogh & K Whelan (eds), *1798: A Bicentenary Perspective*, Four Courts Press, Dublin, 2003, pp. 110–41.

Kelly, MJ, *The Fenian Ideal and Irish Nationalism, 1882–1916*, Boydell Press, Woodbridge, Suffolk, 2006.

Kelly, V, 'Melodrama, an Australian pantomime and the theatrical construction of colonial history', *Journal of Australian Studies*, vol. 17, no. 38, 1993, pp. 51–61.

Kenny, K, *The American Irish: A History*, Longman, Harlow, Essex, 2000.

——, 'Diaspora and comparison: The global Irish as a case study', *Journal of American History*, vol. 90, no. 1, 2003, pp. 134–62.

——, 'Ireland and the British Empire: An introduction', in K Kenny (ed.), *Ireland and the British Empire*, Oxford University Press, Oxford, 2004, pp. 1–25.

——, 'Race, violence and anti-Irish sentiment in the nineteenth century', in JJ Lee & MR Casey (eds), *Making the Irish American: History and Heritage of the Irish in the United States*, New York University Press, New York and London, 2007, pp. 364–78.

Kerr, J, *Artists and Cartoonists in Black and White: The Most Public Art*, The Centre for Cross-Cultural Research, Sydney, 1999.

Kevles, DJ, *In the Name of Eugenics: Genetics and the Uses of Human Heredity*, Penguin Books, Harmondsworth, Middlesex, 1986.

Kibler, MA, 'The stage Irishwoman', *Journal of American Ethnic History*, vol. 24, no. 3, 2005, pp. 5–30.

Kiernan, C, 'Charles Gavan Duffy and "the art of living"', in O MacDonagh & WF Mandle (eds), *Irish-Australian Studies: Papers Delivered at the Fifth Irish-Australian Conference*, Australian National University, Canberra, 1989, pp. 137–54.

——, *Daniel Mannix and Ireland*, Alella Books, Morwell, VIC, 1984.

——, 'Home Rule for Ireland and the formation of the Australian Labor Party, 1883 to 1891', *Australian Journal of Politics and History*, vol. 38, no. 1, 1992, pp. 1–11.

——, 'Irish in Australian politics', in J Jupp (ed.), *The Australian People: An Encyclopedia of the Nation, Its People and Their Origins*, 2nd ed., Cambridge University Press, Cambridge, 2001, pp. 474–78.

Kiernan, TJ, *The Irish Exiles in Australia*, Burns & Oates, Melbourne and London, 1954.

Kildea, J, *ANZACS and Ireland*, Cork University Press, Cork, 2007.

——, 'Ireland Will Be Free: Fanning the flames of sectarianism in Australia', *Australasian Journal of Irish Studies*, vol. 18, forthcoming 2018.

——, 'Killing conscription: The Easter Rising and Irish Catholic attitudes to the conscription debates in Australia, 1916–1917', *Journal of the Australian Catholic Historical Society*, vol. 37, no. 2, 2016, pp. 161–80.

——, 'Paranoia or prejudice: Billy Hughes and the Irish question, 1916–1922', in J Brownrigg, C Mongan & R Reid (eds), *Echoes of Irish Australia: Rebellion to Republic*, St Clement's Retreat and Conference Centre, Galong, NSW, 2007, pp. 155–66.

——, *Tearing the Fabric: Sectarianism in Australia, 1910–25*, Citadel Books, Sydney, 2002.

——, '"A veritable hurricane of sectarianism": The year 1920 and ethno-religious conflict in Australia', in C Barr & HM Carey (eds), *Religion and Greater Ireland: Christianity and Irish Global Networks, 1750–1950*, McGill-Queen's University Press, Kingston and Montreal, 2015, pp. 363–82.

——, 'Where crows gather: The Sister Liguori affair 1920–21', *Journal of the Australian Catholic Historical Society*, vol. 27, no. 1, 2006, pp. 31–40.

King, H, *Richard Bourke*, Oxford University Press, Melbourne, 1971.

King, P, 'Ethnicity, prejudice and justice: The treatment of the Irish at the Old Bailey, 1750–1825', *Journal of British Studies*, vol. 52, no. 2, 2013, pp. 390–414.

Kingston, B, *A History of New South Wales*, Cambridge University Press, Cambridge, 2006.

——, *My Wife, My Daughter and Poor May Ann: Women and Work in Australia*, Nelson, Melbourne, 1975.

——, *The Oxford History of Australia, Volume 3, 1860–1900: Glad, Confident Morning*, Oxford University Press, Melbourne, 1988.

Kirk, N, '"Australians for Australia": The right, the Labor Party and contested loyalties to nation and empire in Australia, 1917 to the early 1930s', *Labour History*, no. 91, 2006, pp. 95–111.

Kleinig, M, 'Peripatetic women: British domestic servants, internal migration and emigration to South Australia in the 1920s and 1930s', in M Kleinig & E Richards (eds), *On the Wing: Mobility Before and After Emigration to Australia*, Anchor Books Australia, Sydney, 2013, pp. 129–34.

Knowlton, SR, 'The enigma of Charles Gavan Duffy: Looking for clues in Australia', *Éire-Ireland*, vol. 31, nos 3 and 4, 1996, pp. 189–208.

Kollar, R, 'An American "escaped nun" on tour in England: Edith O'Gorman's critique of convent life', *Feminist Theology*, vol. 14, no. 2, 2005, pp. 205–22.

Kovesi Killerby, C, '"Never locked up or tied": Early Irish missionary attitudes to the Aboriginal people of Western Australia', in P Bull, F Devlin-Glass & H Doyle (eds), *Ireland and Australia 1798–1998. Studies in Culture, Identity and Migration*, Crossing Press, Sydney, 2000, pp. 124–33.

Kraut, AM, *Silent Travellers: Germs, Genes and the 'Immigrant Menace'*, Basic Books, New York, 1994.

Kuo, M-F, *Making Chinese Australia: Urban Elites, Newspapers and the Formation of Chinese–Australian Identity, 1892–1912*, Monash University Publishing, Melbourne, 2013.

Kwan, E, 'St Patrick's Day procession, Melbourne, 1920: An Australian or Irish event', in J Brownrigg, J Mongan & R Reid (eds), *Echoes of Irish Australia: Rebellion to Republic*, St Clement's Retreat and Conference Centre, Galong, NSW, 2007, pp. 145–54.

——, 'The Australian flag: Ambiguous symbol of nationality in Melbourne and Sydney, 1920–21', *Australian Historical Studies*, vol. 26, no. 103, 1994, pp. 280–303.

Lake, M, '"Essentially Teutonic": E.A. Freeman, liberal race historian. A transnational perspective', in C Hall & K McClelland (eds), *Race, Nation and Empire: Making Histories, 1750 to the Present*, Manchester University Press, Manchester, 2010, pp. 56–73.

——, 'The gendered and racialised self who claimed the right to self-government', *Journal of Colonialism and Colonial History*, vol. 13, no. 1, 2012, <doi:10.1353/cch.2012.0011>.

Lake, M & Reynolds, H, *Drawing the Global Colour Line: White Men's Countries and the International Challenge of Racial Equality*, Melbourne University Press, Melbourne, 2008.

Laster, K, 'Arbitrary chivalry: Women and capital punishment in Vicoria, 1842–1967', in D Phillips & S Davies (eds), *A Nation of Rogues: Crime, Law and Punishment in Colonial Australia*, Melbourne University Press, Melbourne, 1994, pp. 166–86.

Lawson, S, *The Archibald Paradox: A Strange Case of Authorship*, Allen Lane Penguin Books, Melbourne, 1983.

Lebow, N, 'British images of poverty in pre-Famine Ireland', in DJ Casey & RE Rhodes (eds), *Views of the Irish Peasantry, 1800–1916*, Archon Books, Hamden, CT, 1977, pp. 57–85.

Lee, A, 'The nun in the nightgown: The public airing of private prejudice and the Sister Ligouri [sic] scandal, 1920–21', *Journal of Australian Studies*, vol. 21, no. 52, 1997, pp. 34–42.

Lee, D & Kennedy, M, 'The credentials controversy: Australia, Ireland and the Commonwealth, 1950–65', *Australasian Journal of Irish Studies*, vol. 6, 2006/7, pp. 57–81.

Leerssen, J, *Mere Irish and Fíor-Ghael: Studies in the Idea of Irish Nationality, its Development and Literary Expression Prior to the Nineteenth Century*, Cork University Press, Cork, 1996.

Leeson, DM, 'The Royal Irish Constabulary, Black and Tans and Auxiliaries', in J Crowley, D Ó Drisceoil & M Murphy (eds), *Atlas of the Irish Revolution*, Cork University Press, Cork, 2017, pp. 371–84.

Lehane, R, *William Bede Dalley*, Ginninderra Press, Canberra, 2007.

Lemire, E, *'Miscegenation': Making Race in America*, University of Pennsylvania Press, Philadelphia, PA, 2002.

Leon, SM, '"Hopelessly entangled in Nordic pre-suppositions": Catholic participation in the American Eugenics Society in the 1920s', *Journal of the History of Medicine and Allied Sciences*, vol. 59, no. 1, 2004, pp. 3–49.

Levell, D, *Tour to Hell: Convict Australia's Great Escape Myths*, University of Queensland Press, Brisbane, 2008.

Lewis, M, *Managing Madness: Psychiatry and Society in Australia, 1788–1980*, Australian Government Publishing Service, Canberra, 1988.

Lindesay, V, *The Inked-in Image: A Social and Historical Survey of Australian Comic Art*, Hutchinson, Melbourne, 1979.

——, *The Way We Were: Australian Popular Magazines, 1856–1969*, Oxford University Press, Melbourne, 1983.

Lindsay, N, *Bohemians of the* Bulletin, Angus and Robertson, Sydney, 1965.

Lonergan, D, *Sounds Irish: The Irish Language in Australia*, Lythrum Press, Adelaide, 2004.

Lovejoy, V, 'Falling leaves: Chinese family and community in nineteenth-century Bendigo' in C Fahey & A Mayne (eds), *Gold Tailings: Forgotten History of Family and Community on the Central Victorian Goldfields*, Australian Scholarly Publishing, Melbourne, 2010, pp. 91–113.

Lowe, WJ, *The Irish in Mid-Victorian Lancashire: The Shaping of a Working-class Community*, Peter Lang, New York and Bern, 1989.

Luddy, M, 'Women and work in nineteenth- and early twentieth-century Ireland, an overview', in B Whelan (ed.), *Women and Paid Work in Ireland 1500–1930*, Four Courts Press, Dublin, 2000, pp. 44–56.

Lydon, J & Ryan, L (eds), *Remembering the Myall Creek Massacre*, NewSouth Publishing, Sydney, 2018.

Lynch-Brennan, M, *The Irish Bridget: Irish Immigrant Women in Domestic Service in America, 1840–1930*, Syracuse University Press, Syracuse, NY, 2009.

Lynn, P & Armstrong, G, *From Pentonville to Pentridge: A History of Prisons in Victoria*, State Library of Victoria, Melbourne, 1996.

Lyons, M & Russell, P (eds), *Australia's History: Themes and Debates*, UNSW Press, Sydney, 2005.

McCaffrey, LJ, 'Irish-American politics: Power with or without purpose?', in PJ Drudy (ed.), *The Irish in America: Emigration, Assimilation and Impact*, Cambridge University Press, Cambridge, 1985, pp. 169–90.

McCalman, J, 'To die without friends: Solitaries, drifters and failures in a new world society', in G Davison, P Jalland & W Prest (eds), *Body and Mind: Historical Essays in Honour of F.B. Smith*, Melbourne University Press, Melbourne, 2009, pp. 173–94.

McCarron, B, 'The Global Irish and Chinese: Migration, Exclusion, and Foreign Relations between Empires, 1784–1904', PhD thesis, Georgetown University, Washington, DC, 2016.

McCarthy, A, 'Transnational ties to home: Irish migrants in New Zealand asylums, 1860–1926', in PM Prior (ed.), *Asylums, Mental Health Care and the Irish, 1800–2010*, Irish Academic Press, Dublin and Portland, OR, 2012, pp. 149–66.

McCarthy, A, Coleborne, C, O'Connor, M & Knewstubb, E, 'Lives in the asylum record, 1864 to 1910: Utilising large data collections for histories of psychiatry and mental health', *Medical History*, vol. 61, no. 3, 2017, pp. 358–79.

McCartney, D (ed.), *The World of Daniel O'Connell*, Mercier Press, Dublin and Cork, 1980.

McClaughlin, T, *Barefoot and Pregnant? Irish Famine Orphans in Australia*, 2 vols, Genealogical Society of Victoria, Melbourne, 1991 and 2002.

——, '"I was nowhere else": Casualties of colonisation in eastern Australia during the second half of the nineteenth century', in T McClaughlin (ed.), *Irish Women in Colonial Australia*, Allen & Unwin, Sydney, 1998, pp. 142–62.

——, 'Irish-Protestant settlement', in J Jupp (ed.), *The Australian People: An Encyclopedia of the Nation, Its People and Their Origins*, 2nd ed., Cambridge University Press, Cambridge, 2001, pp. 463–65.

——, 'Protestant Irish in Australia', in J Brownrigg, C Mongan & R Reid (eds), *Echoes of Irish Australia: Rebellion to Republic*, St Clements Retreat and Conference Centre, Galong, NSW, 2007, pp. 88–98.

——, 'Vulnerable Irish women in mid- to late-nineteenth-century Australia', in R Davis, J Livett, A-M Whitaker & P Moore (eds), *Irish Australian Studies: Papers Delivered at the Eighth Irish-Australian Conference, Hobart, July 1995*, Crossing Press, Sydney, 1996, pp. 157–65.

McConville, C, *Croppies, Celts and Catholics: The Irish in Australia*, Edward Arnold, Melbourne, 1987.

——, 'Emigrant Irish and Suburban Catholics: Faith and Nation in Melbourne and Sydney, 1851-1933', PhD thesis, University of Melbourne, 1984.

McCracken, D, *Forgotten Protest: Ireland and the Anglo-Boer War*, Ulster Historical Foundation, Belfast, 1983.

MacDonagh, O, *Daniel O'Connell: The Emancipist, 1830–47*, Weidenfeld and Nicolson, London, 1989.

——, *Daniel O'Connell: The Hereditary Bondsman, 1775–1829*, Weidenfeld and Nicolson, London, 1988.

——, 'The Irish in Victoria, 1851-91: A demographic essay', in TD Williams (ed.), *Historical Studies VIII*, Gill and Macmillan, Dublin, 1971, pp. 85–92.

——, 'Politics, 1830-45', in WE Vaughan (ed.), *A New History of Ireland. Volume V. Ireland under the Union I: 1801–70*, Clarendon Press, Oxford, 1989, pp. 169–92.

——, *The Sharing of the Green: A Modern Irish History for Australians*, Allen & Unwin, Sydney, 1996.

McDonald, R, 'The problem with jokes about Irishmen', the *Conversation*, 18 July 2011, <theconversation.com/the-problem-with-jokes-about-irishmen-2370>.

McDonough, T (ed.), *Was Ireland a Colony? Economics, Politics and Culture in Nineteenth-century Ireland*, Irish Academic Press, Dublin and Portland, OR, 2005.

McGarry, F, *The Rising: Ireland Easter 1916*, 2nd ed., Oxford University Press, Oxford, 2016.

McGee, O, *The IRB: The Irish Republican Brotherhood from the Land League to Sinn Féin*, Four Courts Press, Dublin, 2005.

Mac an Ghaill, M, 'The Irish in Britain: The invisibility of ethnicity and anti-Irish racism', *Journal of Ethnic and Migration Studies*, vol. 26, no. 1, 2000, pp. 137–47.

MacGinley, MER, *A Dynamic of Hope: Institutes of Women Religious in Australia*, 2nd ed., Crossing Press, Sydney, 2002.

——, 'The Irish in Queensland: An overview', in J O'Brien & P Travers (eds), *The Irish Emigrant Experience in Australia*, Poolbeg Press, Swords, Co. Dublin, 1991, pp. 103–19.

——, 'A Study of Irish Migration to, and Settlement in, Queensland, 1885-1912', PhD thesis, University of Queensland, Brisbane, 1972.

McGrath, A, 'Shamrock Aborigines: The Irish, the Aboriginal Australians and their children', *Aboriginal History*, vol. 34, 2010, pp. 55-84.

——, 'Shamrock Aborigines: The Irish, the Aboriginal Australians, and their children', in G Morton & DA Wilson (eds), *Irish and Scottish Encounters with Indigenous Peoples: Canada, the United States, New Zealand and Australia*, McGill-Queen's University Press, Montreal and Kingston, 2013, pp. 108-43.

McGuire, J & Quinn, J (eds), *Dictionary of Irish Biography*, 9 vols, Cambridge University Press, Cambridge, 2009.

McGuire, P, *The Australian Theatre*, Oxford University Press, London and Melbourne, 1948.

McHugh, S, 'Not in front of the altar: Mixed marriages and sectarian tensions between Catholics and Protestants in pre-multicultural Australia', *History Australia*, vol. 6, no. 2, 2009, pp. 42.1-42.22.

Macintyre, A, *The Liberator: Daniel O'Connell and the Irish Party, 1830–47*, Macmillan, New York, 1965.

Macintyre, S, *Colonial Liberalism: The Lost World of Three Victorian Visionaries*, Oxford University Press, Melbourne, 1991.

——, *A Concise History of Australia*, Cambridge University Press, Cambridge, 1999.

McKay, B, '"A lovely land ... by shadows dark untainted"? Whiteness and early Queensland women's writing', in A Moreton-Robinson (ed.), *Whitening Race: Essays in Social and Cultural Criticism*, Aboriginal Studies Press, Canberra, 1994, pp. 148-63.

McKenna, M, 'The history anxiety', in A Bashford & S Macintyre (eds), *The Cambridge History of Australia. Volume 2: The Commonwealth of Australia*, Cambridge University Press, Melbourne, 2013, pp. 561-80.

McKernan, M, *The Australian Churches at War: Attitudes and Activities of the Major Churches 1914–1918*, Catholic Theological Faculty and Australian War Memorial, Sydney and Canberra, 1980.

McKibbin, R, 'Britain and Australia: Historical contrasts and comparisons', *History Australia*, vol. 7, no. 3, 2010, pp. 60.1-60.7.

——, 'Conscription in the First World War: Britain and Australia', in R Archer, J Damousi, M Goot & S Scalmer (eds), *The Conscription Conflict and the Great War*, Monash Publishing, Melbourne, 2016, pp. 169-86.

McLachlan, N, 'Patrick O'Farrell on the Irish in Australia', in P Bull, C McConville & N McLachlan (eds), *Irish-Australian Studies: Papers Delivered at the Sixth Irish-Australian Conference, July 1990*, La Trobe University, Melbourne, 1991, pp. 258-74.

——, *Waiting for the Revolution: A History of Australian Nationalism*, Penguin Books, Melbourne, 1989.

McLaren, J & Lindesay, V, 'The war cartoons of Claude Marquet', in A Rutherford & J Weiland (eds), *War: Australia's Creative Response*, Allen & Unwin, Sydney, 1997, pp. 91-99.

Mac Lellan, A, 'Victim or vector? Tubercular Irish nurses in England, 1930-60', in C Cox & H Marland (eds), *Migration, Health and Ethnicity in the Modern World*, Palgrave Macmillan, Basingstoke, Hampshire, 2013, pp. 104-25.

McLoughlin, D, 'Superfluous and unwanted deadweight: The emigration of nineteenth-century Irish pauper women', in P O'Sullivan (ed.), *Irish Women and Irish Migration*, Leicester University Press, London and New York, 1995, pp. 66-88.

McMahon, A, *Convicts at Sea: The Voyages of the Irish Convict Transports to Van Diemen's Land, 1840–1853*, Artemis Publishing, Hobart, 2011.

——, *Floating Prisons: Irish Convict Hulks and Voyages to New South Wales 1823–1837*, Halstead Press, Canberra, 2017.

McMahon, R, 'Anthropological race psychology, 1820-1945: A common European system of ethnic identity narratives', *Nations and Nationalism*, vol. 15, no. 4, 2009, pp. 575-96.

——, *Homicide in Pre-Famine and Famine Ireland*, Liverpool University Press, Liverpool, 2013.

McMahon, TG, *Grand Opportunity: The Gaelic Revival and Irish Society, 1893–1910*, Syracuse University Press, Syracuse, NY, 2008.

McMullin, R, *The Light on the Hill: The Australian Labor Party, 1891–1991*, Oxford University Press, Melbourne, 1991.

MacRaild, DM, '"No Irish need apply": The origins and persistence of a prejudice', *Labour History Review*, vol. 78, no. 3, 2013, pp. 269-99.

——, '"Principle, party and protest": The language of Victorian Orangeism in the north of England', in S West (ed.), *The Victorians and Race*, Scolar Press, Aldershot, Hampshire, 1996, pp. 128-40.

McQuilton, J, 'Doing the "back block boys some good": The exemption court hearings in North-Eastern Victoria 1916', *Australian Historical Studies*, vol. 31, no. 115, 2000, pp. 237-50.

——, *Rural Australia and the Great War: From Tarrawingee to Tangambalanga*, Melbourne University Press, Melbourne, 2001.

——, 'Yackandandah's war', in A Rutherford & J Wieland (eds), *War: Australia's Creative Response*, Allen and Unwin, Sydney, 1997, pp. 41-49.

Mahood, M, *The Loaded Line: Australian Political Caricature, 1788–1901*, Melbourne University Press, Melbourne, 1973.

——, '*Melbourne Punch* and its early artists', *The La Trobe Journal*, vol. 4, 1969, pp. 65-80.

Malcolm, E, '10,000 miles away: Irish studies down under', in L Harte & Y Whelan (eds), *Ireland Beyond Boundaries: Mapping Irish Studies in the Twenty-first Century*, Pluto Press, London, 2007, pp. 39-47.

——, 'After O'Farrell: Writing a new history of the Irish in Australia', *Tinteán*, 6 August 2017, online at: <tintean.org.au/>.

——, '"The house of strident shadows": The asylum, the family and emigration in post-Famine Ireland', in G Jones & E Malcolm (eds), *Medicine, Disease and the State in Ireland, 1650–1940*, Cork University Press, Cork, 1999, pp. 177-91.

——, '"Ireland's crowded madhouses": Institutional confinement of the insane in nineteenth- and twentieth-century Ireland', in R Porter & D Wright (eds),

The Confinement of the Insane: International Perspectives, 1800–1965, Cambridge University Press, Cambridge, 2003, pp. 315–33.

——, 'Irish immigrants in a colonial asylum during the Australian gold rushes, 1848–69', in PM Prior (ed.), *Asylums, Mental Health Care and the Irish, 1800–2010*, Irish Academic Press, Dublin and Portland, OR, 2012, pp. 119–48.

——, *The Irish Policeman: A Life, 1822–1922*, Four Courts Press, Dublin, 2006.

——, 'Irish type and stereotype: from cannibal to alien, via Scythian, Frankenstein and the *doppelgänger*', in E Malcolm, P Bull & F Devlin-Glass (eds), *Ireland Down Under: Melbourne Irish Studies Seminars, 2001–10*, Melbourne University Custom Book Centre, Melbourne, 2012, pp. 62–74.

——, 'Mannix: cartoons, photographs and Frank Hardy', in V Noone & R Naughton (eds), *Daniel Mannix: His Legacy*, Melbourne Diocesan Historical Commission, Melbourne, 2014, pp. 95–100.

——, 'Mental health and migration: The case of the Irish, 1850s–1990s', in A McCarthy & C Coleborne (eds), *Migration, Ethnicity and Mental Health: International Perspectives, 1840–2010*, Routledge, New York and Abingdon, Oxon, 2012, pp. 15–38.

——, '"A most terrible looking object": The Irish in English asylums, 1850–1901. Migration, poverty and prejudice', in J Belchem & K Tenfelde (eds), *Irish and Polish Migration in Comparative Perspective*, Klartext Verlag, Essen, 2003, pp. 115–26.

——, 'A new age or just the same old cycle of extirpation? Massacre and the 1798 Irish Rebellion', *Journal of Genocide Research*, vol. 15, no. 2, 2013, pp. 151–66.

——, 'Obituary: Patrick O'Farrell, 1933–2003', *History Australia*, vol. 1, no. 2, 2004, pp. 321–24.

——, 'Patrick O'Farrell and the Irish history wars, 1971–93', *Journal of Religious History*, vol. 31, no. 1, 2007, pp. 24–39.

——, '"What would people say if I became a policeman?" The Irish policeman abroad', in O Walsh (ed.), *Ireland Abroad: Politics and Professions in the Nineteenth Century*, Four Courts Press, Dublin, 2003, pp. 95–107.

Malcolm, E, & Bull, P, 'Irish studies in Australia, 1980–2012', *Australasian Journal of Irish Studies*, vol. 13, 2013, pp. 29–44.

Malcolm, E & Hall, D, 'Catholic Irish Australia and the labor movement: Race in Australia and nationalism in Ireland, 1880s–1920s', in G Patmore & S Stromquist (eds), *Frontiers of Labor: Comparative Histories of the United States and Australia*, University of Illinois Press, Urbana–Champaign, Chicago and Springfield, Ill, 2018, pp. 149–67.

Malik, K, *The Meaning of Race: Race, History and Culture in Western Society*, New York University Press, New York, 1996.

Malzberg, B, 'Mental disease among Irish-born and native whites of Irish parentage in New York State, 1949–51', *Mental Hygiene*, vol. 47, no. 1, 1963, pp. 12–42.

Mansfield, B, *Australian Democrat: The Career of Edward William O'Sullivan, 1846–1910*, Sydney University Press, Sydney, 1965.

Markus, A, *Fear and Hatred: Purifying Australia and California, 1850–1901*, Hale & Iremonger, Sydney, 1979.

Martin, AW, *Henry Parkes*, Melbourne University Press, Melbourne, 1980.

Martyr, P, '"Having a clean up"? Deporting lunatic migrants from Western Australia, 1924–39', *History Compass*, vol. 9, no. 3, 2011, pp. 171-99.

Marwick, A, *The Deluge: British Society and the First World War*, 2nd ed., Macmillan, Basingstoke,Hampshire, 1991.

Mathews, R, *Of Labour and Liberty: Distributism in Victoria, 1891–1966*, Monash University Publishing, Melbourne, 2017.

Maume, P, *The Long Gestation: Irish Nationalist Life, 1891–1918*, Gill and Macmillan, Dublin, 1999.

——, 'Patrick O'Farrell – A view from Ireland', *Australasian Journal of Irish Studies*, vol. 13, 2013, pp. 11-28.

Maxwell-Stewart, H, '"And all my great hardships endured"? Irish convicts in Van Diemen's land', in N Whelehan (ed.), *Transnational Perspectives on Modern Irish History*, Routledge, New York and London, 2015, pp. 69-87.

——, *Closing Hell's Gates: The Death of a Convict Station*, Allen & Unwin, Sydney, 2008.

Megalogenis, G, *Australia's Second Chance: What Our History Tells Us About Our Future*, Penguin Books, Melbourne, 2015.

Meredith, D & Oxley, D, 'Contracting convicts: The convict labour market in Van Diemen's Land, 1840-57', *Australian Economic History Review*, vol. 45, 2005, pp. 59-60.

Meredith, J & Whalan, R, *Frank the Poet*, Red Rooster Press, Melbourne, 1979.

Miller, KA, *Emigrants and Exiles: Ireland and the Irish Exodus to North America*, Oxford University Press, New York and Oxford, 1985.

Mollenhaur, J, 'Competitive Irish dancing in Sydney, 1994-2003', *Australasian Journal of Irish Studies,* vol. 15, 2015, pp. 35-54.

Molloy, K, 'Tradition, memory and the culture of Irish-Australian identity, 1900-1960', *Australasian Journal of Irish Studies*, vol. 16, 2016, pp. 47-64.

Molony, JN, *An Architect of Freedom: John Hubert Plunkett in New South Wales, 1832–69*, Australian National University Press, Canberra, 1973.

Monk, L-A, *Attending Madness: At Work in the Australian Colonial Asylum*, Editions Rodopi B.V., Amsterdam and New York, 2008.

Moore, A, 'An "indelible Hibernian mark"? Irish rebels and Australian labour radicalism: An historiographical overview', *Labour History*, no. 75, 1998, pp. 1-8.

Moore, B, 'Sectarianism in NSW: The *Ne Temere* legislation of 1924-25', *Journal of the Australian Catholic Historical Society*, vol. 9, no. 1, 1987, pp. 3-15.

Moore, T, *Death or Liberty: Rebels and Radicals Transported to Australia, 1788–1868*, Pier 9, Sydney, 2010.

Morgan, P, *Melbourne Before Mannix: Catholics in Public Life, 1880–1920*, Connor Court Publishing, Melbourne, 2012.

Morgan, S, 'Irish women in Port Phillip and Victoria, 1840-60', in O MacDonagh & WF Mandle (eds), *Irish-Australian Studies: Papers Delivered at the Fifth Irish-Australian Conference*, Australian National University, Canberra, 1989, pp. 231-49.

Morris, E, *Our Own Devices: National Symbols and Political Conflict in Twentieth-Century Ireland*, Irish Academic Press, Dublin and Portland, OR, 2005.

Morrison, E, *David Syme: Man of the Age*, Monash University Publishing and State Library of Victoria, Melbourne, 2014.

Morrison, G & Rowland, A, *In Your Face: Cartoons About Politics and Society, 1760–2010*, Art Gallery of Ballarat, Ballarat, VIC, 2010.

Moynihan, S, *'Other People's Diasporas': Negotiating Race in Contemporary Irish and Irish American Culture*, Syracuse University Press, Syracuse, NY, 2013.

Mulvaney, J, 'F.J. Gillen's life and times', in J Mulvaney, H Morphy & A Petch (eds), *'My Dear Spencer': The Letters of F.J. Gillen to Baldwin Spencer*, Hyland House, Melbourne, 1997, pp. 1–22.

Murphy, DJ (ed.), *Labor in Politics: The State Labor Parties in Australia, 1880–1920*, University of Queensland Press, Brisbane, 1975.

—, 'Religion, race and conscription in World War I', *Australian Journal of Politics and History*, vol. 20, no. 2, 1974, pp. 155–63.

Murphy, W, 'Imprisonment during the Civil War', in J Crowley, D Ó Drisceoil & M Murphy (eds), *Atlas of the Irish Revolution*, Cork University Press, Cork, 2017, pp. 736–40.

Murray, CS, 'Settling the Mind: Psychiatry and the Colonial Project in Australia', PhD thesis, University of Melbourne, 2012.

Murray, R, *The Split: Australian Labor in the Fifties*, Cheshire Publishing, Melbourne, 1970.

Murray, R & White, K, *The Golden Years of Stawell*, Lothian Press, Stawell, VIC, 1983.

Murray-Smith, S, 'On the conscription trail: The second referendum seen from beside W.M. Hughes', *Labour History*, no. 33, 1977, pp. 98–104.

Neal, F, 'A criminal profile of the Liverpool Irish', *Transactions of the Historic Society of Lancashire and Cheshire*, vol. 140, 1991, pp. 161–99.

—, 'Lancashire, the Famine Irish and the poor laws: a study in crisis management', *Irish Economic and Social History*, vol. 22, 1995, pp. 26–48.

Nelson, B, *Irish Nationalists and the Making of the Irish Race*, Princeton University Press, Princeton, NJ, 2012.

Newton, D, *Hell-bent: Australia's Leap into the Great War*, Scribe Publications, Melbourne, 2014.

Niall, B, *Mannix*, Text Publishing, Melbourne, 2015.

Noone, V, 'Class factors in the radicalisation of Archbishop Daniel Mannix, 1913–17', in F Bongiorno, R Frances & B Scates (eds), *Labour and the Great War: The Australian Working Class and the Making of Anzac*, Australian Society for the Study of Labour History, Sydney, 2014, pp. 189–204.

—, *Hidden Ireland in Victoria*, Ballarat Heritage Services, Ballarat, VIC, 2012.

—, 'An Irish rebel in Victoria: Charles Gavan Duffy, selectors, squatters and Aborigines', in J Brownrigg, C Mongan & R Reid (eds), *Echoes of Irish Australia: Rebellion to Republic*, St Clements Retreat and Conference Centre, Galong, NSW, 2007, pp. 108–77.

—, 'People not money: Irish in post-war Australia', in T Foley & F Bateman (eds), *Irish-Australian Studies: Papers Delivered at the Ninth Irish-Australian Conference, Galway, April 1997*, Crossing Press, Sydney, 2000, pp. 122–37.

——, 'Sunburnt Gaelic': Hobby, dream or cultural lifeline', in E Malcolm, P Bull & F Devlin-Glass (eds), *Ireland Down Under: Melbourne Irish Studies Seminars, 2001–2010*, University of Melbourne Custom Book Centre, Melbourne, 2012, pp. 170–82.

Norman, E, *A History of Modern Ireland*, Allen Lane Penguin Press, London, 1971.

Nye, R, *The Unembarrassed Muse: The Popular Arts in America*, Dial Press, New York, 1970.

O'Brien, A, 'Pauperism revisited', *Australian Historical Studies*, vol. 42, no. 2, 2011, pp. 212–29.

——, *Poverty's Prison: The Poor in New South Wales, 1880–1918*, Melbourne University Press, Melbourne, 1988.

O'Brien, CC, *Parnell and His Party, 1880–90*, 1957, Clarendon Press, Oxford, 1968.

O'Collins, G, *Patrick McMahon Glynn: A Founder of Australian Federation*, Melbourne University Press, Melbourne, 1965.

O'Connor, P, 'The Multiple Dimensions of Migrancy, Irishness and Home among Contemporary Irish Immigrants in Melbourne, Australia', PhD thesis, University of New South Wales, Sydney, 2005.

——, 'Rediscovering Irish migration to Australia: The nature and characteristics of post-1980 arrival', in E Malcolm, P Bull & F Devlin-Glass (eds), *Ireland Down Under: Melbourne Irish Studies Seminars, 2001–2010*, Melbourne University Custom Book Centre, Melbourne, 2012, pp. 32–39.

O'Donnell, I, 'Lethal violence in Ireland, 1841–2003: Famine, celibacy and parental pacification', *British Journal of Criminology*, vol. 45, no. 5, 2005, pp. 671–95.

O'Donnell, R, '"Desperate and diabolical": Defenders and United Irishmen in early N.S.W.', in R Davis, J Livett, A-M Whitaker & P Moore (eds), *Irish-Australian Studies: Papers Delivered at the Eighth Irish-Australian Conference, Hobart, July 1995*, Crossing Press, Sydney, 1996, pp. 360–72.

Ó Duigneáin, P, *Linda Kearns: A Revolutionary Irish Woman*, Drumlin Publications, Manorhamilton, Co. Leitrim, 2002.

O'Farrell, P, 'Boredom as historical motivation', *Quadrant*, vol. 26, nos 1–2, 1982, pp. 52–56.

——, *The Catholic Church and Community in Australia: A History*, Nelson, Melbourne, 1977.

——, 'Double jeopardy: Catholic and Irish', *Humanities Research*, vol. 12, no. 1, 2005, <press-files.anu.edu.au>.

——, 'Dreaming of distant revolution: A.T. Dryer and the Irish National Association, Sydney, 1915-16', in P Gray (ed.), *Passing the Torch: The Aisling Society of Sydney, 1955–2005*, The Aisling Society of Sydney, Sydney, 2005, pp. 63–85.

——, *England and Ireland since 1800*, Oxford University Press, London, 1975.

——, 'The image of O'Connell in Australia', in D McCartney (ed.), *The World of Daniel O'Connell*, Mercier Press, Cork, 1980, pp. 112–24.

——, *Imagination's Stain: Historical Reflections on Sectarian Australia*, C O'Farrell (ed.), 2002, <www.patrickofarrell.com>.

——, *Ireland's English Question: Anglo-Irish Relations, 1534–1970*, B.T. Batsford, London, 1971.

——, 'The Irish and Australian history', *Quadrant*, vol. 22, no. 12, 1978, pp. 17–21.

——, *The Irish in Australia*, UNSW Press, Sydney, 1986, 2nd ed. 1993, 3rd ed. 2000.

——, 'The Irish in Australia and New Zealand, 1791-1870', in WE Vaughan (ed.), *A New History of Ireland V: Ireland under the Union I, 1801–70*, Clarendon Press, Oxford, 1989, pp. 661-81.

——, 'The Irish in Australia and New Zealand, 1870-1990', in WE Vaughan (ed.), *A New History of Ireland VI: Ireland under the Union II, 1870–1921*, Clarendon Press, Oxford, 1996, pp. 703-24.

——, 'The Irish Republican Brotherhood in Australia: The 1918 internments', in O MacDonagh, WF Mandle & P Travers (eds), *Irish Culture and Nationalism, 1750–1950*, Macmillan, Canberra and London, 1983, pp. 183–93.

——, *Vanished Kingdoms: Irish in Australia and New Zealand. A Personal Excursion*, UNSW Press, Sydney, 1990.

O'Ferrall, F, *Catholic Emancipation: Daniel O'Connell and the Birth of Irish Democracy, 1820–30*, Gill and Macmillan, Dublin, 1985.

O'Grady, F, *Francis of Central Australia*, Wentworth Books, Sydney, 1977.

Ó Lúing, S, *Fremantle Mission*, Anvil Books, Tralee, Co. Kerry, 1965.

Oliver, B, '"Rats", "scabs", "soolers" and "Sinn Feiners": A re-assessment of the role of the labour movement in the conscription crisis in Western Australia, 1916-17', *Labour History*, no. 58, 1990, pp. 48–64.

O'Neill, P, 'Michael Davitt and John Davitt Jageurs (1895-1916)', *Australasian Journal of Irish Studies*, vol. 6, 2006, pp. 43–56.

O'Neill, PD, *Famine Irish and the American Racial State*, Routledge, New York and London, 2017.

Ormonde, P, *The Movement*, Thomas Nelson, Melbourne, 1972.

O'Sullivan, E & O'Donnell, I, 'Coercive confinement in the Republic of Ireland', *Punishment and Society*, vol. 9, no. 1, 2007, pp. 27–48.

O'Toole, F, 'From Patsy O'Wang to Fu Manchu: Ireland, China and racism', in J McCormack (ed.), *China and the Irish*, New Island, Dublin, 2009, pp. 40–50.

Ou, H-Y 'Ethnic presentations and cultural constructs: The Chinese/Irish servant in *Patsy O'Wang*', *Canadian Review of American Studies*, vol. 43, no. 3, 2013, pp. 480-501.

Overlack, P, '"Easter 1916" in Dublin and the Australian press: background and response', *Journal of Australian Studies*, vol. 21, nos 54–55, 1997, pp. 188–93.

Owens, G, 'Nationalism without words: Symbolism and ritual behaviour in the repeal "monster meetings" of 1843-5', in JS Donnelly Jr & KA Miller (eds), *Irish Popular Culture, 1650–1850*, Irish Academic Press, Dublin and Portland, OR, 1998, pp. 242-69.

Oxley, D, *Convict Maids: The Forced Migration of Women to Australia*, Cambridge University Press, Cambridge, 1996.

——, 'Packing her (economic) bags: convict women workers', *Australian Historical Studies*, vol. 26, no. 102, 1994, pp. 57–76.

Painter, NI, *The History of White People*, W.W. Norton, New York, 2010.

Pakenham, T, *The Year of Liberty: The Great Irish Rebellion of 1798*, Hodder and Stoughton, London, 1969.

Palmer, K & McKenna, C, *Somewhere Between Black and White: The Story of an Aboriginal Australian*, Macmillan, Melbourne, 1978.

Parkinson, C, *Sir William Stawell and the Victorian Constitution*, Australian Scholarly Publishing, Melbourne, 2004.

Patrick, R & Patrick, H, *Exiles Undaunted: the Irish Rebels Kevin and Eva O'Doherty*, University of Queensland Press, Brisbane, 1989.

Pawsey, M, *The Demon of Discord: Tensions in the Catholic Church in Victoria, 1853–1864*, Melbourne University Press, Melbourne, 1982.

——, *The Popish Plot: Culture Clashes in Victoria, 1860–63*, Studies in the Christian Movement, Sydney, 1983.

Pearl, C, *Brilliant Dan Deniehy: A Forgotten Genius*, Nelson, Melbourne, 1972.

——, *The Three Lives of Gavan Duffy*, New South Wales University Press, Sydney, 1979.

Peel, M & Twomey, C, *A History of Australia*, Palgrave Macmillan, Basingstoke, Hampshire, 2011.

Penrose, LS, 'Mental disease and crime: Outlines of a comparative study of European statistics', *British Journal of Medical Psychology*, vol. 18, no. 1, 1939, pp. 1–15.

Pietikainen, P, *Madness: A History*, Routledge, London and New York, 2015.

Pollock, HM, 'A statistical study of the foreign-born insane in New York State hospitals', *State Hospital Bulletin*, vol. 5, 1913, pp. 10–27.

Porter, R, *A Social History of Madness: Stories of the Insane*, Weidenfeld and Nicolson, London, 1987.

Powell, JM, 'Medical promotion and the consumptive immigrant to Australia', *Geographical Review*, vol. 63, no. 4, 1973, pp. 449–76.

Poynter, J, *Doubts and Certainties: A Life of Alexander Leeper*, Melbourne University Press, Melbourne, 1997.

Prentis, M, *The Scots in Australia*, UNSW Press, Sydney, 2008.

Price, CA, 'The ethnic character of the Australian population', in J Jupp (ed.), *The Australian People: An Encyclopedia of the Nation, Its People and Their Origins*, 1988, 2nd ed., Cambridge University Press, Cambridge, 2001, pp. 78–85.

——, *The Great White Walls Are Built: Restrictive Immigration to North America and Australasia, 1836–88*, ANU Press, Canberra, 1974.

Prior, PM, 'Dangerous lunacy: The misuse of mental health law in nineteenth-century Ireland', *Journal of Forensic Psychiatry and Psychology*, vol. 14, no. 3, 2003, pp. 525–53.

Proudfoot, L, 'Landscape, place and memory: Towards a geography of Irish identities in colonial Australia', in O Walsh (ed.), *Ireland Abroad: Politics and Professions in the Nineteenth Century*, Four Courts Press, Dublin, 2003, pp. 172–85.

——, 'Myths, diasporas and empires: Being Irish in the antipodes in the nineteenth century', in PJ Duffy & W Nolan (eds), *At the Anvil: Essays in Honour of William J. Smyth*, Geography Publications, Dublin, 2012, pp. 353–70.

Proudfoot, L, & Hall, D, *Imperial Spaces: Placing the Irish and Scots in Colonial Australia*, Manchester University Press, Manchester, 2011.

—, 'Points of departure: Remittance emigration from south-west Ulster to New South Wales in the later nineteenth century', *International Review of Social History*, vol. 50, no. 2, 2005, pp. 341–78.

Quiggan, A, *Haddon the Headhunter*, Cambridge University Press, Cambridge, 1942.

Quinn, DB, *The Elizabethans and the Irish*, Cornell University Press, Ithaca, NY, 1966.

Reece, B, *Aborigines and Colonists: Aborigines and Colonial Society in New South Wales in the 1830s and 1840s*, Sydney University Press, Sydney, 1974.

—, *Daisy Bates: Grand Dame of the Desert*, National Library of Australia, Canberra, 2007.

—, 'Francis MacNamara: Convict Poet', in S Grimes & G Ó Tuathaigh (eds), *The Irish-Australian Connection*, University College Galway, Galway, 1988, pp. 43–80.

—, 'The Irish and the Aborigines', in T Foley & F Bateman (eds), *Irish-Australian Studies: Papers Delivered at the Ninth Irish-Australian Conference, Galway, April 1997*, Crossing Press, Sydney, 2000, pp. 192–204.

—, *The Origins of Irish Convict Transportation to New South Wales*, Palgrave, Basingstoke, Hampshire, 2001.

—, 'Writing about the Irish in Australia', in J O'Brien & P Travers (eds), *The Irish Emigrant Experience in Australia*, Poolbeg Press, Swords, Co. Dublin, 1991, pp. 226–42.

Rees, L, *The Making of Australian Drama: A Historical and Critical Survey from the 1830s to the 1970s*, Angus and Robertson, Sydney, 1973.

Reeves, K, 'Sojourners or a new diaspora? Economic implications of the movement of Chinese miners to the south-west Pacific goldfields', *Australian Economic History Review*, vol. 50, no. 2, 2010, pp. 179–92.

Reid, R, *Farewell My Children: Irish Assisted Emigration to Australia, 1848–1870*, Anchor Books Australia, Sydney, 2011.

—, 'The history of the INA', <irishassociation.org.au/the-history-of-the-ina/>.

—, *Not Just Ned: A True History of the Irish in Australia*, National Museum of Australia Press, Canberra, 2011.

Reynolds, H, *Dispossession: Black Australians and White Invaders*, Allen & Unwin, Sydney, 1989.

—, *Unnecessary Wars*, NewSouth Publishing, Sydney, 2016.

Richards, E, *Britannia's Children: Emigration from England, Scotland, Wales and Ireland since 1600*, Hambledon and London, London and New York, 2004.

—, *Destination Australia: Migration to Australia since 1901*, UNSW Press, Sydney, 2008.

Richards, E & Herraman, A, '"If she was to be hard up she would sooner be hard up in a strange land than where she would be known": Irish women in colonial South Australia', in T McClaughlin (ed.), *Irish Women in Colonial Australia*, Allen & Unwin, Sydney, 1998, pp. 82–104.

Rickard, J, *Australia: A Cultural History*, Longman, London and New York, 1988.

—, *Class and Politics: New South Wales, Victoria and the Early Commonwealth, 1890–1910*, Australian National University Press, Canberra, 1976.

—, *H.B. Higgins: The Rebel as Judge*, George Allen & Unwin, Sydney, 1984.

Rivett, R, *Australian Citizen: Herbert Brookes, 1867–1963*, Melbourne University Press, Melbourne, 1965.

Robinson, S, 'The Aboriginal embassy, An account of the protests of 1972', in G Foley, A Schaap & E Howell (eds), *The Aboriginal Tent Embassy: Sovereignty, Black Power, Land Rights and the State*, Routledge, Abingdon, Oxon, 2013, pp. 3–21.

Robson, LL, *The Convict Settlers of Australia*, 1965, Melbourne University Press, Melbourne, 1976.

—, *The First A.I.F.: A Study of Its Recruitment, 1914–18*, 1970, Melbourne University Press, Melbourne, 1982.

—, 'The origin and character of the first A.I.F., 1914–1918: Some statistical evidence', *Historical Studies*, vol. 15, no. 61, 1973, pp. 737–49.

Roe, M, *Australia, Britain and Migration, 1915–40: A Study of Desperate Hopes*, Cambridge University Press, Cambridge, 1995.

Roediger, D, *The Wages of Whiteness: Race and the Making of the American Working Class*, 2nd ed., Verso, London, 1999.

Rolfe, P, *Clotted Rot for Clots and Rotters*, Wildcat Press, Sydney, 1980.

—, *The Journalistic Javelin: An Illustrated History of the* Bulletin, Wildcat Press, Sydney, 1979.

Rolls, E, *Sojourners: The Epic Story of China's Centuries-old Relationship with Australia: Flowers and the Wide Sea*, University of Queensland Press, Brisbane, 1992.

Ronayne, J, *First Fleet to Federation: Irish Supremacy in Colonial Australia*, Trinity College Dublin Press, Dublin, 2002.

Rose, L., *'Rogues and Vagabonds': Vagrant Underworld in Britain, 1815–1945*, Routledge, London and New York, 1988.

Rudé, G, *Protest and Punishment: The Story of the Social and Political Protesters Transported to Australia, 1788–1868*, Clarendon Press, Oxford, 1978.

Rule, P, 'Challenging conventions: Irish-Chinese marriages in colonial Victoria', in T Foley & G Bateman (eds), *Irish-Australian Studies: Papers Delivered at the Ninth Irish-Australian Conference, Galway, April 1997*, Crossing Press, Sydney, 2000, pp. 205–16.

—, 'The Chinese camps in colonial Australia: Their role as contact zones' in S Couchman, J Fitzgerald & P Macgregor (eds), *After the Rush: Regulation, Participation and Chinese Communities in Australia, 1860–1940*, Otherland Journal, Melbourne, 2004, pp. 119–32.

Rushen, E, *Colonial Duchesses: The Migration of Irish Women to New South Wales before the Great Famine*, Anchor Books Australia, Sydney, 2014.

Rushen, E & McIntyre, P, *Fair Game: Australia's First Immigrant Women*, Anchor Books Australia, Sydney, 2010.

Russell, P, *Savage or Civilised? Manners in Colonial Australia*, NewSouth Publishing, Sydney, 2010.

—, *A Wish for Distinction: Colonial Gentility and Femininity*, Melbourne University Press, Melbourne, 1994.

Santamaria, BA, *Daniel Mannix: The Quality of Leadership*, Melbourne University Press, Melbourne, 1984.

Scally, G, '"The very pests of society": The Irish and 150 years of public health in England', *Clinical Medicine*, vol. 4, no. 1, 2004, pp. 77–81.

Scalmer, S, 'Crisis to crisis, 1950–66', in J Faulkner & S Macintyre (eds), *True Believers: The Story of the Federal Parliamentary Labor Party*, Allen & Unwin, Sydney, 2001, pp. 90–104.

——, *On the Stump: Campaign Oratory and Democracy in the United States, Britain and Australia*, Temple University Press, Philadelphia, PA, 2017.

Scott, E, *A Short History of Australia*, 4th ed., Oxford University Press, Melbourne, 1920.

Scully, R & Quartly, M, 'Using cartoons as historical evidence', in R Scully & M Quartly (eds), *Drawing the Line: Using Cartoons as Historical Evidence*, Monash ePress, Melbourne, 2009, pp. 11–26.

Serle, G, *From Deserts the Prophets Come: The Creative Spirit in Australia, 1788–1972*, Heinemann, Melbourne, 1973.

——, *The Golden Age: A History of the Colony of Victoria, 1851–61*, Melbourne University Press, Melbourne, 1963.

——, *The Rush to Be Rich: A History of the Colony of Victoria, 1883–89*, Melbourne University Press, Melbourne, 1971.

Shaw, AGL, *Convicts and the Colonies: A Study of Penal Transportation from Great Britain and Ireland to Australia and Other Parts of the British Empire*, 1966, Melbourne University Press, Melbourne, 1978.

Sherington, G, *Australia's Immigrants, 1788–1988*, 2nd ed., Allen & Unwin, Sydney, 1990.

Smart, C '"Excused Only Through the Exigencies of Narrative": Irish-Aboriginal Relations in Colonial Australia and Beyond', Bachelor of International and Global Studies (Honours) thesis, University of Sydney, 2017, <hdl.handle.net/2123/18262>.

Smith, JM, *Ireland's Magdalen Laundries and the Nation's Architecture of Containment*, University of Notre Dame Press, Notre Dame, IN, 2007.

Soper, K, 'From swarthy ape to sympathetic everyman and subversive trickster: The development of Irish caricature in American comic strips between 1890 and 1920', *Journal of American Studies*, vol. 39, no. 2, 2005, pp. 257–96.

Spiers, EM, *The Army and Society, 1815–1914*, Longman, London and New York, 1980.

Stepan, N, *The Idea of Race in Science: Great Britain, 1800–1960*, Macmillan Press, London, 1982.

Stewart, ATQ, *Edward Carson*, Gill and Macmillan, Dublin, 1981.

——, *The Narrow Ground: Aspects of Ulster, 1609–1969*, Faber and Faber, London, 1977.

——, *The Ulster Crisis*, Faber and Faber, London, 1967.

Stocking, G, *Race, Culture and Evolution: Essays in the History of Anthropology*, University of Chicago Press, Chicago, 1982.

Strangio, P, *Neither Power nor Glory: 100 Years of Political Labor in Victoria, 1856–1956*, Melbourne University Press, Melbourne, 2012.

Strangio, P & Costar, B (eds), *The Victorian Premiers, 1856–2006*, Federation Press, Sydney, 2006.

Stratton, J, 'Borderline anxieties: What whitening the Irish has to do with keeping out asylum seekers', in A Moreton-Robinson (ed.), *Whitening Race: Essays in Social and Cultural Criticism*, Aboriginal Studies Press, Canberra, 2005, pp. 222–38.

Sullivan, R & Sullivan, R, 'The Queensland Irish Association, 1898–1928: Heroes and memorials', *Australasian Journal of Irish Studies*, vol. 15, 2015, pp. 13–34.

Swain, S, 'Destitute and dependent: Case studies in poverty in Melbourne', *Historical Studies*, vol. 19, no. 74, 1980, pp. 98–107.

Swift, R, 'Heroes or villains? The Irish, crime and disorder in Victorian Britain', *Albion*, vol. 29, no. 3, 1997, pp. 399–421.

——, 'Historians and the Irish: Recent writings on the Irish in nineteenth-century Britain', in DM MacRaild (ed.), *The Great Famine and Beyond: Irish Migrants in Britain in the Nineteenth and Twentieth Centuries*, Irish Academic Press, Dublin and Portland, OR, 2000, pp. 14–39.

Tavan, G, *The Long Slow Death of White Australia*, Scribe Publications, Melbourne, 2005.

Tedeschi, M, *Murder at Myall Creek: The Trial That Defined a Nation*, Simon & Schuster, Sydney, 2016.

Teo, H-M, 'Multiculturalism and the problem of multicultural histories: An overview of ethnic historiography', in H-M Teo & R White (eds), *Cultural History in Australia*, UNSW Press, Sydney, 2003, pp. 142–55.

Thornton, D, '"We have no redress unless we strike": Class, gender and activism in the Melbourne tailoresses' strike, 1882–83', *Labour History*, no. 96, 2009, pp. 19–38.

Tobin, GM, 'The Sea-Divided Gael: A Study of the Irish Home Rule Movement in Victoria and New South Wales, 1880–1916', MA thesis, Australian National University, Canberra, 1969.

Townshend, C, *The Republic: The Fight for Irish Independence, 1918–1923*, Allen Lane, London, 2013.

Travers, P, 'The priest in politics: The case of conscription', in O MacDonagh, WF Mandle & P Travers, *Irish Culture and Nationalism, 1750–1950*, Macmillan, London and Canberra, 1983, pp. 161–81.

Travers, R, *The Phantom Fenians of New South Wales*, Kangaroo Press, Sydney, 1986.

Troy, J, '"Der mary this is fine cuntry is there is in the wourld": Irish-English and Irish in late eighteenth- and nineteenth-century Australia', in J O'Brien & P Travers (eds), *The Irish Emigrant Experience in Australia*, Poolbeg Press, Swords, Co. Dublin, 1991, pp. 148–80.

Turner, E, 'Not Narrow Minded Bigots – Proceedings of the Loyal Orange Institution of New South Wales, 1845–1895', PhD thesis, University of New England, Armidale, NSW, 2002.

Turner, I, *Industrial Labour and Politics: The Labour Movement in Eastern Australia, 1900–1921*, Australian National University, Canberra, 1965.

Twopeny, R, *Town Life in Australia*, 1883, Penguin Books, Melbourne, 1973.

Urban, A, 'Irish domestic servants, "Biddy" and rebellion in the American home, 1850–1900', *Gender and History*, vol. 21, no. 2, 2009, pp. 263–86.

Urry, J, 'Englishmen, Celts and Iberians: The ethnographic survey of the United Kingdom, 1892–1899', in GW Stocking (ed.), *Functionalism Historicized: Essays on British Social Anthropology*, University of Wisconsin Press, Madison, WN, 1984, pp. 83–105.

——, 'Making sense of diversity and complexity: The ethnological context and consequences of the Torres Strait expedition and the oceanic phase in British anthropology, 1890–1935', in A Herle & S Rouse (eds), *Cambridge and the Torres Strait: Centenary Essays on the 1898 Anthropological Expedition*, Cambridge University Press, Cambridge, 1998, pp. 201–33.

Van Der Krogt, CJ, 'Irish Catholicism, criminality and mental illness in New Zealand from the 1870s to the 1930s', *New Zealand Journal of History*, vol. 50, no. 2, 2016, pp. 90–121.

Vaughan, WE & Fitzpatrick, AJ (eds), *Irish Historical Statistics: Population, 1821–1971*, Royal Irish Academy, Dublin, 1978.

Veracini, L, *Settler Colonialism: A Theoretical Overview*, Palgrave Macmillan, Basingstoke, Hampshire, 2010.

Vertigan, T, *The Orange Order in Victoria: Origins, Events, Achievements, Aspirations and Personalities*, Loyal Orange Institution of Victoria, Melbourne, 1979.

Waldersee, J, *Catholic Society in New South Wales, 1788–1860*, Sydney University Press, Sydney, 1974.

Walker, D, *Anxious Nation: Australia and the Rise of Asia, 1850–1939*, University of Queensland Press, Brisbane, 1999.

——, 'Youth on trial: The Mount Rennie case', *Labour History*, no. 50, 1986, pp. 28–41.

Walker, RB, *The Newspaper Press in New South Wales, 1803–1920*, Sydney University Press, Sydney, 1976.

Walter, B, *Outsiders Inside: Whiteness, Place and Irish Women*, Routledge, London and New York, 2001.

Wang, S-U, 'Chinese immigration 1840s–1890s', in J Jupp (ed.), *The Australian People: An Encyclopedia of the Nation, Its People and Their Origins*, 2nd ed., Cambridge University Press, Cambridge, 2001, pp. 197–204.

Ward, R, *The Australian Legend*, 2nd ed., Oxford University Press, Melbourne, 1966.

Warhurst, J, 'Catholics, communism and the Australian party system: A study of the Menzies years', *Politics*, vol. 14, no. 2, 1979, pp. 222–42.

——, 'Catholics in Australian politics since 1950', in J Jupp (ed.), *The Encyclopedia of Religion in Australia*, Cambridge University Press, Cambridge, 2009, pp. 261–66.

Watters, G, 'Contaminated by China', in D Walker & A Sobocinska (eds), *Australia's Asia: From Yellow Peril to Asian Century*, UWA Publishing, Perth, 2012, pp. 27–49.

Watts, B (ed.), *The World of the Sentimental Bloke*, Angus and Robertson, Sydney, 1976.

Watts, R, 'Beyond nature and nurture: Eugenics in twentieth-century Australian history', *Australian Journal of Politics and History*, vol. 40, no. 3, 1994, pp. 318–34.

Weaver, J, 'Moral order and repression in Upper Canada: The case of the criminal justice system in the Gore District and Hamilton, 1831–51', *Ontario History*, vol. 87, no. 3, 1986, pp. 176–207.

Wechsler, J, *A Human Comedy: Physiognomy and Caricature in 19th-Century Paris*, Thames and Hudson, London, 1982.

West, S, *Bushranging and the Policing of Rural Banditry in New South Wales, 1860–80*, Australian Scholarly Publishing, Melbourne, 2009.

Whitaker, A-M, 'Irish War of Independence veterans in Australia', in R Davis, J Livett, A-M Whitaker & P Moore (eds), *Irish-Australian Studies: Papers Delivered at the Eighth Irish-Australian Conference, Hobart, 1995*, Crossing Press, Sydney, 1996, pp. 413–20.

——, 'Linda Kearns and Kathleen Barry Irish republican fundraising tour, 1924–25', *Journal of the Australian Catholic Historical Society*, vol. 37, no. 2, 2016, pp. 208–11.

——, *Unfinished Revolution: United Irishmen in New South Wales, 1800–1810*, Crossing Press, Sydney, 1994.

White, I, 'Daisy Bates: legend and reality', in J Marcus (ed.), *First in Their Field: Women and Australian Anthropology*, Melbourne University Press, Melbourne, 1993, pp. 46–65.

White, R, *Inventing Australia: Images and Identity, 1688–1980*, George Allen & Unwin, Sydney, 1981.

Wilcox, C, 'Australians in the wars in Sudan and South Africa', in C Stockings & J Connor (eds), *Before the Anzac Dawn: A Military History of Australia to 1915*, NewSouth Publishing, Sydney, 2013, pp. 204–29.

Wilkie, B, *The Scots in Australia, 1788–1938*, Boydell Press, Woodbridge, Suffolk, 2017.

Willard, M, *History of the White Australia Policy to 1920*, rev. ed., Melbourne University Press, Melbourne, 1967.

Willey, K, 'A hard, dry humour for a hard, dry land', in V Burgmann & J Lees (eds), *A People's History of Australia since 1788: Constructing a Culture*, McPhee Gribble and Penguin Books, Melbourne, 1988, pp. 156–69.

Williams, L, '"Rint" and "repale": *Punch* and the image of Daniel O'Connell, 1842–1847', *New Hibernia Review*, vol. 1, no. 3, 1997, pp. 75–93.

Williams, M, *Australia on the Popular Stage: An Historical Entertainment in Six Acts*, Oxford University Press, Melbourne, 1983.

Wilson, D, *The Beat: Policing a Victorian City*, Circa, Melbourne, 2006.

Wolfe, P, *Traces of History: Elementary Structures of Race*, Verso, London, 2016.

Wood, JC, *Violence and Crime in Nineteenth-Century England: The Shadow of Our Refinement*, Routledge, London, 2004.

Woolcock, HR, *Rights of Passage: Emigration to Australia in the Nineteenth Century*, Tavistock Publications, London, 1986.

Wright, D & Themeles, T, 'Migration, madness and the Celtic fringe: A comparison of Irish and Scottish admissions to four Canadian mental hospitals, c.1841–91', in A McCarthy & C Coleborne (eds), *Migration, Ethnicity and Mental Health: International Perspectives, 1840–2010*, Routledge, New York and Abingdon, Oxon, 2012, pp. 39–54.

Wyndham, D, *Eugenics in Australia: Striving for National Fitness*, Galton Institute, London, 2003.

Yarwood, AT, *Samuel Marsden, the Great Survivor*, 2nd ed., Melbourne University Press, Melbourne, 1977.

York, B, *Ethno-historical Studies in a Multicultural Australia*, Australian National University, Canberra, 1996.

Young, R, *Colonial Desire: Hybridity in Theory, Culture and Race*, Routledge, London, 1995.

——, *The Idea of English Ethnicity*, Blackwell, Oxford and Maldon, MA, 2008.

NOTES

Introduction: The Irish in Australia

1   'Craic everywhere – St Patrick's Day 2018', *Irish Echo* (Sydney), 17 March 2018, <www.irishecho.com>.

2   'Professor Patrick McGorry AO', Orygen: National Centre of Excellence in Youth Mental Health, <www.orygen.org.au/about/our/people/leaders>; 'A life of faith, care and Mercy', *Irish Echo*, 24 October 2010, <www.irishecho.com>.

3   *Argus* (Melbourne), 18 February 1848, p. 2; *Port Phillip Gazette and Settler's Journal* (Melbourne), 27 May 1848, p. 1.

4   See Cronin & Adair, *The Wearing of the Green* 2002.

5   Even as late as the mid-1990s, a demographer estimated that Australians of Irish descent, at 12.4 per cent of the population, were the second largest ethnic group after Australians of English descent at 45.3 per cent. See Price, 'The ethnic character of the Australian population' 2001, pp. 78–85.

6   Akenson, *Small Differences* 1988, pp. 62–66, 214–15.

7   Akenson, *The Irish Diaspora* 1993, pp. 68–69, 261–63.

8   O'Farrell, *The Irish in Australia* 1986, p. 25.

9   Proudfoot & Hall, *Imperial Spaces* 2011, pp. 46–59.

10 Delaney, Kenny & MacRaild, 'Symposium' 2006, pp. 35–58.

11 Oxley, *Convict Maids* 1996.

12 Fitzpatrick, *Oceans of Consolation* 1994, pp. 6–14.

13 Rudé, *Protest and Punishment* 1978, pp. 31–40, 145.

14 The Irish transported in 1846–53 numbered around 2400 women and 5100 men. Shaw, *Convicts and the Colonies* 1978, p. 368. See also Kavanagh & Snowden, *Van Diemen's Women* 2015.

15 McClaughlin, *Barefoot and Pregnant* 1991.

16 Donnelly Jr, 'The construction of the memory of the Famine in Ireland and the Irish diaspora' 1996, pp. 26–61.

17 Proudfoot & Hall, 'Points of departure' 2005, pp. 341–78.

18 *Commission on Emigration and Other Population Problems* [1954], pp. 124–25; O'Farrell 1986, pp. 23, 63.

19 Grimes, 'Postwar Irish immigrants' 1988, pp. 137–59; O'Connor, 'The Multiple Dimensions of Migrancy, Irishness and Home among Contemporary Irish Immigrants in Melbourne, Australia' 2005.

20 'More Irish opting for Australian way of life', RTÉ, 9 July 2013, <www.rte.ie>; 'Destination Australia', *Irish Times* (Dublin), 2 June 2018, <www.irishtimes. com>.

21 O'Farrell 1986. Some important subsequent publications include Fitzpatrick 1994; Campbell, *Ireland's New Worlds* 2008; Reid, *Farewell My Children* 2011; Proudfoot & Hall 2011.

22 He had summarised many of these arguments earlier in O'Farrell, 'The Irish and Australian history' 1978, pp. 17–21.

23 O'Farrell 1986, pp. 11–12.

24 For other critiques of Irish–Australian history, see Bolton, 'The Irish in Australian historiography' 1986, pp. 5–19; Reece, 'Writing about the Irish in Australia' 1991, pp. 226–42; Malcolm, '10,000 miles away' 2007, pp. 39–47; Malcolm, 'After O'Farrell' 2017.

25 Hogan, *The Irish in Australia* 1887.

26 Thompson, 'Hogan, James Francis (1855–1924)', *ADB*.

27 Cunneen, 'Cleary, Patrick Scott (1861–1941)', *ADB*.

28 Cleary, *Australia's Debt to Irish Nation-Builders* 1933, pp. 1, 4–5.

29 See, for example, Kiernan, *The Irish Exiles in Australia* 1954; Adam-Smith, *Heart of Exile* 1986; Patrick & Patrick, *Exiles Undaunted* 1989.

30 O'Farrell 1986, pp. 23–24. O'Farrell restricted Irish political offenders to those who had taken part in rebellions, whereas other historians defined them more broadly to include 'social protesters', which increased their numbers to around 2250. See Rudé 1978, pp. 7–10, 249–50.

31 O'Farrell 1986, p. 52.

32 McLachlan, 'Patrick O'Farrell on the Irish in Australia' 1991, pp. 258–74.

33 Lyons & Russell (eds), *Australia's History* 2005, pp. 36, 103–104, 141, 193.

34 Bashford & Macintyre (eds), *The Cambridge History of Australia*, vol. 1, 2013, pp. 207–209, 417–18, 430–31, 480, 602, 618–19, 625–26.

35 Rickard, *Australia* 1988, pp. 37, 187. For a more critical approach to the use of ethnic categories, including 'Irish', see Teo, 'Multiculturalism and the problem of multi-cultural histories' 2003, pp. 142–55.

36 Curthoys, 'History and identity' 1997, p. 26.

37 Hirst, *Australian History in 7 Questions* 2014, pp. 143–52.

38 Ward, *The Australian Legend* 1966, p. 52. By contrast, a recent study of mateship has little to say about the Irish and, when they are referred to, it is usually as either 'British' or 'Catholic'. See Dyrenfurth, *Mateship* 2015, pp. 19, 106, 112, 114.

39 Clark, *A Short History of Australia* 1980, p. 75.

40 Dixson, *The Real Matilda* 1994, pp. 155, 157, 162–63, 169.

41 Blainey, *A History of Victoria* 2006, pp. 114, 117, 123, 134.

42 Scott, *A Short History of Australia* 1920, pp. 60–61.

43 McKibbin, 'Britain and Australia' 2010, pp. 60.4–60.5.

44 O'Farrell 1986; McConville, *Croppies, Celts and Catholics* 1987.

45 2016 Commonwealth of Australia Census: 2024.0 Census of Population and Housing, Australian Bureau of Statistics, <www.abs.gov.au>.

1 The Irish race

1 *Age* (Melbourne), 23 November 1864, p. 4, cited in Bongiorno, *The Sex Lives of Australians* 2012, pp. 47–49.

2 Cited in Kirkpatrick, 'Lynch, Francis Ennis (Guy) (1895–1967)', *ADB*.

3 O'Farrell & O'Farrell (eds), *Documents in Australian Catholic History*, vol. 1, 1969, p. 73.

4 *Argus* (Melbourne), 18 February 1848, p. 2.

5 Topp, 'English institutions and the Irish race' 1881, pp. 9–12. See also Hall & Malcolm, 'English institutions and the Irish race' 2016, pp. 1–15.

6 Correspondent to Patrick O'Farrell, 16 April 1975, O'Farrell papers, National Library of Australia, MS 6265/25/414.

7 McDonald, 'The problem with jokes about Irishmen' 2011.

8 Stocking Jr, *Race, Culture and Evolution* 1982.

9 The literature on settler colonialism and race is extensive but we have been influenced especially by Lake & Reynolds, *Drawing the Global Colour Line* 2008; Wolfe, *Traces of History* 2016; Veracini, *Settler Colonialism* 2010.

10 Malik, *The Meaning of Race* 1996, pp. 80–81; McMahon, 'Anthropological race psychology' 2009, pp. 575–96.

11 Malik 1996, pp. 91ff.

12 Hall, *Civilising Subjects* 2002, p. 17, citing Hall, 'The multi-cultural question' 2001, pp. 209–41.

13 Young, *Colonial Desire* 1995, p. 54.

14 See also Banton, 'The vertical and horizontal dimensions of the word race' 2010, pp. 127–40.

15 Ignatiev, *How the Irish Became White* 1995.

16 Classic works in whiteness studies include Allen, *The Invention of the White Race* 1994 and 1997; Frankenberg, *Displacing Whiteness* 1997; Bonnett, *White Identities* 2000.

17 Ignatiev 1995, pp. 99–112.

18 See also Garner, *Racism in the Irish Experience* 2004, p. 100; for additional perspectives, see Roediger, *The Wages of Whiteness* 1991.

19 O'Neill, *Famine Irish and the American Racial State* 2017, p. 5.

20 As summarised by de Nie, *The Eternal Paddy* 2004, p. 5.

21 De Nie 2004, p. 5; Moynihan, '*Other People's Diasporas*' 2013, p. 17.

22 The literature on this topic is extensive. See as examples: Hayton, 'From barbarian to burlesque' 1998, pp. 5–31; Baker, 'Men to monsters' 2005, pp. 153–69; Leerssen, *Mere Irish and Fíor-Ghael* 1996, pp. 32–76; Carroll, 'Barbarous slaves and civil cannibals' 2003, pp. 63–80.

23 Canny, *The Elizabethan Conquest of Ireland* 1976, pp. 1–44; Quinn, *The Elizabethans and the Irish* 1966, pp. 7–13, 62–90.

24 Canny, 'Protestants, planters and apartheid in early modern Ireland' 1986, pp. 105–15; Canny, *Making Ireland British* 2001, pp. 420–25, 489–91, 506–34.

25 Hickman, 'Reconstructing deconstructing "race"' 1998, pp. 288–307; Mac an Ghaill, 'The Irish in Britain' 2000 pp. 137–47.

26 Garner 2004, p. 115.

27 Recent literature on the histories of Indigenous peoples and the catastrophic effects of racial policies in the past is extensive and growing. For an overview, see Broome, *Aboriginal Australians* 2010.

28 O'Farrell, *The Irish in Australia* 1986, pp. 8, 72–73.

29 O'Farrell, 'Imagination's stain' 2002, pp. 11–12.

30 Stratton, 'Borderline anxieties' 2005, pp. 222–23.

31 McGrath, 'Shamrock Aborigines' 2010, pp. 57, 62–63.

32 Curthoys, 'White, British and European' 2009, pp. 3–24.

33 Topp, 1881, pp. 14–15, 21.

34 There is a substantial literature on the history of 19th-century race science. See Stepan, *The Idea of Race in Science* 1982; Hannaford, *Race* 1996.

35 Kaplan, 'White, black and green' 2004, p. 55.

36 Knox, *The Races of Men* 1850. For an overview of Knox's life, see Biddiss, 'The politics of anatomy' 1976, pp. 245–50.

37 Knox 1850, p. 26.

38 Knox 1850, p. 39.

39 Knox 1850, p. 253–54.

40 Knox 1850, p. 217. For modern writers who have discussed Knox's thinking on the Irish, see Curtis Jr, *Apes and Angels* 1997; de Nie 2004; Bornstein, *The Colors of Zion* 2011.

41 'Knox on the Celtic race' 1868, p. 181.

42 Avery, 'Civilisation' 1869, p. ccxxxi.

43 Avery 1869, p. ccxxxvi.

44 Gould, *The Mismeasure of Man* 1981, pp. 83–88.

45 'Influence of race on disease', *British Medical Journal*, vol. 1, 1870, p. 137.

46 Banton, *What We Now Know About Race and Ethnicity* 2015.

47 For a recent and wide-ranging study of the Irish and race science, see Carew, *The Quest for the Irish Celt* 2018.

48 Richardson, 'Beddoe, John (1826–1911)', *ODNB*.

49 Beddoe, 'Colour and race' 1901, pp. 219–50, and *The Races of Britain* 1885, p. 11.

50 Beddoe 1885, p. 10.

51 Beddoe, *Memories of 80 Years* 1910, p. 192.

52 Fleure, 'Haddon, Alfred Cort (1855–1940)', rev. Rouse, *ODNB*; Quiggan, *Haddon the Headhunter* 1942.

53 Grattan, 'On the importance' 1853, pp. 198–208. See Haddon, *History of Anthropology* 1910, p. 34 for his summary of Grattan's work. Grattan gave Haddon his research materials, now among Haddon's papers in Cambridge University Library. Other material is likely still in the Trinity College, Dublin laboratory, currently being studied by Ciaran Walsh.

54 Haddon, 'Studies in Irish craniology' 1891–93, pp. 759–67.

55 Quiggan 1942.

56 Haddon, *The Races of Man* 1909, pp. 6, 40.

57 AC Haddon to E Haddon, 21 July 1890, Haddon collection, University of Cambridge Library [hereafter UCL], 22.

58 AC Haddon journal, 8 July 1890, p.15, UCL, 22.

59 Several albums of photographs from Haddon's team are now held in Trinity College, Dublin Library and have been analysed by De Mórdha & Walsh, *The Irish Headhunter* 2012, See also Carville 'Resisting vision' 2010, pp. 158–75; Urry, 'Making sense of diversity and complexity' 1998, pp. 201–33.

60 There is an extensive literature on race and colonisation. For a recent erudite addition, see Wolfe, 2016.

61 On Irish convicts, see O'Farrell 1986, pp. 22–53; Reece, *The Origins of Irish Convict Transportation* 2001; McMahon, *Convicts at Sea* 2011, and *Floating Prisons* 2017.

62 Collins, *An Account of the English Colony in New South Wales*, vol. 2, 1802, pp. 74–77.

63 Cited in O'Farrell & O'Farrell, vol. 1, 1969, p. 73.

64 *Colonial Times*, 25 March 1834, cited in Maxwell-Stewart, '"And all my great hardships endured"?' 2015, p. 70.

65 Maxwell-Stewart 2015, p. 70.

66 Lang, *Reminiscences of My Life and Times* 1972, p. 197.

67 Irish uptake of various assisted migration schemes is examined in Richards, *Britannia's Children* 2004, pp. 135–49, 180–81; Proudfoot & Hall, *Imperial Spaces* 2011, pp. 80–82; Reid, *Farewell My Children* 2011, pp. 12–31.

68 *Argus*, 6 June 1891, p. 4.

69 Topp 1881, pp. 24–26.

70 Lake, '"Essentially Teutonic"' 2010, p. 57.

71 Topp 1881, pp. 9–10.

72 *Bendigo Advertiser*, 7 September 1865, p. 3. The women were sent home with their respective husbands, who were charged with keeping them quiet.

73 *South Australian Register*, 16 December 1869, p. 3.

74 *Kiama Independent*, 1 June 1877, p. 4. The case was reported widely throughout the colonies. See, for example, *Age*, 4 June 1877, p. 2.

75 Cited in Hall 2002, pp. 109, 111.

76 Cited in Hogan, *The Irish People* 1899, p. 7.

77 Kingsley (ed.), *Charles Kingsley*, vol. 2, pp. 111–12, cited in Kaplan 2004, p. 54.

78 Turner, *A History of the Colony of Victoria*, vol. 1, 1973, p. 249.

79 Bonwick, *The Wild White Man and the Blacks of Victoria* 1863, p. 32, cited in Damousi, *Colonial Voices* 2010, p. 23.

80 Croly & Wakeman, *Miscegenation* 1864.

81 Croly & Wakeman 1864, p. 120.

82 Lemire, '*Miscegenation*' 2002, pp. 117–21.

83 *Sydney Morning Herald*, 9 May 1864, p. 3. The miscegenation hoax was discussed in the *Brisbane Courier Mail*, 16 March 1866, p. 4.

84 *Argus*, 4 July 1867, p. 7; *Mount Alexander Mail*, 18 June 1867, p. 3; *Geelong Advertiser*, 10 July 1867, p. 10.

85 *Advocate* (Melbourne), 14 May 1881, p. 17, 15 January 1881, p. 7.

86 O'Brien, 'English institutions and the Irish race: A reply' 1881, pp. 111–14; see also Hall & Malcolm 2016, pp. 14–15.

87 McMahon, *Grand Opportunity* 2008.

88 O'Farrell 1986, pp. 178–80; Noone, *Hidden Ireland in Victoria* 2012, pp. 77–108; Sullivan & Sullivan, 'The Queensland Irish Association' 2015, pp. 13–34.
89 M Close to AC Haddon, 1 December 1893, UCL, MS 3058. See E Ó Raghallaigh, 'Hogan, Edmund Ignatius (1831–1917)', in McGuire & Quinn (eds), *Dictionary of Irish Biography*, vol. 4, 2009, p. 738.
90 Hogan 1899, p. 7.
91 *Western Australian Record*, 21 April 1892, p. 3; *Freeman's Journal* (Sydney), 9 April 1892, p. 6. The Irish-Australian nationalist Dr Nicholas O'Donnell owned a copy of Hogan's 1899 book, which is now in the O'Donnell Library, St Mary's Newman Academic Centre, University of Melbourne.
92 Garner 2004, p. 69, citing E Butler-Cullingford, *Ireland's Others* 2001, pp. 99–110.
93 Garner 2004, p. 69.
94 *Advocate*, 28 May 1887, p. 9.
95 Nelson, *Irish Nationalists and the Making of the Irish Race* 2012, pp. 124–25.
96 Cited in McCracken, *Forgotten Protest* 1983, p. 34.
97 Banton, *Race Relations* 1967, p. 8.

2 The Irish and Indigenous Australians: friends or foes?

1 B Burke to J Burke, 18 June 1882, cited in Fitzpatrick, *Oceans of Consolation* 1994, p. 154.
2 MacGinley, 'A Study of Irish Migration to, and Settlement in, Queensland' 1972, p. 184.
3 McDonough (ed.), *Was Ireland a Colony?* 2005; Kenny, 'Ireland and the British Empire' 2004, pp. 1–11.
4 Fitzpatrick, 'Ireland and the empire' 1999, p. 494.
5 Bielenberg, 'Irish emigration to the British Empire, 1700–1914' 2000, pp. 215–34.
6 Fitzpatrick 1999, pp. 510–12.
7 Coolahan, 'The Irish and others in Irish nineteenth-century textbooks' 1993, pp. 59–60.
8 McGrath, 'Shamrock Aborigines' 2010, pp. 55–84; McGrath, 'Shamrock Aborigines' 2013, pp. 108–43; Reece, 'The Irish and the Aborigines' 2000, pp. 192–204. A recent thesis explores some of these issues. Smart, 'Excused Only Through the Exigencies of Narrative' 2017.
9 Smith, 'Lynch, William (Billy) (1839–1913)', *ADB*.
10 McGinness, *Son of Alyandabu* 1971, pp. 1–8; Austin, 'McGinness, Valentine Bynoe (1910–88)', *ADB*.
11 Ellinghaus, *Taking Assimilation to Heart* 2006, pp. 153–60.
12 Ellinghaus, 'Absorbing the "Aboriginal problem"' 2003, pp. 183–207.
13 Ellinghaus 2006, pp. 135–39.
14 *Approved Readers for the Catholic Schools of Australasia* 1908, pp. 137–42; Firth & Darlington, 'Racial stereotypes in the Australian curriculum' 1993, p. 84.
15 Lonergan, *Sounds Irish* 2004, pp. 26, 31.
16 Troy, '"Der mary this is fine cuntry is there is in the wourld"' 1991, pp. 148–80.
17 Broome, *Aboriginal Australians* 2010, pp. 36–68.

18 Buckridge, 'Two Irish poets in colonial Brisbane' 1991, pp. 16–26; McKay, '"A lovely land ... by shadows dark untainted"'1994, pp. 148–63.
19 Chate, 'Moore, George Fletcher (1798–1886)', *ADB*.
20 Cameron, 'George Fletcher Moore' 2000, pp. 21–34; Reynolds, *Dispossession* 1989, pp. 44–46.
21 For Denny Day, see O'Farrell, *The Irish in Australia* 1986, pp. 95–96.
22 Tedeschi, *Murder at Myall Creek* 2016, pp. 76–191; Reece, *Aborigines and Colonists* 1974, pp. 140–74. For recent assessments of the continuing controversy surrounding the massacre, see Lydon & Ryan (eds), *Remembering the Myall Creek Massacre* 2018.
23 For biographies of Plunkett, see Molony, *An Architect of Freedom* 1973; Earls, *Plunkett's Legacy* 2009.
24 Hansord, 'Eliza Hamilton Dunlop's "The Aboriginal Mother"' 2011, pp. 1–12.
25 Hogan, *The Irish in Australia* 1887, p. 314.
26 Gifford, 'Murder and "the execution of the law"'1994, pp. 103–22.
27 Fitzgerald, '"Blood on the saddle"' 1984, pp. 7–15.
28 Wood, *Royal Commission of Enquiry into Alleged Killings and Burning of Bodies of Aborigines in East Kimberley* 1927.
29 Auty, 'Patrick Bernard O'Leary and the Forrest River massacres' 2004, pp. 122–55.
30 Durack, *Kings in Grass Castles* 1974, p. 95.
31 Durack 1974, pp. 329–30; see Devlin-Glass, 'The Irish in grass castles' 2008, pp. 108–109.
32 *Bulletin* (Sydney), 11 December 1897, p. 27.
33 Palmer & McKenna, *Somewhere Between Black and White* 1978, pp. 1–5.
34 Neville, *Australia's Coloured Minority* 1947, p. 72.
35 B Brock Byrne interviewed by L de Paor, in *An Dubh ina Gheal: Assimilation*, director P Kehoe, A Saoi Media Production for TG4/BAI television, Dublin, 2015. Our thanks to Val Noone for facilitating our access to this film.
36 Mulvaney, 'Willshire, William Henry (1852–1925)', *ADB*.
37 Mulvaney, 'F.J. Gillen's life and times' 1997, pp. 1–22.
38 F Gillen to B Spencer, 17 September 1899, in Mulvaney, Morphy & Petch (eds), *'My Dear Spencer'* 1997, pp. 263–64.
39 F Gillen to B Spencer, 23 February 1901, in Mulvaney, Morphy & Petch (eds) 1997, p. 319.
40 Mulvaney 1997, p. 18.
41 Bates, *The Passing of the Aborigines* 1966; Reece, *Daisy Bates* 2007, pp. 125–26.
42 De Vries, *Desert Queen* 2008; White, 'Daisy Bates: Legend and reality' 1993, pp. 46–65.
43 Reece 2007, p. 10.
44 *West Australian* (Perth), 2 December 1905, p. 8.
45 Reece 2000, p. 194.
46 Cited in Reece 2007, p. 18.
47 Cited in Reece 2000, p. 194.
48 *West Australian*, 2 December 1905, p. 8.
49 *West Australian Record* (Perth), 9 December 1905, p. 11.
50 *West Australian Record*, 16 December 1905, p. 11.

51   *West Australian*, 8 February 1910, p. 6.

52   Conor, *Skin Deep* 2016, pp. 226–31.

53   Broome, *Aboriginal Victorians* 2005, pp. 122–25.

54   Noone, 'An Irish rebel in Victoria' 2007, pp. 112–15.

55   Cato, *Mister Maloga* 1976, pp. 43–44, 47, 71. Our thanks to Val Noone and Wayne Atkinson for alerting us to this reference.

56   Haebich, *For Their Own Good* 1988, p. 102; Bolton, 'Connolly, Sir James Daniel (1869–1962)', *ADB*.

57   Wilson, 'Cahill, William Geoffrey (1854–1931)', *ADB*.

58   Finnane, 'The politics of policing powers' 1987, pp. 93, 101–102; Finnane, *Police and Government* 1994, p. 118.

59   Malezer, 'O'Leary, Cornelius (1897–1971)', *ADB*.

60   Franklin, 'Catholic missions to Aboriginal Australia' 2016, p. 46.

61   Kovesi Killerby, '"Never locked up or tied"' 2000, pp. 124–33.

62   *West Australian*, 25 October 1892, p. 3. See also Devlin-Glass 2008, p. 115.

63   O'Grady, *Francis of Central Australia* 1977, pp. 10–12.

64   Carey, 'Subordination, invisibility and chosen work' 1998, pp. 254–56.

65   Grimshaw, 'Faith, missionary life and the family' 2004, pp. 260–80; Carey, 'Companions in the wilderness' 1995, pp. 227–48.

66   Chant, 'Hetherington, Isabella (1870–1946)', *ADB*; Radi, 'Long, Margaret Jane (Retta) (1878–1956)', *ADB*.

67   Robinson, 'The Aboriginal Embassy, an account of the protests of 1972' 2013, p. 8.

68   G Foley interviewed by L de Paor, in *An Dubh ina Gheal: Assimilation* 2015.

69   'Patrick Dodson's speech at the Sydney Aisling Society', *Irish Echo* (Sydney), 12–15 April 2001, p. 3; Dodson, 'Resonance: Irish Australians and Aboriginal Australians' 2005, pp. 265–76. Our thanks to Val Noone for these references.

70   *Age* (Melbourne), 28 April 2001, p. 27. Our thanks to Val Noone for this reference.

71   National Indigenous Television (NITV) news, 27 November 2017, <www.sbs.com.au/nitv/nitv-news/article/2017/10/19/irish-president-acknowledges-role-irish-persecution-aboriginal-people>.

3 The Irish and the Chinese in white Australia

1   B Burke to J Burke, 18 June 1882, cited in Fitzpatrick, *Oceans of Consolation* 1994, p. 154.

2   *Bulletin* (Sydney), 4 July 1896, p. 13.

3   Kenny, *The American Irish* 2000, p. 157.

4   For an overview of Chinese-Australian history, see Couchman, 'Introduction' 2015, pp. 1–21.

5   Rule, 'Challenging conventions' 2000, pp. 205–16.

6   Campbell, *Ireland's New Worlds* 2008, pp. 101–102, 140.

7   McCarron, 'The Global Irish and Chinese' 2016. Our thanks to Barry McCarron for making his research available to us.

8   Markus, *Fear and Hatred* 1979, pp. 14–34.

9   Choi, *Chinese Migration* 1975, pp. 18, 22, 42; Wang, 'Chinese immigration 1840s–1890s' 2001, p. 199.
10 Cronin, *Colonial Casualties* 1982, p. 140; Goodman, *Gold Seeking* 1994, pp. 20–24.
11 Wang 2001, pp. 198–99.
12 The classic study is Rolls, *Sojourners* 1992; for a critique, see Reeves, 'Sojourners or a new diaspora?' 2010, pp. 180–82.
13 *Bendigo Advertiser*, 2 September 1857, p. 3.
14 Finnane, 'Law as politics' 2015, pp. 117–36.
15 McCarron 2016, chapter 6, pp. 20–22, 32–33.
16 Curthoys, '"Men of all nations, except Chinamen"' 2001, pp. 110–16.
17 Price, *The Great White Walls Are Built* 1974, p. 80.
18 Connolly, 'Miners' rights' 1978, pp. 36–37.
19 McCarron, 2016, pp. 265–314.
20 Morris, 'Torpy, James (1832–1903)', *ADB*.
21 Curthoys 2001, pp. 110–11.
22 *Young Witness and Burrangong Argus*, 11 January 1921, p. 2, cited in McCarron 2016, p. 285.
23 Owens, 'Nationalism without words' 1998, pp. 242–47.
24 Dyson, 'A golden shanty' (1889), in Ackland (ed.), *The Penguin Book of 19th-century Australian Literature* 1993, pp. 251–53, 259.
25 Bagnall, 'Rewriting the history of Chinese families in nineteenth-century Australia' 2011, pp. 65–67.
26 Lovejoy, 'Falling leaves' 2010, pp. 98–99.
27 *Young Witness and Burrangong Argus*, 11 January 1921, p. 2.
28 Bagnall, 'Golden Shadows on a White Land' 2007.
29 Bagnall, 'Across the threshold' 2002, pp. 22–23.
30 Choi 1975, p. 30; Markus 1979, p. 68.
31 Bagnall 2007, section 2, p. 96; Bagnall 2002, pp. 22–23.
32 Bagnall 2007, section 1, p. 50.
33 Markus 1979, pp. 258–59.
34 Fitzgerald, *Big White Lie* 2007, pp. xii–xiii; Foord, 'The three promises' 2009.
35 Holst, 'Equal before the law?' 2004, p. 116.
36 Family interviews cited in Bagnall 2007, section 2, p. 94.
37 Bagnall 2007, section 2, p. 98; Rule, 'The Chinese camps in colonial Victoria' 2004, pp. 119–32.
38 Rule, 'Challenging conventions' 2000, p. 206.
39 Bagnall 2007, section 2, p. 114.
40 Walker, *Anxious Nation* 1999, pp. 197–200; see Bakhap's biography at: <biography.senate.gov.au/thomas-jerome-kingston-bakhap/>.
41 *Bulletin*, 11 November 1899, p. 11.
42 Just, *Australia* 1859, p. 209.
43 Dilke, *Greater Britain* 2005, p. 306.
44 Cited in Bagnall 2007, section 2, p. 88.
45 *Victorian Year Book, 1875*, pp. 120–21.
46 *Victorian Year Book, 1886–87*, p. 229.
47 *Australian Town and Country Journal* (Sydney), 16 September 1882, p. 21.

48 Price 1974, pp. 189–90; Finnane, "'Habeas corpus Mongols'" 2014, pp. 165–83.
49 *Leader* (Melbourne), 12 May 1888, p. 26.
50 *South Australian Weekly Chronicle*, 19 May 1888, p. 5.
51 'Ganesha' [Louis Esson], 'Round the corner', *Lone Hand*, 1 December 1908, in Gelder & Weaver (eds), *The Colonial Journals and the Emergence of Australian Literary Culture* 2014, pp. 376–77.
52 Kuo, *Making Chinese Australia* 2013, p. 265, citing *Chinese Australian Herald* (Sydney), 25 March 1898, p. 2.
53 For reviews of the play, see *Windsor and Richmond Gazette* (NSW), 16 October 1914, p. 4; *Mudgee Guardian and North-Western Representative* (NSW), 22 November 1917, p. 22; *Benalla Standard* (Victoria), 14 December 1917, p. 4; *Shoalhaven News and South Coast District Advertiser* (NSW), 30 July 1927, p. 4.
54 O'Toole, 'From Patsy O'Wang to Fu Manchu' 2009, pp. 40–50; Ou, 'Ethnic presentations and cutural constructs' 2013, pp. 480–501.
55 Denison, 'Patsy O'Wang' 1895, pp. 3, 5, 9, 13–14, 28.
56 *Windsor and Richmond Gazette*, 16 October 1914, p. 4.
57 Bagnall 2007, section 2, pp. 80–85.
58 *Sydney Morning Herald*, 29 August 1873, p. 5.
59 *Illustrated Sydney News*, 28 April 1888, p. 6.
60 *Bulletin*, 11 November 1899, p. 11. See also Broinowski, *The Yellow Lady* 1992.
61 *Freeman's Journal* (Sydney), 17 October 1850, p. 3.
62 *Sydney Morning Herald*, 19 November 1851, p. 2; McCarron 2016, chapter 6, pp. 10–13.
63 *Freeman's Journal*, 4 December 1851, p. 8.
64 Pearl, *Brilliant Dan Deniehy* 1972, p. 73.
65 *Goulburn Herald and County of Argyle Advertiser*, 1 July 1854, p. 2. See also McCarron, 2006, chapter 6, pp. 27–29; Price 1974, pp. 78–80.
66 'Speech on Mr. Cowper's Chinese Immigration Bill, April 10th, 1858', in Martin (ed.), *The Life and Speeches of Daniel Henry Deniehy* 1998, p. 62.
67 *Sydney Morning Herald*, 3 October 1860, p. 3. Our thanks to Frances Devlin-Glass for references to Daniel Deniehy. See also Curthoys, 'Race and ethnicity' 1973, pp. 304–305, for other speeches by Deniehy on the topic of immigration.
68 Price 1974, pp. 85–86.
69 Lehane, *William Bede Dalley* 2007, pp. 210, 231–33, 370–72.
70 Watters, 'Contaminated by China' 2012, pp. 32–38, 43.
71 *Freeman's Journal*, 18 August 1866, pp. 520–21.
72 Ayres, *Prince of the Church* 2007, pp. 156, 164, 258.
73 *Bulletin*, 8 September 1888, p. 1.
74 Kuo 2013, p. 279.
75 McCarron 2016, chapter 6, pp. 51–54.
76 Anderson, *The Poet Militant* 1968.
77 Bongiorno, 'Bernard O'Dowd's socialism' 1999, p. 109.
78 Burgmann, 'Revolutionaries and racists' 1980, p. 168; Markus 1979, p. 228.
79 Bryan *John Murtagh Macrossan*, 1958.
80 *Telegraph* (Brisbane), 3 April 1888, p. 4.
81 Cited in Bryan 1958, p. 43.

82 Cited in Bryan, 'John Murtagh Macrossan and the genesis of the White Australia Policy' 1954, p. 899.
83 *Week* (Brisbane), 5 August 1882, p. 12.
84 Anderson, *The Cultivation of Whiteness* 2002, pp. 73–94; see also Griffiths, 'The Coolie labour crisis in colonial Queensland' 2017, pp. 53–78.
85 McCarron 2016, chapter 6, pp. 44–45.
86 Markus 1979, pp. 200–202.
87 *Worker* (Brisbane), 14 May 1892, p. 1; Markus 1979, p. 209.
88 *Advocate* (Melbourne), 15 February 1908, p. 15.
89 On the importance of such self-improvement societies, see Damousi, *Colonial Voices* 2010, p. 119.
90 Connolly, 'Class, birthplace, loyalty' 1978, p. 224, notes that the CYMS was the only Irish organisation to support the British during the Boer War.
91 *Advocate*, 13 November 1880, p. 9; *Kyneton Observer* (Victoria), 7 August 1888, p. 2.
92 *West Australian Record* (Perth), 12 January 1907, p. 12; Hunt, 'Simons, John Joseph (Jack) (1882–1948)', *ADB*.
93 *Advocate*, 19 February 1881, p. 6; Jobson, 'Palmer, Sir Arthur Hunter (1819–1898)', *ADB*.
94 Duffy, *My Life in Two Hemispheres*, vol. 2, 1898, pp. 316–17; Martin, *Henry Parkes* 1980, pp. 268–69.
95 Griffiths, 'The "necessity" of a socially homogeneous population' 2015, p. 141.
96 *Freeman's Journal*, 27 November 1897, p. 13; *Catholic Press* (Sydney), 26 October 1901, p. 13, 6 August 1903, p. 21.
97 *Southern Cross* (Adelaide), 30 March 1906, p. 10.
98 *Freeman's Journal*, 27 November 1897, p. 13; McCarron 2016, chapter 6, p. 55.
99 Garner, *Racism in the Irish Experience* 2004, pp. 135–36; MacRaild, '"Principle, party and protest"' 1996, pp. 136–39.
100 Griffiths 2015, pp. 140–41. See also Serle, *The Rush to Be Rich* 1971, p. 217, for protests by the Scots over the use of the word 'English' instead of 'British'.
101 Kamp, 'Formative geographies of belonging in white Australia' 2010, pp. 411–26.
102 O'Collins, *Patrick McMahon Glynn* 1965, pp. 49, 78, 81–82, 109, 195–96, 246.
103 *Commonwealth Parliamentary Debates (Hansard)*, HB Higgins, 6 September 1901, p. 4659; Rickard, *H.B. Higgins* 1984, pp. 131–35.
104 O'Farrell 1986, pp. 241–42; Tobin, 'The Sea-Divided Gael' 1969, pp. 253–55.
105 Melbourne *Tribune*, reported in Adelaide *Southern Cross*, 8 December 1905, p. 5.
106 Cited in McCracken, *Forgotten Protest* 1983, p. 34.
107 Osborne, *What We Owe to Ireland* 1918, p. 17.
108 Cited in Nelson, *Irish Nationalists and the Making of the Irish Race* 2012, p. 148.
109 *Freeman's Journal*, 23 October 1919, p. 24.

4 Irish immigration, 1901–39: race, politics and eugenics

1 For an article on Irish Americans and whiteness, employing Homi Bhabha's concept of the 'other' being 'almost the same, but not quite', see Eagan,

"'White" if "not quite"' 2003, pp. 140–55; Bhabha, *The Location of Culture* 1994, p. 86.

2 Jones, 'Osborne, William Alexander (1873–1967)', *ADB*.

3 For Osborne's involvement with eugenics and claims that in the 1930s he was an admirer of National Socialism, see Wyndham, *Eugenics in Australia* 2003, pp. 128–29, 143, 154, 157.

4 Osborne, *What We Owe to Ireland* 1918, pp. 18–41.

5 Osborne 1918, pp. 13–16, 71–74.

6 For Osborne's broader involvement with Australian race science, see Anderson, *The Cultivation of Whiteness* 2002, pp. 107–108, 114–15, 130–31, 149, 219.

7 O'Neill, *Famine Irish and the American Racial State* 2017, pp. 1–22.

8 Painter, *The History of White People* 2010, pp. 212–27.

9 Painter 2010, pp. 249, 284–89, 320.

10 For the longstanding interest in Aryanism shown by Protestant Irish scholars, see Ballantyne, *Orientalism and Race* 2006, pp. 19, 35–38.

11 Anderson 2002, p. 108.

12 Anderson 2002, pp. 148–50.

13 For Gobineau's racial theories, see Carlson, *The Unfit* 2001, pp. 285–88.

14 Lyng, *Non-Britishers in Australia* 1935, pp. v–vii, 3.

15 Lyng 1935, p. 2.

16 Lyng 1935, pp. 9–11, 18–22.

17 Huxley & Haddon, *We Europeans* 1935, pp. 25–26, 68, 91, 96–97, 184, 267–68.

18 For discussions of *We Europeans*, see Barkan, *The Retreat of Scientific Racism* 1995, pp. 26–30, 296–310; Bashford, *Global Population* 2014, pp. 259–61.

19 Anderson 2002, pp. 162–63.

20 Bolton, 'Connolly, Sir James Daniel (1869–1962)', *ADB*.

21 Roe, *Australia, Britain and Migration* 1995, pp. 7, 11, 13, 17; Richards, *Destination Australia* 2008, pp. 74–79, 88.

22 Fedorowich, 'The problems of disbandment' 1996, pp. 100–102, 105–106; Malcolm, *The Irish Policeman* 2006, pp. 219–45.

23 Roe 1995, pp. 18, 32.

24 Kleinig, 'Peripatetic women' 2013, pp. 129–34.

25 Roe 1995, pp. 207, 289 n. 144; Richards 2008, p. 99.

26 Borrie, *The European Peopling of Australasia* 1994, p. 184; Roe 1995, p. 211.

27 Vamplew (ed.), *Australians: Historical Statistics* 1987, pp. 8–9.

28 For a discussion of the problems of Irish-Australian immigration statistics, see Akenson, *The Irish Diaspora* 1993, pp. 98–103.

29 Borrie 1994, pp. 184, 189.

30 *Commission on Emigration and Other Population Problems* [1954], pp. 314–17.

31 Borrie 1994, p. 195.

32 For Irish immigration after 1945, see Grimes, 'Postwar Irish immigrants' 1998, pp. 137–59; Chetkovich, 'The New Irish in Australia' 2005; O'Connor, 'The Multiple Dimensions of Migrancy' 2005; Breen, 'Emigration in the age of electronic media' 2015, pp. 198–233.

33 Willard, *History of the White Australia Policy* 1967, p. 125.

34 Kain, 'Preventing "Unsound Minds"' 2015, pp. 190–98.

35 McMinn, 'Reid, Sir George Houstoun (1845–1918)', *ADB*.
36 *Catholic Press* (Sydney), 17 November 1903, p. 16; *Freeman's Journal* (Sydney), 28 November 1903, pp. 23–24.
37 *Sydney Morning Herald*, 23 November 1903, p. 7; *Daily Telegraph* (Sydney), 16 November 1903, p. 6.
38 *Freeman's Journal*, 28 November 1903, p. 23.
39 York, *Immigration Restriction* 1997, p. 2.
40 Kain 2015, pp. 195–96, 234–37, 243–45; O'Collins, *Patrick McMahon Glynn* 1965, pp. 237–45. While minister, Glynn also declined to renew George Reid's appointment as Australian high commissioner in London.
41 York 1997, pp. 2–4.
42 For eugenics in Australia, see Garton, 'Sound minds and healthy bodies' 1994 pp. 163–81; Watts, 'Beyond nature and nurture' 1994, pp. 318–34; Jones, 'The master potter and the rejected pots' 1999, pp. 319–42.
43 In 1930, a papal encyclical on marriage condemned eugenics and especially its advocacy of artificial contraception and sterilisation. For debates between Catholics and eugenicists in the United States, see Leon, '"Hopelessly entangled in Nordic pre-suppositions"' 2004, pp. 3–49.
44 For eugenicist attacks on Catholic Irish working-class immigrants and their families in Britain and the United States, see Kevles, *In the Name of Eugenics* 1986, pp. 72–76, 132.
45 Painter 2010, p. 265.
46 Wyndham 2003, p. 253; Garton, 'Eugenics in Australia and New Zealand' 2012, pp. 247–48.
47 Quoted in Wyndham 2003, pp. 191–96.
48 A Hunt, Melbourne, to Captain R Collins, London, 20 June 1906, Department of External Affairs, National Archives of Australia [hereafter NAA], A2910.417/4/2, pp. 119–21.
49 Examination of persons under the *Immigration Act*. Reports by collectors of customs regarding practice in vogue. Guidance to officers, 1911, pp. 11, 14, NAA, A1, 1911/10657.
50 York 1997, pp. 16–63.
51 Sherington, *Australia's Immigrants* 1990, pp. 95–96.
52 Sherington 1990, pp. 106–17.
53 Tavan, *The Long Slow Death of White Australia* 2005, pp. 27–28.
54 Bashford, 'Insanity and immigration restriction' 2013, pp. 23–24.
55 York 1997, pp. 13–77.
56 *Commission on Emigration and Other Population Problems* [1954], p. 312; Jones, 'Captain of all these men of death' 2001, pp. 127–57.
57 *Commission on Emigration and Other Population Problems* [1954], p. 311; Daly, 'Death and disease in independent Ireland' 2010, pp. 229–50.
58 Bashford 2013, pp. 24–26; Mac Lellan, 'Victim or vector?' 2013, p. 104.
59 Finnane, 'Deporting the Irish envoys' 2013, pp. 403–25.
60 York 1997, pp. 3–4.
61 For papers relating to the attempted Walsh and Johnson deportations, see NAA, 1925, A467, SF12/2–28. For Walsh and Pankhurst, see Hogan, 'Walsh, Thomas (Tom) (1871–1943)', *ADB*.

62   Richards 2008, pp. 106–10, Andreon, 'Olive or white?' 2003, pp. 81–92.
63   Sherington 1990, pp. 117–23.
64   Martyr, '"Having a clean up"?' 2011, pp. 184–87.
65   Wyndham 2003, p. 308.
66   It is not clear from the documentation whether O'Connor had served in the British or the Irish army.
67   RI O'Connor, Deportations 1920–30, NAA, A1, 1927/19900.
68   J Dillon, Memorandum from the assistant secretary, Department of Home Affairs, Canberra, 9 May 1930, NAA, B13, 1930/9443.
69   Jones 2001, pp. 1–3.
70   Deeny, *Tuberculosis in Ireland* 1954, pp. 148–50.
71   Beddoe, *The Races of Britain* 1885, pp. 158–59, 246–49; Dormandy, *The White Death* 1999, pp. 240–42.
72   In the mid-19th century, TB sufferers had been encouraged by doctors and travel writers to immigrate to Australia due to its warm climate. But once the contagious nature of TB was discovered in 1882, the colonies became much less welcoming and the 1901 *Immigration Restriction Act* specifically barred TB sufferers. Powell, 'Medical promotion and the consumptive immigrant to Australia' 1973, pp. 449–76.
73   J McCarthy, Deportations 1920–30, NAA, B13, 1929/6049.

5 Irish men in Australian popular culture, 1790s–1920s

1   Banta, *Barbaric Intercourse* 2003.
2   The literature on cartoons and visual satire is very extensive. For Australia, see Scully and Quartly, 'Using cartoons as historical evidence' 2009, pp. 11–26; Kerr, *Artists and Cartoonists* 1999; Lindesay, *The Inked-in Image* 1979; Lindesay, *The Way We Were* 1983; Mahood, *The Loaded Line* 1973; Morrison & Rowland, *In Your Face* 2010.
3   Curtis Jr, *Apes and Angels* 1997, pp. xvi–xxii; Cowling, *The Artist as Anthropologist* 1989; Wechsler, *A Human Comedy* 1982.
4   Bhabha, *The Location of Culture* 1994, p. 70.
5   Soper, 'From swarthy ape to sympathetic everyman and subversive trickster' 2005, p. 260.
6   Kenny, 'Race, violence and anti-Irish sentiment' 2007, pp. 364–78.
7   Fabian (ed.), *Mr Punch Down Under* 1982; Lindsay, *Bohemians of the* Bulletin 1965; Rolfe, *The Journalistic Javelin* 1975.
8   Mahood, '*Melbourne Punch* and its early artists' 1969, p. 65; Mahood, 'Carrington, Francis Thomas Dean (Tom) (1843–1918)', *ADB*; Hopkins, *Hop of the* Bulletin 1929.
9   See Durkin's death notice in *Williamstown Chronicle* (Victoria), 3 May 1902, p. 4.
10   White, *Inventing Australia* 1981, pp. 85–90; Serle, *From Deserts the Prophets Come* 1973, p. 58.
11   Bagot, *Coppin the Great* 1965, pp. 174–76, 189–98, 251–65, 323–24, 337–39; Irvin, *Gentleman George*.
12   Russell, *Savage or Civilised?* 1980, pp. 114–15.

13 For a set of *Bulletin* 'new chum' cartoons, see Rolfe 1975, pp. 92–93. See also White 1981, pp. 79–80; Ward, *The Australian Legend* 1966, pp. 193–97.

14 For examples, see Lindesay 1979, pp. 147, 167, 171, 182 (Aboriginal people); pp. 99, 133, 139 (Jews); and pp. 86, 116, 169 (Chinese men).

15 Curtis Jr 1997, pp. 29–36.

16 See the Isaac Cruikshank and Gillray drawings reproduced in Douglas, Harte & O'Hara, *Drawing Conclusions* 1998, pp. 10–26.

17 Patten, 'Cruikshank, George (1792–1878)', *ODNB*.

18 See, for example, George Cruikshank's 'Murder of George Crawford and his granddaughter', in Maxwell, *History of the Irish Rebellion* 1866, p. 66; de Nie, *The Eternal Paddy* 2004, pp. 36–70.

19 Curtis Jr 1997, pp. 37–45.

20 Curtis Jr 1997, pp. 99, 101–102.

21 See Lebow, 'British images of poverty' 1977, pp. 57–85.

22 De Nie 2004, pp. 144–200; Gantt, *Irish Terrorism in the Atlantic Community* 2010, pp. 23–65; Jenkins, *The Fenian Problem* 2008, pp. 159–62.

23 *Punch* (London), 8 June 1867.

24 *Punch*, 19 March 1870. See De Nie 2004, pp. 165, 171.

25 RP Whitworth's Australian play, *Catching a Conspirator*, which proved a great success in 1867, was based on an alleged true incident in which the well-known Irish actor Barry Sullivan was arrested as a suspected Fenian. He proved he was not by reciting long extracts from Shakespeare. McGuire, *The Australian Theatre* 1948, p. 99.

26 Amos, *The Fenians in Australia* 1988, pp. 45–77; Travers, *The Phantom Fenians of New South Wales* 1986; Inglis, *Australian Colonists* 1993, pp. 112–23.

27 Hall, '"Now him white man"' 2014, pp. 179–80.

28 *Melbourne Punch*, 28 March 1868, p. 101.

29 McGee, *The IRB* 2005, pp. 66–136.

30 See, for example, 'Hatching Fenianism', *Melbourne Punch*, 18 May 1882, pp. 194–95; Hall 2014, pp. 180–83.

31 Pearl, *The Three Lives of Gavan Duffy* 1979, pp. 205–206, 211.

32 Serle, *The Rush to Be Rich* 1971, pp. 238–39.

33 See 'The Redmond Mission: Seed Time and Harvest', *Melbourne Punch*, 7 June 1883, pp. 224–25.

34 Atkinson, *The Europeans in Australia. Volume 3* 2014, pp. 228–32; McLachlan, *Waiting for the Revolution* 1989, pp. 178–82.

35 *Sydney Morning Herald*, 2 March 1885, p. 11; Lehane, *William Bede Dalley* 2007, pp. 297–323; Wilcox, 'Australians in the wars in Sudan and South Africa' 2013, pp. 214–16. See chapter 9 for further discussion of Dalley and the Sudan contingent.

36 Rolfe 1979, pp. 34–36; Hopkins 1929, pp. 135–36; Lawson, *The Archibald Paradox* 1983, pp. 126–72.

37 *Melbourne Punch*, 19 March 1885, p. 111.

38 Amos 1988, pp. 286–88.

39 The classic study is Duggan, *The Stage Irishman* 1937.

40 *Bulletin* (Sydney), 13 June 1896, p. 13.

41 *Bulletin*, 14 May 1897, p. 10.

42 Earls, 'Bulls, blunders and bloothers' 1988, pp. 1–92.

43 Edgeworth, *An Essay on Irish Bulls* 1999, pp. 5–6.

44 Boldrewood, whose real name was TA Browne, had a complex Irish family background. For the details, see de Serville, *Rolf Boldrewood* 2000, pp. 3–17.

45 GV Brooke, the Irish Shakespearian actor, always made money out of farces featuring comic Irish characters, but usually lost money on Shakespeare. He left Australia broke in 1861. McGuire 1948, pp. 92–99, 106–108.

46 Williams, *Australia on the Popular Stage* 1983, pp. 156–65; Rees, *The Making of Australian Drama* 1972, p. 139; McGuire 1948, p. 87.

47 Dampier & Walch, *Robbery Under Arms* 1985, pp. 29, 65, 92, 34.

48 Denham, 'The Kelly Gang' (1899), pp. 581, 558.

49 Lawson 1983, p. 166.

50 Finnane, *Police and Government* 1994, pp. 9–14, 136–37; Haldane, *The People's Force* 1986, pp. 78–90.

51 Jones, *Ned Kelly* 1995, pp. 283–84.

52 *Melbourne Punch*, 7 April 1881, p. 138.

53 *Warwick Argus*, 19 October 1895, p. 6.

54 Fitzpatrick, *Oceans of Consolation* 1994, pp. 6–7.

55 For the characteristics of Australian humour, see Willey, 'A hard, dry humour' 1988, pp. 156–69.

56 Kelly, 'Melodrama' 1993, pp. 51–61.

57 For similarities between *Dad and Dave* and earlier farces on the Irish Muldoon family, see Williams 1983, p. 93; Nye, *The Unembarrassed Muse* 1970, pp. 151–52.

58 See, for example, the stereotyped Irish characters in Paterson, *An Outback Marriage* 1906.

59 Fotheringham, *In Search of Steele Rudd* 1995, pp. 14–33.

60 In the two collections of stories, there are altogether around 35 individuals or families with distinctively Irish surnames. Rudd, *On Our Selection* 1899; Rudd, *Our New Selection* 1903.

61 Dennis, *The Moods of Ginger Mick* 1916. See also Watts (ed.), *The World of the Sentimental Bloke* 1976, pp. 30–32; Chisholm, *The Life and Times of C.J. Dennis* 1982, pp. 70–76, 95–97.

62 Rickard, *Australia* 1988, pp. 172, 176–78, 182.

63 See chapter 9 for a discussion of the Catholic Irish-born men who served as premiers of some of the Australian colonies during the second half of the 19th century.

64 Hall & Malcolm 2016, pp. 1–15.

65 Strangio & Costar (eds), *The Victorian Premiers* 2006, pp. 17–21, 38–41, 77.

66 See Pawsey, *The Popish Plot* 1983.

67 For Duffy's version of events, see Duffy, *My Life in Two Hemispheres*, vol. 2, 1898, pp. 172–73, 337–41.

68 Deakin, *The Federal Story* 1944, p. 12.

69 *Melbourne Punch*, 24 April 1879, p. 161.

70 *Melbourne Punch*, 22 March 1883, p. 114.

71 Kelly, *The Fenian Ideal and Irish Nationalism* 2006, pp. 2–3.

72 Horne, *The Education of Young Donald* 1967, p. 24.

73 For riots by Irish audiences in Hobart in 1834 and Melbourne in 1844, see *Colonial Times* (Hobart), 11 February 1834, pp. 45–46; McGuire 1948, pp. 80, 102–103.

74 *Advocate* (Melbourne), 18 March 1905, p. 14.

75 There were widely publicised Irish riots in New York theatres in 1903 and 1907. Kibler, 'The stage Irishwoman' 2005, pp. 5–10; Barrett, *The Irish Way* 2012, pp. 157–58.

76 When a sailor named Muldoon was arrested and fined for drunkenness in South Australia in 1945, the police magistrate wondered if he was a 'wild Irishman' because he had resisted arrest. The newspaper report of the case was headed, 'No picnic for Muldoon', *Recorder* (Port Pirie), 28 February 1945, p. 2.

77 'Kodak' [Ernest O'Farrell], 'And the singer was Irish' 1918, pp. 91–93.

78 The ape-like Irish featured in a 1920 Norman Lindsay cartoon commenting on Irish nationalist attempts to gain support for their independence struggle from the new League of Nations. See 'Queer company', *Bulletin*, 30 September 1920, cover.

6 Employment: Bridget need not apply

1 *Irish Echo* (Sydney), 3 March 2012, <pandora.nla.gov.au/pan/100123/ 20160417-0000/www.irishecho.com.au/2012/03/13/perth-builders-no-irish-ad-causes-furore/16667.html>.

2 MacRaild, 'No Irish need apply' 2013, pp. 296–98.

3 Kibler, 'The stage Irishwoman' 2005, pp. 5–30.

4 Lynch-Brennan, *The Irish Bridget* 2009; Walter, *Outsiders Inside* 2001, pp. 54, 63–64, 145.

5 Twopeny, *Town Life in Australia* 1973, p. 51.

6 *Bulletin* (Sydney), 23 June 1883, p. 16.

7 *Bulletin*, 19 October 1889, p. 8.

8 Down, 'Aims and ends; or "Quite Colonial"' (1878), in Jordan & Pierce (eds), *The Poets' Discovery* 1990, pp. 319–20.

9 *Argus* (Melbourne), 22 December 1854, p. 1.

10 Jensen '"No Irish need apply"' 2002, pp. 405–29.

11 MacRaild 2013, p. 277.

12 MacRaild 2013, pp. 269–99.

13 Fried, 'No Irish need deny' 2016, pp. 829–54.

14 MacRaild 2013, p. 271.

15 *Sydney Morning Herald*, 14 June 1862, p. 9; Jensen 2002, p. 407. It is unclear whether the version of the song for sale in Sydney contained the American or the British lyrics.

16 *Melbourne Punch*, 5 November 1857, p. 2.

17 Higman did a manual sampling of advertisements in the *Sydney Morning Herald* (1831–2001) for his research, but did not find any 'No Irish Need Apply' ads. Higman, *Domestic Service in Australia* 2002, p. 63.

18 Higman 2002, pp. 109–21.

19 *Argus*, 12 January 1865, p. 1.

20 *Argus*, 2 October 1854, p. 1.

21 *Sydney Morning Herald*, 5 November 1879, p. 12; 1 March 1880, p. 10; 7 June 1880, p. 8.

22 *Sydney Stock and Station Journal*, 8 October 1920, p. 20.

23 The following results are based on searches completed in December 2017. As the digitisation of newspapers in Trove continues, more ads will doubtless appear.

24 Newspapers researched were: *Sydney Morning Herald; Australian* (Sydney); *Empire* (Sydney); *Commercial Journal and Advertiser* (Sydney); *Evening News* (Sydney); *Age* (Melbourne); *Argus* (Melbourne); *Evening Journal* (Adelaide); *Express and Telegraph* (Adelaide); *Advertiser* (Adelaide); *South Australian Register* (Adelaide); *Brisbane Courier; Courier* (Brisbane); *West Australian; Bendigo Advertiser; Ballarat Star; Geelong Advertiser; Mount Alexander Mail* (Castlemaine); *Launceston Advertiser; Cornwall Chronicle* (Launceston); *Maryborough Chronicle; Rockhampton Bulletin; Inquirer and Commercial News* (Perth); *Kyneton Observer*.

25 *Cornwall Chronicle* (Launceston), 3 February 1838, p. 19.

26 *West Australian* (Perth), 15 May 1908, p. 8.

27 *Advertiser* (Adelaide), 4 January 1916, p. 11.

28 MacRaild 2013, pp. 278–79.

29 *Empire* (Sydney), 15 January 1858, p. 4.

30 Serle, *The Golden Age* 1963, pp. 3, 370.

31 Hamilton, '"Tipperaryifing" the moral atmosphere' 1982, p. 21; Fitzpatrick, 'Irish emigration in the later nineteenth century' 1980, pp. 132–33; Reid, *Farewell My Children* 2011, pp. 98–102.

32 McClaughlin, *Barefoot and Pregnant*, vol. 1, 1991, pp. 1–23.

33 Hamilton 1982, p. 23.

34 *Argus*, 24 January 1850, p. 2; Gothard, *Blue China* 2001, pp. 41–47.

35 *Argus*, 1 July 1854, p. 1; Rutledge, 'Montefiore, Jacob Levi (1819–1885)', *ADB*.

36 Higman 2002, p. 48; Gothard, 'Wives or workers?' 2001, pp. 147–48; Hamilton, 'Domestic dilemmas' 1993, pp. 83–85.

37 Hamilton 1982, pp. 20, 22.

38 Twopeny 1973, pp. 49–62; Russell, *A Wish for Distinction* 1994, pp. 167–88.

39 *Sydney Morning Herald*, 17 November 1920, p. 20.

40 Jupp, *The English in Australia* 2004, pp. 58–60, 119–20.

41 Cited in Meredith & Oxley, 'Contracting convicts' 2005, p. 61; Oxley, 'Packing her (economic) bags' 1994, p. 64.

42 McConville, 'Emigrant Irish and Suburban Catholics' 1984, p. 100.

43 'Stawell Cemetery Register', p. 593, transcribed by M King and held by Stawell Historical Society. For the Scallon and Kinsella brothers, see Murray & White, *The Golden Years of Stawell* 1983, p. 142.

44 Cited in MacGinley, 'The Irish in Queensland' 1972, p. 111.

45 *Bendigo Advertiser*, 1 April, 1859, p. 3.

46 *Bendigo Advertiser*, 2 April 1859, p. 3

47 Pawsey, *The Demon of Discord* 1982.

48 MacRaild 2013, p. 291, citing *Freeman's Journal* (Dublin), 6 September 1841.

49 *Australasian Chronicle* (Sydney), 19 November 1839, p. 4; *Sydney Monitor and Commercial Advertiser*, 22 November 1839, p. 3; 3 January 1840, p. 3; 10 January 1840, p. 4; *Sydney Herald*, 3 January 1840, p. 3; 6 January 1840, p. 2.

50 *Sydney Morning Herald*, 27 May 1850, p. 3.

51 *Adelaide Times*, 18 December 1855, p. 1.

52 *North Australian* (Brisbane), 12 December 1863, p. 3.

53 The case was widely reported: see *Leader* (Melbourne), 30 April 1870, p. 20.

54 *Bulletin*, 26 May 1883, p. 16.

55 Hopkins, *Hop of the* Bulletin 1929, pp. 68–74.

56 *Melbourne Punch*, 20 September 1883, p. 114.

57 MacRaild 2013, pp. 291–92.

58 *Hobarton Guardian, or, True Friend of Tasmania*, 24 February 1849, p. 2. For other examples, see *Argus*, 4 July 1849, p. 2; *Freeman's Journal* (Sydney), 8 August 1857, p. 3.

59 *Age (Melbourne)*, 1 May 1857, p. 6.

60 *Catholic Press* (Sydney), 22 April 1899, p. 7.

61 Newspapers researched were: *Sydney Morning Herald* (1842–); *Daily Telegraph* (1883–); *Empire* (1850–1879); *Evening News* (1869–1922); *Australian Town and Country* (1870–1907); *Australian Star* (1887–1909); *Telegraph* (1872–1947); *Brisbane Courier* (1864–1933); *Courier* (1861–1864); *Queenslander* (1866–1839); *Express and Telegraph* (1867–1922); *Advertiser* (1889–1931); *Evening Journal* (1869–1912); *South Australian Register* (1839–1900); *South Australian Advertiser* (1869–1912); *Register* (1901–1929); *Mercury* (1860–); *Age* (1854–); *Argus* (1848–1957); *Herald* (1861–1990); *West Australian* (1879–); *Daily News* (1882–1950).

62 No regional or rural newspaper used the term before 1860 and none in South Australia or Western Australia had more than one use of the term between 1840 and 1919, so these states have been excluded.

63 *Daily Observer* (Tamworth); *Tamworth Observer*; *Northern Star* (Lismore); *Maitland Mercury*: *Illawarra Mercury* (Wollongong); *Kiama Independent and Shoalhaven Advertiser*; *Goulburn Herald*; *Newcastle Chronicle*; *Wagga Wagga Advertiser*; *Clarence and Richmond River* (Grafton); *Riverine Grazier* (Hay); *Braidwood Dispatcher*; *Goulburn Evening Penny*; *Newcastle Morning Herald*; *Barrier Miner* (Broken Hill); *Maitland Weekly*; *Mudgee Guardian*; *Richmond River Herald* (Lismore).

64 *Darling Downs Gazette* (Toowoomba); *Morning Bulletin* (Rockhampton); *Queenslander* (Ipswich); *Western Star* (Roma).

65 *Geelong Advertiser*; *Albury Banner*; *Gippsland Times*; *Ballarat Star*; *Hamilton Spectator*; *Ballarat Courier*; *Bendigo Advertiser*; *Bendigo Independent*.

66 *Launceston Examiner*; *Cornwall Chronicle* (Launceston).

67 Moran, *Viewless Winds* 1939, pp. 158–59.

68 *Freeman's Journal* (Sydney), 27 June 1868, p. 7.

69 See, for example, 'Wages and patriotism', *Bulletin*, 10 August 1889, p. 12; 'The casus belli', *Bulletin*, 21 November 1891, p. 14.

70 'What they will soon be if they go', *Melbourne Punch*, 5 March 1885, p. 100. This particular cartoon appears from its style to have come from *Puck* (1877–1918), a New York satirical weekly. For examples of *Puck*'s simianised Irish characters, see Curtis Jr, *Apes and Angels* 1997, pp. 61–67.

71 Kenny, 'Race, violence and anti-Irish sentiment' 2007, pp. 366–67.

72 MacRaild 2013, p. 283.

73 Luddy, 'Women and work' 2000, pp. 44–56.

74 Higman 2002, p. 29.

75 Hall, 'Irishness, gender and "An up-country township"' 2005, pp. 81–97.

76 Haskins & Maynard, 'Sex, race and power' 2005, pp. 191–216.

77 MacGinley 1972, p. 188.

78 *Advocate* (Melbourne), 6 October 1883, p. 11.

79 *Age*, 5 February 1870, p. 1.

80 *Evening Journal* (Adelaide), 31 July 1877, p. 1.

81 *West Australian* (Perth), 9 October 1895, p. 5.

82 *Express and Telegraph* (Adelaide), 18 February 1910, p. 2.

83 *Argus*, 12 January 1865, p. 1.

7 Crime and the Irish: from vagrancy to the gallows

1 See, for example, Macintyre, *A Concise History of Australia* 1999, which ignores the Irish at Eureka, jumping from Irish convicts in 1804 to Ned Kelly and then to Mannix and the 1916–17 conscription plebiscites.

2 See, for example, Hocking, *The Rebel Chorus* 2007; Moore, *Death or Liberty* 2010. For a more critical assessment, see Moore, 'An "indelible Hibernian mark"?' 1998, pp. 1–8.

3 Clark, *A Short History of Australia* 1980, p. 87. For Clark's concept of Irish Catholicism as a backward 'counterpoint' to progressive British Protestantism and Enlightenment rationalism, see Berryman, 'The concept of civilization in Manning Clark's "History of Australia"' 2017, pp. 82–98.

4 Akenson, *Small Differences* 1988, p. 60.

5 Hirst, *Australian History in 7 Questions* 2014, pp. 125–27, 27–58.

6 Wood, *Violence and Crime in Nineteenth-century England* 2004, p. 33.

7 O'Farrell, *The Irish in Australia* 1986, pp. 52–53, 36.

8 McMahon, *Homicide in Pre-Famine and Famine Ireland* 2013, pp. 14–15.

9 O'Donnell, 'Lethal violence in Ireland' 2005, Table 1, p. 677. For a useful summary of recent research, see Finnane & O'Donnell, 'Crime and punishment' 2017, pp. 363–82.

10 McMahon 2013, p. 165.

11 Swift, 'Heroes or villains?' 1997, p. 421. Thanks go to Roger Swift for providing a copy of this article.

12 Swift 1997, p. 410; Swift, 'Historians and the Irish' 2000, p. 34.

13 Swift 1997, pp. 402–403.

14 Neal, 'Lancashire, the Famine Irish and the poor laws' 1995, pp. 36–40.

15 Jones, *Crime, Protest, Community and Police in Nineteenth-century Britain* 1982, pp. 166, 178–83, 198–99; Rose, 'Rogues and Vagabonds' 1988, pp. 5–8; Robson, *The Convict Settlers of Australia* 1965, p. 70.

16 Cited in Wood 2004, pp. 92–93.

17 Swift 1997, pp. 405–407.

18 Belchem, *Irish, Catholic and Scouse* 2007, pp. 82–85; Neal, 'A criminal profile of the Liverpool Irish' 1991, pp. 161–99; Lowe, *The Irish in Mid-Victorian Lancashire* 1989, pp. 102–103.
19 Akenson, *The Irish Diaspora* 1993, pp. 118–19.
20 O'Farrell 1986, p. 169.
21 Hall & Malcolm, 'English institutions and the Irish race' 2016, pp. 1–15.
22 Topp, 'A few more words on the Irish question' 1881, pp. 210–11, footnote.
23 Topp 1881, pp. 210–11, footnote.
24 Topp 1881, pp. 210–11.
25 Cited in Topp 1881, p. 211, footnote.
26 Wilson, *The Beat* 2006, pp. 54–56, 123.
27 *Victorian Year Book, 1879–80*, p. 257.
28 *Victorian Year Book, 1879–80*, pp. 254, 261.
29 *Victorian Year Book, 1879–80*, p. 254.
30 *Victorian Year Book, 1879–80*, pp. 251, 253, 19, 255.
31 In 1898, for instance, 55 per cent of total Catholic arrests were for drunkenness, compared to 50 per cent of Protestant arrests. *Victorian Year Book, 1895–98*, pp. 1033–1034.
32 Laughlin & Hall (eds), *Handbook to Victoria* 1914, pp. 240–41.
33 *Victorian Year Book, 1885–86*, p. 578.
34 Morgan, 'Irish women in Port Phillip and Victoria, 1840–60' 1989, pp. 240–44.
35 Central Register of Female Prisoners, vol. 1 (1855–61), nos 1–750, Public Record Office Victoria [hereafter PROV], VPRS 516–P1 Microfiche.
36 Campbell, 'Irish women in nineteenth-century Australia' 1991, pp. 25–38.
37 Richards & Herraman, '"If she was to be hard up she would sooner be hard up in a strange land than where she would be known"' 1998, p. 86.
38 See also McClaughlin, '"I was nowhere else"' 1998, pp. 142–62; McClaughlin, 'Vulnerable Irish women in mid- to late-nineteenth-century Australia' 1996, pp. 157–65.
39 *Victorian Year Book, 1895–98*, pp. 1052–53.
40 Coghlan, *The Wealth and Progress of New South Wales, 1894*, vol. 2, 1896, p. 583.
41 Coghlan, vol. 2, 1896, pp. 583, 587.
42 Hicks, 'Coghlan, Sir Timothy Augustine (1855–1926)', *ADB*.
43 Hayter too had warned against relying on religious affiliation as a means of classifying offenders. Coghlan, vol. 2, 1896, p. 587; *Victorian Year Book, 1875*, p. 108.
44 Coghlan, vol. 2, 1896, p. 588.
45 Coghlan, vol. 2, 1896, p. 586.
46 Francis, *Migrant Crime in Australia* 1981, pp. 62, 172, Table 3.
47 See, for example, King, 'Ethnicity, prejudice and justice' 2013, pp. 390–414; Weaver, 'Moral order and repression in Upper Canada' 1986, pp. 176–207.
48 Finnane, 'The Irish and crime in the late nineteenth century' 1989, pp. 93, 94.
49 Topp 1881, pp. 210–11, footnote. See Lynn & Armstrong, *From Pentonville to Pentridge* 1996, pp. 204–205.
50 *Victorian Year Book, 1892*, p. 203.

51 The classic study of capital punishment in England is Gatrell, *The Hanging Tree* 1994.
52 Douglas & Laster, 'A matter of life and death' 1991, p. 155.
53 McClaughlin 1998, pp. 152–54.
54 Laster, 'Arbitrary chivalry' 1994, p. 168.
55 Between 1842 and 1967 in Victoria, 606 people were sentenced to death, but only 30.5 per cent of them were eventually executed. Those sentenced included 45 women, of whom five were executed. Laster 1994, pp. 167–71.
56 For executions of Indigenous Australians in Victoria, see Douglas & Laster 1991, pp. 152–53.
57 *Argus* (Melbourne), 17 March 1877, p. 4.
58 Lynn & Armstrong 1996, pp. 202–206.
59 Lynn & Armstrong 1996, pp. 202–206.
60 Douglas & Laster 1991, pp. 146, 149, 156.
61 For Irish bushrangers, see West, *Bushranging and the Policing of Rural Banditry in New South Wales* 2009, pp. 78, 214.
62 The two men had been unsuccessfully defended by Irish barrister Redmond Barry, who represented several other Indigenous clients during the 1840s. Davies, 'Aborigines, murder and the criminal law in early Port Phillip' 1987, pp. 315–20; Galbally, *Redmond Barry* 1995, pp. 46–47, 52–57.
63 *Melbourne Times*, 14 May 1842, p. 3, 2 July 1842, p. 3.
64 *Ovens and Murray Advertiser* (Beechworth), 26 March 1859, p. 3, 27 June 1859, p. 3.
65 For documents relating to the case, see Edward Feeney, executed 14 May 1872, Capital Cases Files [hereafter CCF], PROV, VPRS 0264 - P/0000, Box 7.
66 *Argus*, 18 April 1872, p. 4; *Age* (Melbourne), 18 April 1872, p. 3.
67 *Argus*, 6 March 1872, pp. 5–6, 7 March 1872, p. 6.
68 Castieau, '*The Difficulties of My Position*' 2004, pp. 168, 174–75, 177, 181–82.
69 *Freeman's Journal* (Sydney), 23 August 1870, p. 7.
70 James Cusick [also Cusack], executed 30 August 1870, CCF, PROV, VPRS 0264 - P/0000, Box 6; *Argus*, 17 August 1870, p. 6, 31 August 1870, p. 7.
71 Richard Heraghty, reprieved 9 June 1878, CCF, PROV, VPRS 0264 - P/0008; *Melbourne Punch*, 20 June 1878, p. 241.
72 *Argus*, 10 June 1878, p. 2.
73 Douglas & Laster 1991, pp. 145–46.
74 *Geelong Advertiser and Intelligence*, 24 April 1855, p. 2.
75 Francis Brennigan [also Brannigan or Brannagan], prisoner no.2326, Central Register for Male Prisoners, vol. 4, 1855, PROV, VPRS 515-P0000.
76 *Age*, 28 March 1857, p. 4; Barry, 'Price, John Giles (1808–1857)', *ADB*.
77 *Argus*, 2 April 1857, p. 4, 1 May 1857, p. 5; *Age*, 29 April 1857, p. 5. A letter to the *Argus* described ex-convict Thomas Williams, who was one of those executed for Price's murder, as a Catholic Irish man; he was certainly a Catholic, but the *Age* identified him as having been born in Manchester.
78 The most detailed analysis of the trials is offered in Barry, *The Life and Death of John Price* 1964, pp. 104–23.
79 *Age*, 21 April 1857, p. 3. JK Lavater, a Swiss clergyman, published an influential book on physiognomy in the late 1770s.

80 Stephen suffered due to his defence of some of the prisoners accused of killing Price, as an attempt was made to have him disbarred. See 'Stephen, George Milner (1812–1894)', *ADB*.
81 *Age*, 21 March 1857, p. 3; *Argus*, 21 April 1857, p. 5.
82 *Bendigo Advertiser*, 22 April 1857, p. 2.
83 *Age*, 21 March 1857, p. 3; *Argus*, 21 April 1857, p. 5.
84 *Argus*, 28 April 1857, p. 4.
85 Barry 1964, p. 120.
86 Such recommendations were rare. Douglas and Laster, in their statistical analysis of executions in Victoria, found juries recommended mercy in only 3.4 per cent of capital cases, but, unlike the cases of Brennigan and Smith, such recommendations were associated with 'a significantly higher likelihood of commutation'. Douglas & Laster 1991, p. 149.
87 *Argus*, 29 April 1857, p. 7.
88 *Argus*, 30 April 1857, p. 6.
89 Douglas & Laster 1991, pp. 148, 150–51, 156.
90 Ronayne, *First Fleet to Federation* 2003.
91 *Argus*, 24 February 1877, p. 4.
92 *Argus*, 24 February 1877, p. 4.
93 Thomas Hogan, executed 9 June 1879, CCF, PROV, VPRS 0264 - P/0000, Box 9.
94 *Ovens and Murray Advertiser*, 22 January 1879, p. 8, 8 May 1879, p. 3, 10 June 1879, p. 3, 17 June 1879, p. 3.
95 *Hamilton Spectator*, 26 February 1891, p. 3.
96 For the poor working conditions and prospects of aging rural labourers, about a quarter of whom were Irish, in Victoria during the 1870s and 1880s, see Fahey, '"Abusing the horses and exploiting the labourer"' 1993, pp. 109–10.
97 *Advocate* (Melbourne), 28 February 1891, p. 20; *Ballarat Star*, 21 April 1891, p. 2; *Argus*, 21 April 1891, p. 6.
98 *Hamilton Spectator*, 26 February 1891, p. 3, 28 February 1891, p. 4.
99 Cornelius Bourke, executed 20 April 1891, CCF, PROV, 0264 - P/0000-000017.
100 *Hamilton Spectator*, 12 March 1891, p. 4; *Age*, 7 April 1891, p. 4; *Advocate*, 14 March 1891, p. 20, 11 April 1891, p. 19, 25 April 1891, p. 14.

8 Madness and the Irish

1 O'Farrell, *The Irish in Australia* 1986, pp. 169–70.
2 Garton, *Medicine and Madness* 1988, pp. 18, 23, 38. See also the Australian Psychiatric Care website, <www.ahpi.esrc.unimelb.edu.au/index.html>.
3 Australian Bureau of Statistics, Australian Historical Population Statistics [hereafter ABS, AHPS], Table 8.1: Population (a), sex and country of birth, NSW census years 1846–1891, 3105.0.65.001.
4 NSW Inspector-General of the Insane [hereafter NSW IGI], Report, 1881, Table 9, p. 4; 1882, p. 8; 1885, p. 9, Inspector-General of the Insane Reports, 1881–1910, Mitchell Library, Sydney, Q362.2/N.
5 Malcolm, 'Irish immigrants in a colonial asylum' 2012, p. 128.

6   NSW IGI, Report, 1881, Table 9, p. 4; 1891, Table 9, p. 7; 1910, Table 9, p. 15.

7   NSW IGI, Report, 1887, p. 10; 1891, pp. 2–3.

8   Manning, 'Address in psychological medicine' 1889, pp. 151–52.

9   Manning 1889, Table IV, n.p.; ABS, AHPS, Tables 8.1–8.6: Population (a), sex and country of birth, 1891 censuses, 3105.0.65.001.

10   NSW IGI, Report, 1881, Tables 8 and 9, p. 4; 1910, Tables 8 and 9, p. 15. It should be noted that some of the Irish-born in this table could have been Protestant, but the majority would have been Catholic.

11   NSW IGI, Report, 1881, Tables 8 and 9, p. 4; 1910, Tables 8 and 9, p. 15. The NSW inspector-general's annual reports give figures for French, German and Chinese inmates, as well as for those from 'Other Countries'. But the numbers are relatively small in all cases. The French, for example, most of whom were likely to have been Catholic, made up a mere 0.7 per cent of NSW inmates in 1881 and 0.4 per cent in 1910.

12   Vamplew (ed.), *Australians: Historical Statistics* 1987, pp. 26, 421.

13   For an international overview, see Malcolm, 'Mental health and migration' 2012, pp. 15–38.

14   Brennan, *Irish Insanity* 2014, p. 35.

15   Penrose, 'Mental disease and crime' 1939, pp. 4–7, 11.

16   Brennan 2014, pp. 28–35; Healy, 'Irish psychiatry in the twentieth century' 1996, pp. 268–69.

17   Pietikainen, *Madness* 2015, pp. 155–56.

18   For discussions of additional explanations, see Malcolm, 'Mental health and migration' 2012, pp. 21–26; Brennan 2014, pp. 89–92.

19   The best general history remains Finnane, *Insanity and the Insane in Post-Famine Ireland* 1981.

20   Prior, 'Dangerous lunacy' 2003, pp. 525–53.

21   Cox, *Negotiating Insanity in the Southeast of Ireland* 2012, pp. 74–87.

22   Malcolm, '"Ireland's crowded madhouses"' 2003, pp. 324–26.

23   Malcolm, '"The house of strident shadows"' 1999, pp. 177–91; Brennan 2014, pp. 79–85.

24   For Canada and New Zealand, see Wright & Themeles, 'Migration, madness and the Celtic fringe' 2012, pp. 39–54; Van Der Krogt, 'Irish Catholicism, criminality and mental illness in New Zealand' 2016, pp. 90–121; McCarthy, 'Transnational ties to home' 2012, pp. 149–66.

25   Fox, 'Irish immigrants, pauperism and insanity in 1854 Massachusetts' 1991, pp. 315–36.

26   Pollock, 'A statistical study of the foreign-born insane in New York state hospitals' 1913, pp. 10–27; Malzberg, 'Mental disease among Irish-born and white natives of Irish parentage in New York state' 1963, pp. 12–42.

27   Bracken et al., 'Mental health and ethnicity' 1998, pp. 103–105; Scally, '"The very pests of society"' 2004, pp. 77–81.

28   Fox 1991, pp. 330–31.

29   Bhavsar & Bhugra, 'Bethlem's Irish' 2009, pp. 189–90.

30   Bhavsar & Bhugra 2009, p. 194.

31   Gallman, *Receiving Erin's Children* 2000, pp. 28–32, 65–73, 90–102.

32   Cox, Marland & York, 'Emaciated, exhausted and excited' 2012, p. 501.

33 For similar attitudes, see Malcolm, "'A most terrible looking object'" 2003, pp. 127–31.
34 Cited in Cox, Marland & York 2012, pp. 506, 515, 517.
35 For the English lunacy system, see Bartlett, *The Poor Law of Lunacy* 1999.
36 For discussions of committal procedures in NSW and Victoria, see Garton, 'Policing the dangerous lunatic' 1987, pp. 74–87; Coleborne, 'Passage to the asylum' 2003, pp. 129–48.
37 NSW *Dangerous Lunatics Act 1843*, 7 Vic. No. 14.
38 NSW *Lunacy Act 1867*, 31 Vic. No. 19, ss. 1–4.
39 Sinclair, 'Presidential address' 1909, pp. 219–20.
40 See, for Victoria, *Lunacy Statute 1867*, 31 Vic. No. 309, ss. 4–5, 7–9; for Queensland, *Insanity Act 1884*, 48 Vic. No. 8, ss. 23–25.
41 NSW *Lunacy Act 1878*, 42 Vic. No. 7, ss. 4–6; NSW *Lunacy Act 1898*, 62 Vic. No. 45, ss. 4–6.
42 Wilson, *The Beat* 2006, pp. 124–25.
43 Coleborne 2003, pp. 135–37; Wilson 2006, pp. 125–26.
44 For Irish influence on the police, see Finnane, *Police and Government* 1994, pp. 9–14, 29–30, 136–37.
45 Haldane, *The People's Force* 1986, pp. 81–84.
46 Malcolm, "'What would people say if I became a policeman?'" 2003, pp. 100–101.
47 Brennan identifies a 'high tendency to institutionalise' as developing in 19th-century Ireland and enduring throughout much of the 20th century. Brennan 2014, p. 118.
48 As well as many attendants, a number of asylum doctors were also Irish-born. See Malcolm, 'Irish immigrants in a colonial asylum' 2012, pp. 146–47, n. 40.
49 Burdett, *Hospitals and Asylums of the World*, vol. 1, 1891, p. 311.
50 *Argus* (Melbourne), 22 July 1876, p. 4.
51 Malcolm, 'Irish immigrants in a colonial asylum' 2012, pp. 142–44.
52 *Argus*, 29 July 1876, p. 4.
53 Cited in Monk, *Attending Madness* 2008, p. 170, n. 3.
54 Monk 2008, p. 153. French was still working at Yarra Bend nearly 25 years later in 1884.
55 The patient records required under NSW law to be kept by asylums are set out in detail in the appendices to the NSW *Lunacy Act 1898*, 62 Vic. No. 45, schedules 1–19.
56 For the problems of asylums in Victoria, see Crowther, 'Administration and the asylum in Victoria' 2003, pp. 85–95.
57 For a classic study of asylum inmate autobiographies, see Porter, *A Social History of Madness* 1986. For families' interactions with asylums, see Coleborne, "'His brain was wrong, his mind astray'" 2006, pp. 45–65.
58 NSW IGI Report, 1881, Table 9, p. 4.
59 Manning 1889, Table IV, n.p.
60 Manning 1889, Table IV, n.p. Manning believed that the large category of 'Others' in his table was unreliable, having been inflated due to poor record-keeping in Victoria and Tasmania.
61 NSW IGI, Report, 1881, Table 9, p. 29.

62 Winifred Sharkey, 1878–81, State Records NSW, Gladesville Hospital for the Insane, Admissions and Case Books [hereafter SRNSW, Gladesville], NRS 5031/4/8163, folio 17, no. 3382; Catherine Dobson, 1878, SRNSW, Gladesville, NRS 5031/4/8163, folio 157, no. 3452.

63 Connolly, *Priests and People in Pre-Famine Ireland* 1982, pp. 100–20.

64 The word 'friends' as frequently used in the medical notes seems to have usually meant relatives who were not parents or spouses.

65 Hannah McCarthy, 1878–83, SRNSW, Gladesville, NRS 5031/4/8163, folio 217, no. 3482.

66 Joanna Herlihy, 1887–1910, SRNSW, Gladesville, NRS 5031/4/8176, folio 284, no. 6177.

67 For Manning's views on madness and Indigenous Australians and for his efforts to bar Chinese immigrants, see Murray, 'Settling the Mind' 2012, pp. 68–118, 144–63.

68 Coleborne, *Insanity, Identity and Empire* 2015, pp. 143–44.

69 Johanna Flynn, 1887–89, SRNSW, Gladesville, NRS 5031/4/8177, folio 3, no. 6197.

70 For the use of physiognomy by doctors at Melbourne's Kew Asylum, see Day, 'Magnificence, Misery and Madness' 1998, pp. 218–22.

71 James Ryan, 1878, SRNSW, Gladesville, NRS 5031/4/8163, folio 277, no. 3512.

72 Thomas Cahill, 1887–88, SRNSW, Gladesville, NRS 5031/4/8177, folio 33, no. 6227.

73 John Larkin, 1887, SRNSW, Gladesville, NRS 5031/4/8176, folio 274, no. 6167.

74 Garton 1988, p. 187.

75 O'Brien, *Poverty's Prison* 1988, pp. 51–52.

76 Garton 1988, pp. 103, 118.

77 Garton 1988, p. 104.

78 Malcolm, 'Irish immigrants in a colonial asylum' 2012, pp. 130–31.

79 Cage, *Poverty Abounding* 1992, pp. 14–15.

80 McCalman, 'To die without friends' 2009, pp. 173–76.

81 Margaret Cuthbert, 1897, Public Record Office Victoria, Yarra Bend Asylum, Case Books, VA2839, VPRS 7400/12/9. For similar cases of friendless Irish women committed to NSW and Queensland asylums, see McClaughlin, '"I was nowhere else"' 1998, pp. 159–61.

82 Manning, *The Causation of Insanity* 1880, pp. 2–3.

83 McCarthy, 'Transnational ties to home' 2012, p. 155; Fitzpatrick, 'Emigration, 1801–70' 1989, p. 616.

9 Colonial politics: Daniel O'Connell's 'Tail' and the Catholic Irish premiers

1 Moore, 'An "indelible Hibernian mark"?' 1998, pp. 1–8.

2 Pakenham, *The Year of Liberty* 1969; Malcolm, 'A new age or just the same old cycle of extirpation?' 2013, pp. 151–66; Kelly, '"We were all to be massacred"' 2003, pp. 110–41.

3   Whitaker, *Unfinished Revolution* 1994; O'Donnell, '"Desperate and diabolical"'
    1996, pp. 360–72.
4   For O'Connell's life, see Geoghegan, *King Dan* 2008; Geoghegan, *Liberator*
    2010.
5   MacDonagh, *Daniel O'Connell* 1989, p. 119; Owens, 'Nationalism without
    words' 1998, pp. 242–47.
6   For varying assessments of O'Connell, see McCartney (ed.), *The World of Daniel
    O'Connell* 1980.
7   Earls, '"The opportunity of being useful"' 2008, pp. 170–82.
8   King, *Richard Bourke* 1971, pp. 139–243.
9   *Sydney Herald*, 11 January 1836, p. 2. The paper became the *Sydney Morning
    Herald* in 1841.
10 For other examples of the term the 'O'Connell Tail', see *True Colonist* (Hobart),
    18 September 1835, p. 5; *Sydney Monitor*, 30 January 1836, p. 2; *Sydney Herald*,
    11 February 1836, p. 2; and *Courier* (Hobart), 16 October 1840, p. 4.
11 Henry Parkes's newspaper attacked government parliamentary nominees in
    1854 for their 'slavish subserviency', comparing them to 'Daniel O'Connell's
    tail'. *Empire* (Sydney), 7 November 1854, p. 4.
12 Macintyre, *The Liberator* 1965, pp. 154–59.
13 *Sydney Gazette*, 5 September 1840, p. 2.
14 *Sydney Gazette*, 17 October 1840, p. 2. The 'St Bartholomew Massacre' referred
    to the killing of large numbers of Protestants by Catholics in Paris and other
    parts of France in 1572.
15 *Sydney Morning Herald*, 2 October 1844, p. 2.
16 *Morning Chronicle* (Sydney), 30 November 1844, p. 2.
17 MacDonagh, *The Sharing of the Green* 1996, pp. 81–82.
18 O'Farrell, 'The image of O'Connell in Australia' 1980, pp. 112–24.
19 Kiernan, 'Irish in Australian politics' 2001, pp. 474–78.
20 Campion, *Australian Catholics* 1987, pp. 27–35; Hall, 'Defending the faith' 2014,
    pp. 207–23.
21 Campion 1987, pp. 34–35; Freudenberg, *A Certain Grandeur* 1978, p. 24.
22 Franklin, Nolan & Gilchrist (eds), *The Real Archbishop Mannix from the Sources*
    2015, pp. 159–68.
23 James, '"From beyond the sea"' 2015, pp. 81–109.
24 For an account of Ireland in 1860–1925 written specifically for Australian
    readers, see MacDonagh 1996, pp. 89–159.
25 Amos, *The Fenians in Australia* 1988; Harris, *The Prince and the Assassin* 2017;
    Fennell & King, *John Devoy's 'Catalpa' Expedition* 2006.
26 Jackson, *Home Rule* 2003.
27 Kingston, *The Oxford History of Australia, Volume 3* 1988, pp. 237–308.
28 The word 'premier' is used throughout to describe the chief ministers of
    colonial, as well as state, governments. In the early decades, other terms were
    employed, but 'premier' provides consistency and so avoids confusion.
29 Some premiers served multiple terms in office, but the numbers given
    in Tables 1 and 2 are for individuals not governments. Self-government
    commenced in Victoria in 1855, in NSW, Tasmania and South Australia in
    1856, in Queensland in 1859 and in Western Australia in 1890.

30 Tables 1 and 2 of colonial premiers, 1855-1900, are both based on entries in the *Australian Dictionary of Biography* and lists of premiers in *Australians: The Guide and Index* 1987, pp. 44-47.

31 McClaughlin, 'Irish-Protestant settlement' 2001, pp. 463-65.

32 McClaughlin, 'Protestant Irish in Australia' 2007, pp. 88-98.

33 Kiernan, 'Irish in Australian politics: Irish Protestants' 2001, p. 478.

34 Prentis, *The Scots in Australia* 2008, p. 125; Vamplew (ed.), *Australians: Historical Statistics* 1987, pp. 8-9.

35 For CC Kingston, premier of South Australia (1893-99), see Glass, *Charles Cameron Kingston* 1997.

36 MacDonagh, 'The Irish in Victoria in the nineteenth century' 2001, pp. 467-71; Coughlan, 'The coming of the Irish to Victoria' 1965, pp. 68-86.

37 MacDonagh, 'The Irish in Victoria' 1971, pp. 85-92.

38 McCaffrey, 'Irish-American politics' 1985, p. 175.

39 Duffy, *My Life in Two Hemispheres*, vol. 2, 1898, p. 169.

40 Hogan, *The Sectarian Strand* 1987, pp. 102-103; 'Garryowen' [E Finn], *The Chronicles of Early Melbourne*, vol. 2, 1888, pp. 680-87. We saw in chapter 6 that 'No Irish Need Apply' newspaper advertisements reached a peak in Melbourne during the 1850s, which suggests that anti-Irish and anti-Catholic sentiment was still strong in the city throughout the 1850s.

41 Pawsey, *The Popish Plot* 1983.

42 Hall & Malcolm, 'English institutions and the Irish race' 2016, pp. 10-13.

43 Travers, *The Phantom Fenians of New South Wales* 1986; Inglis, *Australian Colonists* 1993, pp. 112-23.

44 Brett, *The Enigma of Mr Deakin* 2017, pp. 27, 81-83, 164.

45 For O'Shanassy's career, see Pole, 'O'Shanassy, John (1818-83)', in McGuire & Quinn (eds), *Dictionary of Irish Biography*, vol. 7, 2009, pp. 933-34.

46 Deakin, *The Crisis in Victorian Politics* 1957, p. 64.

47 *Age* (Melbourne), 5 March 1860, p. 4.

48 Macintyre, *Colonial Liberalism* 1991, pp. 129-31.

49 Morrison, *David Syme* 2014, pp. 48, 71-72.

50 Bryan O'Loghlen was sometimes caricatured as an Irish farmer: not a 'peasant', but a fat prosperous-looking farmer with an equally fat pig. In some cartoons O'Loghlen was the pig. See, for example, *Melbourne Punch*, 22 March 1883, p. 114, 15 December 1881, p. 235.

51 For Michael, Colman and Bryan O'Loghlen, see their entries by Geoghegan in McGuire & Quinn (eds), *Dictionary of Irish Biography*, vol. 7, 2009, pp. 649-52. Bryan O'Loghlen inherited the title in 1877 on his older brother Colman's death.

52 Duffy, vol. 2, 1898, p. 133.

53 Duffy, vol. 2, 1898, pp. 172-73; Macintyre 1991, p. 130.

54 Knowlton, 'The enigma of Charles Gavan Duffy' 1996, pp. 189-208.

55 Doyle, 'Sir Charles Gavan Duffy's land act, 1862' 1986, pp. 145-55.

56 Serle, *The Golden Age* 1963, p. 250. For more positive assessments of Duffy, see Noone, 'An Irish rebel in Victoria' 2007, pp. 108-17; Kiernan, 'Charles Gavan Duffy and "The art of living"' 1989, pp. 137-54.

57 Serle, *The Rush to Be Rich* 1971, p. 242.

58   Duffy, *Young Ireland* 1884, pp. 127-30.
59   *Australasian* (Melbourne), 22 July 1871, p. 20.
60   *Melbourne Punch*, 27 July 1871, p. 5, 23 May 1872, p. 4.
61   Scalmer, *On the Stump* 2017, pp. 106-20.
62   *Melbourne Punch*, 23 May 1872, p. 4, 30 May 1872, p. 5.
63   Duffy, vol. 2, 1898, p. 384; Pearl, *The Three Lives of Gavan Duffy* 1979, pp. 212-31.
64   Serle 1971, p. 17.
65   Deakin 1957, pp. 15, 55-57, 63, 78-80. Bent's father had been an English convict, while his mother was a free Irish immigrant.
66   Glass, *Tommy Bent* 1993, pp. 44-73.
67   *Melbourne Punch*, 3 April 1879, p. 138.
68   Hall & Malcolm 2016, pp. 11-12.
69   Morgan, *Melbourne Before Mannix* 2012, p. 27.
70   Serle 1971, pp. 17, 238.
71   *Leader* (Melbourne), 21 October 1882, p. 27.
72   Macintyre 1991, pp. 166-67.
73   Ingham, 'O'Shanassy, Sir John (1818-1883)', *ADB*.
74   Strangio, *Neither Power nor Glory* 2012, pp. 106-108, 120.
75   Strangio 2012, pp. 162-73, 181-203.
76   James Martin, NSW premier (1863-65, 1866-68 and 1870-72) and chief justice (1873-86), was born into a County Cork Catholic family in 1820, but during his rise to high colonial office he converted to Protestantism. Grainger, *Martin of Martin Place* 1970.
77   Cahill, 'Jennings, Sir Patrick Alfred (1831-1897)', *ADB*; *Evening News* (Sydney), 8 January 1887, p. 5.
78   Kingston, *A History of New South Wales* 2006, pp. 69-73.
79   Hamilton, 'Irish Catholics of New South Wales and the Labor Party' 1958, p. 256.
80   *Australasian Pastoralists' Review*, 16 August 1897, pp. 298-99; *Protestant Standard* (Sydney), 15 January 1887, p. 4; *Freeman's Journal* (Sydney), 15 January 1887, pp. 10, 12.
81   Walker, 'Youth on trial' 1986, pp. 28-41; Bavin-Mizzi, *Ravished* 1995, pp. 157-70; Bellanta, *Larrikins* 2012, pp. 86-105.
82   *Daily Telegraph* (Sydney), 6 January 1887, p. 6.
83   *Sydney Mail and New South Wales Advertiser*, 8 January 1887, p. 63.
84   Cited in Ayres, *Prince of the Church* 2007, pp. 156-57.
85   *Freeman's Journal*, 8 January 1887, p. 16, 15 January 1887, p. 13; *Age*, 8 January 1887, p. 9.
86   Davitt, *Life and Progress in Australasia* 1898, pp. 433-34. For Dalley's comments, see *Sydney Morning Herald*, 6 January 1887, p. 4.
87   Inglis, *The Rehearsal* 1985; Reynolds, *Unnecessary Wars* 2016, pp. 48-58.
88   Cited in Lehane, *William Bede Dalley* 2007, p. 301.
89   Dalley may not have known it, but there were at least 20 Orangeman among the contingent. Inglis 1985, pp. 90-91, 147.
90   Hogan 1887, pp. 303-305.
91   Froude, *Oceana* 1886, p. 173.

92 Inglis 1985, pp. 85, 152–53.

93 Lehane 2007, pp. 303, 310.

94 Inglis 1985, pp. 68–70, 118, 140–41, 151–53.

95 For a survey of the Queensland Irish community, see MacGinley, 'The Irish in Queensland' 1991, pp. 103–19.

96 Gill, 'Byrnes, Thomas Joseph (1860–1898)', *ADB*; St Ledger, *Thomas Joseph Byrnes* 1902.

97 Davitt 1898, pp. 252–55.

98 Murphy, 'Queensland' 1975, pp. 130–65, 218–19, 222–23; McMullin, *The Light on the Hill* 1991, pp. 1–7, 23–29.

99 *Worker* (Brisbane), 29 February 1896, p. 2.

100 Davitt 1898, p. 303.

101 Woolcock, *Rights of Passage* 1986, pp. 316–17.

102 O'Farrell, *The Catholic Church and Community in Australia* 1977, pp. 234, 244, 274, 306–308.

103 *Worker*, 29 February 1896, pp. 2–3.

104 TJ Byrnes is identified as a conservative, although political labels were in transition in Queensland during the 1890s; he was certainly anti-labour. Murphy 1975, p. 140.

105 *Warwick Argus*, 4 April 1896, p. 2; *Warwick Examiner and Times*, 8 April 1896, p. 3.

106 *Brisbane Courier*, 13 March 1896, pp. 5–6; *Telegraph* (Brisbane), 21 March 1896, p. 3.

107 *Telegraph*, 4 March 1896, p. 4; *Brisbane Courier*, 15 January 1896, p. 4, 18 February 1896, p. 6.

10 Catholic Irish Australians in the political arena after 1900: from sectarianism to the split

1 For simplicity and clarity, the terms ALP and Labor Party will be used throughout, although the labour parties of the 1890s and the early federal party initially used a variety of different names.

2 Malcolm & Hall, 'Catholic Irish Australia and the labor movement' 2018, pp. 149–67.

3 Camm & McQuilton (eds), *Australians: A Historical Atlas* 1987, pp. 147–48.

4 Hamilton, 'Irish Catholics of New South Wales and the Labor Party' 1958, p. 265. For Victoria, see Bongiorno, *The People's Party* 1996, pp. 164–87.

5 Ford, *Cardinal Moran and the A.L.P* 1966, pp. 97–103, 257–58, 274.

6 Redmond, *Through the New Commonwealth* [1906], pp. 16–17; O'Brien, *Parnell and His Party* 1968, pp. 140–43.

7 O'Brien 1968, pp. 126–33.

8 More research is required to substantiate Kiernan's analysis. Kiernan, 'Home rule for Ireland and the formation of the Australian Labor Party' 1992, p. 9.

9 Brett, 'Class, religion and the foundation of the Australian party system' 2002, pp. 39–56.

10 *Census of the Commonwealth of Australia, 30 June 1933*, vol. 2, pp. 1927–28.

11 McConville, 'Emigrant Irish and Suburban Catholics' 1984, pp. 108 (a) and (b), 116–23, 134–38.

12 Hogan, 'The Sydney style', pp. 39–46.

13 O'Farrell, *The Catholic Church and Community in Australia* 1977, p. 288.

14 See *Australian Dictionary of Biography*; *Australians: The Guide and Index* 1987, pp. 44–47.

15 Crisp, *The Australian Federal Labour Party* 1955, p. 316.

16 See the entries on these eight 1904–49 prime ministers in the *Australian Dictionary of Biography*.

17 The maternal grandparents of JC Watson, Australia's first Labor prime minister in 1904, were Irish. The seven other prime ministers in Table 2 all had either one or both parents born in Ireland.

18 Hogan, *The Sectarian Strand* 1987, pp. 138–45, 170–71.

19 Rickard, *Class and Politics* 1976, pp. 199–202, 249–50.

20 Ayres, *Prince of the Church* 2007, pp. 197–204; Ford 1966, pp. 202–18, 235–36.

21 Irving, 'Making the federal Commonwealth' 2013, p. 259.

22 O'Farrell 1977, pp. 265–66; Field, *The Forgotten War* 1995, pp. 44–46, 68–69, 210–11 n. 168.

23 McHugh, 'Not in front of the altar' 2009, pp. 42.1–42.22.

24 Hogan 1987, p. 193.

25 O'Farrell, *The Irish in Australia* 1986, pp. 241–51.

26 Davis, *Arthur Griffith and Non-violent Sinn Fein* 1974, pp. 23–24, 74–79; Maume, *The Long Gestation* 1999, pp. 48–59.

27 Foster, *Vivid Faces* 2014, pp. xv–xxiii.

28 Broome, 'Dill Macky, William Marcus (1849–1913)', *ADB*.

29 Ford 1966, pp. 258–60. For the animosity between Moran and Dill Macky in Sydney, see Cunningham, *The Price of a Wife?* 2013.

30 Hamilton, 'Catholic interests and the Labor Party' 1959, pp. 62–73.

31 Kildea, *Tearing the Fabric* 2002, pp. 35–36, 57–63, 249–50; Hogan 1987, pp. 182–85.

32 Stewart, *The Ulster Crisis* 1967.

33 Newton, *Hell-bent* 2014, pp. 61, 282.

34 Hennessey, *Dividing Ireland* 1998, pp. 86–97.

35 Vaughan & Fitzpatrick (eds), *Irish Historical Statistics* 1978, p. 81; Vamplew (ed.), *Australians: Historical Statistics* 1987, pp. 27, 40.

36 Fitzpatrick, 'Militarism in Ireland' 1996, p. 388.

37 Fitzpatrick 1996, p. 388; Vamplew (ed.) 1987, p. 412.

38 Kildea, *ANZACS and Ireland* 2007, pp. 82–88; Irish Anzacs Project, database, University of NSW, <hal.arts.unsw.edu.au>.

39 *Census of the Commonwealth of Australia taken on 2 and 3 April 1911* pp. 753, 757, 772.

40 Robson, 'The origin and character of the first A.I.F' 1973, pp. 740–41, 748.

41 Spiers, *The Army and Society* 1980, pp. 50–51, 297–98.

42 JD Jageurs to M Jageurs, 20 February 1915, in O'Neill, 'Michael Davitt and John Davitt Jageurs' 2006, pp. 50–52.

43 *Advocate* (Melbourne), 16 September 1916, p. 16.

44 Marwick, *The Deluge* 1991, pp. 219–21.

45 Stewart, *Edward Carson* 1981, pp. 96–100; Bowman, 'The Ulster Volunteer Force' 2006, pp. 247–58.
46 Travers, 'The priest in politics' 1983, pp. 162–63.
47 McKernan, *The Australian Churches at War* 1980, p. 112.
48 *Advocate*, 5 June 1915, p. 22.
49 *Watchman* (Sydney), 3 June 1915, p. 5.
50 *Worker* (Brisbane), 27 May 1916, p. 1.
51 *Australian Worker* (Sydney), 4 May 1916, p. 3.
52 Beaumont, *Broken Nation* 2013, pp. 219–31.
53 Marwick 1991, pp. 101–102, 116–25.
54 McKibbin, 'Conscription in the First World War' 2016, pp. 169–86.
55 Bew, 'The politics of war' 2008, pp. 102–103; aan de Wiel, *The Catholic Church in Ireland* 2003, pp. 114–27, 203–55.
56 The 1916–17 votes were plebiscites, not referendums, as they were not aimed at amending the Constitution, but at the time and in many later histories they have frequently been referred to as referendums. See Kildea, 'Killing conscription' 2016, pp. 162–63.
57 Archer, 'Stopping war and stopping conscription' 2014, pp. 43–67.
58 Beaumont 2013, pp. 184–216, 315–63; Vamplew (ed.) 1987, p. 414.
59 Goot, 'The results of the 1916 and 1917 conscription referendums re-examined' 2016, pp. 111–46.
60 Kildea, 'Paranoia and prejudice' 2007, pp. 155–66.
61 Inglis, 'Conscription in peace and war' 1968, pp. 34–45.
62 Hughes cited in Fitzhardinge, *William Morris Hughes*, vol. 2, 1979, pp. 215, 276.
63 Cusack, *With an Olive Branch and a Shillelagh* 2004, pp. 86–93, 106–109; Inglis 1968, pp. 30–31; Walker, *Anxious Nation* 1999, pp. 197–200.
64 Noone, 'Class factors in the radicalisation of Archbishop Daniel Mannix' 2014, pp. 189–204.
65 *Advocate*, 3 February 1917, pp. 12–13.
66 Bollard, 'Economic conscription and Irish discontent' 2015, pp. 139–56.
67 *Freeman's Journal* (Sydney), 8 November 1917, p. 27.
68 Franklin, Nolan & Gilchrist, *The Real Archbishop Mannix from the Sources* 2015, pp. 32–33.
69 Aan de Wiel 2013, pp. 203–40.
70 Franklin, Nolan & Gilchrist 2015, p. 33.
71 *Catholic Press* (Sydney), 21 June 1917, p. 20; *Advocate*, 11 November 1916, p. 17.
72 Holroyd, 'Parker, Frank Critchley (1862–1944)', *ADB*.
73 *Australian Statesman and Mining Standard* (Melbourne), 26 October 1916, p. 260.
74 *Australian Statesman and Mining Standard*, 15 February 1917, p. 97
75 For distribution of Parker's pamphlets in Western Australia, see *Tribune* (Melbourne), 26 July 1917, p. 3, and in NSW and South Australia, see *Southern Cross* (Adelaide), 6 April 1917, p. 9.
76 Holroyd, 'Parker, Frank Critchley (1862–1944)', *ADB*.
77 *Australian Statesman and Mining Standard*, 8 March 1917, insert.
78 *Melbourne Punch*, 4 May 1916, p. 5.
79 *Bulletin* (Sydney), 18 April 1918, cover. Thanks to Stephanie James for alerting us to this cartoon.

80 *Catholic Press*, 25 April 1918, p. 21.
81 Doyle, 'Allegations of disloyalty at Koroit during World War I' 2000, pp. 165–76.
82 Proudfoot & Hall, 'Points of departure' 2005, pp. 341–78.
83 Hall, '"God sent me here to raise a society"' 2015, pp. 319–39.
84 Goot 2016, pp. 123–25, 133–34.
85 Australian Electoral Commission, *Australian Referendums* 2000. Note that, as informal votes have not been included in Table 3, the figures do not add up to 100 per cent.
86 Gilbert, 'The conscription referenda' 1969, pp. 54–72; Murphy, 'Religion, race and conscription in World War I' 1974, pp. 155–63.
87 Franklin, Nolan & Gilchrist 2015, pp. 93–97.
88 Lang, *I Remember* 1956, p. 81.
89 Fraser cited in Megalogenis, *Australia's Second Chance* 2015, pp. 171, 174–75.
90 Warhurst, 'Catholics in Australian politics since 1950' 2009, pp. 262–63.
91 McConville, *Croppies, Celts and Catholics* 1987, pp. 108–17.
92 Santamaria, *Daniel Mannix* 1984, p. 91.
93 Cronin & Adair, *The Wearing of the Green* 2002, pp. 116–18; *Age* (Melbourne), 22 March 1918, p. 17; *Argus* (Melbourne), 19 March 1918, p. 5.
94 Rivett, *Australian Citizen* 1965, pp. 62, 64–68, 70–71.
95 O'Farrell, 'The Irish Republican Brotherhood in Australia' 1983, p. 183.
96 Collins, '"A one-battalioned mind"' 2013.
97 O'Farrell, 'Dreaming of distant revolution' 2005, pp. 62–85; O'Farrell 1986, pp. 254–60, 273–78.
98 For the INA, see the documents deposited by Albert Dryer with the Irish Bureau of Military History, Dublin, W.S. 957 and W.S. 1526, <bureauofmilitaryhistory.ie>.
99 Reid, 'The history of the INA', <irishassociation.org.au/the-history-of-the-ina/>.
100 Bielenberg, 'Fatalities in the Irish revolution' 2017, pp. 758–59.
101 Leeson, 'The Royal Irish Constabulary, Black and Tans and Auxiliaries' 2017, pp. 371–84.
102 Kildea 2002, pp. 232–33.
103 *Age*, 14 December 1920, p. 7.
104 Townshend, *The Republic* 2013, pp. 218–19.
105 *Advocate*, 24 January 1920, p. 4; Cronin & Adair 2002, pp. 120–26.
106 Griffin, *John Wren* 2004, pp. 240–45; Niall, *Mannix* 2015, pp. 146–48.
107 Kwan, 'The St Patrick's Day procession, Melbourne, 1920' 2007, pp. 145–54; Kwan, 'The Australian flag' 1994, pp. 280–303.
108 Kildea, *'Ireland Will Be Free'*, forthcoming 2018.
109 Kildea, '"A veritable hurricane of sectarianism"' 2015, pp. 363–382; Kildea 2002, pp. 204–205, 208–13, 211, 254.
110 *Northern Champion* (Taree, NSW), 5 August 1922, p. 4. *Warwick Daily News*, 12 October 1922, p. 4.
111 Fitzpatrick, 'Exporting brotherhood' 2005, p. 310.
112 Davis, *Orangeism in Tasmania* 2010, p. 68.
113 Kildea 2002, p. 229.

114 Hogan 1987, pp. 191–94; Kildea 2002, pp. 242–45; Moore, 'Sectarianism in NSW' 1987, pp. 3–15.
115 Hopkinson, *Green Against Green* 1988, pp. 6–46.
116 J O'Flaherty, Adelaide, to K Barry and L Kearns, 19 January 1925, Kathleen Barry Maloney papers, University College Dublin [hereafter UCD] Archives, P94/56.
117 Niall 2015, pp. 182–84.
118 O'Farrell 1986, pp. 276–77; Hall, 'Irish republican women on tour', forthcoming 2019.
119 Dutton, 'The Commonwealth Investigation Branch' 1998, p. 163.
120 O'Farrell 1986, p. 293.
121 Finnane, 'Deporting the Irish envoys' 2013, pp. 409, 415–16.
122 Kildea 2002, pp. 247–49.
123 Whitaker, 'Linda Kearns and Kathleen Barry' 2016, pp. 208–11.
124 Murphy, 'Imprisonment during the Civil War' 2017, p. 736.
125 Hall, forthcoming 2019.
126 Ó Duigneáin, *Linda Kearns* 2002, p. 95.
127 *Sun* (Sydney), 24 February 1925, p. 9.
128 K Barry Maloney to J Maloney, 26 February 1925, Maloney papers, UCD Archives, P94/127; Hall, forthcoming 2019.
129 Roe, *Australia, Britain and Migration* 1995, pp. 17, 211.
130 Whitaker, 'Irish War of Independence veterans in Australia' 1996, pp. 413–20.
131 Foster, 'Locating the "Lost Legion"' 2017, pp. 744–47.
132 Santamaria 1984, pp. 248–49.
133 Lee & Kennedy, 'The credentials controversy' 2006/7, pp. 57–81.
134 Niall 2015, p. 330; Santamaria 1984, pp. 219–20.
135 Warhurst, 'Catholics, communism and the Australian party system' 1979, pp. 222–42.
136 Crisp 1955, pp. 312, 316, 327; Murray, *The Split* 1970, pp. 26, 66.
137 Scalmer, 'Crisis to crisis' 2001, pp. 90–100.
138 Duncan, *Crusade or Conspiracy?* 2001, pp. 57–107; Ormonde, *The Movement* 1972; Mathews, *Of Labour and Liberty* 2017, pp. 227–96.
139 BA Santamaria to D Mannix, 11 December 1952, in Morgan (ed.), *B.A. Santamaria: Your Most Obedient Servant* 2007, pp. 74–75.
140 Murray 1970, pp. 334–42.
141 Duncan 2001, pp. 388–90; Strangio, *Neither Power nor Glory* 2012, pp. 212, 232.
142 O'Farrell 1977, pp. 397–403.

Epilogue: Irish Australia in the 21st century

1 Delaney, *The Irish in Post-War Britain* 2007, pp. 1–11.
2 Grimes, 'Irish immigration after 1945' 2001, pp. 480–83.
3 For unpublished studies of late 20th-century Irish immigrants in Western Australia and Melbourne, see Chetkovich, 'The New Irish in Australia' 2005; and O'Connor, 'The Multiple Dimensions of Migrancy, Irishness and Home among Contemporary Irish Immigrants in Melbourne, Australia' 2005.
4 Grimes 2001, pp. 480–83.

5   Noone, 'People not money' 2000, pp. 128–35.
6   O'Farrell, *The Irish in Australia*, 3rd ed., 2000, p. 312.
7   O'Connor, 'Rediscovering Irish migration to Australia' 2012, pp. 35–36.
8   Aileen Garry interviewed by Seamus O'Hanlon, 30 May–4 June 2012, for the
     Australian Generations Oral History Project, National Library of Australia
     [hereafter NLA], ORAL TRC 6300/61.
9   See, for example, online interview with Limerick-born Bishop David
     Cremin by Siobhán McHugh, 24 and 31 March 2014, for the Irish National
     Association Centenary Oral History Project, NLA, ORAL TRC 6570/18, <nla.
     gov.au/nla.obj-220503090/listen>.
10   For Irish women recruited during the 20th century into Australian religious
     orders, such as the Sisters of Mercy and the Josephites, see MacGinley,
     A Dynamic of Hope 2002, pp. 291–92; Doyle, *Mercy, Mater and Me* 2010; and also
     'Sister Brenda Browne and the "49ers"', in Reid, *Not Just Ned* 2011.
11   Walker, 'Memories of a 1950s Irish leftie in St Kilda, Melbourne' 2016, *Tinteán*,
     <tintean.org.au>.
12   Molloy, 'Tradition, memory and the culture of Irish-Australian identity' 2016,
     pp. 47–64; Mollenhauer, 'Competitive Irish dancing' 2015, pp. 35–54.
13   Walker 2016.
14   Collins, '"A one-battalioned mind"' 2013.
15   Noone, *Hidden Ireland* 2012, p. 150.
16   Noone, 'Sunburnt Gaelic' 2012, p. 172.
17   Malcolm & Bull, 'Irish studies in Australia' 2013, pp. 29–44.
18   Breen, 'Emigration in the age of electronic media' 2015, pp. 198–233;
     Ballantyne & Burke, 'People live in their heads a lot' 2017, pp. 10–24.
19   The term 'Anglo-Celtic' appears to have been first used by the Irish-Australian
     journalist and NSW politician, Edward W O'Sullivan (1846–1910). See
     Mansfield, *Australian Democrat* 1965, p. 263.
20   Evans, Moore, Saunders & Jamison, *1901* 1997, pp. 15, 40, 156.
21   Dixson, *The Imaginary Australian* 1999, pp. 33–35, 93–94.
22   Curthoys, 'History and identity' 1997, pp. 23–24.
23   Hage, *White Nation* 2000, pp. 57, 19.
24   Hage 2000, pp. 198–204.
25   O'Farrell, 'Double jeopardy' 2005, <press-files.anu.edu.au>. For a similar view,
     see Teo, 'Multiculturalism and the problem of multi-cultural histories' 2003,
     p. 144.
26   *Daily Mail* (London), 3 June 2015, <www.dailymail.co.uk/news/article-
     3107579>.
27   Grahame Morris's mention of failed potato growing is presumably a reference
     to the Great Famine of the late 1840s, which was due to a crop disease, not
     to any lack of skill on the part of Irish farmers. The 'mutant lawn weed' is
     presumably the shamrock, but this is not Ireland's 'national symbol' – that
     symbol is the harp. As for 'th', it is pronounced in Hiberno-English, although
     some localised dialects reflecting Irish-language pronunciation render it as 't'.
     Rather than highlighting Irish stupidity, Morris was simply demonstrating
     his own ignorance and prejudice. See Bourke, *'The Visitation of God'* 1993,

pp. 129–58; Morris, *Our Own Devices* 2005, pp. 14–15, 73–75, 199; Dolan (ed.), *A Dictionary of Hiberno-English* 1999, p. 269.

28 *Brisbane Times*, 12 March 2018, <www.brisbanetimes.com.au/national/ queensland/border-force-has-been-targeting-the-wrong-foreigners-20180312-p4z414.html>.

29 For favourable reviews, see *Australian* (Sydney), 5 April 2014, <www. theaustralian.com.au/arts/review/david-hunts-girt-delivers-our-history-with-humour/news-story/9b74f40096dcfbb748e8b8c08fb66a13?sv=2ac82286155 b8704857254dcdbbc00a9>; *Sydney Morning Herald*, 20 October 2016, <www. smh.com.au/entertainment/books/true-girt-review-david-hunts-satirical-look-at-australian-history-20161020-gs6mug.html>.

30 Hunt, *Girt* 2013, pp. 147, 149, 178–79.

31 Hunt, *True Girt* 2016, pp. 427, 360 note 10, 399 note 18, 259, 357, 308. It seems only fair to inform readers that one of the authors (Malcolm) of this book is the descendant of an Irish Famine orphan.

INDEX